Beatriz Allende

Beatriz Allende

A Revolutionary Life in Cold War Latin America

TANYA HARMER

THE
UNIVERSITY OF
NORTH CAROLINA
PRESS
Chapel Hill

© 2020 The University of North Carolina Press
All rights reserved

Set in Miller and Klavika types
by Tseng Information Systems, Inc.

Cover photograph courtesy of Fundación Salvador Allende,
Santiago de Chile

Library of Congress Cataloging-in-Publication Data
Names: Harmer, Tanya, author.
Title: Beatriz Allende : a revolutionary life in cold war Latin America / Tanya Harmer.
Description: Chapel Hill : The University of North Carolina Press, 2020. |
Includes bibliographical references and index.
Identifiers: LCCN 2019046694 | ISBN 9781469654294 (cloth) |
ISBN 9781469679150 (paperback) | ISBN 9781469654300 (ebook)
Subjects: LCSH: Allende, Beatriz. | Socialists—Chile—Biography. | Revolutionaries—
Latin America—Biography. | Exiles—Cuba—Biography. | Suicide victims—Biography.
Classification: LCC F3101.A39 H37 2020 | DDC 983.06/46092 [B]—dc23
LC record available at https://lccn.loc.gov/2019046694

For Tom

Contents

Introduction *1*

1. An Awakening *18*
2. University and Politics *39*
3. Youth and Women *65*
4. Reform and Radicalization *84*
5. Love and Revolution *106*
6. Revolutionary Upheaval *135*
7. Working for the Revolution *154*
8. The Battle for Chile *183*
9. Another Life *213*
10. Disillusionment *236*

Onward March *262*

Acknowledgments *275*

Appendix *279*

Notes *281*

Bibliography *333*

Index *353*

Illustrations

Map of Chile *x*

Salvador Allende and his daughters, ca. 1950 *21*

Beatriz with friends and cousins, Algarrobo, 1956 *21*

Allende family at home in Guardia Vieja, 1964 *67*

Student doctors at the Hospital San Juan de Diós, no date *86*

Beatriz and Renato, 1965 *93*

Beatriz and Salvador Allende, Cuba, 1967 *111*

Luis and Beatriz, Cuba, 1968 *130*

Sketch, Beatriz to Luis, no date *133*

Fidel Castro and Beatriz, Havana, no date *162*

Beatriz and Salvador Allende, Santiago, no date *166*

Beatriz and Luis, Havana, 1972 *176*

Beatriz and Maya, no date *186*

Beatriz and Juan Carretero, Cajón del Maipo, no date *190*

Meeting in Havana, no date *199*

Beatriz, Havana, 28 September 1973 *217*

Beatriz, Alejandro, and Luis, Havana, 5 November 1973 *219*

Beatriz, Stockholm, December 1973 *226*

Isabel, Beatriz, and Patricia, Havana, ca. 1975 *232*

Beatriz, Havana, 1977 *259*

Beatriz Allende

Introduction

Sitting in his home in Havana, Luis made me the strong, sweet coffee you instantly miss when you leave Cuba. We had taken a break from discussing his career in Cuban intelligence and begun to talk a bit about our lives. There, hanging next to the table we sat around, was a framed picture of a young woman. I knew it was Beatriz Allende and that the man I was talking with, Luis Fernández Oña, had been married to her. I knew that Beatriz was the revolutionary daughter of Chile's socialist president, Salvador Allende. And I knew she had died in Cuba after a right-wing military coup in 1973 deposed her father's democratically elected government.

Over the many hours I had spoken to Luis before this, Beatriz's name had also come up sporadically as someone who had worked in Allende's presidential administration, had intimate links to Cuba's leaders, and had mediated relations between them. But for the most part she had remained a smiling, tragic, and mysterious presence watching over us as we delved into Luis's memories of revolution in Cold War Latin America.

It was only years after we first met—drinking coffee—that I finally broached the possibility of learning more about Beatriz. Compared with our earlier conversations, I now felt more confident asking Luis difficult questions. I had interviewed him in the stifling Cuban heat, made more oppressive when power cuts stopped the fan next to us. The tape recorder that had once sat awkwardly between us had also become a habitual and forgotten accessory.

I therefore seized the opportunity to ask Luis about his relationship with Beatriz, about the role she played in Chile's revolutionary past, and why she died so young. The answers he gave me only raised more questions. And that is where a decade-long project to write a history of her life began.

That it had taken me so long to ask him about her also spoke to the way, like so many other women in Latin America's revolutionary history, Beatriz had been subsumed within narratives driven by men. Historians, myself included, had found it hard to situate women like her who held offstage, but highly influential, roles. And we had rarely probed their historical significance.

Inevitably, the more I learned about Beatriz, the more she showed herself to be a protagonist worthy of study in her own right: a revolutionary who revealed the promises, paradoxes, and problems of a revolutionary age. The more I delved into her life, the more I also understood her in relation to the world she came from and the times she lived through. In turn, the lens Beatriz provided opened up these times to me. She witnessed remarkable changes in Chile, Cuba, and Latin America—changes determined by the rise and fall of a revolutionary moment stretching from the late 1950s to the early 1970s. And she helped drive these forward while ultimately being consumed by them. Yet to comprehend her as a revolutionary, her milieu and her world required further research. In turn, Beatriz's story became the history of her life and an account of revolutionary times told from her perspective. Combining the personal and political, it is about a life in its context: a new textured history of revolution in Chile at the height of Latin America's Cold War and how it impacted a life.

Born on 8 September 1942, Beatriz Ximena Allende Bussi was the second of Salvador Allende and Hortensia Bussi's three daughters. She had a middle-class, left-wing upbringing in Santiago before going on to study medicine and work in public health as a pediatrician and university lecturer in her late twenties. When her father won Chile's presidential election in September 1970 as the head of a left-wing coalition seeking to bring about a peaceful, democratic transition to socialism, she left medicine to work full-time as his private secretary. It was an easy decision. Beatriz had been politically active from a young age, accompanying her father on his numerous election campaigns for senator and president in the 1950s and 1960s. As a member of the Chilean Socialist Party, she had actively participated in its youth section and the Brigada Universitaria Socialista (Socialist University Brigade, BUS). And, in doing so, she formed part of a radicalized generation of young Chileans deeply inspired by the Cuban Revolution. After Ernesto "Che" Guevara's death in Bolivia in 1967, she had also been a leading figure in the attempt to instigate a second transnational guerrilla insurgency in that country. And she was close to the Movimiento de Izquierda Revolucionaria (Revolutionary Left Movement, MIR), which stood to the left of the Communist and Socialist Parties in Chile.

Together, this combined—but divided—Left forged one of the most significant experiments of socialist transformation in twentieth-century Latin America: *la vía chilena al socialismo* (the Chilean road to socialism). However, on 11 September 1973 it came to an abrupt end. That day, a military coup brought a seventeen-year dictatorship to power. Led by

General Augusto Pinochet, it would destroy Chile's constitutional democratic past, forcing the country toward neoliberalism, killing more than three thousand, and torturing at least forty thousand more. Beatriz's life—and the lives of everyone she knew—changed irrevocably. Her father and many of her friends died as a result, as did the revolutionary future she had worked toward for over a decade.

As an exile in Havana, living with Luis and their two young children, she subsequently worked tirelessly as a figurehead for the global solidarity campaign with Chileans resisting the dictatorship. Then, in 1977, when Pinochet's regime was at its strongest, having decimated the country's left-wing parties and consolidated its institutional power, Beatriz took her own life. She was thirty-five years old.

Brief as it was, Beatriz's life contains multitudes of historical meaning. On one level, she exemplified the Cuban Revolution's influence on young Latin Americans. Like so many of her generation, frustrated by underdevelopment, poverty, inequality, and the pace of transformation at home, she was drawn to the idea of armed struggle and internationalism à la Cuba as a way of bringing about decisive change. Her experience is therefore representative of the rise of a particular revolutionary project that emerged in the late 1950s and 1960s and its power to shape militancy, behavior, friendships, and romance. On another level, Beatriz was also a loyal collaborator and confidant to her father's democratic experiment to move Chile along a *peaceful* road to socialism in the early 1970s. She was influenced by her experience of having grown up comfortably in one of Cold War Latin America's few constitutional democracies. And perhaps her greatest legacy is her work in building up a global solidarity campaign after 1973, not with arms but with typewritten words, administrative toil, and diplomacy, emphasizing human rights and a return to democracy rather than promising imminent socialist revolution. As a member of the Chilean Socialist Party, though not formally part of its governing structures, she stood at the margins of institutional party politics but at the center of a guerrilla insurgency and her father's democratically elected presidency. And as a female militant amid Latin America's hypermasculine guerrilla decade, Beatriz challenged gendered conventions prevalent in society even while remaining constrained by them.

These ambiguities and contradictions are attractive features of Beatriz's life that help us study Chile's revolutionary past. Tracing her life as it evolved also allows us to probe teleological and romanticized accounts of her political commitment—and that of others in her social and political circle. Examined up close, individuals rarely tally with historical typologies and neat frameworks.¹ As Linda Colley concluded in her biography of Elizabeth Marsh, the inherent messiness and contours of a human life permit historians to "cross boundaries."² In this respect, Beatriz lets us explore the disjuncture between Cuba's example and Chile's distinct experience; a revolutionary moment dominated by men and the women who participated in it; the relationship between political groups across private, public, local, transnational, and global spheres. Her life—and microhistorical approaches to individual lives generally—can thus offer insight into larger political, cultural, and social processes.³

At its broadest level, Beatriz's story was unmistakably affected by ideological conflicts at the heart of the Cold War. True, for her and the Left, *la guerra fría* was a U.S. construct, an imperialist tool to fight revolutionary forces imported into local spheres by domestic "imperialist" collaborators.⁴ Yet, like the majority of historians studying the conflict today, this book adopts the Cold War as a conceptual framework for explaining a wider twentieth-century struggle between different visions of "modernity," pitting various interpretations of capitalism and Marxism against one another. And the Left was obviously a key player in this struggle rather than an object of others' machinations.⁵

The point here is to examine this conflict through a young Chilean woman's lived experience. In doing so, we see the way ideas at the heart of the global Cold War intersected with local concerns, developments, and circumstances and how they were enmeshed into the fabric of society, politics, and individuals' worldviews. As Greg Grandin and Gilbert Joseph argued, the "internationalization and politicization of everyday life" is key for understanding the Cold War's character, violence, and resonance in Latin America.⁶ And in exploring how everyday life was affected in this way, I take inspiration from historians who have examined how the conflict overlapped with struggles endogenous to local environments.⁷ I also add to those underlining the obvious but all-too-often-forgotten point that Latin Americans—women included—were not simple objects, victims, and passive recipients of conflicting ideologies but often "progenitors" of contestation.⁸ Contingency and agency mattered, driving social change and political imaginations. And because the Cold War had human dimensions, studying people at its heart, preferably in tandem with broader geopolitical and institutional narratives, helps us grasp its evolution and meanings.

There are obvious methodological and conceptual challenges with writing this kind of history. As Jill Lepore has stressed, "Finding out about people ... is tricky work. It is necessary to balance intimacy with distance while at the same time being inquisitive to the point of invasiveness. Getting too close to your subject is a major danger, but not getting to know her well enough is just as likely."[9] And Beatriz is not a particularly easy or straightforward subject to get to know intimately or otherwise. She was a private person, not least because of her role in clandestine revolutionary ventures. Those who knew her described her as simultaneously strong and vulnerable. She was also fiercely political and sectarian in some respects and open in others. She compartmentalized her life and moved between groups with apparent ease—a characteristic that allowed her to operate covertly for revolutionary movements and play the role of intermediary between others but one that makes her position harder to pin down. Even on a basic level, her friends' accounts differ. Some said she chain-smoked, for example, others claimed that she did not (she did, increasingly, but avoided doing so around some of her medical school peers). Because she stood at the margin of party politics and was skeptical of them, she is also largely silent in institutional archives, insofar as they exist (as the Chilean feminist scholar Julieta Kirkwood lamented, women's historical participation in Chilean political parties was largely undocumented).[10] Histories and memoirs of political leaders or accomplices often mention her in passing as someone who was present but opaque.[11] Until 2017, when the Chilean historian Marco Álvarez Vergara published the first historical biography of her including reference to her birth certificate, even her age was questioned (archivists of East German state security files curiously disputed that Beatriz was born in 1942 rather than 1943 before indicating that the archive had no documents related to her). Student publications from the 1960s that she contributed to were mostly destroyed after the coup. Beatriz's personal role in burning documents and sending others to Cuba for safekeeping in 1972–73 compounds the problem of getting to know her. That the Cubans have never released such files blocks this avenue of research. Being a revolutionary and a woman thus made Beatriz doubly invisible. Her agency in her own historical censure has not helped. There are also stark imbalances in how sources relating to different parts of her life were regarded. Revolutionary groups she belonged to, facing powerful counterinsurgent states, regarded record keeping as a vulnerability, whereas written documents propelled global solidarity forward.

These challenges partly explain why no studies of Beatriz's life existed when I began this project. In the last decade, two biographies have subsequently been published. The best is Marco Álvarez's biography, based on interviews and published sources. But in claiming her as a predestined, "forgotten revolutionary" whose example can inspire contemporary political actors, he romanticizes her.[12] As a biography rather than a microhistory of her life, the broader story she sheds light on is also missing. The other account, a fictional biography by the Spanish journalist Margarita Espuña, has copious references to Beatriz crying, despite friends and family remembering her as stoic and self-controlled, at least until the final months of her life.[13] Espuña's portrayal of Beatriz as a victim and passive recipient of events is doubly problematic. As well as being inaccurate, the stereotypically gendered depiction of an emotional, vulnerable woman gives weight to the notion that women were insignificant adornments of history. A third study of Beatriz's life is Eduardo Labarca's "sentimental" biography of Salvador Allende, although it deals with her in relation to her father rather than as a study of her in her own right.[14]

One of the fixations of all three works and scattered media coverage of Beatriz's life has been her relationship with Luis Fernández Oña. This intimate part of Beatriz's life is important for both its political significance and what it reveals about the affective dimensions of revolution. As a member of Cuba's intelligence community involved in the island's operations in Latin America, his relationship with her has been read through preconceived ideas regarding Cuban revolutionary operations. International Telephone and Telegraph (ITT) documents leaked to the *Washington Post* in 1972, for example, cited Luis's presence in Santiago as a "grim" sign of Cuba's efforts to "strangle" democracy in Chile. Rumors his relationship with Beatriz was inauthentic, an excuse for his presence in the country, and a way of gaining privileged access to Salvador Allende have circulated ever since 1970.[15] But, interestingly, even accounts sympathetic to Cuba and the revolutionary Left depict Luis as being in control of the relationship. If, at one extreme, he was the embodiment of a sinister Cuban revolutionary state, using Beatriz to intervene in Chile, to those sympathetic to revolution, he caused her death as a result of his infidelities and alcoholism.[16] My exclusive conversations with Luis might have been expected to confirm his centrality or obscure such flaws. Yet he was open about them. Where he sat in on initial interviews with those he introduced me to, he always encouraged me to conduct follow-up interviews without him present. Crucially, this book also argues that he and the Cuban Revolution have had too much power to determine Beatriz's story. As we shall see, Beatriz *chose* Luis as someone who personified the revolutionary project she identified with, rejecting her first husband in the process and becoming a willing conduit of information between Cuba's leaders and Chile's left-wing parties. While the breakdown of her marriage to Luis and his self-confessed failings as a husband undoubtedly contributed to her suicide, they were neither the sole cause nor the most important. In short, although Luis is where my interest in Beatriz started,

I argue her relationship with him should not define her; it was a part of her life, but it was not its entirety. And the same goes for Cuba's influence over Chile's revolutionary Left.

To assemble a fuller picture of Beatriz's life and times, I have cast the net wide. What follows draws on research conducted in seven countries and exclusive access to Beatriz's private correspondence, her handwritten love letters to Luis in the late 1960s included.[17] I have also used archival collections, extensive online sources, published memoirs, and detailed interviews with her closest friends, fellow militants, and family members. Interviews and written memories obviously need to be treated carefully. What one person remembers as having happened fifty years after an event is clearly not the same as having records from the time. When dealing with the history of Chile's contested revolutionary past, interviewees were also understandably keen that *their* version be privileged. And it must be noted that by interviewing those close to Beatriz, I did not gain a picture representative of all Chileans or even all those on the Left but rather the branch of the revolutionary Left Beatriz belonged to that is the focus of this book. The inability to interview those who have died or to persuade some who were reticent to share their stories was also problematic. And, in this respect, although all efforts were made to interview women, men, more comfortable with seeing themselves as historical actors, were more willing to be interviewed.[18]

Yet, even with these caveats, oral history and written testimonies can be immensely valuable for "filling in the historical record" and providing "access to undocumented experience," something especially important in the case of bringing women to the foreground.[19] With many protagonists of Latin America's revolutionary past getting older and dying, they are imperative sources for recording the past before it is gone forever. For a microhistory of an individual, oral history can also simultaneously help understand the quotidian, personal ways people experienced events, processes, conflicts *and*, as Patricia Leavy argues, the "macro-level environments that shape and contain those experiences."[20] Conducting as many interviews as possible, cross-referencing them, critically reading them, and using them in combination with newspapers, magazines, archival sources, and written memoirs can meanwhile ameliorate the pitfalls of "mistaken memories."[21]

A note on names and scope is necessary before moving on to the book's contributions. I specifically refer to Beatriz rather than "Tati," the name by which she was more commonly known. To do otherwise would be to suggest a familiarity and friendship I do not pretend—nor want—to have. To avoid confusion with her father, I do not refer to Beatriz by her surname and have generally opted to use first names for others once introduced to correspond with the way I deal with her and avoid infantilizing her next to her peers—and particularly her male peers. An exception is Salvador Allende, who was hardly ever known by his first name. The Chilean tendency to use nicknames and revolutionaries' covert aliases ("Marcela," in Beatriz's case) complicates the picture further, because, like Beatriz, individuals were very often known by these. Except when it obscures the past, I have noted them but stayed with formal given names for the same reason.

Finally, on scope, this book does not pretend to tell the history of all women and all revolutionary currents in Chile. It is neither a history of Chile's left wing as a whole nor the origins and course of its Unidad Popular government, about which there exists an ample bibliography.[22] Rather, it zooms in on Beatriz's particular experience as a female revolutionary at a particular moment in time within a particular left-wing circle. It does not, therefore, provide detailed insight into the Communist Party, for example. In dealing with gender, about which I write more below, its focus is predominantly on revolutionary socialist circles rather than grassroots communities or right-wing attitudes, both of which have received more attention elsewhere.[23] Beatriz was obviously middle class and privileged as a result of both who her father was and the life she lived in affluent districts of Santiago and Havana. She belonged to a specifically pro-Cuban revolutionary Left group in Chile that came of age in the 1960s. And this book tells the history of her life within this world.

In charting the history of Chile's revolutionary Left through an individual life, *Beatriz Allende: A Revolutionary Life in Cold War Latin America* aims to makes four significant contributions. First, responding to such scholars as Katherine Hite and Kirsten Weld, who have complicated isolated periodizations by exploring lived experiences and historical memory, it expands and probes the chronology of Chile's revolutionary moment and demise.[24] I ask how different periods fed into one another over a thirty-five-year period and where turning points occurred. A longer-term perspective also affords the opportunity to grapple with the progressive politicization and internationalization of Chilean life. National and international markers of time, such as presidential terms, were important in shaping this process. But Beatriz's experience—and individual lives generally—attests to inflections between and within these episodes that determined the course of Chile's revolutionary history. To a large extent, for example, her perspective supports scholars' understanding of a "long sixties," characterized by a "combination of crisis and creations," stretching from the late 1950s to the early 1970s (ca. 1957–73 in Chile's case).²⁵ However, Beatriz's experience also helps us explain change within this period. The 1960 earthquake that struck southern Chile, for example, stands out as a catalyst for national soul-searching and mobilization. The year 1967 also marked a decisive shift in Beatriz's life and leads us to probe the significance of Che Guevara's death in stoking the allure of revolutionary violence in Chile.²⁶ Her radicalization in the mid-1960s, meanwhile, forces us to explore the transitional character of Eduardo Frei's reformist government (1964–70), during which frustration progressively replaced initial hopes of change. And this process, in turn, is essential for understanding *la vía chilena*.

Indeed, Beatriz's trajectory prior to Allende's presidency and after the Chilean coup obliges us to view the early 1970s in context. These years—known for political mobilization—have all too often been studied separately from preceding decades. But to understand them and the Chileans who lived through them, it is essential to grasp the period before. Chile had a relatively stable and robust constitutional democracy from the late 1950s to 1973. The country's electorate divided consistently in thirds comprising the Left, the Right, and a strong middle-class-led reformist center most obviously represented by the Radical and Christian Democratic Parties. These years also witnessed progressive democratization as new sectors were brought into the political sphere.²⁷ Participation in presidential elections rose dramatically from 29.1 percent and 33.8 percent of the voting-age public in 1952 and 1958, respectively, to 66.1 percent in 1964. Quite simply, twice as many people voted in 1964 as in 1958. Opinion polls also show Chileans' formal identification with individual parties grew.²⁸ However, as Nancy Bermeo has argued and we shall see, rather than being confined to formal institutional political spaces, political contestation increasingly began spilling into the public sphere before 1970.²⁹ With economic growth and political leaders unable to keep up with rising demands for participation and benefits of reform by the late 1960s, Chile's social system, to quote Federico Gil, Ricardo Lagos, and Henry Landsberger, was already experiencing "extraordinary strain."³⁰ Politicization and mobilization in the early 1970s, in other words, did not appear out of nowhere. Beatriz's death in 1977, meanwhile, requires us to take stock of the Chilean Left's position in this year when the end of the dictatorship still seemed far off and the reconfiguration of its parties was incipient. Which in turn leads us to question the specificities of the late 1970s, rather than subsuming it within a teleological process of democratization at the Cold War's denouement.

A second contribution of the book relates to the question of youth as examined through Beatriz's perspective and the insight she offers into young people's prominent role in politics and society. It is difficult to separate youth from the long sixties. As Valeria Manzano has argued in relation to Argentina, this was quite simply the "Age of Youth." Stuck ambiguously between childhood and adulthood with different signifiers across time and place, "youth" is admittedly a tricky construct.[31] But, at least in Beatriz's immediate world, it denoted groups in their late teens and early twenties. Militants in the Chilean Juventud Socialista (Socialist Youth, JS), for example, were aged from fourteen to twenty-five.[32] There were, of course, many who retained "youthful" identities longer, including Cuba's revolutionary leaders, already in their thirties when they epitomized their country's "young" revolution. And although Beatriz turned twenty-seven in 1968, officially separating her from the youthquake of that year, as a university lecturer and recruiter for internationalist revolutionary ventures, she was directly involved in young people's political and societal mobilization. Indeed, as a growing body of literature has underscored, youth in the long sixties was often about more than age: it was associated with the impulse for change, directly related to postwar demographic shifts, rapid modernization projects, and the questioning of hegemonic practices and authority.[33]

Chile experienced this "age of youth" for many of the same reasons as other countries worldwide. A postwar baby boom meant a growing sector of its population was young. Modernization drives also brought more young people into the public sphere, imbuing them with a sense of power and entitlement. And, in this respect, improved access to secondary and higher education was key. In Chile, university student numbers rose from 7,800 in 1940 to just over 20,000 in 1957 and 120,000 by 1970.[34] True, it is just as ahistorical to talk about a "student movement" as it is a singular "youth" sector. And although politicized young students on the revolutionary Left—*la juventud revolucionaria*, or revolutionary youth—are the focus of this book, young men and women were by no means always students, political, or left-wing. Student politics were also heterogeneous, and Beatriz's revolutionary tendencies certainly did not represent all her contemporaries, even on the Left. For much of the 1960s, in fact, her political circle was in a minority compared with reformist actors and more established left-wing parties, the Communist Party included.

However, the impulses driving her to participate actively in politics and the politicized intrusion of student sectors into Chilean public life were similar across the political spectrum. They related to students' growing tendency to interact with the wider population and participate in societal mobilization. The increasingly popular practice among Catholic and left-wing students of social, voluntary work in impoverished urban shantytowns, or *poblaciónes*, and rural areas connected them to realities they were not otherwise in contact with. Young people's frustrations with the pace and model of "development" in Chile concurrently grew. Students participated in strikes and unionization drives, fought political campaigns, initiated university reform, contributed to public health initiatives, and took part in guerrilla insurgencies. During Allende's presidency in the early 1970s, many of Chile's sixties generation also held influential roles in government and opposition. Youth mobilization during this period, to quote Patrick Barr-Melej, was "exceptional."[35]

To grasp this exceptionality—and Beatriz's own politicization—domestic and international contexts are both vitally important. Political, economic, and social crises during the Carlos Ibáñez del Campo (1952–58) and Jorge Alessandri (1958–64) governments were pivotal. The conscious use of "youth" as a campaigning tool, and target constituency, by candidates in Chile's 1964 presidential election was vital in leading young people to view themselves as protagonists of their country's future. During Frei's presidency, young Chileans were then explicitly mobilized to remake Chile.[36] They were also among those most galvanized when expectations fell short or the state responded to calls for change with repression. And, although they would never have admitted it, young revolutionary Chileans such as Beatriz were shaped by the combined frustrations and opportunities Chile's reformist environment provided.

Meanwhile, transnational influences, facilitated by improvements in mass communication, travel, displacement, and exile, contributed to Chile's age of youth and to radicalization of particular circles within it.[37] To contest local phenomena, young Chileans read, heard, and appropriated an "international language of dissent."[38] Through such youth encounters as the Soviet bloc–sponsored meetings of the World Federation of Democratic Youth or Cuba's transnational revolutionary organizations, they also had the opportunity to share ideas beyond their immediate worlds. As Fernando Purcell and Marcelo Casals have argued, universities were a "fundamental theatre" of ideological exchange and contestation in this regard.[39] Indeed, Beatriz's story shows that influences from abroad—with the Cuban Revolution front and center—overlaid and interacted with local mobilization, ideas, and processes to shape young Chileans' worldviews. Certainly, as we shall see, it was the juxtaposition of Cuban developments with local realities that gave the Cuban example its potency among young revolutionary left-wing Chileans like Beatriz.

Third, this book also contributes to histories of Chile's "revolutionary Left" that emerged in the 1960s, espousing the inevitably of violent struggle and a rejection of gradual, institutionally based strategies for gaining power in stages. There has been ample scholarship of Latin America's Left—or lefts.[40] As in the case of Chile, knowledge has mostly been driven by histories of parties through their institutional records or through (male) leaders and theorists.[41] However, a number of significant contributions have told a broader history of politics, rank-and-file militancy, and culture.[42] Even so, intra-Left divisions and radicalization sparked by the Cuban Revolution deserve more attention. We know much more than we did about Cuba's foreign policy in Latin America but far less about its resonance on the ground.[43] Of course, Patrick Iber reminds us that differences over Cuba added a new chapter to a much longer "international left-wing civil war" driven by different interpretations of Stalin and the Spanish Civil War.[44] Yet intense debates following the Cuban Revolution regarding paths to revolution, as well as fears that Cuba's revolutionary experience generated from non-left-wing sectors, are particularly significant for understanding Latin America's Cold War experience.

Chile is an interesting case to study within this context. With the exception of the periods 1948–58 and 1973–90, the country's constitutional democracy allowed long-established left-wing parties, the Communist Party (PCCh) and the Socialist Party (PS), to participate formally in Congress, giving them a stake in the country's governing institutions and the possibility of changing the country using such instruments. For this reason, in a Latin American context, Chile was considered exceptional: a place where revolutionary change could conceivably occur peacefully and democratically. Although this logic governed the majority of left-wing thinking in Chile, underpinning *la vía chilena*, by the 1960s a new revolutionary Left, Beatriz included, had begun questioning such logic. To be sure, as Alfredo Riquelme has argued, their "revolutionary imagination" and "bellicose ethos" contrasted with reformist impulses, even though the latter were deepening in Chilean society and transforming it in revolutionary ways at precisely the same time.[45] Having seen revolution succeed by force of arms in Cuba and witnessing systemic constraints on change at home—not least, through repressive state violence—a young radicalized sector of the PS and the MIR nevertheless began challenging electoral strategies for gaining power. Adherents of this sector did not advocate a rural guerrilla insurgency (many, the Cubans included, thought one unsuitable for Chile) but began preparing defensively to meet "reactionary" violence, disavowing constitutionality as the sole source of power and legitimacy.

Even so, the boundaries between lefts were more porous than previously understood.[46] Certainly, the idea that Beatriz was neatly divided from her father is simplistic. Differences between them definitely existed.

As an article written shortly after Beatriz's death put it, "Salvador and Beatriz Allende represented two political schools, two generations of Latin American revolutionaries."[47] Salvador Allende referred to himself explicitly as being from a different—1930s—generation when he spoke to young Chileans in the mid-1960s.[48] His parliamentary service and four presidential election campaigns, his espousal of peaceful ways of gaining power, and cross-party alliances made him a representative of the so-called old or traditional Chilean Left. As president, Allende, like the pro-Soviet Communist Party, also put faith in the constitutionality of Chile's armed forces and the opportunities state institutions offered for revolutionary change. By contrast, Beatriz was adamant about preparing militarily for counterrevolution. She and those advocating this line of thought berated their parents' generation for failing to solve Chile's political and social crisis through its reliance on electoral politics. Referring to older leaders as *guatones* (roughly translated as "fat and bloated"), they berated what they saw as the traditional Left's "reformism" when contrasted with their prescriptions for surpassing the state and preparing for class conflict.[49] And, crucially, from the late 1960s onward, these radicalized sectors gained increasing power in the Socialist Party's hierarchy.

However, what is surprising is not that Beatriz and her father differed—nor that Beatriz's familial and political loyalties seemed to pull her in different directions—but how interdependent they were. Beatriz participated in her father's government in a way that fused her loyalties together, bringing her intimate relationship with Cuba as well as her training in covert intelligence and security to the job of assisting her father's democratically elected government. And, in doing so, she served as his confidant and an architect of his presidential team. For his part, close strategic allegiance with the Communist Party, as well as advocacy of negotiation and institutionally based change as a means of averting a crisis, did not make Allende a simple defender of an "old" Left. He was a key proponent of closer relations with Cuba. And he supported, integrated, and used younger radicalized sectors of Chile's revolutionary Left, drawing on their ideas, training, and military resources in private. Beatriz's personal contacts and affective relationships mattered enormously in this respect.[50] Indeed, her perspective shows informal networks, beyond institutional party structures, determined and complicated power and politics. And when it came to Allende's presidency, she reveals the relationship between different left-wing factions to be as entangled and intimate as it was uncomfortable—a mix that helps explain the evolution, course, and demise of Chile's revolutionary project.

Beatriz's viewpoint also shows the fallacy of simplistic "old" versus "new" Left categorizations in other ways. As Eric Zolov has underlined, Latin America's "new Left" was far broader culturally, socially, and politically than the "revolutionary" Left it is often associated with and to which Beatriz belonged.[51] Indeed, more tied the "old" Left to the revolutionary Left when it came to musical tastes, behavior, sociability, and gender relations. It was this world Beatriz belonged to rather than other "new" Left groupings such as Chile's countercultural movement. She did not experiment with recreational drugs, attend youth festivals, challenge sexuality norms, or embrace Chile's burgeoning rock scene (an outlier to prevailing left-wing preferences for the Nueva Canción, or New Song, movement).[52] To the contrary, she belonged to what was a relatively socially conservative left-wing at the time.

Which brings us to this book's fourth and perhaps most significant contribution: the insight Beatriz's life offers into what it meant to be a female revolutionary in the era of Che Guevara and Allende. As other scholars have attested, deeply embedded patriarchal systems of power often proved immune to political and social upheaval.[53] Despite efforts to radically transform the world around them, the Latin American Left's attitude to gender was part of this story. This is not to say left-wing parties were more conservative than religious or conservative groups at the time.[54] As we shall see, left-wing Chilean parties—and particularly the Communist Party—championed women's legal rights and access to fair working conditions, encouraging women's participation and militancy. As one scholar argues, it would also be unfair to expect the Left to have adopted practices not found anywhere else in society.[55] The Right, meanwhile, linked—and vigorously fought—revolutionary change precisely because they saw its proponents as threatening gendered power structures and societal norms.[56]

Even so, to revolutionaries in the 1960s and early 1970s, wider feminist goals were considered a "bourgeois deviation" from the priority of class struggle. Women's liberation would come after, and as a secondary feature of, class liberation, not before or in competition with it.[57] Women very rarely became Central Committee members or assumed leadership roles; those few who did were regarded as "exceptional."[58] The way the Cuban Revolution was framed also exacerbated gendered ideas about who should preside over revolutionary change.[59] The idea of it as being driven by men, as well as a particular construction of masculinity, embodied by Fidel Castro and Che Guevara, established parameters around the roles women could play. The glorified "heroic guerrilla" understood as driving Cuba's revolution forward was unmistakably male, while the quest for "the new man" underpinned notions of a new revolutionary consciousness and society.⁶⁰ Chile's own revolutionary heroes, Salvador Allende and the MIR's leader Miguel Enríquez, confirmed contemporaneous understandings of Chilean politics as a "masculine affair."⁶¹ There were, as Jeffrey Gould reminds us, hierarchies in revolutionary circles.⁶²

In this context, even a privileged woman such as Beatriz faced considerable limitations when trying to follow in Che's footsteps and fight for Chile's revolutionary future. Exploring why and with what consequences adds to our understanding of gendered dimensions of Chile's revolutionary Left and long sixties while simultaneously inserting women as subjects into political histories of the period. As feminist historians have done for decades, *Beatriz Allende* is therefore an effort to "both include and account for women's experience." Taking Joan Scott's definition of gender as an analytic category for examining "relationships of power," what follows explores the structural opportunities and constraints Beatriz faced, in comparison with male peers, as she tried to fulfill her ambitions. And, to do this, it zooms in on how she related to constructed ideals of "womanhood" in her immediate political and social circles.⁶³

These questions obviously need historicizing within Beatriz's lifespan and specific environment. Women's positions changed substantially in the thirty-five years she was alive. When she was born, Chilean women did not yet have the right to vote in national presidential elections. By the time she died, global second-wave feminism was in full swing. Shifts in the intervening years gave Beatriz the space to rebel and choose a future that would have been far harder for her mother's generation. But such shifts still fell short of radically altering society in ways that would have enabled her to live the same life as men in her milieu. Even as the daughter of Chile's foremost left-wing politician, with advantages and access far above most of her male friends, Beatriz craved acceptance into a man's world that she was only partially granted. The relationship she had with her father, for example, was intimate, affectionate, respectful, and conspiratorial. But it was also overshadowed by Allende's disappointment at not having a male heir and Beatriz's inability, not for want of trying, to fully become what my interviewees invariably referred to as the "son he never had."

Allende's belief—shared widely across society at the time—that women were ultimately predestined to be mothers and revolutionary dependents, to be protected and shielded by men, also affected Beatriz's ability to participate as actively in Chile's revolutionary process as she would have liked. As someone with intelligence and communications training who knew how to use firearms, she was ready to fight next to him when the coup struck. Pivotally, however, as a woman who was seven months pregnant, Allende forced her to leave the presidential palace before it was bombed.

And it was in this moment "she broke forever," Beatriz's son would reflect.[64] Like many Chilean left-wing women who fought the dictatorship in the 1980s, she did not believe a choice between motherhood and militancy had to be made.[65] But she was unable to persuade her father otherwise. In exile, she was then prohibited from fighting against the dictatorship inside Chile, and it was assumed she would be at home to look after her children and her husband rather than traveling the world to campaign for solidarity. Partly because she did not fulfill this role, her marriage broke down, leaving her increasingly unable to cope as a single working mother.

These circumstances did not preclude Beatriz from actively participating in the political, social, and cultural processes that intersected with her life. Rather, this book is a call to take the role of offstage secretaries, the urban underground in revolutionary organizations, and solidarity campaigners seriously; to look at their significance in shaping history as agents of change; and to explore the extent to which they were able to challenge the roles society expected of them (subconsciously or consciously). As Beatriz's friend Carmen Castillo lamented, compared with the history of violence against left-wing women, female militancy still needs further research.[66] This is particularly so when it comes to the women who embraced armed struggle.[67] Women's lives may have been more constrained than men's. And as they pushed boundaries in the 1960s and 1970s in combining careers and family, they inevitably faced the double burden of fulfilling new roles without being relieved of expected domestic and caring responsibilities.[68] But the past quite simply would not have unfolded the way it did without them.

In this regard, what follows adds to recent studies of Cold War Latin America that put women and gender at the center of narratives and challenge the idea of women's history as separate history, disconnected from politics and confined to the private sphere.[69] When it comes to the Chilean Left, this book also contributes to the few but growing studies of women who instigated social and political change and the effect such changes had on their lives.[70] In telling the story of one woman in her particular context, it is an explicit call to make women, as Scott urged, "a focus of inquiry, a subject of the story, an agent of the narrative" as a means of not simply "recounting great deeds" but also revealing "often silent and hidden operations of gender."[71]

As Beatriz's father quipped in 1961, "Some think ... Chile is at the end of the world, and it is completely the opposite, [Chile] is where a new world begins."[72] And what follows probes a particular revolutionary moment in Latin America's Cold War from inside out, starting with Beatriz and her world and looking outward. I begin with Beatriz's childhood, adolescence, and political awakening in Chile at a moment of mobilization in the late 1950s. Moving forward to Beatriz's university years as a young medical student in Concepción and Santiago, we see her growing politicization and radicalization emerge. Beatriz's subsequent role in a Cuban-sponsored transnational guerrilla insurgency in Bolivia after Che Guevara's death follows. I examine how she managed covert life with public health work during the troubled final years of Frei's government and how she related to the rise of the revolutionary Left in Chile during this period. I then look at Beatriz's involvement in her father's presidential campaign and his government between 1970 and 1973, focusing on her role in security and relations with regional revolutionary groups. Following an account of the Chilean coup the book turns to Beatriz's position in the global solidarity campaign for Chile and what it meant to live in exile in Cuba. Finally, I explore Beatriz's political and personal disillusionment leading to her death.

This story is ultimately a tragedy. It is about the rise and fall of a revolutionary project inspired by Cuba and an urgent impulse for change amid dissatisfaction at home. It is also concurrently about the failure of an individual to live the life she wanted to—why she aspired to the ambitions she did, and why she was unable to fulfill them. But to establish where her ideas and inspiration came from, we need to start at the beginning. From a framed picture of Beatriz hanging in Havana, we thus travel back to 1940s and 1950s Chile, to her family life and political awakening at a moment of crisis and change.

1 : : : An Awakening

Beatriz would remember she became politically conscious of Chile's socioeconomic problems when she was fourteen or fifteen, between 1956 and 1958. She had started accompanying her father—a Socialist deputy from 1937 and senator from 1945—on his tours of Chile when she was seven or eight. And from an early age he had been keen to show her and her sisters "Chilean reality." "From an early age we were integrated into all political activities," she would explain. "Our father ... pushed us to engage, study, and instruct ourselves." But in Beatriz's words, until she reached adolescence, she had observed the world around her "without understanding anything." As part of a middle-class urban elite, the daughter of a politician and a state-employed librarian, Beatriz had lived a sheltered and privileged upbringing. It was only later that Salvador Allende explained the significance of what she saw around her.[1] And what she learned from him would shape her future.

As Salvador Allende perceived it, Chile faced a profound crisis of inequality, poverty, and "underdevelopment" caused "overexploitation" by domestic and foreign ruling classes. As a founding member of Chile's Socialist Party, he had argued for socialist transformation of the country since the 1930s, proposing nationalization of Chile's mining industry and banking sector, agricultural reform, and state-led welfare projects. As a medical doctor and then health minister between 1939 and 1941, he had campaigned to improve standards of living. As a Socialist, he used Marxism, which he had first encountered as a university student, as a broad framework for interpreting history. Yet Allende rejected the Soviet Union as a model. In fact, he was deeply wedded to Chile's democratic tradition, believing its political institutions and practices allowed radical change by peaceful means.[2] Increasingly critical of U.S. intervention in Latin America and its dominance of Chile's economy by the 1950s, he was also a fervent anti-imperialist, describing his position as one of "national liberation."[3] He was not alone. By the fifties, a growing current of radical nationalism challenged the established order in the region and throughout what would be known as the Third World, often looking to Marxist-inspired alternatives.

Influenced by her father, Beatriz would join the Juventud Socialista (Socialist Youth, JS) and become politically active in the late 1950s. This was an important and particular juncture in Chile: a moment of crisis, left-wing mobilization, and resurgent political activism. And, as her friends remembered, distinct from her two sisters, she had a "very strong political commitment" to Allende.[4] Yet, as much as he influenced her, Beatriz's gender, generational distance, and rapidly changing circumstances in Chile and abroad in the late 1950s—not least the Chilean Left's defeat in the 1958 presidential election and the Cuban Revolution in 1959—would differentiate her politics and experience from his. Indeed, there was something very particular about the confluence of forces in the late 1950s that would shape Chile's 1960s generation. This was the context in which Chile's future revolutionary current was born. And to grasp Beatriz's trajectory, it is therefore important to understand it. The advantages and constraints she faced, as well as her upbringing, childhood, and character, are also vital for comprehending who Beatriz was and would become. They reveal why she had such a close relationship with her father. They also indicate the origins of the rebellious energy, determination, and confidence she devoted to the cause of revolution in later years.

Family, School, and Society

As a young girl growing up in the 1940s and 1950s, Beatriz was part of her father's political world insofar as she and her sisters would listen to his conversations with friends at the dinner table or would, on occasion, tour Chile with him. With Allende a candidate for deputy, senator, and president all before Beatriz was ten years old, family holidays often dovetailed with election campaigns.[5] However, steep rates of infant mortality, or the experience of child labor and poverty against which Allende fought, did not pervade the life of such middle-class children as Beatriz. This did not mean her family was immune to hardships. Beatriz's older sister, Carmen Paz, was born on 10 January 1941 partially paralyzed. Then, in 1953, Beatriz's family suffered two tragedies: Hortensia's father, having lost much of his money and unhappily married for a third time, died of suicide by shooting himself (Beatriz's parents told people that he had been ill). Months later, Hortensia and Salvador lost a son, stillborn at six months.[6]

How much Beatriz knew of these events and how much they affected her is hard to determine. By all accounts, she grew up a happy child: outgoing, "adventurous," and confident.[7] She was "brave," Carmen Paz and childhood friend Cecilia Viel explained, and "tenacious." She liked to raid neighboring gardens for tangerines. Together with friends, she also spent time playing in the street roller-skating and riding bikes.[8] Believing it was good for young children to have fresh air, Hortensia had frequently sent her daughters and their nanny to Santiago's Parque Forrestal.[9] At the weekend, Salvador also took Beatriz, her sisters, and their friends on weekend walks in Santiago's San Cristobal Hill and to football matches. He flew kites with them, joined in games at their birthday parties, and taught them how to swim, which Beatriz particularly enjoyed.[10] On occasion, the Allende family was also invited to an estate in the countryside where Beatriz rode horses.[11] Then, in her teenage years, Beatriz went to a friend's house in southern Chile where she honed her riding skills, swam in the river, hiked, and camped.[12] An active life for children outdoors was encouraged at the time. Public health programs since the 1930s had promoted it, and women's magazines in the 1950s encouraged sports and fresh air as the essence to good health (and, for women, good looks).[13] But, even in this context, Allende, athletic himself, was particularly insistent his daughters appreciate physical pursuits.[14]

The family's happiest moments occurred during its extended summer holidays in Algarrobo, a beach resort frequented by Chile's center-left politicians and intellectuals. Arriving in late December, Beatriz and her sisters would stay over a month. And those who spent their childhood there remembered it as idyllic.[15] Beatriz and her sisters played with their cousins—the children of Salvador's sister Laura—and with other friends they spent successive summers with.[16] Beatriz particularly loved beach bonfires. As Cecilia and Carmen Paz remembered, she was often the ringleader of midnight excursions, waking other children up and sneaking out to light them.[17] During the day, her father taught them how to jump across rocks or took them out on a small boat. With Allende's house the center of social life and politics at the beach, the Allende girls were also witness to visits from such Chilean intellectuals as Pablo Neruda and Manuel Rojas, as well as leaders of Chile's emerging reformist Christian Democratic movement, Eduardo Frei and Gabriel Valdés.[18] This was unmistakably a privileged upbringing, giving Beatriz confidence and a sense of entitlement. And, by all accounts, she enjoyed the opportunities it offered.

When not at the beach, from early 1953 on, the Allende family lived in the affluent neighborhood of Providencia. Having moved from their downtown apartment next to Santa Lucia Hill, where their neighbors included prominent left-wing Latin American exiles, Chilean intellectuals, politicians, and lawyers, they now had a garden and more space. The Allendes were middle class but not rich; Salvador had to take out a loan to buy the house and had side businesses to complement his senatorial work.[19] Successive election campaigns also put pressure on the family's finances.[20] But Beatriz could count on her own bedroom, a family cook, and access

Salvador Allende and his daughters, ca. 1950. *Left to right*: Carmen Paz, Isabel, and Beatriz. Colección Alejandro Witker, Archivo Fotográfico de la Biblioteca Nacional de Chile.

Cecilia Viel, Carmen Paz Allende, Beatriz Allende, Billy Pascal, Carmen Montt, Ximena Echenique y Denise Pascal.

Beatriz with friends and cousins on holiday in Algarrobo. "Balnearios de Chile: Algarrobo," *Zig-Zag*, 7 January 1956.

to her father's library, where a photo of her skiing would later hang beside signed photos of dignitaries, including Aguirre Cerda, Chile's former president; Fidel Castro; and Mao Zedong.[21] She and her sisters also went to a small private girls' school near their house, La Maisonette, famed for its open teaching style.[22] Then, at fourteen, Beatriz and her younger sister, María Isabel (known as Isabel), transferred to the elite British girls' college, Dunalistair, also walking distance from their house. As Carmen Paz remembered, Beatriz wanted to learn English; she had an impatient curiosity, was always reading, wanting to know about the world. And she believed English would help her.[23]

Beatriz was a good student and made close friends at Dunalistair but never really adapted to it. It was "very strict" and "very traditional," her contemporaries remembered. They studied Latin and played hockey, lacrosse, and tennis. Days were longer than usual school days, and when students ate lunch they did so at long tables in silence, watched over by their teachers.[24] They were also punished for small misdemeanors. Regardless, Beatriz broke rules related to conduct, etiquette, and appearance. She had no interest in improving her handwriting, for example, much to her teachers' "desperate concern." She drew a line on the back of her legs to avoid wearing stockings, and she took her gloves off on the way home despite instructions to keep them on in public.[25] In an era when women's attire—particularly in middle- and upper-class urban areas—was scrutinized and idealized, when foreigners commented frequently (and positively) on Chilean women's high heels and makeup as testimony to the country's beauty and modernity, and when women wearing trousers was considered a topic worth debating in women's magazines, Beatriz's rebellion is noteworthy.[26] In 1960s Chile (and Cuba), Beatriz's informality would win her praise as an indication of her disinterest in material concerns.[27] But, at the time, it earned her multiple detentions.[28] And it was also one of a series of growing tensions between her and her mother.[29]

Indeed, Beatriz was increasingly distant from Hortensia. One reason was that her mother suffered from episodic pulmonary tuberculosis, which left her bedridden. Fearing contagion, she avoided physical contact with her daughters, creating a long-lasting distance between her and Beatriz in particular.[30] With their mother ill, their father attended school events.[31] He also played an active role in pushing Beatriz and her sisters to do well at school, helping them with homework. As Carmen Paz recalled, without being austere and strict, he demanded "responsibility and commitment" to obtain university degrees.[32] "He argued that you could not be a good fighter [*luchador*] if you did not study," Beatriz would explain. "In a society you had to study to contribute."[33] She also remembered him fondly as "joyful, jovial."[34] As Beatriz and Carmen Paz would describe Allende to a journalist in the early 1960s, he was a "loving father" who gave them time, "in spite of his multiple concerns."[35]

Even so, Isabel remembered that "time with him was scarce," leaving her and her sisters wanting more of it.[36] There were also other cleavages in the Allende family: first and foremost, Salvador's infidelities—initially discreet but less so by the early 1950s. Although, like many other married women in Chile at the time, Hortensia stood by her husband, and he never considered leaving her (divorce was illegal in Chile but marriage annulments were possible), the two increasingly lived different lives. While Allende dedicated his to politics, Hortensia resisted electoral campaigns and, having given up work in the early 1950s, inclined toward artistic and intellectual circles. In this context, Carmen Paz stayed close to both of them, but their younger two daughters took sides, with Isabel leaning toward their mother and Beatriz gravitating toward their father.[37] Beatriz was "very attached" to Allende, Carmen Paz explained.[38] He was "the best, best ... everything" to her, a friend remembered.[39]

The attachment was mutual. Family friends would recall Beatriz sitting next to her father and holding his hand at the dinner table.[40] She was also the most eager to learn from him when it came to physical pursuits and politics. Indeed, she was widely and openly regarded as Allende's favorite—his *regalona*, to use a Chilean colloquialism.[41] There was also complicity between them. As a young student at La Maisonette, Beatriz had pushed a girl who was making fun of her father and whose family opposed him politically.[42] Beatriz also tended to go to her father when she wanted something. When she was eight and wanted a dog, for example, her mother said no but her father agreed, and she got one.[43]

This puppy also had a broader significance. When it became seriously ill, Allende helped Beatriz give it injections. As she recalled, she learned to "appreciate the immense kindness" of "father's efforts" and "became aware of the importance of taking care of others," explaining that "it was in that moment" she "decided to become a doctor."[44] For a girl who idolized her father, Allende's medical training was also undoubtedly important in making this decision.[45] In modeling her future career on him, Beatriz almost certainly had a particular concept of what medicine was about. Salvador had been a key figure in the promotion of "social" and "integrated" medicine in Chile in the 1930s and 1940s, which, as we shall see, shaped the medical profession—and Beatriz's studies—in the decades that followed.

When it came to Beatriz's choice to study medicine, the Allendes' family background and changing attitudes to gender and education were also important. The aspirational middle classes to which the Allendes belonged emphasized education's worth. And it was increasingly accepted by the 1950s that women should enjoy the benefits of university.[46] The percentage of female students almost doubled between the mid-1940s and mid-1960s, when it reached 40 percent.[47] Even so, societal norms still meant women's experiences differed from their male counterparts, and degree choices remained highly gendered. True, the first female doctors had graduated from the University of Chile in 1886, and by the 1950s, women had good professional opportunities relative to their Latin American counterparts.[48] Of 8,000 women who had graduated from the University of Chile between 1910 and 1960, 494 also did so as doctors. But the 3,200 who graduated as schoolteachers dwarfed these figures.[49] Aside from teaching, women tended to study for degrees in the arts, social work, or nursing, deemed more suitable to their gender.[50] And many of Beatriz's generation still had to convince their parents to let them study courses traditionally regarded as male. One of her university friends, for example, fought her mother to be a psychologist rather than a bilingual secretary.[51] The enduring expectation that the majority of women would abandon their professions to get married and have children was concurrently a disincentive for universities to train them. It was for this reason, for example, that the number of women accepted to medical school was capped at 15 percent.[52] As Beatriz's classmate remembered, "The idea was that women should get married and have children and, that if they went to university, it was to look for a husband, so you had to compete fiercely."[53] And this fiercer competition was a vivid example of how Beatriz's gender affected her experience. It tested her determination and cultivated her will to succeed. Even with her parents' support, she had to excel at school to pass two-day university entrance exams (the *bachillerato*).[54]

When it came to politics, meanwhile, Beatriz's choices were shaped by the simple fact that men still dominated Chile's formal political world. It was no secret that Allende "would have liked a son to follow in his footsteps," explained his friend Victor Pey. "He loved his daughters very much," but the idea one of them could succeed him politically was not something considered possible.[55] There *were* a number of significant women in public life in Chile by the 1940s and 1950s, such as feminist leaders of Chilean women's movements Elena Caffarena, Marta Vegara, and Amanda Labarca. Carmen Lazo and Julieta Campusano were pioneering left-wing female politicians. The internationally acclaimed Nobel Prize–winning poet Gabriela Mistral had also blazed a trail for female intellectuals in the 1920s and 1930s, just as Violeta Parra would do for music from the late 1940s.[56] Foreign visitors remarked on the "greater prominence of women in the professions, the arts, and even public life" in Chile compared with other countries in Latin America.[57] Twenty-five percent of the workforce was female between 1940 and 1960, with the majority employed in manufacturing or personal services.[58]

However, women still lacked access to power and representation. Beatriz was almost seven when women could vote in presidential elections and nine before the first woman was elected to Congress. Three more followed in the 1950s, but they were in a stark minority.[59] When the press reported their arrival, it was to announce "beauty" had entered Congress.[60] And although many more women entered politics in the 1950s, opposition to their participation remained strong.[61] On the Left, men were suspicious of feminist demands, believing they diverted attention from working-class solidarity.[62] Within new women's sections of left-wing parties, the Chilean feminist Julieta Kirkwood also bemoaned a history of "passivity" and "silence."[63] Conservative and religious groups, meanwhile, argued that political women would damage family structures; that women were inferior and not prepared to assume political responsibilities; that they were too "emotional."[64] Warnings that women would lose their femininity by spending time on social and political problems were also commonplace.[65] And even in the mid-1950s, teachers at Beatriz's private girls' school did not tolerate discussion of politics.[66] As Isabel would recall, political conversations she and her sisters were privy to "separated" them from their classmates.[67] Moreover, women could not escape the prevalent expectation—promoted by the state's growing welfare system—that they should prioritize motherhood.[68] Since the 1930s, like his contemporaries, Allende had made much of what he called the "mother-child binomial" as a pillar of Chilean society and future development.[69] Magazines written by, and aimed at, women also ardently called for safeguarding "women's roles" in the home. When a man wrote for advice on his wife's determination to keep working after having a child, female readers' letters resoundingly berated her. As a prize-winning letter writer insisted, it was time women returned to their "proper roles."[70]

It is unsurprising, therefore, that 65 percent of women were not active members of political parties in 1950 and that more than 60 percent of those eligible to vote had not registered.[71] Having achieved the right to vote in national elections and hit by broader ideological and party-political divisions, examined below, the Chilean women's movement of the 1940s had largely disbanded by the 1950s. As such, societal attitudes toward women regressed in the 1950s, reasserting traditional gendered norms and expectations just as Beatriz reached adolescence. True, as Allende's daughter, Beatriz escaped many common constraints. Her family status and upbringing gave her freedom other women did not have. As one of her friends remembered, Allende women did not have to conform to traditional gendered roles (housework or cooking, for example).[72] Beatriz thus felt empowered to fight against restrictions by dint of who she was and who her father was. Her childhood friends remember her, in addition to disobeying dress codes, intentionally challenging expected behavior—climbing rocks only boys tended to climb, for example.[73] Her father, an early proponent of women's suffrage, also encouraged his daughters to engage in politics.[74] "From early on I realized ... I was from a very different family," Isabel would explain. Yet, for now, politics were "part of ... daily life" rather than the Allende girls' own ideology and convictions.[75] As a confident and determined teenager, with rebellious tendencies, Beatriz was equipped to push against constraints and assert herself within a man's world. But, as a woman, the question was to what extent she would be able to do so and in what capacity.

A Political Awakening: Context

If we accept Beatriz's explanation of her political awakening at fourteen and fifteen, then it occurred at a moment of a crisis in Chile. When she was fourteen, for example, riots erupted across Chile. For six consecutive days at the end of March and the beginning of April 1957, spontaneous protests took place in Valparaiso and Santiago. Public spaces, Congress, the presidential palace, and courts were attacked. Thousands of students marched.[76] Having deployed police who used water cannons and fired live bullets into the air, the populist president, Carlos Ibáñez del Campo, a former military general, then ordered the armed forces to intervene on 2 April. Official figures recorded more than twenty people dead and eighty-two badly injured, but there were rumored to be many more casualties. The army also destroyed the left-wing printing press Horizonte, attacked the Socialist Party headquarters, and cut telephone lines.[77] The name of one young women killed—Alicia Ramírez, a nursing student—would resonate and be commemorated by left-wing activists for decades.[78]

There were good reasons for societal unrest in the late 1950s. The immediate catalyst for the riots had been a sudden increase of transport costs, primarily affecting students and workers.[79] However, this measure was symptomatic of a deeper crisis. Commentators pointed to a "moral and material chaos," to a government "each day ... more divorced from reality," and of a population running out of patience.[80] Opinion polls conducted in Santiago in 1958 would also find that 70 percent believed Chile's national predicament was bad, whereas only 20 percent had faith the future would be brighter.[81] With living costs rising, unemployment doubling, and inflation soaring, in 1955 the government had imposed a U.S.-sponsored stabilization plan—the Klein-Saks Plan, named after the private consultancy firm that brokered it. It cut public spending, restricted credit, ended subsidies for public services, brought in wage controls, and suspended the right to strike.[82] Yet this effort had not stopped labor unrest, especially as copper prices fell sharply in 1956–57 and austerity measures hit poorer sectors hardest.[83] Students had increasingly joined workers in demonstrations and general strikes.[84] Six months after the riots, hundreds of slum dwellers, supported by priests and left-wing parties, also participated in one of the first land occupations on the outskirts of Santiago, establishing La Victoria settlement. As one of those who took part recalled, "living conditions were truly inhumane" prior to this, with families sleeping along the city's sewerage canals.[85] And among the sympathetic politicians who went to La Victoria was Beatriz's father.[86] Touring coal mining districts in southern Chile the same year, one of Allende's staffers recalled dire poverty: "Misery is not only visible but breathable," he wrote.[87]

This crisis Beatriz awoke to in the late 1950s built on decades of frustrated efforts to deal with the country's underlying economic, social, and political problems. Chile's "social question" had become an increasingly pressing concern from the late nineteenth and early twentieth centuries.[88] By the late 1930s, Beatriz's father was calling for urgent improvement of living standards while decrying high infant mortality rates (half of Chilean children in the 1930s would not live past their ninth birthday).[89] In 1942, the year Beatriz was born, the mood was still bleak. As the middle-class weekly *Ercilla* noted, "Wherever you look, tiredness and sadness are visible."[90] Visiting Chile that year, U.S. essayist and intellectual Waldo Frank had observed "poverty pitiful and painful." Venturing "beyond ... bourgeois squares"—not uncommon to the Allende family—he found "sordid barricades of moldy and rancid houses." With the exception of a few "seriously devoted men in government"—Salvador Allende included—he argued that politicians were playing a "morbid ... game," cushioning their failure with talk of democracy.[91]

Indeed, successive coalition governments led by the Radical Party between 1938 and 1952, wracked with ideological divisions, constrained by conservative elites in Congress, and, from the late 1940s on, derailed by "obsessive" anticommunism, had failed to resolve deep-seated inequality.[92] True, the reformist governments during this period, led by Chile's ascendant middle class, had done much to change Chile's political, social, and cultural reality. Viewing the social question and politicization of the working-class as a "powder keg" but opposed to the Chilean aristocracy's stubborn resistance to change, intellectuals, educators, bureaucrats, and politicians in this middle sector of society had fought to forge an anti-oligarchic, meritocratic, and modern alternative. This entailed constructing and promoting a new "inclusive nationalism," building the basis of a welfare state, expanding public education, encouraging mass participation in politics, and increasing the state's role in everyday life and society.[93] Between 1930 and 1952, life expectancy had also subsequently risen from 37.7 for women and 35.4 for men to 53.8 and 49.8, respectively. And infant mortality rates of 220–60 deaths per thousand live births were halved as a result of the introduction of penicillin, state-led postnatal care, nutritional advice, and food distribution.[94] As an "archetypal middle-class politician," albeit one who devoted his energies to helping Chile's poorer sectors, Beatriz's father, first as health minister for Pedro Aguirre Cerda's Popular Front government of 1938–41, then as a senator and chair of the Senate's Health Committee, had played a leading role in the creation of the National Health Service: the Servicio Nacional de Salud (SNS) in 1952.[95]

However, the situation had been so drastic before this that improvements to Chile's social and political life had fallen short of expectations.[96] With President Juan Antonio Ríos prioritizing stability over social reform from 1942, Chile's political center had also moved right.[97] Allende and other Socialists in government had resigned in 1943.[98] And, for all the Popular Front's gains, workers' real income had fallen between 1938 and 1952, while dependency on foreign capital and food imports grew.[99] The improved infant mortality rate was still one of Latin America's worst by the early 1950s. Malnutrition remained a serious problem in 1960.[100] And steep inequalities within and between urban centers and rural provinces were stark.[101] In 1952, a Chilean women's magazine referred to homeless children as a "problem without solution," despite having predicted a swift solution to child poverty a decade earlier.[102]

Three major factors contributed to the sense of crisis that engulfed Chile in the 1950s. As Aníbal Pinto, a Chilean economist working at the United Nation's Economic Commission for Latin America, argued, Chile had experienced "frustrated development" since the 1930s, characterized by "excessive specialization" in exports (primarily copper), making Chile more vulnerable to falling commodity prices such as those following the Korean War. The lack of diversification, as well as the need for foreign technology and credits to invest in industrialization, left Chile dependent on imports and credits, increasingly from the United States.[103] Moreover, as Allende argued, despite 65 percent of revenue coming from copper, Chileans had no control over or expertise to determine its production, with private U.S. companies owning mines and reaping profits.[104] On another level, successive governments' failure to initiate agrarian reform for fear of a conservative backlash upheld an inefficient and underperforming agricultural system.[105] While landowners remained powerful, rural workers were prohibited from forming unions and repressed, their real wages and living conditions declining in the 1940s and 1950s.[106]

Finally, Chile suffered a democratic deficit, which exacerbated political and societal tensions. Even after women were given the vote, Chileans under twenty-one or illiterate remained disenfranchised. Many also did not participate in politics. In 1952, for example, only 17.6 percent of six million Chileans (29.1 percent of the country's voting-age public) registered to vote.[107] Frustrations with the Popular Front governments and coalition infighting, meanwhile, meant Ibáñez campaigned on an antipolitics ticket that year. State-sanctioned violence was also frequently used to quash strikes and protests, leading to massacres.[108] Chile's celebrated constitutional democracy, stable as it was, thus hid an exclusionary and repressive environment that allowed conservative elites to resist change and bred resentment.

The Law for the Permanent Defense of Democracy, or "Ley Maldita," introduced by President Gabriel González Videla in 1948, outlawing the Communist Party, had further circumscribed Chilean democracy. Anticommunism had been prevalent in Chile before this.[109] But its institutionalization by a Radical president who had previously relied on Communist Party electoral support was an "atomic bomb" detonated against Chile's "social coexistence," Beatriz's father told the Senate.[110] A reaction to the PCCh's strong showing in 1947 congressional elections and a wave of Communist-supported strikes provided the impetus.[111] With U.S. praise and financial incentives, the government henceforth interned nitrate workers and Communists in camps in northern Chile, which the army, including a young Captain Augusto Pinochet, guarded. More than twenty-three thousand Communist Party members were struck off voter registers; publication of the Communist Party's newspaper, *El Siglo*, was shut down; and the government launched anticommunist propaganda campaigns.[112] Communist women who had led the fight for women's equality in the 1940s were now marginalized as "subversive" and expelled from organizations they had helped found.[113] And as Cold War language penetrated society, establishment figures and the media used "communist" and "pro-Soviet" labels to attack many of those who fought for equality in areas such as education and health care.[114]

Anticommunism in the late 1940s and 1950s—legitimized by and dovetailing with a new global Cold War climate—had been part of a more pervasive decline of left-wing influence throughout Latin America since the 1930s.[115] For Beatriz's father, these were "difficult years."[116] The Socialist

Party he had helped found in 1933 was in pieces by the mid-1940s, having broken into at least three factions and lost much of its electoral strength.[117] Having served as general secretary of the Socialist Party (PS) for two years, from 1943 to 1945, Allende was replaced by Raul Ampuero, and he left the party's Central Committee.[118]

In this context, he had increasingly struck out on his own, representing a new coalition of Socialists and Communists and establishing himself as a future leader of a reunited, pluralistic Left. Vigorously opposing the Ley Maldita and refusing to back Ibáñez as presidential candidate in 1952, given his dictatorial legacy from the 1930s, he had decided to stand as a candidate on behalf of a coalition known as the Frente del Pueblo (People's Front) formed by a faction of the Socialist Party and the clandestine Communist Party. He asked Chileans to "fight ... for bread and freedom; for work and health; for peace and culture, against imperialism; for agrarian reform and industrialization; and for democracy, against oligarchy and dictatorship." And yet, with limited funds and publicity, it was a campaign he and supporters expected to lose. When he received 5.5 percent of the vote, he was nevertheless disappointed.[119] As Volodia Teitelboim, Allende's election secretary, later reflected, "The repression had taken its toll ... We had to start again, and that's where we began."[120]

A Political Awakening: Mobilization

Five years later, the riots and repression of March–April 1957 — amid a broader economic, social, and political crisis — spurred left-wing reunification and mobilization. For Beatriz's generation, this was a significant moment of political awakening.[121] As explained by one of her university friends, who, as a secondary school student, took part in the protests, he decided to join the Socialist Party then.[122] For the Left, caught somewhat off guard by the protests, it also signaled a need to better guide anger that had given rise to the riots.[123] Subsequently, the Socialist Party's three factions reunited in early July.[124] Unified and stronger, the PS was now also part of the Frente de Acción Popular (Popular Action Front, FRAP), a coalition formed in 1956, uniting them with the clandestine PCCh and its legal front organizations.[125] By the late 1950s, it was clear the Ley Maldita had failed, with the PCCh not only having endured prohibition but also won sympathy.[126] However, the Left was not immune to divisions after this. The invasion of Hungary caused vehement disagreements between Socialists and Communists, for example, who were described by one observer as having "daggers drawn."[127]

Even so, in September, the month Beatriz turned fifteen, eighteen hundred FRAP delegates met in Santiago to agree on a platform for the country's forthcoming presidential elections and nominated Allende to run as the coalition's candidate.[128] Two electoral reforms in 1958 then stood the Left in good stead: the Ley Maldita was finally revoked, and a unitary ballot was introduced, curbing bribery (*cohecho*), which was particularly endemic in rural areas, where parties and landowners supplied their own voting slips.[129]

The election that followed offered voters a three-way choice. On the right, Jorge Alessandri, a businessman and son of Chile's former president Arturo Alessandri, stood for the Liberal and Conservative Parties on a platform of improved economic efficiency, productivity, and order.[130] Standing for a resurgent Left, Salvador Allende campaigned for agrarian reform, nationalization of mining and banking, and the creation of a social area of the economy.[131] He also emphasized fighting for Chilean "independence" from "imperialist" intervention.[132] And in the middle stood Eduardo Frei, representing the newly formed Christian Democratic Party, a religious and socially oriented reformist party.[133] Two other candidates ran with far less support: Luis Bossay, for a depleted Radical Party, and Antonio Zamorano, a priest standing as an independent. But it was the Left's campaign that shook up the race. Far more radically framed than anything that had come before, the FRAP proposed a revolution by peaceful democratic means. Fearing the geopolitical ramifications of a FRAP victory and concerns for $750 million worth of U.S. investments in Chile, State Department officials in Washington held their breath.[134]

Indeed, mobilization for the FRAP far exceeded Allende's 1952 presidential campaign. Supporters formed committees, composed songs, and staged marches.[135] In a pattern familiar in the 1960s, Allende supporters—or Allendistas, as they were known—formed brigades, painted slogans on walls across the country, and volunteered in poorer neighborhoods.[136] (One observer noted that "every available yard of wall space was plastered with the name of one of the four candidates."[137]) Allende, himself, also campaigned intensely. With the help of railway unions, he boarded a locomotive train to Puerto Montt in southern Chile—the "Victory Train"—making 136 stops in eleven days.[138] An innovative publicity device, Allende's Victory Train brought musicians, intellectuals, and political figures to parts of Chile they did not usually reach.[139]

For their part, Beatriz and her sisters were with their father on the campaign trail more than ever before. In Santiago, she and Carmen Paz joined Socialist Youth militants working at Allende's campaign headquarters. This was very much an initiation into youth politics for them, and because they did not know other members of the JS, a family friend's daughters were asked to look after them.[140] Isabel remembered spending three weeks in Chiloé with their father; "we traveled by plane, bus, boat, horseback," she recalled, witnessing their father's "tireless energy."[141] Beatriz also accompanied her father to campaign rallies in Santiago and would spend weekends with him outside the city.[142] Now that his daughters were older, Allende "was eager" to put them in contact with "workers, campesinos, and the unemployed to illuminate ... naked reality," Beatriz recalled. "In those exhausting trips he met with 20 or 30 people in one place, and 40 or 50 others a considerable distance away. On one occasion, tired after walking and walking, I asked him ... 'why father? If there were [groups of] thousands....' I will never forget his answer: 'We are planting, Beatriz, planting ideas.... Our people deserve the best and in order to achieve this we shouldn't let fatigue or sacrifices stop us.'"[143] However, beyond this, it is hard to find traces of the Allende daughters' teenage experiences in the campaign. As with Allende's previous presidential campaign, there was hardly any media coverage of his family—or any other candidate's personal life. Days before voters went to the polls, one small, out-of-date photo of Hortensia and her daughters on the inside pages of *El Siglo* stood without comment.[144]

What *is* clear, however, is that young Chileans of Beatriz's generation played an important part in this election and that youth involvement in politics—comprising secondary school–age children and university federations—grew significantly at the end of the 1950s as a result of mobilization against Ibáñez. "Many years have passed since something similar was seen," one observer noted, calling "the reappearance of youth in popular demonstrations ... impressive."[145] Young Chileans were called to canvas potential voters door-to-door, distribute pamphlets, and organize marches.[146] In early August, FRAP supporters took part in a Festival of Youth in Santiago, reported to have had a carnival atmosphere.[147]

Enthusiasm turned to bitter disappointment when the election results were announced. Allende lost by just 33,000 votes, prompting the FRAP to argue it had been robbed. Zamorano took 41,000 votes and was rumored to have been financed by the right wing to divert votes away from the FRAP.[148] The Left's inability to match the Right's campaign funds was also regarded as crucial.[149] And 34 percent of women had voted for Alessandri, compared to only 22 percent for Allende, confirming fears raised a decade earlier that the Right would benefit from women's suffrage as a result of the church's influence over female voters and higher literacy rates within conservative circles. Indeed, the Christian Democratic Party secured more female support than the FRAP, winning 24 percent of the vote (see appendix).[150] That anticommunist propaganda targeted Allende as an enemy of the church, one who would destroy families and take children away from parents—reflecting what would become a virulent right-wing "campaign of terror" against him later—was also important.[151]

Overall, the FRAP's 1958 defeat was "a hard blow." Rather than call people out onto the streets to protest, however, Allende asked supporters to go home quietly, knowing there would be other opportunities.[152] That the FRAP had won in agricultural regions that were traditionally right-wing strongholds was significant, underlining the impact of electoral reform in ending cohecho.[153] And yet, for Beatriz's revolutionary generation, awaking to politics precisely at this time, the defeat was important in demonstrating what elections failed to accomplish. As Beatriz's cousin, Andrés Pascal, remembered, children of those who had been architects of the left-wing's participation in the Popular Front, and who had led the Left until this point, now began to reevaluate their parents' insistence on electoral strategies and cross-class alliances. Indeed, to understand Beatriz's politics, he explained, one had to "place her in the context of this tipping point." She had a profound "love for her father, absolute; she was always going to be at her father's side." However, the seeds of what would be her "critical reflection on the traditional Left's politics" were sown.[154] As explained by another member of Chile's revolutionary Left who would volunteer to fight alongside Venezuela's guerrilla insurgency a decade later, "The last time I believed in elections was in 1958 and I think that defeat, as well as the Cuban Revolution, closed one era in this continent and opened another."[155]

Cuba

Victorious four months after Allende's defeat, the Cuban Revolution had a profound impact on left-wing Chileans. The internal, domestic crisis of the 1950s followed by the hope and disappointment generated by Allende's 1958 campaign meant the Chilean Left was searching for—and particularly receptive to—news of revolutionary change elsewhere. In this context, it is no exaggeration to say Cuba transformed domestic politics, sparking a new revolutionary impulse on the left and counterrevolutionary fears on the right. And, with these currents, a new phase of a Cold War struggle to determine Chile's future began.[156]

Beatriz remembered her initial "curiosity about Cuba came from the little newspapers published on the last stage of the struggle against Batista."[157] The Socialist Party—more so than the Communist Party, whose relations with its Cuban counterpart made it initially suspicious of guerrilla insurgencies—had established relations with Cuban groups fighting against Batista from 1957. The JS had also invited Cuban delegates to its national conference in 1958.[158] Before 1959, it was nevertheless hard to get information. Much of the news Chileans read from the island came from U.S. publications like *Time, Newsweek,* and *Life* or international press agencies.[159] For example, Isabel Jaramillo, Beatriz's friend and a fervent Cuba supporter in later years, remembered learning about the island when she read U.S. journalist Herbert Matthews's interviews with Fidel Castro in the library at her private girl's school. She was captivated, just as U.S. audiences were.[160] It was only at the end of January 1959 that Luis Rodríguez, a reporter from *Las Noticias de Última Hora,* began sending back direct reports from Havana unmediated by international press agencies.[161] And when it came to the tribunals the new government imposed on members of the old regime, the difference in Chilean left-wing reporting and U.S.-filtered news was stark. According to Rodríguez, many of the Cubans he had spoken to thought executions of former Batista forces were "insufficient."[162] Left-wing Chilean commentators also quickly tended to support the charge of hypocrisy leveled by Havana's leaders against those, primarily in the United States, who denounced executions but had stayed silent on Batista's violence.[163]

Even so, Chilean observers initially found the revolution's character and its leaders' ideology ambiguous. "Castro is an enigma," one left-wing newspaper columnist wrote. "He has the making of a romantic caudillo, with neither a clear ideology nor a concrete political position. Where is he heading?"[164] Beatriz, too, admitted that she did not initially have a "clear picture. I had a very clear, negative image of Batista, but I didn't realize what this process was going to signify." "We became hungry for information," she told a journalist a decade later. "At times we had an intuition about things, but not a clear one. I thought: I have to do everything possible to go and see this."[165]

The visit Beatriz's father made to Cuba in February 1959 was pivotal in disseminating more information about the revolution. Henceforth Allende would become a key interlocutor between the Chilean Left and Cuba, an interpreter of the island's reforms, and a supportive voice in Santiago—a factor determining Beatriz's own appreciation of the island. He also came back with a signed photo of Che Guevara dedicated to Beatriz and her sisters with "love." As Allende later told the French intellectual and revolutionary theorist Régis Debray, his meetings with Fidel and Ernesto "Che" Guevara had convinced him of the revolution's promise.[166] On his return, friends and advisers then sat quite literally at Allende's feet to listen to what he had seen. As Osvaldo Puccio recounted, "He told us it was a mistake not to have paid more attention to events on the island. That it was a mistake not to have known how to take advantage of them in the election campaign; but, above all, [a mistake] that we had not helped

Cuban comrades." In the immediate aftermath of the FRAP's defeat, Cuba was now a "beacon of hope."[167]

In the following months, as Chilean reporting of and visits to Havana increased, and as developments unfolded on the island, left-wing Chilean impressions of Cuba centered on a number of key issues. One was a romanticized fascination with the Cuban guerrillas' armed insurgency, seemingly unrelated to distant Chilean electoral campaigns. In contrast to the harsh climate of the Andes, the Sierra Maestra was described as a paradise filled with bountiful food and tropical fruits.[168] And, among the Left, the guerrilla struggle launched by Castro's forces from the Sierra Maestra raised the question of armed struggle as an alternative route to power.

Other themes in Chilean left-wing reports were the youth and appearance of Cuba's revolutionary leaders. *Gente Joven*, a new youth publication printed by the Communist Party's press, celebrated young people as the "inspiration" and "motor" of Cuba's revolution.[169] And when revolutionary emissaries arrived in Santiago in March 1959, their beards made headlines (local journalists were so excited they felt it necessary to explain a female delegate was the only one not to have one).[170] Only when agricultural reform was complete—and the revolutionary process was fulfilled—would revolutionaries shave, Cuban visitors proclaimed, as if the revolution's progress depended on facial hair.[171] Looks mattered because they provided an obvious contrast to established politics. Fidel "with his beard is even in his appearance" their "antithesis," one Chilean commentator argued, adding, as if an afterthought, "The Cuban Revolution is also the antithesis of this world."[172]

However, perhaps most significant, in early reporting of the Cuban Revolution, Chilean readers learned of Cuba's Latin Americanist discourse and the mounting threats seemingly poised against the island's revolutionary regime. Left-wing Chileans identified with the idea of a new, unified region working together to tackle problems of development and dictatorial rule.[173] With Prensa Latina, the Cuban news agency launched in 1959 as the voice of *América Morena* (dark-skinned and dark-haired America), Chileans celebrated Cuba's authenticity.[174] More so than other governments in the region, one Chilean editorial argued, Castro spoke for Latin America.[175]

This interpretation of the Cuban Revolution's significance was stoked by left-wing parties in the buildup to a meeting of inter-American foreign ministers held in Santiago in August 1959. In late March, left-wing Chilean commentators had already begun referring to Chileans' "obligation" and "responsibility" to defend Cuba should U.S. sugar quotas be dropped.[176] In the context of Cuba's agrarian reform and opposition to it, coupled with growing U.S.-Cuban tensions in June, Chilean calls for solidarity grew.[177] By July, with the foreign ministers meeting approaching, FRAP parties and the Christian Democrats organized a solidarity movement and were subsequently joined by the national workers' federation, the Central Única de Trabajadores (CUT), and by the Federación de Estudiantes de la Universidad de Chile (Federation of Students at the University of Chile, FECH).[178] Together, they warned that the meeting was being framed as a "new Guatemala"—an allusion to the U.S.-sponsored 1954 Caracas Conference and Washington's efforts to mobilize support to overthrow the democratically elected reformist leader, Jacobo Arbenz, through the Organization of American States (OAS).[179] In Guatemala's case, Chilean "protest ... was late and unorganized," an editorial in *Las Noticias de Última* lamented, arguing now for preemptive action.[180] On the eve of the conference, statements were issued by both the Communist Party and the Socialist Party promising defense of Cuba.[181]

During the OAS foreign ministers meeting, nongovernmental delegations from Latin America also arrived in Santiago to pledge support.[182] Argentines representing more than twenty regional youth organizations called for Latin Americans to "form voluntary brigades ... to defend the Cuban Revolution."[183] On 11 August, more than two thousand people congregated in Santiago's Plaza Bulnes to hear speeches by Cuban delegates to the conference; the veterans of the Sierra Maestra, Armando Hart and Haydée Santamaria; and left-wing Chilean leaders, Allende included.[184] Rumors that Fidel Castro would arrive, whipped up by the left-wing press, heightened excitement.[185] According to the British ambassador, Salvador Allende even went to Havana, hoping to bring Fidel to Santiago.[186]

Then, finally, with the conference almost over, Raúl Castro arrived in his place, citing threats against the revolution as the reason his brother had not come. He also made an unconventional and delayed entrance aboard a military Britannia airplane called "Libertad," accompanied by his wife, Vilma Espín, and Manuel Piñeiro, both veterans of the Sierra Maestra, and forty others. Dressed in army fatigues, none of them had passports, but symbolically, they carried small arms.[187] Beatriz's father—and quite possibly Beatriz as well—was there to greet the Cuban delegation. In Chile, Raúl then denounced OAS efforts to intervene in Cuban affairs, toured La Victoria settlement, and visited Santiago's tourist sights with Allende and Salomón Corbalán, secretary general of the PS. Pivotally, for Beatriz, Raúl and his comrades also attended a reception at the Allendes' home.[188]

Raúl's presence somewhat eclipsed the conference's inauspicious conclusions.[189] Yet the rhetorical and performative mobilization for Cuba in its wake was highly significant: a catalyst for formal Chilean pro-Cuban organizing to begin and the pretext for a visit to Chile by the revolution's leaders. This was the kindling for a much larger movement in future years. And for Beatriz, still only sixteen and at school, the encounter was momentous. As she remembered, "Cuban comrades started visiting my house. I clearly remember Comandante Raúl Castro's visit ... and Comandante Manuel Piñeiro's, and they spoke to us a lot."[190]

It was also an encounter that would leave Beatriz—and other left-wing young Chileans—eager to know more. During his brief visit to Santiago, Raúl handwrote a greeting to young revolutionaries in Chile, which was reprinted in *Gente Joven*.[191] And following a collective decision taken by more than twenty youth organizations congregating in Santiago during the OAS meeting, plans for a Latin American youth conference got under way. At a subsequent preparatory meeting in Santiago in November, 160 young representatives from fourteen countries, including members of Cuba's 26th of July Movement, championed regional coordination and unity. Delegates agreed to work together for a "more dignified present and future," focused on "economic development ... democracy ... the right to work, to education and culture, to health and wellbeing, and to leisure and rest." Delegates in Santiago also agreed that this Latin American Youth Congress would take place in Cuba in July 1960.[192]

A year after seizing power, Cuba's revolutionary leaders expressed appreciation for Chilean support. As a Cuban envoy to Santiago had told a press conference earlier in 1959, "We could never have imagined events occurring in our country ... were going to have such profound repercussions in fraternal [Latin] American countries."[193] The gratitude he expressed for Chilean solidarity would grow in subsequent years as left-wing groups, reenergized and inspired by the Cuban Revolution, sought closer ties with the island and looked for ways to support it and, in some cases, emulate it.

Certainly, Beatriz's graduation yearbook at the end of 1959 noted her desire to visit Cuba. "She will get there," a brief caption read, "as long as she is not shot for being a rebel." It also joked about her missing afternoon classes to wait at Santiago's international airport for her father returning from one trip or another. "With her intelligence and personality she should go far," it predicted.[194] For now, however, Beatriz got ready to go to university. Because quotas limited places for women in medical programs, she did not get into the University of Chile (her first choice), home to three-quarters of Chilean students, the most prestigious place to study medicine and where her father had studied.[195] Instead, she would go to the University of Concepción, a private but progressive secular university in southern Chile. Getting ready to leave the capital and embark on a new chapter in 1960, she could not have known her disappointment would turn into opportunity when it came to discovering her own political identity. Already, at seventeen, she was known as a rebel. As we have seen, her upbringing also imbued her with confidence, a thirst for politics, an interest in the world around her, and a determination to succeed.

2 : : : University and Politics

Beatriz arrived at the University of Concepción in March 1960. It was a long way from Santiago. Students from the capital took an eight-hour night bus if they wanted to visit their families for the weekend and would arrive back just in time to shower and run to classes on Monday morning.[1] It also had a different feel: it was smaller and cold. Yet it was in Concepción that Beatriz found her own political voice and strengthened her vocation for medicine. The modern university campus, home to three thousand students, was a buzzing and intimate place to find her feet. Replete with bars and cafes where students exchanged ideas, there was a sense, as those at the university remembered, "everyone knew everyone."[2] It was also here—and especially at the Faculty of Medicine, a left-wing hub on an already left-leaning campus—that Beatriz became an activist for Cuba and made friends with people who would shape Chile's revolutionary future.

This revolutionary generation was profoundly influenced by the world around them. Concepción, Chile's third largest city, was home to just 150,000 people and thus had a provincial feel compared with the capital's two million inhabitants. Although it was considered a middle-class city, poverty was visible and proximate. Its surroundings were marked by industrialization drives, which, since the late nineteenth century, and more so in the 1950s, had stimulated the growth of coal mines; textile, ceramics, and glass factories; a petroleum refinery; and Chile's first modern steel mill. Migration to the province by those seeking work pushed the population up from 310,663 in 1940 to 539,521 in 1960, when Beatriz arrived. But living conditions were hard. The concentration of workers and the conditions they worked in encouraged unionization, mobilization, and left-wing influence. And in the middle was Concepción with its university campus. As Marian Schlotterbeck and Danny Monsálvez have argued, "urban poverty" was "never far away"; middle-class students were "conscious of daily reality" beyond their immediate world and upbringing.[3]

By the early 1960s Concepción's university had a growing cosmopolitan and international feel. As well as having long-standing links to academic institutions around the world—primarily in the United Sates and Latin America—the city's university welcomed artists, intellectuals, and students from abroad.[4] Global concerns—Algeria's struggle for independence, the Cold War in Asia and Africa, the superpowers' space race, and the drive for accelerated development—resonated in local newspapers, student publications, and the national youth press.[5] And on all sides of Chile's political spectrum, Cuba occupied front-page headlines, its example of revolutionary change jarring with a stifling economic environment and political stalemate at home. Cuba's influence was not something everybody embraced. In the context of student mobilizations in defense of its revolution, for example, one reader wrote to the city's newspaper, *El Sur*, to express the concern that students worried "more and more about problems that are totally alien to our interests. Are these young people blind? Are they not able to understand the misery our own people struggle with?"[6]

What this reader missed, however, was that for Beatriz and her peers beginning university in the early 1960s, Chile seemed intricately tied to the rest of the world. The United States' role in Latin America was certainly central to how left-wing Chileans conceptualized the world around them, often being seen as the primary source of local problems. When U.S. president Dwight Eisenhower visited Chile in January 1960, for example, the Federación de Estudiantes de la Universidad de Chile (Federation of Students at the University of Chile, FECH) wrote him a letter condemning U.S. regional policies. "Has the United States become a 'satisfied nation,' that fights 'to preserve the existing world order?'" students asked. "In Latin America, defending the 'existing order' signifies upholding the privileges of a small strata that controls power and wealth, while surrounded by an ocean of misery." Significantly, centrist Christian Democrats, rather than anti-imperialist Communists or Socialists, controlled the FECH.[7]

Politically active young Chileans also had direct and growing transnational ties to their counterparts in other countries. At the Juventud Socialista's national conference in 1960, for example, invited delegates from Colombia, Bolivia, Brazil, Venezuela, Peru, Cuba, and Yugoslavia attended. The Socialist Party's new youth-focused "Instituto Lenin," established in Santiago in 1961, organized events on Cuba's agrarian reform and the Non-Aligned Movement.[8] In fact, international politics would increasingly infuse Chile's ideologically charged scene in the 1960s. As Chileans debated the future of their country, ideas and influences from abroad informed their choices. In many aspects of life, the local status quo seemed tired, old, and untenable. A devastating earthquake that hit southern Chile in May 1960 further challenged ideas of modernity in Chile, making the need for change seem suddenly more urgent.[9] Not only did the disaster attract worldwide attention, bringing people from the Americas to Concepción to help, but it also catapulted Beatriz abroad on a life-changing mission that took her across Latin America and, most important, to Cuba.

University Life and Medicine

When Beatriz arrived in Concepción accompanied by her father, she could not have known what lay around the corner. For now, she moved into a large university house for female students close to campus. Lina Boza, Beatriz's classmate from Dunalistair, now shared a room with her and remembered them having fun. "We chatted until the small hours," she recalled. "We shared joys and pains and even clothes when we went to parties."[10] Yet how many parties Beatriz actually went to is unclear. Her male university friends remembered living well, dating a lot, and partying. But they recalled Beatriz was often absent from social occasions because, as a woman, she lived under strict supervision.[11]

Indeed, Beatriz's experience was circumscribed by the persistent conservative attitudes toward gender and morality. For Chilean women growing up in the early 1960s, the "rhetoric of the restrained 'lady'" remained pervasive, while "direct regulation of girls' behavior (e.g., controlling their dating)" was common.[12] Young women were advised to be softly spoken, to listen, and to be caring, loyal, and grateful. As the women's magazine *Eva* advised, its younger readers should be "aware of national and world events" but avoid being "a know-it-all."[13] Instead of knowledge, women were mostly celebrated for their beauty—depicted in formal, racialized, and class-based terms. Chile's newspapers published pictures of white society women, replete with diamond broaches and dreams of becoming beauty queens, suggesting this was something to aspire to.[14] *Eva* meanwhile counseled that a woman should kiss a man only if she was ready to marry him. Only when daughters exhibited "moral and physical maturity"—around 19—should parents condone this behavior. If young girls kissed a number of men, however, *Eva* warned parents to intervene: "This denotes a weakness of character ... that will very soon have no limits."[15] To supervise female students, "inspectors" ran the boardinghouse Beatriz lived in and imposed a strict curfew of 10:00 P.M. From the house's balcony at this hour, the girls waved good-bye to their boyfriends before rushing to their rooms for inspection. No boyfriends were allowed in the building.[16]

As someone brought up in a house full of visitors and political debates, showing very little interest in fashion, Beatriz must have found these attitudes difficult, particularly as areas outside Santiago tended to be more conservative than was the capital.[17] Those who lived with her remember she also missed home, and her father especially. It was therefore a great comfort to Beatriz when Allende visited the south, as he did from time to time to support coal miners who had initiated a prolonged strike at the beginning of 1960.[18] On other occasions, Beatriz received calls from home when he was going to be in Santiago for the weekend and, desperate to grab the chance to see him, made the long trip home.[19]

Indeed, to Beatriz, her father and his opinions still mattered enormously. María Eugenia Lorca Robles, a student who lived with her, remembers that Beatriz was suddenly very friendly when she discovered their fathers had been politically close since the Socialist Party's founding.[20] In fact, many of those whom Beatriz befriended at university were the sons and daughters of Chile's center-left political elite her father knew. As part of a generation with parents linked to the university or politics, she found a supportive network in Concepción thanks to family connections, including her father's friend from his own university days, the director of the Faculty of Medicine, Rafael Darricarrere.[21]

This network also helped Salvador Allende, who could call on friends in the city to keep an eye on Beatriz. One of them, a young socialist professor at the university, Jorge Peña Delgado, acted as her *apoderado*—a tutor, one to whom she could turn and who invited her for lunch on the weekends.[22] Allende was also reassured when Beatriz made friends with the actor and radio presenter Inés Moreno, with whom he was romantically involved.[23] Every month, he nevertheless sent Carmen Paz to Concepción with money to buy Beatriz food, clothes, and anything else she needed. As Carmen Paz remembered, it was a way of checking up on her, even if buying her clothes was difficult because Beatriz did not like "material things." The only treat Beatriz accepted was *café helado*—a Chilean dessert made from Nescafé, milk, and vanilla ice cream—which the two sisters, sometimes with Isabel in tow, enjoyed at a small restaurant near her boardinghouse.[24]

The University of Concepción was an interesting place to study. Generally absorbing just over 10 percent of the country's student population, it had grown rapidly from two thousand to three thousand students between 1957 and 1960.[25] Rising student numbers did not yet reflect significant social—or gender—mobility. In Chile, less than 3 percent of students came from low-income backgrounds, below 10 percent in Latin America as a whole.[26] (The Christian Democratic president of the FECH complained this reflected Chile's "hateful social inequality."[27]) And yet, conscious of their elitist position, universities emphasized their "social debt" either through the way they trained their students or through cultural projects for wider audiences.[28] The University of Concepción's founders, for example, had envisaged the institution having a "vanguard" role in technological and educational development of the region.[29] "To say Concepción is to say University," one former student wrote to *El Sur*. "Our University has been the 'foundry' in which guiding elements of knowledge ... are refined.... The University gives study, work, life."[30]

By the late 1950s and early 1960s, the idea that universities were pivotal for modernization had gained new traction in Latin America. Although the University of Concepción had always been outward looking, it embarked on a series of reforms in the 1950s sponsored by international organizations and U.S. private foundations, such as the Ford and Kellogg Foundations. As part of a pilot project for the hemisphere, experts at the Organization of American States (OAS) and the United Nation's Educational, Scientific, and Cultural Organization (UNESCO) spearheaded these reforms, believing the university could be a "strategic motor." In practice, they brought the University of Concepción more in line with U.S. universities through structural reorganization and a student credit system. Rather than focusing on professional preparation, the university was also encouraged to emphasize general education and foster academic research. By expanding the university's remit in this way and increasing student numbers, the hope was that it could better contribute to the "cultural, economic and social development of Chile."[31]

It was as the university was implementing these reforms that Beatriz arrived in Concepción and was caught up in student debates and protests about them. Medical students at the University of Concepción, for example, complained about being required to study general sciences and mathematics at central institutes designed to raise educational standards.[32] In an era when anti-imperialism was surfacing as a key issue among students, U.S. funding and inspiration also met with criticism.[33] And although she had friends in both camps, Beatriz opposed the reforms.[34] Debates regarding the reform process thus provided an instant introduction to student mobilization. Stemming from changing ideas of education and development, this ferment was also emblematic of the tangible reverberations national and global debates could have at a local level.

Associated with accelerating developmental goals was improved access to health care.[35] Since the 1930s, Beatriz's father had been at the forefront of arguing for improved public health as a means of raising living standards and development. By the time Beatriz started university, these arguments had become mainstream with those who had been students alongside Allende, such as Rafael Darricarrere, now university professors instructing a new generation of doctors. Chile's foremost medical journal, the *Revista Médica de Chile*, had also inaugurated a public health section in 1959, responding to the profession's growing "preoccupation" with the links between the population's health and standards of living.

The accepted idea of public health as a developmental pillar reflected global trends.[36] In September 1960, at an inter-American conference on "development" in Bogotá, delegates called for particular attention to tackling infant mortality, nutrition, the elimination of key diseases, sanitation, access to health care, and training across Latin America.[37] Teaching medical students like Beatriz to deal with these problems in turn depended on how "health" was defined. According to a 1946 World Health Organization definition, it was conceived as "a state of complete physical, mental, and social wellbeing and not merely the absence of disease."[38] And this required an approach to medicine that simultaneously addressed "psychological, moral, religious, aesthetic, sociological, cultural, and economic" needs, known by Chilean medical professionals at the time as *medicina integral* (integrative or holistic medicine). As a seminar at the University of Chile in 1960 concluded: "The individual and society itself—and therefore its health—are an indivisible and complex whole, subject to multiple interrelations." Trainee doctors thus had to be taught to perform interdisciplinary tasks: technical, educative, administrative, research, advisory, and informative. They also had to observe economic, social, and cultural conditions around them.[39]

For Beatriz, the idea of medicine as a way to promote development and alleviate Chile's social ills was ingrained in her upbringing. And, in this respect, Chile's specific socioeconomic context at the start of the 1960s mattered enormously. Among health care professionals' concerns were inequalities in access to health services and living conditions between urban and rural populations, malnutrition, infant and maternity care, and access to primary education. As two Chilean doctors in 1960 noted, socioeconomic and political conditions were "the most important factor in determining the risk of getting ill and dying." And because living standards were widely regarded as falling ("every day more precarious"), health deficiencies were considered increasingly serious as the 1960s began.[40] As medics at a symposium on mortality, held in Santiago in September 1960, concluded, medicines and hospitals could not solve Chile's health problems alone unless "the Government, politicians, public authorities, businessmen, and citizens" created "conditions to make illnesses less common and medicine more effective."[41]

It was in this context that professors at the University of Concepción encouraged students like Beatriz to think about medicine's relationship to "the social question."[42] "The School of Medicine, under ... Darricarrere, initiated a great change," one of Beatriz's peers recalled. "They tried to train doctors for Chilean reality ... professionals who understood and made the profound problems Chilean society was experiencing their own."[43] This attention to Chile's sociomedical problems inclined many doctors toward reformist and revolutionary stances. Jorge Peña, the young doctor in the faculty who had been assigned as Beatriz's apoderado, for example, explained that the hope of alleviating poverty had driven him to socialism.[44] In this respect, he was not alone. As a study of Communist and Socialist Chilean university students in the late 1950s had found, "there were few serious students of Marxism ... support of the Marxist parties seemed to stem more from the direct experience and observation of injustice and economic deprivation than from intellectual impulse."[45]

Certainly, when Beatriz recalled what underpinned her socialism years later, she remembered the coal miners near Concepción she had met with fellow students: "Those men, extractors of coal, lying under the sea, crossed galleries and underground tunnels and, exhausted, after hours of work in terrible conditions, returned lacking oxygen, intoxicated by gasses.... They had nothing, neither physical protection, nor social security laws, nor logical time to rest nor enough pay, nor hours to share with family. They exploited them in an inhuman way. The siren announcing collapsed mines was heard often. As students we rushed to the mines to wait, with their wives, with their children, instilling courage or as quiet as a grave, until they brought out the dead and survivors."[46] These were the kinds of images that influenced students like Beatriz who were coming of age at the beginning of the decade. Local experiences informed the way they perceived the challenges confronting Chile. But, as we have seen, national, regional, and global developmental debates had significant local consequences. Increasingly, Chile seemed to be rocked by the tensions between global aspirations of modernity and the reality of "inhuman" exploitation and misery at home. It was not just that Chile seemed to be suffering the ills of poverty and inequality but also that these problems seemed so out of step with broader narratives of progress at the start of the decade. When major earthquakes hit southern Chile on 21 and 22 May 1960, these tensions became even starker, feeding into growing mobilization and ideologically charged opposition to the government, which would infuse Chilean politics in the years ahead.

Earthquakes

Measuring 9.5 on the Richter scale, the earthquake that hit Chile on 22 May 1960 was (and remains) the most powerful ever recorded. Along with two previous earthquakes measuring above 7.0 the day before, fierce aftershocks, the eruption of at least five volcanoes, and tidal waves, it devastated Chile. Although the death toll from both earthquakes was relatively low because they struck on a weekend (numbers vary between fifteen hundred and three thousand dead and missing),[47] the material damage was enormous: 129 towns and cities were affected, with ports, roads, bridges, hospitals, schools, industry, and agriculture hit. A year later, the cost was estimated at $600 million.[48] In this respect, the earthquakes came at a particularly bad time, halting already frustrated development. Despite Alessandri's promise to tackle inflation and improve economic performance at the start of the year, the country found itself in much the same situation as before, with tensions over reconstruction now adding to political battles regarding wages and austerity.[49] The international scene—and revolutionary Cuba in particular—provided a stark counterpoint. As aid flooded into Chile from abroad, the solution to the country's problems increasingly seemed to lie elsewhere. Certainly, in a decade that had begun celebrating space travel and promising rapid modernization, the earthquake seemed to underline how far Chile had to go.

When it came to the earthquakes themselves, Beatriz and her friends were lucky. Because the first one struck on a Saturday at dawn, all girls were at their boardinghouse. It was a solid building, suffering little damage. Even so, the impact of the earthquake caused water and electricity to be cut off (the girls relied on a small fish pond at the entrance to flush toilets). Phone lines also stopped working, so it was impossible for the students to communicate with their families to let them know they were safe. Without any way of contacting her, María Eugenia's father drove through the night from Santiago to collect her. Beatriz's family was also anxious and relieved when Darricarrere managed to contact them to say she was okay. Allende, who was in Cuba when the earthquake hit, immediately sent two aides to Concepción to get Beatriz. Having traveled home, he then flew to areas affected by the disaster to offer support.[50]

Beatriz and María Eugenia were not the only students to leave Concepción. The university closed indefinitely. Students from the north were sent home so the university could concentrate on housing local students and those from the south. The central library and administration building were also deemed irreparable. The university therefore faced the task of managing the crisis, rebuilding, and replacing equipment destroyed by the earthquake. By the end of May, the cost was estimated at almost $5 million.[51] Its director, David Stitchkin, called the earthquake's impact "doubly serious" given the university's recent investments on reforms.[52]

For those who stayed in Concepción and surrounding areas, life was difficult. Close to 60 percent of all houses in the city had been destroyed.

With winter approaching at the beginning of June, 150,000 Chileans in the region were believed to be without a roof.[53] The army and volunteers set up tents in public spaces, while the Chilean air force organized an airlift of supplies to affected areas and the navy dispatched ships.[54] More than one thousand people were evacuated to hospitals in Santiago, while medical staff in the capital who could be spared traveled south to affected regions. As well as injuries sustained, fears of infection were rife. Doctors, nurses, and medical students treated patients for physical and psychological effects and organized vaccination campaigns.[55] A month after the earthquake, challenges included setting up emergency hospitals, building temporary accommodations, launching hygiene campaigns, treating drinking water, repairing sanitation facilities, and distributing food.[56]

However, it was not just southern Chile that had been affected by the earthquake; the whole country appeared to reel in shock. Politics and commemorations planned for Chile's 150th anniversary stopped, and labor disputes—including a coal miners' strike begun months earlier—were put on hold.[57] The earthquakes had served to "make the dreadful conditions of local construction" and the inadequacies of reconstruction after Chile's 1939 earthquake "tragically evident," Concepción's newspaper reported.[58] It had also starkly revealed—or forced people outside the region to engage with—poverty in affected areas. Panelists at a University of Chile seminar described "subhuman living conditions." Reconstruction could not be "mere restitution," they argued, but had to provide a new "economic, social, and cultural foundation" to "guarantee these areas' inhabitants a stable and prosperous life."[59] Indeed, the idea that earthquake relief should initiate a new phase of regional development was widely shared.[60] "We must set our sights on a constructive vision," a columnist in *El Sur* argued. "To cry, lament, criticize everything means nothing."[61] On the left, in particular, politicians, including Beatriz's father, argued the earthquake should provoke radical change.[62]

Conservative and right-wing public voices echoed the need for change, albeit on a different scale, putting more emphasis on their idea of modernity than inequality and poverty. As a result of the earthquake, *El Mercurio* reported that "the country appeared to wake up" to inadequacies of the south's infrastructure: "the inexistence of any airfields, the deficiency or lack of roads and ports ... [and] wireless communications, which were few and of poor quality." As the paper retrospectively bemoaned, these were all "fundamental factors for the first stage of development in any civilized community." Reconstruction efforts needed specialists Chile lacked. Development required greater literacy and more-skilled workers.[63]

Without specialists of its own and lacking in large financial reserves for reconstruction, Chile welcomed international support. The noteworthy speed and scale of such aid was possible thanks to postwar advances in international organization and communication.[64] As one Chilean remembered, it seemed as if Santiago's international airport would collapse with airplanes delivering aid.[65] Indeed, more than 127 air force planes from around the Americas, together with domestic and international commercial airlines, took part in the airlift.[66] Meanwhile, Latin American nongovernmental and governmental responses were impressive. Voluntary collections in Venezuela, Argentina, and Colombia raised hundreds of thousands of dollars. The Mexican government sent more than seven tons of food, clothing, medical aid, and construction materials; Peruvian and Ecuadorian navies dispatched supply ships; Brazilian military planes and Chilean merchant ships transported thousands of tons of food and medicine; Uruguay sent medical equipment; and Argentinean aid convoys crossed the Andes. Around the world, Red Cross societies organized campaigns. Japan sent earthquake experts, while Britain's Queen Elizabeth and the Dalai Lama wrote messages of support. Other notable aid came from West Germany ($2 million), the Soviet Union (7 tons of supplies), and, overwhelmingly, the United States ($20 million, 900 tons of aid, 600 auxiliary personnel, and, later, $100 million in credits).[67]

In fact, the 1960 earthquake resonated to such an extent worldwide that Lenka Franulic, director of *Ercilla*, would reflect in an interview for *El Mercurio* that it caused world leaders to "forget, for a moment, their differences, their Cold Wars."[68] And yet international earthquake assistance was immensely politicized within Chile itself. Parties emphasized the altruism of their international allies, celebrating their contribution. Cold War divides were thus refracted through local politics even during a moment of natural catastrophe, with the right-wing press emphasizing support from the United States, the OAS, and Western Europe, bemoaning delays in Soviet aid. The Communist daily *El Siglo* conspicuously ignored U.S. support and celebrated Soviet supplies.[69] And the socialist newspaper *Las Noticias de Última Hora* emphasized assistance from Cuba, East Germany, Czechoslovakia, and Yugoslavia.[70] Even when it came to disaster relief, then, the politically charged internationalization of everyday life was palpable.

Within this broader context, university students throughout the Americas joined the relief effort. Almost two thousand University of Concepción students constructed housing and organized street collections.[71] Brigades from the United States offered to travel to Chile, and Cuban students collected money on Havana's streets.[72] With volunteers came news from abroad. As María Eugenia, Beatriz's friend in Concepción, remembered, she first learned about General Alfredo Stroessner's dictatorship from a Paraguayan student who arrived to build a school in the area.[73] A delegation comprising fifty volunteers from five continents also came to Concepción to take part in a month-long project to build a medical center under the university's auspices in Población Andalién.[74] A small city in southern Chile famed for being at the "end of the world" thus became a hub for transnational encounters encouraging Chileans' identification with the world beyond its borders.

Beatriz's participation in this student-led activism certainly had a profound impact on her understanding of Latin America. As a result of contacts made at summer schools in Chile earlier that year, the University of Buenos Aires's student federation invited socialist militants from the University of Concepción to collect donations for rebuilding the campus. Beatriz, supported by her father on the condition it did not affect her studies, was one of six students chosen to go. And it fed her political interests, offering her the chance to become part of a new Latin Americanist moment. "We began to realize, without knowing it concretely, that we were entering a different political dimension in Latin America—regional," one of those accompanying her remembered.[75]

From Santiago, Beatriz and her five fellow students hitched a ride on a postal plane across the Andes.[76] As they sat among mailbags en route to Buenos Aires, they hoped they might somehow use Argentina as a stepping-stone to other Latin American countries and, if possible, to Cuba, in time for the Latin American Youth Congress. And they were in luck. In Buenos Aires, they met Uruguayan students who invited them to Montevideo. And, while there, they were asked to visit Rio de Janeiro. From Brazil, they went to Venezuela, where thanks to contacts made between exiled Venezuelans and Allende in the 1950s, the country's senator, Luis Beltrán Prieto Figueroa, looked after them. With help from Venezuelans, they then went to Cuba. At each stop they met local students and participated in solidarity events for Chile. They also talked about local, national, regional, and global politics, exchanging ideas and perspectives. It was an unexpected, improvised journey that would last weeks. As Beatriz later explained, "We didn't have money.... In each country we arrived we linked up with left-wing students. We stayed in universities. We travelled in cargo planes, in postal planes."[77]

Hernán Sandoval, one of those on the trip, remembered it was an incredible journey: "I was 19! I was not even 20! I had never left Chile ... it was a cultural shock." He also recalled that he and Beatriz were struck by the mobilization of opposition groups to President Betancourt's reformist, pro-U.S. government in Venezuela. They became particularly close to the country's pro-Cuban Movimiento de Izquierda Revolucionaria (Revolutionary Left Movement, MIR), formed in April 1960 by a young breakaway faction of Betancourt's own party. At a constituent conference the same month Beatriz and her friends arrived in Caracas, the MIR underlined its commitment to Marxism-Leninism and "national liberation" as a route to socialist transformation.[78] Now, welcomed by its founding members, the Chilean students accompanied the MIR on antigovernment demonstrations, regarding the protests as much bigger and more serious than their Chilean equivalents.[79] Probably referring to the raid of the MIR's headquarters and the murder of a 26th of July Movement representative in Venezuela the previous month, Beatriz also recalled "a lot of repression."[80] (By October–November 1960, the MIR would take part in large-scale protests, and faced with more government repression, it became the first left-wing party to declare the necessity of armed struggle.[81]) In more ways than one, in fact, politics gradually overtook solidarity with earthquake victims as the trip's main focus.[82]

Cuba was the resounding highlight of this trip. For months, preparations for the Latin American Youth Congress planned in Santiago in late 1959 had been under way with active Chilean involvement.[83] When Cuban representatives visited Santiago in June, they had promised "a truly transcendental event" that would establish "the pillar of continental liberation." And young Chileans read that "enthusiasm was indescribable" in Cuba.[84] Now, arriving just after the Congress had begun on 26 July, Beatriz and her friends participated in a two-week encounter bringing together delegates from 183 regional organizations.[85] Although accounts of numbers attending ranged from a few hundred to fifteen hundred, there was no mistaking the event's significance.[86] U.S. government observers later reflected that it was Cuba's "first mass effort to recruit youngsters for guerrilla training."[87] Yet it was far more opaque than this, attracting a mix of young Latin Americans ranging from social democrats to Christian Democrats and armed revolutionaries. Guatemala's deposed democratic president, Jacobo Arbenz, was a special guest. Representatives from the Soviet bloc, Western Europe, China, Algeria, Iraq, the World Federation of Democratic Youth, and the World Federation of Trade Unions were also present as observers.[88] Not formally delegates for the thirty Chilean youth organizations attending, Beatriz's group had met a Cuban representative in Uruguay, who personally invited them at the last minute. This was what the students had hoped for when they left Santiago unsure—but hopeful—of reaching Cuba. For Beatriz, who was invited to stay with Raúl Castro and Vilma Espín when she arrived, it was also one of life's chance encounters that proved decisive.[89]

The congress also played a big role in Cuba's hemispheric position, forging links between its leaders and revolutionary hopefuls. As a decidedly "young" revolution, Cuba was an obvious location to host such a congress. For the new Cuban revolutionary regime, the congress was also an opportunity to promote its vision of revolutionary change across Latin America, communicate directly with people from the region, share Cuba's reality with them, and ask for support. Although it focused on such broad topics as Latin America's political, economic, and social reality, delegates were specifically asked to consider how young people should position themselves, what problems they faced, and how they might participate in solidarity groups to cooperate or exchange information with one another.[90] Che Guevara explained in an opening address that one of the revolution's greatest strengths was its ability to rely on transnational support. And he underlined such solidarity as being "a duty." As he reminded delegates, Cuba's revolutionary leaders had all been young—"young in age, young in character, and in hopes [*ilusiones*]." However, since gaining power, they had matured "in the extraordinary university of experience and by living contact with the people." He invited delegates to "verify" its positive aspects during their visit.[91]

Beatriz was profoundly impressed by what she saw. "The impact was definitive," she recalled. "When I saw the [Cuban] people so dedicated, organized and consistent, I realized that they were invincible."[92] Visiting the island "marked her," a friend explained; she subsequently talked about Cuba at length as a "a model, a wonder ... she thought everything was excellent ... to her, there was nothing discordant or dissonant about it." She also saved photos, newspaper cuttings, and letters from her trip in a wooden box under her bed at university.[93] Indeed, as Beatriz would later say, she felt "lucky" to have seen the revolution's "first moments."[94] And she was not alone. Chilean visitors to the island told of an infectious urge to make the most of their stays and of militias training daily, learning to use arms, organizing talks on topics like patriotism and advances in science.[95] Mireya Baltra, a young Chilean kiosk seller, union delegate, and future Communist Party leader, felt as if she had "awoken to a different reality," leaving "the cultural bubble the ruling classes had confined [her] to" behind. "Maybe for the first time," she remembered, "I understood that life had meaning. It was like a lightning bolt to my brain."[96] It was "like a Catholic seeing God," a friend of Beatriz's explained.[97] "I want to see everything," another Chilean told the Cuban newspaper *Revolución*. "I want to smell the land, go fishing for stars, feel myself saturated in this vigorous spirit ... which will ultimately, and hopefully soon, be that of all our America."[98]

During what turned out to be weeks in Cuba, Beatriz joined delegates gathered in university halls to discuss problems of war, peace, and imperialism.[99] She met fellow Chilean student groups and founding members of Nicaragua's Sandinista movement and Peruvian guerrilla insurgencies. Alongside other young Latin Americans, she also met Che Guevara face-to-face in the lobby of the Hotel Habana Libre.[100] And she had the opportunity to meet him briefly at Cuba's National Bank. When she was introduced as Allende's daughter, she answered back "No! I am Beatriz!," asserting a new independent voice that life at university and on the road had given her.[101]

The most powerful event of the congress, however, was Fidel Castro's closing speech on 6 August. A month earlier, Cuba had announced it was seizing foreign-owned oil refineries that would not process Soviet oil—and had received active solidarity from sympathetic Chilean followers.[102] Now, losing his voice and at times handing the microphone to Raúl, but willed on by a crowd of young Latin Americans, he listed the nationalization of twenty-six private U.S. companies. Beatriz would vividly recall "the love between the people and Fidel.... I will never forget this rally."[103] Another young delegate remembered it was "deeply moving because from above, the whole stadium was watched over by armed militia who danced alongside the public."[104] Indeed, Fidel celebrated Cuba's defensive militias and promised military training for all workers, peasants, and students. Castigating U.S. democracy and inter-American efforts to sanction the island, he also proclaimed a new style of Cuban armed democracy comprising "more than a vote that you falsify, that you prostitute, and that you buy ... Cuban democracy gives each Cuban a rifle to defend their rights, to defend their homeland." He warned that the United States—described earlier by Guevara as "the greatest colonial force on the face of the Earth"—would do everything possible to stop revolution in Latin America.[105] However, Fidel reassured delegates that Cuba was a "homeland" for the region's peoples.[106] After this, Hernán, Beatriz's companion from Concepción, remembered a carnival atmosphere infused Havana's streets. Crowds removed signs from buildings of U.S. companies, paraded them to Havana's seawall, and threw them into the water.[107]

The Latin American Youth Congress's final resolution spelled out the lessons its participants had derived. "The peoples of the world are waging great and heroic battles for freedom, national independence, and a better future," it stated. "Latin America's young people are conscious that they belong to the frontline of action and thought in these struggles."[108] Certainly, this is the message that Beatriz took home. It reflected a growing rebellious mood in Chile and the increasingly prominent role students played in politics. As the left-wing youth newspaper, *Gente Joven*, told its readers, Chile's ongoing economic and political crisis meant there were dark days ahead but a "youth-led renovation movement" had shaped 1960. As editors noted, young Chileans were now part of a global awakening of youth from countries as far apart as the Congo, Algeria, Argentina, Japan, and Venezuela: "It seems as if they have realized that they are the ones with most energy. That they are the ones most interested in a new, more just, and human world."[109]

Leftward Turns and Student Politics

The year after the earthquakes, Chile shifted politically, in part owing to continued frustration with the status quo, austerity, and the slow pace of change in the country, which seemed especially so when contrasted with Cuba's revolutionary example.[110] "On the one hand, life, risk, and hope, and on the other, hypocrisy, conformity, and despondency," one Socialist commentator argued in late 1960.[111] The Chilean government's delays in reconstruction aggravated the sense of localized morass in the country. Imports rose by 45 percent to cover the demands of rebuilding.[112] And although the opposition on the right and the left obstructed Alessandri's Reconstruction Bill, albeit for different reasons, its delay exacerbated affected communities' difficulties. This, combined with ongoing battles regarding wage increases to match inflation, meant many were angry with the government as the country approached congressional elections in March 1961. Alessandri was able to claim some success when inflation rose by only 6 percent in 1960 (compared with 33 percent the previous year). However, this decrease in inflation rises was not considered enough. Nor did agreed wage increases satisfy demands or significantly alleviate workers' scarcities.[113] When Chileans went to the polls, they therefore voted overwhelmingly for the opposition, blocking the president's ability to use his veto and fundamentally shaking up the country's politics. It was the first time in the twentieth century that Chilean Conservatives and Liberals lost out to center and left-wing parties, with the Christian Democrat Party (PDC) now holding more seats than the Conservatives in Congress.[114]

The combined parties in the Frente de Acción Popular (Popular Action Front, FRAP) also did well, securing 27.5 percent of seats in the Chamber of Deputies (forty) and thirteen of forty-five seats in the senate.[115] The Communist Party, outlawed between 1948 and 1958, received 154,000 votes on its own, winning sixteen seats in the Chamber of Deputies and four in the Senate.[116] And left-wing commentators celebrated younger voters' contribution.[117] The 1958 electoral reforms had also bolstered the opposition's chances, and its constituent parties made concerted efforts to win over rural voters with calls for land reform.[118] In a country where 7 percent of landowners owned 80 percent of the land, where the majority of Chile's rural families were landless, and where the price of food imports exceeded exports by $100 million, the idea of change resonated.[119]

Partly as a result of his successful campaign in rural areas—often accompanied by Beatriz and Isabel—Salvador Allende also celebrated winning the Senate seat for Valparaiso and Anconcagua against all predictions. Had he not done so, his hopes of standing as a presidential candidate in 1964—already discussed widely as a possibility—would have been doomed. Throughout the campaign he had driven daily between Santiago and the region he was campaigning in, leaving at dawn and arriving home after midnight.[120] As well as underlining the need for land reform in the Anconcagua valley, where rural poverty was rife, he converted a bus for campaigning, assembling loudspeakers and a cinema screen to it. As one of his assistants remembered, it had a particular impact among communities with no access to electricity or television. Films with sound donated by Cuba depicting battles against Batista and life on the island drew especially large crowds. "Every time one of the heroes of the Revolution appeared," a witness remembered, "the crowd applauded."[121] Even so, Allende complained bitterly about negative media reports.[122] And, on one occasion, campesinos had to defend his bus against right-wing opponents, using farm tools as "weapons."[123]

Beatriz and Isabel witnessed the intensity of this campaign. Although classes in Concepción had started early to make up time for months lost after the earthquake, Beatriz skipped university, spending two months living at her Aunt Inés's house in Viña del Mar.[124] As Isabel would recall, she and Beatriz stood in for their father when he was not able to meet everyone personally, going to meetings, and campaigning "house by house": "We knocked on the door, delivered pamphlets, we began to speak to people or we went to the edges of settlement constructions." As she remembered, "it was very moving because peoples' standard of life was very bad."[125] Ultimately, their efforts contributed to Allende's unexpected victory. Nationally, those on the right were rudely awakened to traditional elites' declining power. Anticommunist international observers were also concerned by what one diplomat called the "disturbed and potentially dangerous political state of affairs."[126]

A month after the elections, the CIA-backed invasion of Cuba by Cuban exiles and its defeat by Castro's government boosted the Left and further perturbed the Right. Of course, Cuba had become politically contentious before this. By June 1960, with growing Soviet-Cuban ties, anti-Cuban fervor had grown. Cuba had become a "platform for communist penetration of our continent," *El Mercurio* reported.[127] As one columnist for Concepción's *El Sur* wrote in July 1960, it was impossible to "view it with indifference."[128] Eight months later, the same columnist warned that Cuba had become a decisive battleground of the global Cold War: "a serious international risk."[129] Political cartoons depicted guillotines manned by bearded revolutionaries and Fidel as Nikita Khrushchev's puppet.[130]

For those sympathetic to the revolution, however, growing hostility to Cuba had spurred them to action. The Socialist Party maintained a particularly close relationship with the island, empathizing with its Latin Americanist stance and playing a key role in disseminating news about it.[131] Salvador Allende was a key actor in this respect, traveling to the island three times in the first eighteen months after the revolution and speaking at length about it in Congress.[132] Having seen the revolution firsthand, Beatriz was also now invited to speak about Cuba at events in Concepción, doing so enthusiastically.[133] According to a senior Cuban intelligence official, both she and her father were local contacts for visiting Cuban delegations and important links on which the island's leaders relied.[134]

Beatriz also undoubtedly had a receptive audience when she talked about Cuba on campus. At universities across the country, left and center-left students—accounting for the majority of politically engaged students at the time—sympathized with the revolution. As a declaration by Socialist, Communist, and Radical students at the University of Chile at the start of 1961 proclaimed, "The Cuban Revolution embodies the greatest yearnings for peace, liberty, independence, and progress that we, Chilean students, wish for the peoples of the world. To defend it against attacks from its enemies—which are ours—is to defend our own future."[135]

Indeed, broadly speaking, the Chileans involved in mobilizations identified Cuba's revolution and struggle against the United States as their own.[136] As Allende proclaimed at one of many solidarity events for Cuba in early 1961, "The Cuban Revolution is also Latin America's Revolution."[137] And in the context of President Eisenhower's decision to break diplomatic relations with the island in January 1961, Chile's Movimiento de Defensa y Solidaridad con la Revolución Cubana (Cuban Revolution Defense and Solidarity Movement)—comprising political parties, trade unions, writers, and artists—had responded immediately as if the move had been an affront to their own political futures.[138]

In this context, the Bay of Pigs prompted wide-scale protest. The day the invasion began, Allende presided over a FRAP emergency meeting and Socialist senators in Congress issued denunciations.[139] In the following days, Chile's national workers' federation, the CUT, called a national strike, and the Socialist Party (PS) and Communist Party (PCCh) met at their respective headquarters and issued declarations supporting Cuba. As the PS declared, "To defend Cuba is the popular movement's fundamental task."[140] Expressions of solidarity for Cuba spread across the country. From Havana, Giraldo Mazola Collazo, head of Cuba's Instituto Cubano de Amistad con los Pueblos (Cuban Institute of Friendship with Peoples, ICAP) received a telex from Chile indicating "coal miners [in Lota] had organized a battalion of two or three hundred people."[141] This battalion remained on alert in the following weeks, growing to five hundred young volunteers between nineteen and twenty-seven years old who undertook symbolic physical training.[142] Reflective of the power events outside the country had to affect life at home, the Chilean government sent *carabineros* (Chile's armed police officers) to repel protestors, guard the U.S. embassy, and protect private U.S. businesses and banks.[143] As one columnist wrote, the invasion taught Latin Americans "a magnificent lesson" of the lengths "imperialism" would go to protect its interests.[144]

Young Chileans played a leading role in this mobilization.[145] Because the invasion coincided with a meeting of the socialist bloc–sponsored World Federation of Democratic Youth in Santiago, attended by delegates from 41 countries and 110 Latin American organizations, news resonated in a ready-made forum. It was a "burning topic, the topic that inspired concern," one delegate proclaimed. Participants issued a unanimous solidarity declaration and resolved to return quickly to their own countries to mobilize support.[146] On the day of the invasion, one thousand students also took to Santiago's streets chanting "Cuba yes! Yankees no!" and were fired on with tear gas.[147] As Alejandro Rojas, a secondary school student who had never participated in politics before this, remembered, he found himself suddenly joining a pro-Cuban group of classmates heading downtown and shouting "Fidel, Fidel" and "Viva Cuba Libre" until hoarse. That night he went to a friend's house where—as a new Fidelista—he listened to Nicolás Guillen poems and Carlos Puebla songs. Not long after he joined the Socialist Party.[148] "Our generation awoke to politics expressing our unconditional solidarity with Cuba in the streets," another future left-wing student leader would recall of the Bay of Pigs. "Thousands of young Chileans signed up as volunteers to go and fight for the Cuban Revolution."[149]

In Concepción, Beatriz took part in a student demonstration that turned violent, with around forty protestors breaking off and throwing stones at the U.S. Consulate's windows.[150] A U.S. flag stolen from the U.S.-Chilean Cultural Institute was burned, while three protestors and two police were injured.[151] The violence was actually mild compared with future demonstrations. It was not the first time students had burned the U.S. flag or effigies of U.S. policymakers.[152] Compared with outpourings of anger across Latin America, it was also moderate. In Venezuela, for example, a sixteen-year-old was killed, 36 were wounded, and 30 detained in demonstrations; in Mexico City, 25,000 burned an "Uncle Sam" puppet.[153] Even so, columnists and readers of *El Sur* described student protesters as "mentally ill"—"an ungrateful and irresponsible mob" and "emerging spirits, won over by demagogy."[154]

Of course, the students involved, Beatriz included, saw their actions differently. As she would tell a Cuban journalist years later, "We felt tremendous angst that we were not able to help the Cuban people. We burned American flags. We threw stones at buildings. The [Cubans'] victory was a party."[155] Although not responsible for the march, the Christian Democrat-led Federación de Estudiantes de Concepción (Concepción Students' Federation, FEC) issued a declaration to "emphatically repudiate" the invasion. Underlining the right to self-determination, it warned of "a serious danger for world peace and ... Latin American peoples."[156]

Across Chile, in fact, the Bay of Pigs increased support for Cuba. Chilean students had warned Eisenhower in January 1960 that intervention against the island would be "enormously stupid.... [The United States] would lose respect and trust."[157] Now, in the aftermath of the invasion, a group of young Chileans who had been in Cuba at the time of the invasion came home in awe of the Cubans' resilience and willingness to sacrifice their lives for their country.[158] At 1 May celebrations in Santiago, workers carried Cuban flags and large pictures of Fidel and Che, while the CUT's president, Clotario Blest, one of the earliest supporters of the revolution and a regular visitor to the island, demanded the need to "follow Cuba's example."[159] The Instituto Chileno-Cubano de Cultura (Chilean-Cuban Cultural Institute) hosted a photo exhibition of life on the island.[160] In July 1961, the PS also named a new recruitment drive after Fidel Castro and by November had enlisted seven thousand new members.[161] Young Socialists initiated into politics by the Bay of Pigs henceforth spent free time volunteering in poblaciónes, teaching literacy, and spreading "information about national and international politics focusing on Cuba and the revolution."[162]

Anticommunist observers were notably concerned, jumping to conclusions about the implications of Cuba's influence. "There are ugly rumors going around about armed groups being formed in the countryside (though we have no hard evidence of any kind to support this)," the British ambassador reported. "Pessimists are inclined to hint that some Chilean Fidel Castro may appear; others consider that a FRAP (i.e., extreme left wing) president is inevitable in 1964."[163]

Beyond Cuba's influence, there were many other reasons for the growing ranks of left-wing militants and the rising temperature of politics in the country. Strikes multiplied in mid-1961 in protest at rising living costs and inadequate wages (inflation rose again by 10 percent in 1961).[164] In July 1961, in Santa Adriana, south of Santiago, Socialists and Communists also supported a new *toma* (land seizure) by poor migrants and the establishment of a shantytown, or *callampa*.[165] A few weeks later, another toma in the rural south stoked fears that some sort of larger rural uprising was on the horizon.[166] In addition to the question of land, left-wing parties and the PDC denounced falling levels of public health and malnutrition amid government stabilization policies.[167] A damning UNICEF report in mid-1961 highlighting infant mortality rates in southern Chile also put the idea of Chile as a country on the road to development into stark relief, positioning it, in a reporter's words, "at the level of the most underdeveloped countries in Africa."[168] Compounding matters, the Canadian ambassador reported, the government appeared stuck in a state of "paralysis."[169]

Frustration grew as promised reconstruction of the south failed to materialize, with one observer describing it as "torturously slow."[170] A year later, the Servicio Nacional de Salud found the majority of emergency poblaciónes to be "unhealthy," affecting fifteen thousand people.[171] With the government insisting the region was on the road to recovery, local residents complained that nothing had been done to help them.[172] And with "strong discontent" growing, support for the FRAP grew.[173] When students went on strike in southern Chile to protest delays in rebuilding schools, this added to a revolutionary feeling in the air. By mid-1961, approximately fifteen thousand young Chileans and teachers had joined the students' protest movement.[174] At university level, Chile's student federations amplified the antigovernment mood in the country and joined workers' mobilization. As the third largest university student federation in Chile, the FEC, together with the FECH, had long been dominated by Christian Democrats and left-wing parties, albeit with the FEC having a reputation for being to the left of its sister federation. In the run-up to student elections in September 1961, Marco Antonio Rocca, the Christian Democrat leader of the FECH, made no secret of the organization's stance on national questions. As he told a reporter, "young people cannot be at the margins of social inequality that is holding all of Chilean development back." Reflecting opposition to Alessandri's government, Marco Antonio urged students to become even more aware of their country's predicament. "There is a crisis in the air that affects young people directly," he told the paper. "There is a crisis of values, disorientation, concern for what is happening outside. There is an awareness that options for professionals are becoming scarcer every day. They [students] observe, with trepidation, how every day those trained at universities go abroad. Can we untangle a student of pedagogy from the teachers' problems ... ? Low wages, terrible working conditions ... the big socioeconomic problems that affect all students. The crisis outside is felt inside the university."[175] In this respect, the Christian Democrats' position did not differ much from socialists' view. As Juventud Socialista's president, Jaime Ahumada, would argue in early 1962, student concerns were intricately linked to "the general workers' movement."[176]

Despite agreeing on opposing the government, there were intense disagreements between political factions within universities, and especially between FRAP militants and their strongest rivals, the Christian Democrats. Student elections at the University of Concepción were infused with "ideological clashes," one of Beatriz's contemporaries remembered.[177] As a result of architectural reforms instigated in the late 1950s, the university had perfect spaces for political meetings, such as the Foro Abierto, an amphitheater-like space in the center of campus that, as Eugenia Palieraki has argued, gave budding leaders a platform on which to launch political careers.[178] Sometimes these debaters became self-absorbed. As one observer of the FECH noted, students would descend into "contrived and tiresome attempts to give a political cast to issues with no relation to party position." Even so, they represented a revived spirit of student activism dating back to the early twentieth century underpinned by attributes such as "the courage to hold and defend a point of view on fundamental issues, a readiness for self sacrifice, loyalty in friendship, love of country, hatred of dictators and distrust of the military, a sentimental identification with the working classes, and solidarity with the youth of other Latin American countries."[179]

Militancy and Revolution

With these unspoken values, Beatriz became an active militant for the Brigada Universitaria Socialista (Socialist University Brigade, BUS) in Concepción. Now in her second year, rather than living in the female dormitory, she lodged with Jorge Peña and his family. It was a friendlier environment. When her father passed through Concepción, he would also stay with them. And from what Jorge remembered, Beatriz impressed him by studying hard. Perhaps more important, Jorge Peña gave Beatriz and her friends political guidance (*formación política*), directing them through socialist "principles." Although her father was a former presidential candidate and senator, Beatriz was only "half left-wing" when she arrived, Peña recalled; "she didn't have things very clear yet." Jorge, who had become a Socialist during his own medical studies at the University of Concepción in the 1940s, now helped her and a younger generation refine them.[180]

Specifically, once a week, at their request, Jorge met Beatriz and a group of other medical students at the new Instituto de Biología—one of the institutes created by the university's reforms—to guide them through Marxist theory and teach them about the Socialist Party's history. As Ariel Ulloa, one of this group's members, explained, saying that everyone read *Das Kapital* would be wrong. However, students did read Lenin's *State and Revolution* and *What Is to Be Done?* Lenin "was sacred," he remembered.[181] In their effort to share what they had learned, Peña's study group also reproduced Lenin's writings in student newspapers. As Ariel remembered, "If you did not publish something you were nobody." The socialists in the medical faculty (both teachers and students) produced a newspaper called *Horizonte* during this period, which Beatriz wrote for. And at a university level, Beatriz coedited a Socialist-produced newspaper called *Revolución*.[182]

Beatriz and the students who studied with Peña meanwhile formed a small nucleus of the BUS in Concepción. As was normal, these nuclei tended to be determined by faculty. Consisting of twenty-five to thirty people, medical students named theirs the "Sierra Maestra." As Ariel explained, "We were Fidelistas.... Fidel and his comrades were our guiding light and compass." As if to make the point, the nucleus made a membership card with a picture of Fidel carrying a rifle in the Sierra Maestra.[183] Around this time, the University of Concepción also became an information hub on Cuba. As the organizer of a regional solidarity institute in the early 1960s explained, it was through the University that the Cuban organizations like ICAP would send newspapers, magazines, and films.[184]

One of those who joined Jorge Peña's tutorials and formed part of the Sierra Maestra nucleus at this time was Miguel Enríquez, a medical student a year below Beatriz.[185] Having been a member of the PS since he was a secondary school student in the late 1950s, he would subsequently go on to lead Chile's far left movement, the MIR, in the 1960s.[186] He also became a close friend of Beatriz's. As she would explain, there were "lots of ties, bonds," between them, and "apart from [our] studies, we were united by friendship, work, and shared political development."[187] Like her, he also came from a privileged background and had chosen to study medicine because his father had. However, much more so than she, quite possibly as a result of gendered ideas about women and men's political roles, he was a leader. Silvia Funke, a fellow student at Concepción in the early 1960s, remembered that Miguel and his friends "were attractive young men ... charismatic, charming."[188] As Beatriz recalled, Miguel was "an organizer, you could see in him someone that led students with ease, who could easily understand the language of the shantytown inhabitants [*pobladores*] and miners, that interpreted their problems well."[189]

Indeed, Miguel and his friends, Bautista van Schouwen and Luciano Cruz, together with Beatriz, often volunteered in neighboring communities while at university. "We went to Lota, to Coronel, to Huachipato," Beatriz recalled, "we talked to people, we helped with their strikes."[190] This kind of work echoed a longer student tradition of volunteering in poorer neighborhoods. From its inception, the traditionally left-leaning FECH, for example, had extended medical, legal, and educational services.[191] The Catholic Church had also instigated youth volunteering in the late 1950s. From 1959 onward, Catholic students' summer volunteering work, while "initially altruistic," had also included what Palieraki called "a certain proselytism that sought to politicize and raise potential voters' consciousness."[192] Other political parties and youth groups followed suit. As a young Communist deputy in Concepción explained, militants arranged "football tournaments between various rural teams concluding with parties and award ceremonies" as a way of organizing and incorporating new groups.[193] Young Socialist militants such as Miguel and his friends would similarly go to poblaciónes to offer "literacy courses ... basic health assistance" and, as Beatriz explained, contribute to pobladores' "political development."[194] This activity did not mean that this was all they did. As Beatriz remembered, "Miguel organized weekend trips and travelled around the whole area."[195] Another of Miguel's friends also recalled they went to the beach and to dances; "the only thing that differentiated us was that we dedicated an important part of our free time to political reflection," he explained.[196]

Given his role in Chilean politics and his close relationship to Beatriz in the decade that followed, Miguel is important. Far more so than she, and well before he joined Jorge Peña's tutorials, he had a fascination with history and theory. Influenced by his older brother, Marco Antonio, he "devoured" stories of the French Revolution and those who resisted the Roman Empire (Viriathus). Marco Antonio had also introduced him to politics, taking him to his first meetings in support of Allende's presidential campaign in 1958. Coming from a political (Radical) family, Miguel, like Beatriz, had also been exposed to politics from a young age and had accessed his father's large library. Then, at the University of Concepción, he began studying Lenin "systematically." However, as Beatriz's cousin and future MIR member (*mirista*) Andrés Pascal Allende recalled, Miguel also had "a more open, non-dogmatic conception of Marxism.... We read Leon Trotsky's *The Permanent Revolution* and *The Revolution Betrayed*, the

Belgian professor Ernst Mandel, the *New Left Review* magazine."[197] As Beatriz explained, Miguel's interests included "history, economics, Marxism, and ... books of a military character."[198]

Indeed, Miguel's interest in military topics, revolutionary insurrection, and armed struggle increasingly separated him from the rest of the Sierra Maestra nucleus. By 1962, together with his closest friends, including Bautista van Schouwen and Marcello Ferrada, he formed a factional movement known as the Movimiento Socialista Revolucionario (Revolutionary Socialist Movement, MSR). The idea, according to Marcello, was to underline the group's opposition to what they considered as the PS's "reformism" and to ensure students played a role in establishing an insurrectional force of the "working class, campesinos, pobladores, and students."[199] In this respect, their ideas chimed with older Trotskyist groups rejecting electoral strategies and inspired by Soviet and Chinese examples.[200] Ariel Ulloa recalled that Miguel's fascination with China and the Sino-Soviet dispute during these years was also a source of contention between the MSR and the rest of the Sierra Maestra nucleus.[201] Arguments on Chile's university campuses were thus fought through the lenses of ideologically charged global conflicts that would increasingly become a feature of local politics.

Despite factional tendencies within the BUS, friendships and personal contacts persisted and ensured coordination in student campaigns. Certainly, Beatriz, with a loyalty to the PS stemming from her father's politics, remained close to Miguel's group. Had it not been for her father, she might well have gravitated to the left with members of the MSR. Although she did not, this did not prevent her close affiliation with them. To the contrary, these close ties would define her politics and her role in Chile's future revolutionary history. Familial ties also linked her directly to the MSR, when Andrés Pascal joined its Santiago wing.[202]

These types of personal relationships proved important in allowing left-wing students to collaborate when confronting their opponents. The decision to campaign together on one list in student federation elections, for example, gave them a greater chance of defeating the Christian Democrats. And, significantly, in 1963, the MSR was in charge of the combined Movimiento Universitario de Izquierda (Left-Wing University Movement, MUI), which brought together the PS, the PCCh, and the Trotskyist party, the Vanguardia Revolucionaria Marxista (Revolutionary Marxist Vanguard, VRM). When the MUI won the FEC's elections in 1963, Beatriz's friend Ariel was then narrowly elected the FEC's president.[203] Although by this point Beatriz had left Concepción and returned to Santiago, and although Ariel had won the presidency by just fifty votes, it was a significant victory for the Sierra Maestra nucleus she had belonged to. Indeed, the

MUI's success in Concepción, as well as the growing influence of the MSR within the Sierra Maestra nucleus under Miguel's leadership, was an indicator of radicalization of a group of left-wing students. With FRAP parties having increased the number of representatives in the FECH, which the Christian Democrats retained control of, student politics pointed to the combined opposition's strength as the country approached presidential elections in 1964.[204]

For the time being, Chile seemed to stand at a crossroads. Although the British ambassador noted that "nothing resembling a 'Sierra Maestra' situation as yet exists," the mood in the country pointed to radical changes.[205] As he observed, from 1961 onward, "the majority of Chileans, even among the ruling oligarchy, came to realize that their country could no longer afford to go on living in conditions resembling those of the 19th century." For those previously reluctant to countenance change, the consequences of standing still amid domestic political ferment in a divided Cold War world seemed dangerous.[206] Reporting in late 1962, he warned of "economic liberalism and political democracy under fire" and mounting calls for change. "The only question," he added, "is whether they will take place through evolution or through revolution."[207] Clearly, the earthquake, Cuba's influence, and left-wing gains in Chile's 1961 congressional elections meant the country appeared to be on a very different path by the end of 1962 from that when Beatriz first arrived in Concepción in 1960.

As Beatriz prepared to transfer to the University of Chile to enroll in her fourth year of medicine at the start of 1963—a popular and frequent transfer made by many of her contemporaries—she could look back on three years of political activism and experience that would shape her future. She could also be relatively proud of her academic performance. Although her first-year grades were lower than in subsequent years—probably a result of her Latin American trip—she passed comfortably.[208] Indeed, when she had not been involved in politics, she devoted her time assiduously to her studies. In this respect, she had benefited from inclusion in a close-knit study group comprising a different set of friends from those she was politically affiliated with.[209] Her ability to make friends across political divides was testament to her capacity for compartmentalizing her life depending on the exigencies of the moment—a skill that would become increasingly important in future years of combined intensive medical training and political commitments.

For now, Beatriz had found her political voice at a particularly interesting time. Although we tend to think of Chile's revolutionary moment starting much later and student mobilization being characteristic of 1967–68, the national and international contexts at the start of the decade were ripe with revolutionary impulses. Opposition to Alessandri's government and solidarity with Cuba offered opportunities to become politically active. Over the course of 1962, Chile's economic situation worsened as its imports rose, exports dropped, and foreign reserves fell. In these circumstances, Chile's leaders—in government and in opposition—looked abroad for help, drawing international actors further into the national politics. And when Alessandri turned to the United States, John F. Kennedy's administration responded with extensive aid under the Alliance for Progress despite its criticism of the government's refusal to enact reforms envisaged by the program. The decision reflected growing fears in Washington by early 1962 that the FRAP—and its most likely candidate, Salvador Allende—stood a good chance of winning Chile's 1964 elections. Although Alessandri eventually agreed to a devaluation of Chile's currency and enacted a limited land reform bill in late 1962 (dismissed by opponents as "flowerpot reform"), U.S. observers acknowledged his readiness to embrace reforms were "essentially a fiction."[210] In April 1962, the Kennedy administration therefore turned its attention to providing covert funds for the Christian Democrats as the party that could satisfy demands for change and ward off the Left.[211]

3 : : : Youth and Women

Beatriz returned to Santiago in late 1962 more politicized than she had been when she left and more aware of Chile's economic, social, and political reality. This in turn shaped her life back in the capital. Returning to Chile's political center on the eve of the country's 1964 presidential elections, she was clear where her loyalties lay. Although some of her friends from Concepción, such as Miguel Enríquez and her cousin, Andrés Pascal, were part of a group of twenty-two young Socialists who publicly denounced an electoral route to socialism as a "revisionist façade," Beatriz declined to join them. This did not mean her friendship with them ended, only that she prioritized loyalty to her father and was not prepared to leave the Brigada Universitaria Socialista (BUS), where she found a political home at the University of Chile.[1] Indeed, with Allende being declared the presidential candidate of the Frente de Acción Popular (FRAP) on 27 January 1963, Beatriz threw all of her energies when not studying—itself highly demanding as we shall see in chapter 4—into supporting his campaign.

Rarely a year had gone by in Beatriz's life when Allende was not involved in some form of political campaigning. But this election—overshadowing daily life in Chile for almost two years—was different. Not only was Beatriz now politically active in her own right, but two of the election's central issues also intersected directly with her life: youth and women. As a militant in the BUS she was active in youth campaigns and imbued with the idea that young people could be protagonists of Chile's future, something candidates directly fostered by explicitly targeting them. When it came to women, and by association ideas about family life, Beatriz's relationship with her father—not to mention her ability to speak publicly about it, to be on show as a model daughter—was also important. More so than ever, Allende's family was part of his campaign. And this had a lot to do with the unprecedented attention women received in this election.[2] As young adults, the three Allende daughters were repeatedly interviewed by journalists and pictured in newspapers. Writing for *Ercilla*, Erica Vexler reported that Allende's wife and daughters "talk to different organizations, unions, neighborhood committees, they take part in demonstrations and accompany the candidate on nearly all his provincial tours."[3] On one occasion, Beatriz and her sisters stood next to their father at a rally for striking health workers as he received a standing ovation.[4] On another, Beatriz walked into a packed hall of thousands of women supporters with him and stood aside as he danced the *cueca*, Chile's national dance, in the aisles before ascending to the podium with him.[5]

Indeed, Beatriz's involvement stood out. Far more so than her sisters or mother, she accompanied her father to the countryside and towns across Chile.[6] Not only was she a Socialist Party militant unlike them, but compared with Carmen Paz and Isabel, who trained to be a teacher and studied sociology, respectively, she had followed in her father's footsteps to study medicine—a fact the media underlined.[7] In one of the most famous pictures of the Allende family from the 1964 campaign, Beatriz sits smiling on the floor with her father, who looks directly at her and indicates approval, presumably for the way his candidacy is going, while her sisters and mother, seated next to them, look on. More so than ever, in fact, Beatriz shared a special political affinity with her father.

Mobilizing for Change

Chile's 1964 presidential election was particularly tense, aggressive, and ideologically fought. It seemed all the more important as it was perceived as happening at a decisive moment in the Cold War battle to determine Latin America's future. In Chile, a democratic country where the majority of the politically active population was wedded to electoral processes, neither violent socialist revolution nor right-wing military intervention—as was happening elsewhere in the region—seemed serious options.[8] With Chile's Conservative and Liberal Parties largely discredited and the status quo seemingly untenable, essentially two choices were left: on one side, Salvador Allende on behalf of the FRAP, running on a similar platform to the one he had run on in 1958, and, on the other, Eduardo Frei, the Christian Democrats' candidate and representative of a centrist alternative, increasingly supported by all those fearing socialism. When the FRAP triumphed unexpectedly in a by-election in Curicó in March 1964, this conclusion was amplified, leading shocked right-wing parties to support Frei as a means of stopping Allende in what became a two-way race between different visions for radical change. As a *New York Times* columnist put it, Chilean elections presented the hemisphere's "most critical test since the Cuban Revolution."[9]

This test related to what Chilean politicians in the early 1960s referred to as an "integral crisis."[10] The University of Chile's rector inaugurated the 1964 academic year warning students of "urgencies" that could not be

The Allende family at home in Guardia Vieja.
"¡Allende en la intimidad!," *El Clarín*, 26 April 1964.

delayed. "Humanity ... calls for a new order," he proclaimed.[11] And such concepts as "development," "progress," and "modernity" infused political discussions, mirroring global debates. Certainly, U.S. and Soviet leaders fought bitterly over whose system represented the best model for "underdeveloped" countries, expending energy to win adherents. While the Soviets championed nationalization and state-led planning, U.S. leaders embraced modernization theory as a supposedly scientific alternative that, with U.S. funding and reformist programs like the Alliance for Progress, would lead Third World countries to capitalist prosperity and liberal democracy. After 1959, Cuba had also put forward its own model of rapid revolutionary change, borrowing from the Soviets but buoyed by its own idiosyncratic nationalist appeal and mass mobilization.

Faced with a sense of growing crisis and the call for change at home, Chileans were among those to import, take ownership of, and use these ideas to fight domestic battles, albeit arguing they stood for *Chilean* alternatives to them. As Inés Bordes, a Chilean singer, told *El Siglo*, she was voting for Allende for "Chile's incorporation in a modern world in which capitalism ... will have to turn into socialism."[12] Allende, meanwhile, explicitly criticized the Alliance for Progress for asking Chileans to wait thirty years to see a significant improvement. Development could not be "inspired by personal profit and safeguarding what exists," he argued. Faster, unattached, revolutionary change was needed.[13] Even so, with a "terror campaign" launched against him arguing that FRAP's ties to Cuba would establish a communist dictatorship and bring Cuban firing squads to Chile, Allende's team spent considerable time underlining the specificity of a Chilean revolutionary process. "Cuba made its revolution flavored with rum and sugar," he insisted. "Chile will make its own favored with wine and empanadas."[14] It was precisely to ward off the possibility of "another Cuba," he ended up arguing, that voters should support the FRAP: "We were the first, the only ones, who pointed out the need for ... transformations, precisely to avoid, sooner or later, or because of brutal injustice, the birth of an insurgency without destiny, an adventurous attitude, a social rebellion without content."[15] His efforts to carve out a new road to socialism as an alternative to violent revolution did not convince everyone.[16] But for now, at least, Allende's proposition served as the basis for the left wing's position.

On the other side of the election, the Christian Democratic Party (PDC) put forward a campaign that championed its own reformist vision for modernizing Chile. To be sure, Frei's campaign received $2.6 million in covert funds from the United States, amounting to more than half its total spending.[17] Fearful that instability, shortages, and rising costs would push people to vote for Allende, Washington also shipped food to Chile under its PL 480 aid program and disseminated extensive pro-American propaganda. As Frei associated himself with Kennedy, supported the Alliance for Progress, and viewed his program as an integral part of it, these messages, whether linked explicitly or not, benefited him.[18] However, Frei also insisted the Christian Democrats represented a *unique* Chilean "modernity."[19] Specifically, he called for a "Revolution in Liberty"—the transformation of Chile without class conflict, an alternative to both capitalism and socialism.

In substance, Frei's recipe for third-way reform was actually similar to the FRAP's program. The PDC called for agrarian reform and nationalization of the copper industry (albeit not total expropriation). He vowed not to replace the old state but to improve it, to create new institutions, increase suffrage and union rights, and to strengthen local communities' power while protecting private property.[20] The PDC also drew on the ideas of Roger Vekemens, a Jesuit of Belgian origin resident in Santiago, to argue for the incorporation of "marginal" sectors into society, that is, those who had previously been excluded either passively, as nonrecipients of state services, or actively by refusing to participate. The Catholic Church's social doctrine, galvanized by the Second Vatican Council (1962–65), added weight to the PDC's reformist platform and its efforts to address societal problems. And when it came to identifying these "marginal" sectors, the PDC consciously avoided class-based categories. As Eugenia Palieraki notes, age, gender, and where people lived became important, as Frei targeted young people, women, campesinos, and pobladores.[21] In doing so, Frei was able to count on the Catholic Church's experience in working with these groups and on U.S. funds, a third of which in 1963 were spent on small loans and grants for PDC-operated community-level health and education services. Reconstruction efforts in the south funded by the United States, meanwhile, reflected an awareness of the earthquake's significance.[22]

Ultimately, then, Allende and Frei *both* advocated profound transformation. And in the period leading up to the election, Chile experienced unprecedented mobilization for change. Santiago, Beatriz's home once again, was central to campaigns. Partly as a result of improved public health and longer life expectancies, but also due to large-scale rural-to-urban migration to the city, its population had risen sharply. By the early 1960s, it was seven times the size of any other Chilean city and where a third of all registered voters lived.[23] Santiago's privileged position and power thus meant PDC and FRAP candidates staged frequent rallies in the city, garnering national attention and bringing thousands of Chileans together—Beatriz included—at famous landmarks such as the Avenida Bernardo O'Higgins, Parque Bustamante, Parque Cousiño, and the Teatro Caupolicán.[24] Indeed, as politicized spaces, the media depicted them as perpetually filled and echoing with political speeches.[25]

Thousands of Chileans also came to Santiago especially to take part in "national encounters" in the run-up to the election. And with emphasis on incorporating marginalized sectors and winning their votes, these visitors' pilgrimages "from the provinces" were celebrated and romanticized. "Young people will arrive in caravans, marching hundreds of kilometers by foot, in trucks, carts, bicycles, buses, and special trains," one announcement of a forthcoming Allendista youth encounter proclaimed.[26] Elsewhere, tens of thousands of young Christian Democrats organized themselves into five columns, advancing from Chile's geographic extremes toward the capital, picking up adherents along the way. Camping outside the city, they then marched to the Parque Cousiño, where they took part in a rally of three hundred thousand.[27] Just as important as those arriving were communities which volunteered to host delegations. They prepared parties, waited at train stations with musical groups and placards, and organized communal kitchens. For one national encounter of Allendista youth in May 1964, organizers went "house by house, family by family" asking for volunteers to host ten thousand visitors.[28] While most political journies during 1963 and 1964 brought visitors to the capital, young Chileans like Beatriz and politicians also went out of the city to volunteer and campaign. Politics therefore encouraged a mass circulation of people, stimulating an effervescent environment for young militants to engage with and facilitating contacts between different sectors of the population.

Youth

Beatriz's age was significant in boosting her involvement in her father's 1964 campaign. Having turned twenty-one in 1963, she and her generation were now eligible to vote. Youth involvement in politics had been an increasingly important phenomenon in Chile for some time before 1964. And in a country where more than 50 percent of the population was under thirty, this demographic was set to become more significant still.[29] Mobilizing young Chileans—even before they reached twenty-one—was therefore considered vital. Frei campaigned for a new, youthful nation: what he called a "Patria Joven" (young homeland). And with an active Juventud Democrata Cristiana (Christian Democratic Youth, JDC) taking to the streets, he was particularly successful. Indeed, the PDC had a more elaborate discourse on youth than did left-wing parties in 1963–64, ascribing values of morality, honesty, integrity, and sacrifice to young people.[30]

"Our youth's sun shines!" Frei's supporters sang, while he pointed to young Chileans as the answer to Chile's future.[31] Grasping the youth vote's significance, the CIA aimed projects at "wrestling control of Chilean university student organizations from the communists."[32] With the country gearing up for an election widely regarded nationally and internationally as a turning point for Chile, Latin America, the Third World and the global Cold War, Beatriz and her generation coming of age in the early 1960s were thus at the heart of political campaigning.

This required active commitment from Chile's politically minded youth. Visiting the University of Chile in October 1963, Allende told students he had come to "demand [their] participation."[33] In a letter to young Chileans in early 1964, the Allende campaign had asked for "the most enthusiastic and sacrificial" support. "Surely you have noticed that everyone today talks about politics," it challenged readers. "The election results will determine if things stay the same or worse than they are, or a new era begins." It urged Allendistas to join youth centers, march in the streets, disseminate propaganda, and organize sports competitions or artistic activities. And, of course, the campaign specifically underlined the urgency of improving living standards for young people by voting for Allende. With those under fifteen accounting for 48 percent of all deaths in Chile, the Allende campaign charged that the incumbent regime offered Chile's youth "death, ignorance, misery, and frustration."[34] Young people stood to benefit from revolutionary change, the FRAP insisted.

Beatriz actively took part in youth campaigns, participating in traditional Chilean election repertoires ranging from large-scale assemblies to localized youth volunteering. Her involvement in the BUS and friendships with its leaders—as we shall see in more detail in chapter 4—also gave them a direct link to Allende.[35] Together with new friends she met through the BUS in Santiago, she spent evenings and weekends on the city's outskirts visiting poblaciónes, talking to people, and persuading them to vote for her father. This was not always easy. The FRAP did not have resources to pay for transport or food and so campaigning was often based on creative solutions. Beatriz and her friend Edith Benado Calderón, for example, snuck onto the train coaches that the more amply funded Christian Democrats—counting, as we now know, on covert U.S. financing—put on for their young campaigners. With FRAP pamphlets hidden in their bags, they would eat the PDC's empanadas and then disappear when they reached their destination. Their first strategy was to find a restaurant or shop and start talking to local people, asking how they could meet others in the community and disseminate campaign materials.[36]

On other occasions, as in previous campaigns, and as Beatriz's cohort had been doing near Concepción, medical students would provide health services in poorer districts, telling patients that if Allende won, there would be health centers in all poblaciónes.[37] "Because we arrived in white coats, they welcomed us immediately," a Socialist militant in his second year of medical training remembered; it allowed them to do political work more easily: "They asked us to carry out surveys, for example. And you found people who were convinced communists ate babies, or Russian tanks were coming ... as a result of a terror campaign."[38] Elsewhere, Socialist students painted murals and street propaganda on walls, sometimes being arrested for graffiti and being bailed out by party elders.[39] Mostly, however, campaigning consisted of canvassing house by house: "lots of walking, lots of pamphlets, talking to people," Edith remembered.[40]

Indeed, voluntary work was central to both the PDC and the FRAP campaigns. In the buildup to the election, students were reported as "expand[ing] their activities" beyond university campuses and "out into the community."[41] As the president of the Federación de Estudiantes de la Universidad de Chile insisted at the beginning of the 1964 academic year, they did not want to be separated from Chile's reality.[42] And at a provincial meeting of two thousand Allendista youth in Santiago, students agreed to volunteer in the countryside during the summer vacation to collect money and register voters.[43] Young Allendistas from around the country subsequently got together to paint houses, burn rubbish, clean canals, arrange irrigation systems in poblaciónes, construct children's playgrounds, and create sports facilities.[44] As a history student at the University of Chile explained, "Political work in the callampas ... and rural zones was an essential contribution ... awakening people's sense of their needs and rights."[45]

The students involved in these experiences also learned from them, in some cases becoming more militant as a result. Beatriz would recall she and fellow Socialist militants returned to classes after volunteering in poorer mining communities near Concepción, "ashamed of [their] better life, [their] opportunities to study, torn but with [their] willingness to fight for socialism strengthened at the same time."[46] As another young Chilean who began volunteering in poblaciónes at age fourteen recalled, it "moved [him] to the left." Though his own voluntary work tended to be church-organized, he got to know "poverty ... the social question," which "sharpened" his perspective.[47] Or as another student campaigning for the FRAP put it, "Observe malnutrition and then try to side with the ones that preach moderation and upholding tradition."[48]

The reality and immediacy of urban poverty in Greater Santiago was significant in this regard. Migrants coming to the capital in search of work, living in growing callampas around the city, made up half the city's workforce by 1963. In sharp contrast to wealthy upper- and middle-class districts in which Beatriz grew up, 30 percent of the city's inhabitants had no electricity, and 40 percent lacked access to running water.[49] Bringing students into direct contact with different groups of the population and underlining the reality experienced by people from poorer and marginalized communities, volunteering both enabled students to disseminate campaign messages and radicalized them.

Medical students who interacted with patients from all walks of life in Santiago's big public teaching hospitals experienced something similar on a daily basis. By 1963, for example, hospital staff were bemoaning the high number of children they saw with hunger-related illnesses like dystrophy (73 percent of admitted children in one central hospital).[50] And this had consequences for medical students' political engagement. As a study of students at the University of Chile in the runup to the 1964 elections found, there was an "important shift in attitude" among students after their hospital internships. They began to have less faith in medicine alone as means of improving Chileans' health and a "bigger interest in the vaster problems posed by society's transformation." This did not always lead them to the left, with the majority of students studying medicine in the early 1960s more inclined toward the Christian Democrats, but increasingly, they found it "more difficult to separate professional life from politics."[51]

Even apolitical university students found it hard to ignore mobilization in the two years preceding the election. One observer reported "a steady stream of every imaginable kind of political action engulfed student activists."[52] Certainly, at the Hospital San Juan de Dios, where Beatriz was interning, a course mate remembered a "clear separation" and "polarization" between students.[53] Although these differences did not hinder camaraderie between internees, everyone knew which parties students supported, and political groups tended to socialize separately, as we shall see in chapter 4. Although professors tried to keep politics outside the Faculty of Medicine, "numerous discussions" also "took place in the cafeteria," and propaganda was plastered on the building's walls.[54] Indeed, "virtually all students" were "subjected to pressure to commit themselves to a political party" when they enrolled at the university.[55] Some students even believed politics should take precedence over studying, given the country's "urgent problems." Jaime, a history student campaigning for the FRAP, insisted "that to give studying and the desire to become a competent professional primordial importance would be to betray the needs of countless armies of the dispossessed." In medicine, which was regarded precisely as a means of addressing such necessities, this attitude did not resonate as much. Even so, across university campuses, witnesses described an "exaggerated politicization."[56]

Beyond the confines of the university, politicized students were part of wider youth movements during the campaign, participating in major national encounters that brought secondary school children, young workers, miners, and campesinos together. The largest FRAP encounter—and the biggest youth gathering before Frei's Patria Joven march a month later—took place in May 1964, reportedly involved 9,873 students "from the provinces" alongside 25,000 young people from the capital and an additional 10,000 from nearby towns and villages.[57] At its main ceremony in the Caupolicán Theatre, thousands waited outside, while those indoors interrupted Allende's speech with thirty minutes of applause and singing.[58]

As a university student in the early 1960s, Beatriz was thus part of unprecedented youth mobilization. This occurred on both sides of the campaign. As Beatriz's teacher explained, she was part of "a generation ready to change the world."[59] Whether for the FRAP or the PDC, campaigning cemented the idea that young people had a significant role to play in the country's future and more specifically in changing it. It also brought university students increasingly into contact with people and circumstances beyond their immediate worlds. As delegates to a youth meeting in Santiago in December 1963 had decried, the Chilean university system was still a relatively "hermetic organism" when it came to class.[60] And educated about everyday life, young militants mobilized for change. The fight against poverty was not a mere campaign slogan but a conviction gained from personal observation. And the experience of volunteering to provide services and infrastructure to local communities would imbue young people with a sense of ownership over the country's future. If youth politics gave an indicator of Chilean politics for demographic reasons if nothing else, a survey of students at the University of Chile in the buildup to the election proved prescient. Only 2–6 percent of students identified themselves as right wing, one-third identified with the FRAP, and two-thirds with the Christian Democrats.[61]

Women and Family

The Christian Democrats' margin over the FRAP had a lot to do with the conscious construction of the idea—supported by the right wing and its media—that Chileans faced a choice between democracy and dictatorship, freedom and totalitarianism.[62] Because it was widely accepted that Alessandri had won the presidency in 1958 thanks to 34 percent of women voting for him compared with 22 percent for Allende, this narrative was effectively targeted at female voters.[63] By 1964, women's registration had increased from 35 percent to 70 percent, accounting for 45.7 percent of voters.[64] And because women and men voted in different locations, the precise significance of their share of the vote was visible.[65] Women were generally assumed to be more conservative and religious than men, but they also had to be mobilized to vote.[66] Believing women could once again defeat Allende, the PDC and its U.S. sponsors therefore devoted enormous efforts to persuading women to support Frei.

A "scare campaign" targeting women and equating an Allende win with an atheistic communist dictatorship thus ensued.[67] In the dystopian future propagandists painted, a FRAP victory would destroy Chilean families and women's position in society.[68] And, as Marcelo Casals has argued, the PDC emphasized that women—the fundamental "affective and moral" pillars of family life—were key to saving the Chilean nation from communism.[69] To articulate the supposed threat posed, *El Mercurio* ran features on women forced into work in the Soviet Union fulfilling jobs "extraordinarily hard for them, ones which no civilized country makes their sex perform."[70] The women's magazine *Eva* also ran an exclusive report on Moscow life published in six weekly installments before the election. It presented a deeply depressing picture: women walked freezing in the snow, were forced to work long hours for low salaries, queued endlessly for basic food, and lived in tiny, cramped apartments. Fashion was "practical" and bereft of color, makeup was banned as a "Western vice," everyone ate in canteens as there was no one to cook at home, and while being "free" of child-care responsibilities, mothers had to live with their children being indoctrinated as atheists.[71] News of tens of thousands of Cuban children being sent to Russia or forced into militias also circulated widely.[72] Then, in a last-minute intervention, one of Fidel Castro's sisters, Juana, addressed "Chilean mothers" in a radio broadcast, begging them not to vote for Allende. "I am sure that you will not allow your small children to be taken from you and sent to the Communist bloc, as happened in Cuba. ... The enemy is stalking, it is at your doors.... Be alert!" Behind Juana, the United States government, working with anticommunist groups such as Acción Mujeres de Chile (Women's Action of Chile), helped disseminate her message. Broadcast the day before the election in contravention of the forty-eight-hour moratorium on campaigning before polling opened, Juana's intervention was the culmination of a campaign that, as Margaret Power argues, "relied on Chilean constructions of gender that conflated womanhood with motherhood." This association was not unsurprising. As Power noted, "Motherhood defined many Chilean women's identity, as well as much of their lived reality."[73]

Without knowing precisely of its existence but suspecting "multimillion" dollar U.S. financing for Frei, the Allende campaign repeatedly denounced its opponent's tactics.[74] Even before the official start of the U.S.-funded "scare campaign" in June 1964, efforts to instill fear of an Allende win used alarmist propaganda and distorted information. As Allende told the Senate, the FRAP had suffered "systematic disfiguration" of its positions.[75] His campaign expended considerable energy—somewhat reactively—to underline what an Allende presidency would offer women.[76] As well as setting up an active National Feminine Command led by his sister, Laura, who was soon to be a Socialist deputy, for example, it staged rallies and national encounters similar to those organized for young people. At one national event in December 1963, four thousand women attended, with hosts from every commune in Santiago housing visitors to the capital. This national assembly promised the "direct participation of women in the future popular government."[77] At subsequent national events in July 1964, thousands of women joined rallies and marched through Santiago, displaying what *El Siglo* called a new "political consciousness."[78] Apparently showing her devotion to the cause, one delegate, Eliana Puente, even gave birth in the balcony of the Caupolicán Theatre just as a campaign event was beginning, and the baby, having been attended by a doctor, was wrapped in large handkerchiefs embroidered with the words, "Women Workers."[79]

Extraordinary stories of childbirth aside, there was a familiar performative character to these events, each of them following an established repertoire invariably including standing ovations and campaign speeches culminating in one given by Allende himself. He would make a grand entrance after the proceedings had started, often accompanied by one or more of his daughters, invariably including Beatriz, and less frequently by his wife or sister, Laura.[80] Like events for other groups in society, they also always had a cultural component, albeit in this case, like the speeches themselves, spearheaded by women. Inés Moreno's "Himno de la Mujer Allendista" (Hymn of an Allendista woman) was regularly performed.[81] In Valparaíso, the local Allende team meanwhile established the Instituto de Cine Popular, which employed what it called "guerrilla cinema"—documentary films to combat "artistic hierarchy" and "reflect reality." And its second film was aimed precisely at encouraging female participation in Allende's campaign. As *El Siglo* reported, it was important that women were empowered with a "responsibility for solving national problems."[82]

Allendista women meanwhile took the initiative to mobilize on their own accord. Ana Eugenia Ugalde, who defected from the Radical Party to become a leading figure in the campaign, decided to stitch the letter A for Allende into cloth nappies, which thousands of other Chilean women copied. Women also set up their own literacy groups and reportedly initiated local campaign events "spontaneously," including marches during which they banged empty pots and pans to signify food shortages, a practice that would become a powerful political tool in future years.[83]

And yet, despite positive left-wing reports of these events, the FRAP was not able to replicate the size of youth events. Only 631 women attended an assembly of Santiago women compared with 2,000 attendees at an analogous youth event (only 30 percent of whom were women).[84] Similar to the PDC's campaign, there was also frequently a paternalistic and stereotypically gendered dimension to the way in which women were described, represented, and involved. Journalists (male and female) referred to female Allendistas as "emotional," and in celebrating their acts of spontaneity, they revealed that FRAP leaders, the majority of whom were men, far more commonly managed events from above.[85] Fashion and appearances were also deemed important; women's events were reported as looking "extraordinary" because of the "variety of feminine clothes."[86]

When Jeanette Gallo, a journalist for *El Siglo*, interviewed Beatriz and Carmen Paz about their father for a piece on the women in Allende's life, she also asked them more about his preferences for how women should do their hair than about politics or the election. ("Allende's daughters say their father fervently hates seeing them and his wife with hair rollers.... 'He says that we look monstrous,'" Beatriz explained. As Gallo informed readers, Beatriz revealed her father preferred that she and her sisters wear "a simple and natural hairstyle."[87]) Indeed, hairstyles seemed to be a favorite focus for journalists, with *Ercilla's* Erica Vexler reporting that Allende gave Beatriz money to cut her hair so it would not fall in her face "during surgery."[88] Mirroring societal norms, Allendista women were tasked with organizing teas designed for "the private, specific world of women" that male politicians joined to hear about "women's" problems related to the home and children.[89]

Reflecting the gendered dynamics of politics in Chile at the time, women were unsurprisingly also represented in the campaign (for both candidates) as *incorporating* themselves into a male endeavor rather than being part of it automatically, of being given entry—"the wonderful opportunity," as *El Siglo* put it—into a world they had not previously belonged to.[90] Beatriz and her female friends in the BUS agreed women should participate next to men and not form their own autonomous groups. They campaigned furiously against the few women-only cells in the Socialist Party that existed in the early 1960s, arguing women should not separate themselves in this way.[91] And, in doing so, they were not alone. When a female leader of Uruguay's Communist Party raised the idea of reinstating women-only cells in 1962, there was strong opposition by many who saw it as an anachronism. As Gerardo Leibner has argued, "For the majority of young females, the ongoing modernizing process of women entering most public spaces and institutions was an important advancement and they did not want to be pushed back into segregated spaces."[92] Even so, when Beatriz accompanied her father to a national women's event at the Caupolicán Theatre in July 1964, she heard him welcoming women in the audience as newcomers to politics: "I raise my voice, broken with emotion, before this extraordinary meeting unlike anything I have seen before. Your presence here, the human warmth you offer, the trust you place in us; all of this is saying ... women have incorporated themselves next to men in the great struggle to make Chile a different country."[93] Gatekeepers of this political world, male Allende and Frei supporters were now asked to "facilitate" their wives' attendance at campaign events by looking after children and organizing babysitting pools.[94]

If the goal of incorporating women into politics was championed, changing the way women's issues were discussed or their place in society proved more difficult. The ideological Cold War conflict over Chile's future that intensified in 1963–64 did not offer competing ideas on gender so much as focusing on which program for radical change—reformed capitalism or socialism—could fulfill expected norms *better*. And, partly because it was forced on the defensive by the Christian Democrats' terror campaign, the FRAP underlined its commitment to upholding, rather than challenging, such norms. True, the FRAP made more references to the fight for women as workers than its opposition did, campaigning for women to have equal pay, access to work, and union rights.[95] Compared with Frei, who praised his wife for being home to look after their children and openly stated husbands and wives could not "be politically involved at the same time," Allende included female members of his family in campaigning (and would probably have liked Hortensia to be more politically active than she was).[96] As Casals notes, the FRAP's campaign also emphasized class dynamics of poorer women's needs, focusing on what it would do to improve material conditions and alleviate poverty forced on them by "reactionaries" and "imperialism."[97]

But, across the political spectrum, little had substantively changed since the 1950s regarding popular conceptions of women's place in the home, caring for their family, as appendages to men: wives, sisters, daughters, or mothers.[98] As the national Allendista assembly of women in December 1963 concluded, "Every woman's aspiration" was to "build a home" and to look after her children. "What do we want?" asked Mireya Baltra, at the time a Communist militant and trade union leader, "happiness for our children, schools so that our children ... can get to University." True, she called for agrarian reform and "fundamental changes" to Chile's economy, but these were seen as a means by which all women—from whatever background—could fulfill their primary role of raising families.[99] And linked to the idea revolution meant progress, Allende argued paying attention to mothers as children's principal guardians—the mother-child binominal—was essential for bringing about societal change and building a modern nation.[100] Serving the interests of women was thus considered as synonymous with looking after mothers. And he urged women to be "mothers of the [people's] victory."[101]

The principal issues at the heart of such campaigns help us understand the way ordinary Chileans experienced a wider Cold War struggle. The battle to secure women's votes made many false promises and threats, amplified thanks to generous U.S. sponsorship. But the way they were constructed and propagated by both sides is important. Ultimately, from this perspective, the ideological conflict shaping the election revolved not only around economic and political arguments or international alignments (with U.S. "imperialism" or Soviet "totalitarianism")—these were discussed mostly as root causes—but also around the nature of the Chilean family, children, and future of everyday life. Chileans believed the election would have a significant impact on how they were born, grew up, and lived in private.

And with "the family" taking center stage in this presidential campaign, it was vital that Allende was perceived as a devoted family man. Throughout 1963 and 1964, the spotlight therefore turned on Beatriz, her sisters, and their mother to vouch for him as a father and husband. Allende's mother was also asked to comment on his presidential potential, and her answer fed into the idea that family roles were qualifications for government: he would be a good president, she said, because he was a good son and "a great father."[102] When asked to comment, Beatriz reiterated this message. Whether describing Allende joking with her and imitating voices, playing games, teaching her how to swim, or going for walks, she and her sisters depicted him as a dedicated father who had been present and invested in building a family. As if to emphasize his commitment to peaceful, pluralistic revolution, Beatriz and her sister also underlined their father's reluctance to dominate decision making. "In the Allende house there is a total and absolute democracy," Beatriz and Carmen Paz explained. His "wife and daughters are called on to debate all issues," Gallo reported.[103] There were revealing anecdotes that undermined the idea of a radically democratic family—too out of step with prevailing societal norms.[104] In detailing the way Hortensia called her husband "Salvador" rather than

"Chicho," the nickname he was most commonly known by, when she asked him for money, Beatriz revealed the decision-making power her father had through control of the family's finances. And when Salvador praised his wife's public speaking by saying he preferred it to her requests to complete household chores, he underlined that she ran the home.[105]

Whether scripted or spontaneous, in fact, Beatriz and her sisters were thus adept at getting across key messages of the campaign, particularly when it came to countering the scare campaign aimed at women. Allende came across as revolutionary but not *too* revolutionary. "My daughters are so extreme they often accuse me of being a bit reactionary," he joked with *Ercilla*'s reporter. When Isabel replied, "If young people do not have this position they are not young," it suggested he had the political maturity to be a more reasoned choice.[106] When it came to religion—a major feature of efforts to engender fear in voters, and particularly women voters—Beatriz explained her grandmother was "fervent Catholic." Far from coming from an atheistic household, in fact, she told readers how she had "attended religious services" until her father had allowed her to stop going. "If you have rationally convinced yourself you do not believe in Catholic faith, then I accept you don't have to go to church but if you still have faith but don't go because of laziness I will force you to attend," she reported him saying, as if to emphasize his respect for true believers.[107] In an effort to confront spurious right-wing allegations the Allendes lived in a "fabulous mansion," sympathetic reports and pictures described it as "soberly elegant" and filled with "tranquility." Left-wing journalists also wrote about Guardia Vieja as "a happy home."[108] Interviewed for *El Siglo*, Beatriz and Carmen Paz spoke of their father's sense of humor, his love of birthday celebrations. As Beatriz revealed, he never accepted a "long or grumpy face." "The intimate life of Salvador Allende," Gallo concluded, "is imbued with a definitive joie de vivre."[109]

Of course, such reports of a happy Allende family need to be read in context. Behind the scenes of a public family on show as never before, home life was, unsurprisingly, more complicated. Salvador's extramarital affairs continued. In particular, his relationship with Inés Moreno, Communist Party member and singer, whom Beatriz had spent time with in Concepción, deepened during the campaign. Not only did she accompany him at campaign events, but she was also designated as a leader of Allende's cultural campaign team. When the Communist Party asked her to stop seeing him for fear the affair would become public, she refused. Hortensia meanwhile knew about and suffered through it.[110] And then, of course, there were the wider demands of a national presidential campaign, which disrupted any semblance of a "tranquil" home. Osvaldo Puccio, Allende's campaign coordinator and private secretary, for example, would get to Guardia Vieja early every morning to have breakfast before he and Allende met Salomón Corbalán, secretary general of the Socialist Party and coordinator the FRAP's campaign.[111] In the evenings, if he was in Santiago and not touring the country as he did incessantly, Allende would attend rallies. And brief insights into the election's impact on family life slipped into otherwise glowing reports of an idyllic home. At one point, Hortensia bemoaned the constant telephone calls. "My dream is to live one day without this artifact," she revealed.[112]

However, rather than these uncomfortable truths, the main problem for Allende when it came to winning over women voters was that the FRAP's campaign messages did not have the opposition's reach. From June 1964, the CIA-sponsored scare campaign consisted of twenty radio spots a day in Santiago alone, with special twelve-minute programs running five times a day on three main stations in addition to media and press advertising. Three thousand posters were also being distributed daily by the end of the month.[113] Congratulating itself on how it had manipulated the threat of an Allende victory, the CIA later concluded the single most important factor determining the election had been the fear of communism.[114] While this was an oversimplification born of U.S. analysts' priorities, there is no doubt this fear became more pervasive in 1963–64 and that its relevance now reached to the most intimate spaces and relationships in Chilean society. As one male campesino who voted for the FRAP told interviewers, women were "fooled ... they voted for Frei so that nobody would take their babies."[115]

Ultimately, on election day, 62.8 percent of women voters chose Frei. And although the percentage of female support for Frei was stronger in wealthier districts (above 70 percent in the middle-class and affluent areas of the city), more than 50 percent in working districts areas also backed the Christian Democrats.[116] In comparison with the presidential election of 1958, Allende had increased his share of the women's vote by almost 10 percent. But compared with the high levels of female support for Frei, this was simply not enough.[117] Indeed, Frei won the presidency with 56.1 percent of the popular vote, a striking majority for a relatively new ideological program.

This result was a not completely unexpected blow to the Left, with most observers predicting the PDC's victory from mid-1964.[118] Having received the news, Beatriz, her sisters, and their mother accompanied Allende downtown to the Casa del Pueblo. There, at midnight, they emerged on the balcony as a family to greet supporters in the street outside. As Allende proclaimed the struggle would go on, one supporter in the crowd below remembered seeing Beatriz standing next to her father.[119] Having been in the spotlight for over a year, the Allendes now publicly lost together as a family.[120] There was no escaping the fact this third presidential loss was difficult. As Isabel remembered, it was "so ... aggressive ... it distanced a lot of people who were once friends."[121] Interviewed years later, Hortensia would similarly describe cumulative, repeated losses as "tough."[122] Salvador was particularly disappointed women had voted against him. He would also never forgive Frei for the way the campaign had been fought. The question was how to respond. And while Hortensia, Carmen Paz, and Isabel retreated from politics, Allende and Beatriz became more—rather than less—committed to revolution in the years ahead.

The politicization of the family in 1960s Cold War Chile therefore had a direct bearing on Beatriz's home life and vice versa. She was part of the 1964 campaign not only because of her politics but also because she was Allende's daughter. And she suffered the defeat of the election by his side. Indeed, back in Santiago at the heart of Chilean political life for the presidential election, the relative autonomy and independence she had in Concepción was overshadowed by her relationship to him. Behind the scenes, though, Beatriz continued to forge her own political trajectory begun in Concepción, running parallel to her father's ideas but sometimes intersecting with them and defined by his experience.

Meanwhile, Chile geared itself up for Frei's inauguration and the beginning of his reformist program. The PDC faced an uphill struggle. To succeed, it had to find the money to enact social programs and service Chile's external debt.[123] Until congressional elections in March 1965 when it won a majority in Congress, the PDC also controlled only 28 out of 147 seats in the Chamber of Deputies and 4 of 45 seats in the Chilean Senate. Its resounding victory in 1965 and the support it received from the Chilean public in the first few years of government helped boost its agenda. But Frei still faced political opposition from the Right, particularly on the question of agrarian reform.[124] Increasingly, he also faced left-wing opposition from within his own party.

Moreover, the idea of the Christian Democrats forging a new middle way between capitalism and socialism—of offering a radically new "communitarian" alternative—was contradicted by the way the election campaign had been fought. The terror campaign, funded by the CIA and framed in global Cold War terms, constructed the election as a stark choice between Frei as the defender of the U.S.-led "free world" and "totalitarian communism" driven by Cuban firing squads, Soviet tanks, and baby-stealing Bolsheviks. Rather than moving beyond the Cold War, then, the PDC's rhetoric ingrained its logic and lexicon further into Chilean society. That the PDC explicitly took the campaign to "marginal" sectors and expended efforts to bring them into the body politic accentuated the politicization of everyday life further still. By explicitly targeting and incorporating women, youth, pobladores, and campesinos, in other words, the PDC's mission expanded the resonance and traction of ideological frameworks, embedding them deeper than ever before.[125]

For FRAP's parties, there was also no such thing as a middle-way alternative. True, Allende's 1964 platform promised socialism without violent revolution, a Chilean electoral road to revolutionary change. But supporters fervently believed that the replacement of capitalism with socialism was needed to guarantee Chileans would live, thrive, and prosper. And they, too, took this message to youth groups, to women, to campesinos, and to trade unions more than ever before. With the right wing in disarray, having failed to articulate its own vision for addressing the country's perceived crisis and "underdevelopment," the Left would be the Christian Democratic government's alternative, decisively beaten and bruised by the 1964 election but not defeated. And while the political gravity in Chile would remain firmly rooted in the center for the next few years, left-wing militants and parties readied themselves to contest Frei's government. Socialist Party militants, in particular, were embittered by the way the 1964 campaign had been fought and opposed the new government from day one.[126]

Young Chileans, meanwhile, were galvanized by the Frei administration. Although some saw themselves as part of the PDC's reformist program—drivers, even—others believed it was their duty to oppose it, redirect it, or speed it up. And while the Communist Youth, the second largest student force at the University of Chile, tended to work with its Christian Democrat counterpart to support reforms, young Socialists like Beatriz positioned themselves further to the left. Frustrated with the 1964 defeat, reacting to significant events that occurred in the first years of Frei's presidency, some militants of the Juventud Socialista moved increasingly away from the "traditional Left's" reliance on electoral strategies for gaining power. As a pamphlet distributed by its members in October 1964 stated, "We declare a state of revolutionary emergency within our Party. We demand a political judgment on our Party's current leadership. We demand an honest, frank, and revolutionary balance of what has happened, we demand a policy that truly opens ways to conquer power."[127]

4 ::: Reform and Radicalization

When Beatriz was not campaigning and militating for the Brigada Universitaria Socialista (BUS), medical school absorbed her life. A friend remembered her sitting for hours on the floor in her bedroom surrounded by large spiral binders, memorizing university notes while eating biscuits.[1] She had kept her studies and politics mostly separate since returning to Santiago, especially when it came to her social life. But the two informed each other. The contact with poverty and inequality during medical training at one of the capital's largest public hospitals reinforced her commitment to radical change. And her political views, in turn, shaped the way she approached medicine. As a young, left-leaning teacher of hers explained, Beatriz was part of a group of students, doctors, and professors who met regularly to discuss how to "fix Chile." When it came to practicing medicine, she was not simply concerned about patients' "pathology, but their social condition" as well, asking not only "what illness does this child have?," for example, but also "why did he get ill? She looked for answers that, in many cases, medicine could not offer as an isolated specialty."[2] And these, in turn, led her back to revolution.

In the dynamic context of the first few years of Frei's reformist government, Beatriz was not the only one asking new questions of the world and wanting to transform it. The issue was what kind of transformation should occur and how. As it was, Chile changed significantly during the mid-1960s as the new Christian Democratic government pushed its reformist agenda forward. As well as passing a new labor code for rural workers and initiating agrarian reform, the administration brought about "Chileanization" of mines—the name given to a negotiated takeover of half of Chile's copper industry from foreign investors. And in its effort to address "marginality," it extended state programs and funding to areas that previously had not been reached, encouraging disenfranchised sectors to participate in society and politics. Under its Promoción Popular program, for example, the government created twenty thousand new organizations, including mothers' centers, neighborhood committees, and youth clubs.[3]

Beatriz saw much of the positive impact state-led reforms had on health care and community-led development firsthand as a medical student and graduate. Reforms during the Frei period also provided the space, environment, and framework for young militants to practice their political activism when it came to unionization drives, volunteering in poorer communities, intellectual development, and university politics. In many ways, in fact, "the very decried 'system,'" as Diana Sorensen has argued regarding youth politics in the sixties, "made ... expansive utopian thinking possible."[4] But Beatriz was also radicalized by what she and others within an emerging revolutionary Left regarded as inadequate progress and tired left-wing strategies. Frustrated by Allende's 1964 defeat, angered by Frei's recourse to force, and inspired by news of guerrilla insurgencies abroad, they increasingly sought faster, urgent revolutionary strategies, ultimately leading them toward armed struggle. The speed with which radicalization of young Chilean socialists occurred between 1964 and 1967 is noteworthy, emerging as it did out of a combined response to the opportunities and indignation Frei's Chile provided. In Beatriz's case, Allende's position as the epitome of the Left's electoral strategies and as president of the Senate beginning in 1966—together with her unbending loyalty to him—complicated her ability to shift left openly and decisively as many of her peers did. It also affected her private life as she conformed to societal norms expected of her so as not to undermine her father's reputation. She therefore kept a relatively low profile and was consumed by the rigorous nature of her studies. But this did not mean she was unsympathetic to a revolutionary Left emerging during these years.

Practicing Medicine in Changing Times

As those in Beatriz's year at university remembered, practical medical training was intense. Students spent their fourth, fifth, and sixth years at an assigned hospital studying the key branches of medicine and surgery alongside specialist subjects such as obstetrics, gynecology, and pediatrics. Any spare time was spent at the hospital's library reading up on cases. As most medical texts were in English, they also made sure to attend lunchtime lectures (Beatriz and her cohort read English but were understandably more confident listening to Spanish). Getting a place at the Hospital San Juan de Dios in Santiago's Quinta Normal district, as Beatriz did, was considered lucky. As Beatriz's course mates remembered, this was the Medical Faculty's "golden age." It was a privilege to be taught by professors attached to the hospital, such as Rodolfo Armas Cruz, pediatrician Adalberto Steeger, and Victorino Farga, a world-renowned respiratory and tuberculosis expert. Within this context—and the obvious fact they were dealing daily with "matters of life and death"—they felt immense pressure to succeed.[5]

Student doctors at the Hospital San Juan de Diós, no date. *Left to right*: Felipe Cabello, Manuel Oyarzún, Daniel Pizarro (professor of surgery), Beatriz, Andrés Zahler, Hector Guzmán, Horacio Zepeda, and Arturo Jirón. Archivo Fundación Salvador Allende.

Beatriz thrived in this atmosphere. Her teachers despaired trying to decipher her handwriting and bad spelling (she wrote *volver*—to return—with a *b* and *hypertension* without *h*) but she was generally considered "brilliant."[6] Her relationship with patients—and empathy for them—were particular strengths. As a classmate remembered, she had a "sensibility towards the sick . . . [she was] very close to the patients." Beatriz found some of the work she had to do difficult and was affected emotionally by it.[7] But she worked well with her peers, studying closely with them, catching lifts to and from hospital with a small group that lived nearby, thereby sharing the intensity of their learning experience. She also got on well with her professors, many of whom she was able to joke with. It helped that some of her teachers were her father's friends whom she had known since childhood, such as Benjamin Viel, the University of Chile's public health and family planning specialist. But it was not just her father's connections that allowed her to get on well with others. As her friend at medical school, Manuel Oyarzún, explained, people had a special "predilection for her."[8] Another student recalled Beatriz as "a very strong woman, with a VERY attractive personality," recalling decades later that "the study group gyrated around her (perhaps at the time we were all a little in love with her)."[9] Given women made up only 15 percent of medical students, it was unsurprising she was surrounded by men, many of whom admired and flirted with her but to whom, as we shall see, she was never romantically attached.

In 1966, her seventh and final year, Beatriz was required to do a ten-month internship.[10] More so than previous years of training, this was the students' baptism of fire. They practically lived at the hospital and often slept there. Once, when Salvador Allende stopped by to see Beatriz and deliver a box of cakes for her, she was asleep in between rounds.[11] Wary of what was coming, Beatriz strategically asked Manuel Oyarzún if they could do rotations of the internship together. As with many of her course mates, he was not political, but they became close.[12] As another friend, Marcela, remembered, she had a knack of attaching herself to students who took good notes and were well prepared.[13]

It was from the vantage point of the Hospital San Juan de Dios that Beatriz was able to get a sense of the major problems and challenges affecting health care in Chile, as well as what the state was doing to alleviate them. The most common medical issues interns dealt with, for example, were problems arising from illegal abortions.[14] The Hospital San Juan de Dios treated around ten thousand obstetrics and abortion cases annually by the mid-1960s, reflecting a crisis in Chile described by health care professions as having reached "epidemic proportions."[15] By 1965, record numbers of Chilean women sought illegal abortions (over fifty-six thousand cases were documented). Of those who did, a third would be admitted to the hospital with complications derived from the unsanitary and violent methods employed in terminating pregnancies.[16]

From their direct contact with patients, medical students were thus among health professionals campaigning for access to safe abortion and family planning.[17] In this respect, they chimed with the spirit of reform sweeping through Chile. For at the same time as Beatriz and her cohort were training, the Frei administration was beginning to address this crisis head on. Responding to pressure from doctors, the government invested money and resources in family planning. By 1966, 102 family planning centers had been set up around the country offering 58,000 women free contraception (mostly intrauterine devices, or IUDs). Thanks to government funding and expertise developed by internationally funded projects at the University of Chile, 100,000 further women gained access to these services in 1967, the year that Beatriz and her course mates graduated. As a doctor, she would also be in a position to write prescriptions for the contraceptive pill for her friends, still controlled and difficult to get hold of.[18]

Indeed, she and her cohort were interns at a transformative moment in reproductive health, when a rare consensus between health care professionals, the government, progressive sectors of the Catholic Church, and global paradigms regarding population control propelled change. This consensus not only tackled the effects of illegal abortions but also freed women to take control. There were also conservative dimensions to population control by the 1960s. International programs advised developing countries to stave off social revolution arising from poverty quite simply by encouraging poor people not to have children or, more extreme, preventing them from doing so through sterilization campaigns. However, in Latin America, resistance to population control limited such measures.[19] And, in Chile, even if conservative calculations fed into new projects, they reinforced an established desire to improve access to contraception as a means of alleviating the human cost of illegal abortions rather than driving them in the first place.[20]

Another serious problem at San Juan de Dios—and, across the country, the most common cause of death—was tuberculosis (TB). Working for Victorino Farga, Beatriz had the opportunity to participate in monitoring the disease in Quinta Normal. For over a year, she was among a group of paid interns who spent two or three lunchtimes a week at the hospital's TB laboratory examining sputum samples to see if they contained bacteria. This technical work was part of an innovative and successful project directed by Farga of "direct observed treatment (DOT)." And such projects, alongside improved access to health care during the Frei years, led to cases of TB dropping from 48.9 cases per 100,000 in 1964 to 29.6 five years later.[21] On a more practical level, working for Farga helped with student expenses.[22]

Beyond the Hospital San Juan de Dios, all final year interns undertook rural internships in preparation for possibly becoming a médico general de zona (MGZ) after graduation. Primary care physicians in provincial areas of the country responsible for delivering health services, MGZs were a significant piece of Chilean state-led development in the late 1950s and 1960s. They aimed to tackle inequalities and extend the welfare services to previously marginalized sectors.[23] As one MGZ in the early 1960s in the province of Melipilla, part of Chile's agricultural central valley, remembered, he had to establish medical services from scratch. As the only medic in town, a bell rang to alert him when he was needed, and he did rounds on horseback.[24]

In the climate of reform and voluntarism in the mid-1960s, medical students were enthusiastic about the prospect of becoming an MGZ after graduating.[25] Certainly, Beatriz spoke to Manuel about her desire to work as one in Llanquique, southern Chile, although why she chose Llanquique is unclear.²⁶ With professors at the University of Chile teaching students to think of what the medical profession could contribute to society, there was broad agreement that doctors had a role to play in extending public health by physically relocating themselves. As Manuel remembered, even if apolitical, "it was unusual not to feel the call to serve the country, for social medicine.... It was a way of paying the country back for what it had invested in us." And medical students considered rural internships as "very important to get to know reality" beyond the confines of what was for most a privileged middle- or upper-class urban life.²⁷

Beatriz and Manuel were also assigned to Melipilla province for their internship, although they were stationed in the town of Melipilla rather than its surrounding countryside. The municipality was less than two hours southeast of Santiago and had a population of just over forty thousand at the start of the 1960s, with over half engaged in agricultural work on large haciendas. Its lower levels of infrastructure and education also reflected steep inequality between the capital and other areas of Chile—precisely the kind Frei's government was attempting to address.²⁸ Having arrived at Melipilla in Beatriz's blue Citronetta, she and Manuel moved into the Hospital San José—a renovated old colonial building. As Manuel and Felipe Cabello, who also did his internship there, remembered, it was a welcoming environment. Interns were invited to social events, and when they escaped their duties at the hospital, they also visited the town's small, new open-air cinema.²⁹ But the internship was also difficult, with students thrown in at the deep end at a hospital with very little equipment or provisions. Manuel's most vivid memory was of him and Beatriz operating alone on a case of appendicitis (it went well).³⁰ Felipe remembered assisting a woman in complicated labor. And as testimony to unequal modernization in Chile at the time, he also recalled being shocked at the "drastically" different standards of medicine he encountered; in Melipilla it seemed that ideas about antimicrobials, hormone therapies, and insulin treatment were behind those his generation had learned in the capital. Doctors working in Melipilla's hospital had been trained in the 1940s and 1950s and practiced "old medicine," whereas he felt he was equipped with a new, more modern, scientific outlook.³¹

Indeed, the practice of sending doctors out to be MGZs was emblematic of a particular idea—prevalent at the time—about development spreading out from the cities to the countryside. As Heidi Tinsman has argued, many in the Frei administration, particularly those involved in agrarian reform, believed they were involved in a "mission of class uplift" when it came to rural communities, commonly considered as "junior partners."³² And, although driven by altruistic intentions, the attitude of political student militants when coming into contact with Chile's poorer communities was often similar.

Militancy, Friendship, and Love

Despite the intensity of medical training, Beatriz was still able to socialize, fall in love, and be politically active. On one level, she spent time with those she met at the Hospital San Juan de Dios. In addition to her classmates, she had particularly close relations with younger left-leaning teachers such as Arturo Jirón and Manuel Ipinza, a young pediatrician and Communist militant.[33] Elena Gálvez, a recent graduate, also became a close friend and one of the few people in whom Beatriz would confide over the course of her life.[34] Whenever they could get away, students and staff would eat together at a small restaurant in front of the Hospital San Juan de Dios called the Estrella. The restaurant had a television, and in 1963 it was there that Beatriz had been shocked to learn of John F. Kennedy's assassination.[35] On two or three occasions, toward the end of her medical degree, Beatriz also invited her internship group to Guardia Vieja for dinner, and Salvador Allende would drop by to talk with them.[36]

Medical students enjoyed themselves socially in effervescent 1960s Santiago. As one female medical student remembered, they met to drink beer or wine in popular venues and escaped to the snow in winter or the seaside in the summer.[37] Although they did not share political views, Marcelo Trucco, Beatriz's friend from Concepción, also recalled going to the Peña de los Parra to listen to folkloric music with her.[38] As a new music venue that had opened in April 1965 in downtown Santiago, the Peña de los Parra, run by Violeta Parra and her son and daughter, became a center of the la Nueva Canción (the New Song) movement that flourished during this period.[39] And Beatriz was part of this emerging cultural scene.

Generally, however, she socialized with those who were in the BUS, only some of whom were medical students. As one BUS militant remembered, "We were very sectarian in our social relations."[40] Indeed, politics—and political divides—permeated personal lives and social practices, helping to cement differentiated political cultures and imaginaries in Chilean society. Beatriz's group of socialist friends met in one another's homes, where Beatriz listened to her friends play guitar and sing old Spanish Civil War songs or hits by Los Chalchaleros, an Argentine folk band that was influential in Chile at the time. And in between singing, they would talk politics.[41] She invited them to Guardia Vieja, where they used her father's library and Allende greeted them affectionately as "revolutionary youth." On at least one occasion, the group also went to the Allendes' house in Algarrobo.[42] Meanwhile, they had an "everyday partisan life," participating in grassroots organizations, regional meetings, and party congresses. Although the BUS was generally centered on university politics and the Federación de Estudiantes de la Universidad de Chile (FECH), they had to know what was happening in the countryside and with urban workers so as to be able to participate in national campaigns.[43] And in 1965, Beatriz's BUS nucleus provided support to areas hit by an earthquake, helping to rebuild a town.[44]

She and her fellow socialist militants also spent time mobilizing rural workers in the context of Frei's new rural labor code and agrarian reform bill. The effects of such reforms were already being felt across Chile. Melipilla, where Beatriz did her internship, for example, had experienced one of the first major rural *tomas* (land seizures) that would characterize the Frei administration months before she arrived. On 17 October 1965, following a dispute over pay and conditions, rural workers had taken control of the Culiprán estate. It was not the first time Culiprán workers had mobilized. But this time, in anticipation of Frei's agrarian reform, the government had responded by expropriating the estate and establishing a land colony (*asentamiento*), which lasted three years before the land was divided up peacefully into individual and collective plots.[45] And when it came to such tomas, Socialist Party leaders put significant pressure on the government to avoid it using force to repress workers.[46]

It was in this context, responding to advice from Salomon Corbalán, leader of the Comisión Nacional Agraria Socialista (National Socialist Agrarian Commission, CONAS), that students in the BUS spent university holidays in 1966 and 1967 outside Santiago organizing and talking to rural communities.[47] As one of those who came into contact with Beatriz's immediate group recalled, they arrived from Santiago wanting to understand the problems local communities faced and what they were doing to assert their needs.[48] In an atmosphere in which the Left criticized Frei's agrarian reform program for not going fast or far enough, young militants felt that they could speed things up. They were driven by revolutionary zeal and altruism. And also by the guilt of having a privileged life that Beatriz had described feeling when volunteering near Concepción. To make up for this, students shared their knowledge and education. They invited pobladores to their university for evening classes—the idea being to "take them out of the poblacióne so that they could see there was something else."[49] In the mid-1960s, Rolando Calderón, a recipient of such efforts, met Beatriz during a visit by Socialist students to the small town of Asiento, north of Santiago. As he reflected, Beatriz's group essentially adopted him and decided it was their duty to help raise funds to enable him to continue the education in humanities that he had been unable to finish. Although, as we shall see, he subsequently became highly significant in national politics—and would marry a student leader in the Faculty of Medicine a few years below Beatriz—he recalled initially feeling discomfort in the students' world, which was still predominantly Santiago-based and middle class.[50] But of course Socialist students never talked about themselves or their goals in such terms. As one of Beatriz's friends in the BUS remembered, they spoke of themselves as being on the same side as the workers and the oppressed.[51] And their reach beyond university confines broke down barriers, fostering a new sense of purpose.

As in Concepción, the BUS's nuclei tended to organize themselves around individuals or groups of faculties. Those in Beatriz's closest circle were students of medicine, psychology, and pedagogy (including history, journalism, and sociology). This combination was shaped, at least in part, by romantic relationships. Edith Benado, a psychology student, remembered getting to know Beatriz because their boyfriends were friends.[52] Indeed, Beatriz's relationship with Renato Julio, a student of history and sociology and an active student leader, shaped her involvement in the BUS. Having campaigned together during the 1964 election and become friends, they began dating soon after. A couple of years older and already a young father, Renato was the son of Republican exiles who had fled the Spanish Civil War. He had been a Communist until the early 1960s when the international context had persuaded him to shift away from the Soviets' insistence on peaceful coexistence and join the Socialist Party (PS). He was attractive, dressed formally, spoke well, and was "active everywhere." He had a knack for telling stories, chain-smoked, sang, and played the guitar. He also drank too much, which would be a serious problem for him and for his relationship with Beatriz. But he was "cultured," his friends remembered, with a reputation for being an intellectual. He read avidly, always carried a newspaper, and devoured the beatniks, Jean-Paul Sartre, and Frantz Fanon (BUS militants, remembered a friend of Beatriz and Renato, read every page of *Wretched of the Earth* repeatedly).[53] Having earned a history degree in 1963, Renato then, along with his best friend and fellow militant, Ricardo Núñez, switched to sociology. From 1965 onward, the two of them studied with Enzo Faletto and Clodomiro Almeyda, left-wing intellectuals contributing to the development of dependency theory at the time.[54] Renato also served on the editorial board of the Socialist Party's journal, *Arauco*, from 1964 (even if he was not the most reliable contributor).

As recalled by one of those who knew them early on in their relationship, Beatriz "gravitated around Renato's political activities." She never sought leadership herself (very few women did in the PS, although there were more young female leaders in the Communist Party [PCCh]), but she

Beatriz and Renato (*both seated at right*) at the wedding of Benny and Gloria Pollack (*both standing*), 1965. Benny Pollack private collection.

supported him and was by his side.⁵⁵ As a couple, they were also central to their particular group of the BUS and socialized together with other couples, eating at restaurants or going to bars in Macul, near the Pedagogical Institute, where they ate hotdogs and drank (although Beatriz never liked alcohol).⁵⁶

This was Beatriz's most serious relationship to date and would last throughout her time at the University of Chile. Before Renato, it is difficult to trace her romantic ties. Her friends and sisters cannot remember her having any serious long-term boyfriends, although she had male friends and admirers.⁵⁷ To Salvador, his daughters' boyfriends were "temporary sons-in-law," and he made them feel welcome as long as they were cheerful.⁵⁸ While in Concepción, Beatriz had had a brief relationship with a student in Santiago who supported the Christian Democrats. However, when he demanded she stop participating in student politics, the relationship ended quickly.⁵⁹ And after that, although she spent much time with her course mates and was attracted to some, her friend Carmen Noemi remembered she refused to date them because they were not left wing.⁶⁰ She had also had a relationship with Luis Villalón in Concepción. He was handsome, liked art and literature, transferred to study philosophy in

Santiago around the same time as Beatriz moved to the capital, and got on well with her family.[61] However, their relationship did not last, probably because Luis was gay. (In May 1966, a few years after they broke up, Beatriz was one of the first to find out that he had taken his own life, tormented by the prospect of living as a homosexual in a patriarchal and homophobic Chile.)[62]

As Beatriz's friend from Concepción remembered, with lots of admirers, Beatriz found it difficult to know whether she was liked for whom she was or for whom her father was.[63] But Renato was apparently different. Like other men she fell for in her life, he was charismatic but vulnerable—someone who needed her. He also supported her in the final years of her medical degree. During her internship, for example, he would drive to pick her up in the evenings and often sat waiting for hours in his car, smoking and reading while she finished her rounds.[64] She, in turn, was close to his family and would often treat his father's diabetes (although she had to take Manuel along because Renato's father did not trust a female doctor to be qualified enough).[65] They were "very young" and "very in love," friends remembered, "very physical with each other."[66]

Radicalization

To understand Beatriz and Renato's relationship, as well as the political commitment of their immediate circle of socialist militant friends, it is important to understand their shared passion for socialism and the environment in which it was nurtured. As Ricardo, their friend and fellow socialist militant, explained, "It was a relationship that took place in the context of transformation ... not only from a political point of view, but also from a cultural point of view, transformations of great importance ... of readings that opened up a different world for us ... [and] different paths to those that had traditionally been used by the Left."[67] A glimpse at discussions within the Christian Democratic–led FECH at the time reveals these changes. At the Convention on University Reform in June 1966 convened by the FECH and attended by left-wing student militants, for example, hundreds of students defined Chilean society as being shaped by three processes: global capitalism, Latin America's frustrated modernization process, and a specific national social process aimed at replacing "unjust" and "out-of-date" institutions. And while the last imbued young Chileans with a messianic and revolutionary sense of purpose, the former two provided reasons for justifying significant change. "We are witnesses to a global process that has never been registered in history, in which man in all areas of the world is present for the disintegration of a decadent society and sees the possibility of a new, more dignified, and human one getting closer," one of the convention's commissions concluded.[68] That Christian Democrat and Communist students rather than Socialists led this convention makes such revolutionary statements more significant. Meanwhile, young Socialists like Beatriz's nucleus, active in university politics at the time, argued that proposed reforms did not go far enough and pushed for more proactive and urgent ownership of change.

The radicalization of the Socialist Party—particularly its youth wing—had begun almost immediately after Allende's 1964 defeat. As a leader of the Socialist Youth recalled, the experience had shown that the Left would never be able to reach power by electoral means and that the "bourgeoisie" would find a way of blocking their chances. Anti-imperialism and anger at U.S. intervention in Chilean affairs—albeit without full knowledge of its backing for Frei—was important.[69] At the party's congress at Linares in 1965, militants also defined the Christian Democratic Party (PDC) as "reactionary and anti-socialist, reformist, and patronizing."[70] But when it came to what to do about it, there were sharp divisions between "moderates"—referred to as "reformists" and "social democrats" by their opponents—and radical groups. At this congress, a young faction including Ricardo and Renato—and by extension Beatriz, although she was not there—successfully pushed for the party to embrace Marxism-Leninism more explicitly than before. This is not to say the radicals won over the party entirely; rifts persisted and grew deeper in subsequent years. Although Allende showed affection and sympathy for his daughter's "revolutionary youth" friends, for example, he was one of those resisting changes in formal party settings. The radical students' preferred candidate, Clodomiro Almeyda, director of the University of Chile's Sociology School and an intellectual on the left of the party, also refused to stand against the more moderate Aniceto Rodríguez for secretary general of the party, meaning it was still governed by those opposed to change. However, Linares signaled a shift.[71] "We all radicalized," Edith remembered; the goal was to change the makeup of the Central Committee so revolutionaries rather than so-called reformists governed it.[72]

In the following years, Chile's political and social environment contributed to this radicalization. The government's reformist agenda increasingly politicized life, from cities to the countryside, hospitals to factory floors, and university campuses to poblaciónes. Agitation and division also often accompanied dynamism and innovation. Reforms faced resistance in some quarters. Others believed they did not go far enough. Marginalized groups, previously unable to voice their demands or facing fierce repression, now felt empowered to insist on significant change.[73] And this empowerment, in turn, created a growing sense of uncertainty and upheaval. Strikes, land seizures, and demonstrations, for example, occurred frequently in towns, cities, and the countryside, focused on securing better salaries, the right to homes, education, and health care.[74] Societal mobilization during the Frei administration also had a lot to do with raised expectations, with impatience, and with a sense Chile needed to move forward urgently to address a crisis the 1964 election campaign had articulated. And all this was buttressed by the "hyperbole of 'revolution,'" as Heidi Tinsman argues, embedded in the PDC's pledge to bring about a "*Revolution* in Liberty."[75]

Part of the government's problem in responding to such demands was money. Although Frei had been successful in renegotiating a substantial part of Chile's external debt and the United States government provided generous aid and assistance—half a billion dollars in 1964–65[76]—Washington's support diminished after this. This change resulted partly from a shift in Alliance for Progress priorities toward stabilization and conditionality in return for aid. When Frei proposed raising salaries for public sector workers by 25 percent, for example, the Johnson administration opposed the move. Only by acquiescing in Washington's priorities (keeping copper prices low, for example, for the United States' Vietnam War commitments) could Frei guarantee support. But playing by U.S. rules threatened his national credentials vis-à-vis left-wing political rivals who already regarded him as "Washington's candidate."[77]

Within this context, left-wing students did not need much excuse to demonstrate. "The street was our preferred place for politics," Ricardo remembered; there was an intense "social upheaval," and any opportunity to protest against the United States or its links to Frei became socialist militants' "favorite sport."[78] However, there were moments that rocked the country decisively, such as the massacre of eight workers and the injury to over thirty people at the El Salvador mine on 11 March 1966. Proclaiming a "strong hand [*mano dura*]" against the strike days before, the government had illegally decreed a zone of emergency, intimidated workers, and detained journalists before sending in the army and carabineros.[79] Frei falsely blamed workers for the confrontation and suggested they had fired on the army first as part of a Cuba-orchestrated plan of subversion, which generated further condemnation.[80] When evidence showed workers had been shot in the back and two women, both mothers, were killed, anger spread.[81] The BUS sent a delegation to the funerals of those killed.[82] Left-wing parties mobilized in protest, Chile's national trade union federation (CUT) called a twenty-four-hour strike, and even PDC members, student leaders of the FECH included, decried the violence employed.[83] As the Radical Party senator Hugo Miranda, who had been at the mine before the massacre, challenged rhetorically, surely no one was accusing him of being a Cuban-inspired "red guerrilla."[84]

In fact, El Salvador and how it was explained became a significant sign of a reformist government opting for repression and Cold War threats to quell disquiet. As such, it is also a familiar story of state violence and repression being the spark that radicalized local people to take a different course from what they might have followed otherwise. Certainly, for those close to Beatriz who would later embrace armed struggle as an inevitable ingredient for revolutionary change, El Salvador was significant.[85] Hernán Coloma, a militant in the BUS a few years younger than Beatriz, for example, had initially been sympathetic to the PDC's Revolution in Liberty. But like many other young people in Chile, he became disillusioned. Encouraged by childhood friends, he had therefore joined the PS in 1965, and he remembered that a year later, he had a "very strong response" to what happened in El Salvador. "That is where I convinced myself this [the electoral road] was not the way [forward]," he would explain, "that there were not going to be social solutions without another way. It was there I thought of the armed struggle."[86] Or, as Ricardo explained, El Salvador "meant that the step from social and political radicalism to the possibility of organizing violence ... was an obvious move justified by the violence deployed by the state against unarmed people." Certainly, the massacre confirmed the expectation that Chilean elites and institutions would not allow "real changes" and that "the exacerbation of 'class struggle' other areas of Latin America were living through" was inevitable.[87] Henceforth, young Socialists, albeit mostly rhetorically for now, argued "all forms of struggle"—and implicitly armed struggle—would be needed to secure radical change. Any future revolutionary process, in other words, had to be ready to defend itself against those who resisted transformations.[88]

The government's efforts to blame Cuba also illustrate the internationalization of local phenomena at the time. According to the Left, Frei's "mano dura" was evidence of his willingness to serve imperialist interests (and, more specifically, Anaconda, the private U.S. company that refused to recognize the legality of striking workers).[89] A war of words also ensued between Fidel Castro and Frei, dominating local reporting of the event. As Castro declared, El Salvador had shown that the PDC was driving Chile toward "blood without revolution" rather than a "revolution without blood." When accused of interfering against Chile, Castro also raised questions at the heart of the struggle to determine the country's future. Who represented Chile and its interests: the workers or Frei, the protector of U.S. imperial interests?[90] Even the pro-Soviet Communist Party, no fan of Cuba's advocacy of guerrilla insurgency, denounced Frei as a spokesman for U.S. imperialism—which in the context of the U.S. invasion of the Dominican Republic in 1965 and the spiraling war in Vietnam was increasingly condemned throughout Chile.[91] When no evidence of provocation emerged, the government was forced to backtrack from its initial allegations. Yet it is significant that it had immediately used the specter of Cuban-inspired subversion to justify what had happened locally.[92] As commentators worried, it seemed the government was looking abroad for pretexts to instigate anticommunist legislation at home, much as Gabriel González Videla had done in the late 1940s. Now, however, as the Communist senator Volodia Teitelboim proclaimed, the Christian Democrats had a "new red phantom: the Tricontinental Conference."[93]

Children of Latin America's Revolution

There is no doubt the meeting of revolutionary leaders from Africa, Asia, and Latin America in January 1966, known as the Tricontinental Conference—or the inaugural meeting of the Organización de Solidaridad con los Pueblos de Asia, África y América Latina (OSPAAAL)—provided powerful inspiration to those seeking alternatives to Frei's reformist government and left-wing electoral strategies. Beatriz's father had attended the conference and participated actively in it. As well as hearing from delegates in Havana for the conference, news from the island and revolutionary insurgencies throughout Latin America captivated young Chileans like Beatriz and her milieu. "We read a lot about everything from abroad," remembered one medical student and revolutionary hopeful who would become a close friend of Beatriz in later years. "We were like sponges, we absorbed everything."[94] By the mid-1960s, it was not only Cuba's revolution capturing attention; guerrilla insurgencies throughout Latin America were at their height. Cuba's news agency, Prensa Latina, reported on them, and Cuban publications openly instructed readers how to launch their own operations. Che Guevara's *Guerra de Guerrillas* resonated among young Chilean militants. First published in Havana in 1960, it became especially popular after it was reissued in 1963 with updated prescriptions on "methods" that included discussion of the legitimacy of guerrilla warfare in democratic countries. Followed by Régis Debray's *Revolution in the Revolution?*, published in January 1967, Havana provided the conceptual tools to justify commitment to armed revolution.[95] And Chile's far left publications voraciously reported them. Compared with the early days of Cuba's revolution when it was hard to get news of what was happening on the island, reports of regional revolutionary activity now filled pages of the new pro-Cuban magazine *Punto Final*.[96]

Feeding into this context, the Tricontinental Conference brought together more than eighty revolutionary, left-wing, and nationalist groups from three continents, including twenty-seven Latin American delegations. Over six hundred attendees and more than two hundred journalists arrived for the event. Participants celebrated revolutionary violence as a necessary and desirable response to "Yankee imperialism."[97] Even Allende noted that the U.S. invasion of the Dominican Republic proved "imperialists will respond with violence to any popular movement that has any chance of coming into power." Although he said Chileans would determine appropriate methods in their own country, he reasoned that U.S. actions entailed an "obligation to intensify our struggle; mobilizing the masses, linking anti-imperialist actions to every demand of the population; and strikes, land occupations, and collective mobilizations." Strikingly, he noted a growing "awareness" of the need to oppose "reactionary violence ... with revolutionary violence."[98] As those traveling to Cuba also undoubtedly hoped, the conference caused alarm in the United States. A U.S. Senate subcommittee predicted "the immediate and massive intensification of terrorism and guerrilla activity throughout the Americas, as well as in Asia and Africa."[99] Indeed, when it came to the Americas, Tricontinental delegates resolved to offer "the most determined support to the revolutionary movements of Colombia, Venezuela, Peru, Panama, Ecuador, and other countries of the Caribbean area and the southern part of the hemisphere."[100]

To provide a regional logistical framework for this kind of assistance, Beatriz's father had also called for the establishment of a special Latin American grouping—the Organización Latinoamericana de Solidaridad (Latin American Solidarity Organization, OLAS). Thereafter, an organizing committee consisting of representatives from nine countries (Chileans included) prepared for OLAS's first conference in July–August 1967. In Chile, this caused political tension, as the Right and the PDC accused those who were involved of promoting subversion. When Allende, by now president of the Senate, said he would attend the conference, he was threatened with a vote of no confidence and forced to cancel his trip, though he sent a telegram to Cuba vaunting OLAS as a decisive move toward the "liberation of Latin America and the overthrow of imperialism."[101]

Haydée Santamaria, a veteran of the Sierra Maestra who presided over OLAS, told television reporters, "The highest expression of revolutionary struggle—armed struggle—was the prevailing theme of the conference."[102] In fact, at one preparatory meeting, a Chilean participant remembered, "The pressure in favor of armed struggle was tremendous. The hosts offered guerrilla courses with great ease. [People] talked about FAL and M-1 rifles, and those that had not mastered the jargon were classified as 'soft.'"[103] The OLAS conference also emphasized efforts to "continentalize" this armed revolutionary fervor.[104] As sympathetic Chilean reports noted, the region was under "one great political structure," and "national powers [were] merely delegations of this super entity" dominated by the United States. As a result, one person's struggle was everyone's.[105]

Socialist militants like Beatriz keenly adopted this militarized and continentalized message. As Ricardo Núñez reflected, by the mid-1960s they were no longer "children ... of the Chilean Revolution" but, thanks to the "Cuban Revolution's enormous influence," now "children of a Latin American Revolution."[106] Defining themselves in favor of Latin America was very important in the process of radicalization, Beatriz's friend and fellow *brigadista* (brigade member), Edith, explained.[107] And to show their solidarity with insurgencies abroad, students frequently took to the streets, engaging in direct action. When Raúl Leoni, Venezuela's Christian Democrat president, visited Chile in April 1967, for example, Felix Huerta, a young fourth-year medical student in the BUS, painted "LEONI ASESINO" in tar on the walls of La Moneda, the presidential palace, to protest Venezuela's use of force against a Cuban-inspired insurgency.[108] That year, Ricardo was also among the first young socialists to travel to Cuba to receive two months of armed training, reflecting the political shift that had taken place over the previous two years.[109]

Radicalization born of local frustration and indignation had made influences from abroad resonate more so than they might have otherwise. In an era when revolution of one sort or another was embraced widely across the political spectrum as necessary and desirable, the question was whether change could avoid violence. But, as we shall see, faced with state repression and with revolutionary insurgencies romanticized, "avoiding" violence lost much of its relevance. For Beatriz and others in the radical wing of the Socialist Party, waiting for electoral processes and union struggles was not enough. "We live in a time of revolutions," an editorial in *Las Noticias de Última Hora* reminded readers. "What matters is to continue revolutionizing our Chilean reality."[110] That Frei's project struggled to keep up with the demand for change exacerbated these trends. By the end of 1966, even observers sympathetic to his government admitted the PDC's Revolution in Liberty "creaked, rather than leapt forward."[111] A year later it seemed that it was "grinding to a halt" and that Frei had failed to meet expectations.[112] And when people grew disillusioned with the Christian Democrats, they tended to turn left. The Socialist Party recruited five thousand new militants in 1966 and a further ten thousand a year later.[113] In Chile's April 1967 municipal elections, the PS and PCCh collectively gained over six percentage points, whereas Christian Democrats lost eight.

And by the end of the decade, the Communist Party could count sixty thousand members.[114] Although, as we shall see, the Right and the call for a return to the status quo also accompanied disillusion with the PDC, demands for change rose rather than diminished during the mid-1960s. The government had opened a Pandora's box, a member of Chile's new revolutionary Left reflected.[115]

Revolutionary Differences

In search of a decisive revolutionary path, young Socialists in Beatriz's group increasingly clashed with other left-wing youth sectors. By 1966–67, the Frente de Acción Popular (FRAP)—and, in particular, its younger militants—was consumed by a growing ideological struggle, at least in part reflective of the split between the USSR and Cuba within the international communist movement. At this stage, radicalized socialists like Beatriz were in a minority in the University of Chile's political scene, even if hindsight tells us that they were in the ascendance. Their interest in "all forms of struggle" was also still incipient. But intransigence against any hint of collaboration with Frei's reformist program—even to the extent of refusing to work with Christian Democratic (DC) and Communist youth groups to support agrarian reform considered by the PS as too moderate— led to fierce arguments, dividing the Socialist Party and separating Socialists from Communists.[116] When Communist students refused to back down to Socialists' demands that the FECH leave the Union of Chilean University Federations—accused of acting as an "agent of imperialism" by boycotting the Cuban-led Congreso Latinoamericano de Estudiantes (Latin American Congress of Students)—the two parties fielded separate candidates for the FECH's elections for the second year in a row. And when Renato and Beatriz's close friend, Ricardo, stood as the Socialist candidate in 1966, he did so with the slogan, "We are the only revolutionary alternative." The meaning was twofold: It sent a message to the DC and the Communists that they weren't revolutionary enough, and it also sought to stave off challenges from the far Left. At a moment when all student factions were claiming to be "revolutionary," the question was who could prove themselves to be the *right* kind of revolutionaries for Chile's circumstances. As Ricardo and his backers claimed, only the Socialists were revolutionaries "pure, tough, and mature."[117] Yet, by campaigning separately, the Left relinquished any chance of beating the Christian Democrats, who won comfortably with 5,232 votes to the Communists' 2,628 and the Socialist Party's lackluster 1,137.[118] Because PS radicalization took place more prominently within youth sectors of the party, these left-wing divisions at a university level were particularly acute when compared with those of the collective Left. And yet young Chileans' growing involvement in national politics, their visibility, and their view of themselves as protagonists, encouraged by national party leaderships, meant splits over revolutionary legitimacy were far more significant than they might have been a decade before.

This was certainly the case when it came to youth involvement in a new far left Chilean political party established at a congress in Santiago in August 1965. Attended by ninety delegates, this new party—the Movimiento de Izquierda Revolucionaria (Revolutionary Left Movement, MIR)—brought together small, disparate extraparliamentary left groupings. Young dissident Socialists joined older Trotskyists, Maoists, anarchists, and former Communists to form the "movement," so labeled to identify with Castro's 26th of July Movement and to distinguish itself from established political parties. Although there were significant differences within the MIR regarding strategy and international alignments, as well as between an older generation of Trotskyists and a younger generation of Socialist students, such as Beatriz's friends from Concepción, including Miguel Enríquez, Luciano Cruz, and Bautista van Schouwen, members were united by their disdain for the "traditional Left," identified as "fossils of the glacial age."[119] The MIR's founding declaration insisted that, because capitalism was in crisis, the conditions existed for immediate revolution. Accordingly, miristas (MIR members) argued, to support reformism—either that of the PDC or of what they argued as traditional left-wing parties—was to betray and disarm the proletariat, leaving it defenseless against those with a vested interest in violently defending their power. While the PCCh and the PS denounced the MIR as "ultra-left" and divisionist, miristas criticized established left-wing parties in Chile as "tacit sellouts and collaborators of capitalist and imperialist domination."[120] Miristas also regarded Allende's 1964 defeat as confirming that elections could not bring revolutionary change.[121]

While Beatriz was still a student, the MIR remained a relatively minor party in Santiago. By 1967 it had only a few hundred militants and small pockets of support at the University of Chile concentrated in the Pedagogical Institute (it won only 465 votes in the 1966 FECH elections, for example).[122] As Eugenia Palieraki has underlined, the University of Chile's decentralized campus, with faculties spread across Santiago, made it harder to organize mass meetings and gain traction than it was in Concepción, where the MIR had its stronghold.[123] There, Luciano and Miguel, members of the MIR's Central Committee, became charismatic leaders of a radicalized student population—which would place them in a stronger position vis-à-vis the MIR's older Trotskyist leadership. Their emphasis on armed struggle and action over theory had been particularly effective. This was largely symbolic—comprising marches in hills around Concepción and some shooting practice—but it proved popular among students.[124] Young mirista leaders also received national attention through staged acts designed to gain publicity, according them prestige beyond their power. Miguel had fought "imperialism" when he confronted Robert Kennedy verbally during his visit to the University of Concepción and suggested he visit Chilean poblaciónes to see the results of the United States' misguided foreign policy. Luciano was arrested for briefly kidnapping a journalist on the university's campus and was feted when he escaped from prison.[125] In May 1966, Sergio Pérez Molina, a former Communist militant recruited to the MIR at the University of Chile and a friend of Beatriz, had stood up in the public gallery when Frei delivered his annual speech to Congress, shouting, "Down with workers' oppression! Long live the MIR!" and throwing pamphlets into the air denouncing the El Salvador massacre.[126] Later that year, the MIR carried out its first robbery, of an arms depot.[127]

Beatriz's friendship with and sympathy for the MIR's leaders during these years meant she began to stand even to the left of her close radicalized Socialist friends and, increasingly, to the left of Renato as well. Ricardo remembered she was increasingly absent from BUS politics and, unlike Renato, was not particularly involved in his 1966 campaign for the FECH.[128] In part this was due to the demands of medical training. But it was also because her political alliances were shifting. She never left the Socialist Party because of loyalty to her father.[129] But, from 1965 onward, her Concepción friends had begun traveling frequently to Santiago and meeting with students at the University of Chile, such as Hernán Sandoval (who transferred to Santiago with Beatriz) and Miguel's brother, Edgardo.[130] Beatriz's cousin Andrés Pascal, in Santiago, was also in their inner circle. And Beatriz remained in close contact with them.

Operative in student politics before the university reform of later years, Beatriz may also have been attracted to the MIR's inclination for capturing national attention. Divided left-wing student politics, which the Christian Democrats had dominated for over a decade and to which her friends and boyfriend were wedded, seemed increasingly irrelevant when faced with day-to-day challenges she witnessed as a trainee doctor and Socialist activist. Significantly, in 1967, after two relatively good years, living costs rose again.[131] Although Chile's economy under Frei fared relatively well compared with what had come before and what would come after, the government's inability to grow the economy fast enough to address rising demands created a sense of crisis.[132] The number of strikes in 1966–67 were double what they had been in 1964–65, and increasing.[133] That younger miristas positioned themselves as Cuba's most faithful defenders despite having no concrete links to Havana until late 1967 was important, particularly for Beatriz.[134]

Even so, Beatriz kept a low profile when it came to the diverging strands of her life and her support for the MIR, fearful of harming her father's reputation. Dedicated to her medical training by day, close friends with those in the BUS in the evenings and on weekends, and a sympathetic collaborator with miristas when they needed help, Beatriz assumed different roles and personalities depending on the situation. In fact, the different groups in her life knew very little about one another or about Beatriz's place within them. As she neared graduation, she appeared to be searching for a cause she could contribute to in her own right as opposed to being her father's daughter, Renato's girlfriend, or the MIR's accomplice. University education had been not only about professional training but also about a personal process of political radicalization that intersected with, reflected, and fed into wider political and social processes.

Graduation and Work

For now, when Beatriz graduated on 10 May 1967, she worked part-time for Benjamin Viel's newly established Consultorio Ismael Valdés in Quinta Normal.[135] Her graduation had taken place at the University of Chile's Casa Central. And as was customary in the university's medical school with children of former graduates, her father presented her degree certificate.[136] There was no formal party to commemorate the students' achievement. But separate private celebrations took place across Santiago.[137]

Beatriz also married Renato on 6 July 1967 at a small ceremony in Guardia Vieja.[138] It is difficult to know why they got married, given their emerging differences. But it was not unusual for couples to formalize their relationships after graduating. Beatriz's sisters and many of her friends also chose to do so.[139] In this way, the shift from young romance to marriage mirrored the transition from adolescence to adulthood and independence. But Isabel Jaramillo, who got to know Beatriz at this time, also remembered her decision being driven by societal expectations and a desire not to embarrass her father by being in a long-term relationship unsanctioned by marriage. "Chile was a very conservative, Catholic, and provincial country," Isabel explained. "She had to protect his name and political activity."[140] Now married, they found a small apartment close by. And Renato juggled various jobs, including part-time university teaching and journalism for *Las Noticias de Última Hora*.[141]

Newly qualified and married, it was also time for Beatriz to work. And as a student who had specialized jointly in public health and pediatrics, it was fitting Beatriz should join the growing team at the Consultorio Ismael Valdés, an innovative medical center focusing on women's and children's health. With its emphasis on local community building, family planning, and international funding, it was a typical venture of the reformist Frei period.[142] It was also emblematic of an increasingly popular belief in "integrative medicine." Its team consisted of six pediatricians (Beatriz and Manuel Ipinza were two), a psychiatrist, a psychologist, a sociologist, a statistician, a gynecologist-obstetrician, two nurses, and three social workers. In time, it established a kindergarten to address child malnutrition and poverty in the area.[143] It also established a local health council, bringing community representatives and staff together.[144]

By all accounts, Beatriz's colleagues regarded her highly. That this was a particularly left-wing team helped, even if Viel was more aligned to the Christian Democrats (when conservative colleagues accused him of employing "communists," he excused himself by saying these were the people who wanted to work in public health).[145] As a pediatrician, Beatriz was responsible for treating children and attending emergencies, describing her clinical work as "serious but affectionate."[146] According to the Consultorio's director, Gilda Gnecco, she arrived promptly and was often seen tying her hair back with a rubber band before getting down to work. "She always showed love for families, mothers and children," Gilda recalled, adding that she had a "capacity to analyze the relationship [between] socioeconomic reality and the health and well-being of individuals, families and the community."[147]

Shortly after starting work at the Consultorio Valdés, Beatriz nevertheless left Chile to accompany her father on a trip to Cuba and the Soviet Union. She was supposed to be away for only a couple of weeks, but as we shall see, she would not return for more than two months. When she did, she was also distracted. Beatriz could not stay at meetings all day because she had to go and see "this *compañera* or that *compañero*," Gilda remembered.[148] Increasingly in the late 1960s, in fact, Beatriz's time would be divided between political, professional, and personal commitments. And in all respects, she was tied to an intensifying ideological conflict in the country in which global conflicts resonated loudly, fusing with domestic concerns. By 1967, for example, Latin American guerrilla insurgencies and the Vietnam War mobilized young people.[149] For those like Beatriz, who believed revolutionary change at home was linked to revolution abroad, the question was not just whether to show solidarity from afar but also how to participate directly.

5 ::: Love and Revolution

Although she could not have known when she arrived in Havana, Beatriz's trip to Cuba in 1967 would change her life. There, she began a secret love affair with a Cuban intelligence official, giving her an emotional link to Cuba and entangling her in its revolutionary operations. Partly because of this affair, partly because of her infatuation with Cuba, but also due to existing differences, her marriage to Renato ended months after it started. Early in 1968, she also became a covert revolutionary, helping coordinate a new guerrilla insurgency in Bolivia after Ernesto "Che" Guevara's death. Juan Carretero, a senior Cuban intelligence official involved in Bolivian operations, went so far as to describe Beatriz as its "soul."[1] She played an "extraordinary" role, a Bolivian leader of the insurgency recalled.[2] This was a decisive shift in her personal and political life. And she seized the opportunity to follow in Che's footsteps. Yet, as Beatriz found out firsthand, Latin America's "Guerrilla Decade"—with its allure of mystery and potential—was costly. Only two years later, writing to her Cuban lover, she acknowledged her experience had made her "older and more serious."[3]

Beatriz's new connection with Cuba and her covert role in Bolivia—carefully delineated by her gender and her father's position in Chile—was extraordinary but not unusual. By 1968, the CIA calculated that "at least 2,500 Latin Americans" had received training in Cuba since 1961.[4] On the other side of the Cold War divide, the Bulgarian ambassador in Havana—hostile to Castro's support for revolution abroad—reported the Cubans had organized "about 40 small guerrilla groups" in the region by 1967.[5] As we have seen, Cuba actively encouraged young people to take up arms and provided the framework to justify revolutionary action. As well as disseminating news of revolutionary struggles, writing and sharing practical manuals for would-be guerrillas, or organizing conferences, Havana's leaders also concretely facilitated young Latin Americans' involvement in insurgencies, providing money, training, and logistical support.

Even so, interpretations differed as to how applicable armed struggle was to Chile. Militants in the Brigada Universitaria Socialista (BUS) exploring "all forms of struggle," for example, tended to view military training as defensive—a means of resisting Frei's "strong hand" and a reserve force in case the Left won power electorally. The Movimiento de Izquierda Revolucionaria (MIR), by contrast, saw armed struggle in Chile as an alternative to elections and a means of bringing about decisive revolutionary change, although in 1966–67 its efforts had yet to get off the ground. There was another vision as well: participating in guerrilla insurgencies abroad to further a transnational battle against imperialism and, in doing so, weakening its ability to block radical change in Chile.

When it came to this latter vision, Che Guevara's call to create "two, three, many Vietnams" as a means of bringing imperialism to its knees, published by the Tricontinental in April 1967, became a manifesto. Bemoaning lackluster support for the Vietnamese in their war against the United States, Guevara insisted revolutionaries "share their fate, accompany them in death or victory." And, in this respect, he celebrated Fidel Castro's dictum, outlined in February 1962, that revolutionary internationalism was a revolutionary's duty.[6] Death and sacrifice abroad in the name of revolution, Guevara now argued, could serve as a lesson for those who survived back home. The road ahead would be long and costly, but revolution would triumph if enough people were committed to success. "Our every action is a battle cry against imperialism, and a battle hymn for the people's unity against the great enemy of mankind: the United States of America," he wrote. "Wherever death surprises us, let it be welcome, provided that this, our battle cry, may have reached some receptive ear." He also insisted that Latin America—with its common language, customs, religion, "common love," and exploitation—would have an important task: "that of creating the second or third Vietnam."[7]

Vietnam had already been a focal point of the Tricontinental and Organización Latinoamericana de Solidaridad (OLAS) Conferences.[8] Vietnamese delegates attending these events were heralded, and participants were told to emulate their example.[9] *Punto Final* was among left-wing publications devoting space to vehement condemnation of the U.S. war in the country, including statements from Chile's national solidarity commission for African and Asian peoples.[10] Yet what made Che's message significant was his explicit invitation to young Latin Americans to participate immediately in a broader regional and global battle. For socialist militants, who were persuaded by armed struggle's merits but unsure of its suitability for Chile, internationalism provided a solution. As one Chilean revolutionary wrote to his family, "The revolution is one and the same. You cannot liberate all countries at the same time. All forces must be concentrated where the best conditions reside."[11]

For Beatriz, in search of a cause and a means of speeding up decisive change, this idea hit a nerve. It now formed the basis of her commitment to revolutionary activism and freed her from local constraints. It also allowed her to covertly embrace armed struggle without undermining her father's domestic position. As sympathetic as she was to the MIR, she had never believed Chile was suitable for a Cuban-style rural—or even urban—guerrilla insurgency initiated by a small vanguard of revolutionaries of *foco*. And in this respect she was guided both by her father, who had always insisted Chile was different from other Latin American countries, and by Cuba.

To Be Like Che

The Cubans had always doubted armed revolution's applicability in Chile. Although Allende had proposed the establishment of OLAS, Chile was never its focus. To the contrary, at the organization's inaugural meeting in Havana, the idea of guerrilla insurgency in Chile was considered "crazy and absurd."[12] The problem, as Fidel explained to a Chilean journalist, was the absence of "geographical conditions": the inhospitable conditions of the Atacama Desert and Patagonia made guerrilla warfare difficult, and with the Pacific and the Andes on either side of the country, insurgents had nowhere to retreat. "If you want to be involved in guerrilla warfare there are conflicts on your doorstep, there in Bolivia," Castro added.[13]

Of course, when Castro pointed to Bolivia, Cuba was already heavily committed to bringing about revolution in the country. In November 1966, Che Guevara had arrived to organize a guerrilla column and established what became known as the Ejército de Liberación Nacional (National Liberation Army, ELN) in southeastern Bolivia. Despite its name and in keeping with the ideas espoused by OLAS, the ELN's objectives were anything but "national." Instead, Guevara's plan was to establish a base camp and "mother column" that would eventually incorporate other guerrilla forces from neighboring countries and span out throughout South America to bring about the "continental" revolution he had long since championed.[14] Although the Bolivian Communist Party (PCB) had initially offered conditional support, this ended when Che insisted on remaining in control and misunderstandings arose regarding ultimate objectives. Even so, a network within the party, including the Peredo brothers Roberto ("Coco") and Guido Alvaro ("Inti"), who had received Cuban guerrilla training and collaborated with previous operations in Argentina and Peru, stayed with Che. Before the guerrilla insurgency ever got off the ground, its base camp was nevertheless discovered, and the ELN's members found themselves trekking through inhospitable, sparsely populated terrain, lost and starving. After the column divided, half the ELN's forces were killed on

31 August 1967. Guevara was then captured on 8 October 1967 and executed the next day. The six survivors of Guevara's column, including three Cubans and Inti, who would henceforth become the ELN's leader, went into hiding.[15]

For Cuba's regime, the news was devastating. Castro called Guevara's death "a hard blow."[16] In a posthumous letter to Che, Haydée Santamaria, who presided over OLAS, mourned his death's regional impact: "With your eyes open," she lamented, "Latin America would have found its way forward."[17] In the United States, CIA analysts similarly believed Guevara's death would undermine revolution in the region. Despite nine years supporting insurgencies, they concluded, "no guerrilla group" constituted "a serious threat to any [Latin American] government."[18]

In their rush to celebrate, however, U.S. analysts failed to grasp the mobilizing effect of Guevara's death. True, no regional government was significantly endangered by a revolutionary insurgency in subsequent years, and OLAS was more symbolic than operationally powerful.[19] Che's death also prompted many revolutionaries—particularly in the Southern Cone—to turn to urban, rather than rural, guerrilla tactics. And Cuba's leaders would eventually distance themselves from armed insurgencies. Yet, for now, Guevara's failure paradoxically sparked a new revolutionary fervor.[20]

This was certainly the case in Chile. In the weeks after it was announced, demonstrators condemned his "assassination," shouting "Comandante Guevara. Here!" as they marched through Santiago's streets. University students flew flags at half-mast, secondary students appointed Che as the "supreme leader of our people's struggle for liberation," and the Senate held a two-hour vigil.[21] Left-wing politicians committed to constitutional democracy in Chile lined up to pay homage to the fallen guerrilla. In a letter demanding Guevara's remains be returned to his family, Salvador Allende wrote to Bolivian president General René Barrientos that Che had become "synonymous with the most untarnished loyalty to ... social progress."[22] Although the Communist Party had disagreed with Guevara's armed tactics, *El Siglo* also unequivocally praised his willingness to risk his life for revolution.[23] Even Chilean center and right-wing politicians suggested Guevara deserved "respect for a bravely defended ideal."[24]

As tributes filled Chilean newspaper pages, those who had idealized Che before his death grieved. A young medical student remembered the "blow" he felt when he learned of Che's death walking past a newsstand.[25] In Concepción, Miguel Enríquez "suffered intensely, he became ill."[26] Hernán Coloma, a BUS militant, remembered it being "a catastrophe."[27] Across town, Beatriz left work and reportedly ran to Osvaldo Puccio's house nearby. As her father's private secretary and a close family friend, Osvaldo had often welcomed Beatriz. Now, she asked for privacy. From behind a bedroom door, Osvaldo's son, Carlos, heard her crying, lamenting not having done more to save Che.[28]

Chilean left-wing leaders meanwhile waited for Fidel to respond.[29] Finally, over a week later, Castro spoke, insisting Che's ideas would continue, that Guevara had always understood the revolutionary struggle would be long: "Five, ten, twenty years, a whole lifetime if necessary!" Although Che was dead, the important thing, according to Castro, was that others—"millions"—follow in his footsteps. "If we want to express how we aspire our revolutionary combatants to be, our activists, our men to be," he proclaimed, "we must say without any hesitation of any kind: let them be like Che!"[30]

A week later, *Punto Final* echoed Fidel's message: "Che did not forge his revolutionary personality ... for it to be cried over. The homage this great captain of Latin America deserves is for his example to be copied many times over."[31] Only in following his example, left-wing Chileans argued, would Latin America achieve its true independence. Che's body, now evoked alongside Emiliano Zapata, Augusto César Sandino, and the Colombian guerrilla priest Camilo Torres, was imagined as the seed of a new revolutionary struggle with roots spreading across the region.[32]

Cuba and the Soviet Union

It was in this context that Beatriz and her father arrived in Cuba in late October 1967.[33] Before leaving Santiago, Allende had bemoaned Chileans' lackluster support for Che. "As organizers of OLAS," he stated, "we must recognize—it hurts us to say so—that in the tough moments of Guevara's struggle, our people's response did not materialize."[34] Now, arriving in Havana, the senator told a Cuban reporter he wanted to express his "sorrow"; Guevara's "life was a lesson," he added.[35]

It must have been a strange time to return to Cuba and very different from the celebratory atmosphere that had greeted Beatriz in 1960. But she was excited to be back. She and her father stayed at the Habana Libre, and one evening, when "Demid Crespo," the Cuban intelligence official assigned to look after them, arrived at the hotel, she gave him an enthusiastic hug and a kiss on the cheek. He had been out with friends drinking and so lied it was his birthday to excuse himself. Even so, Beatriz's effusive birthday greeting was unusual, and he stepped back surprised, not least because he was attracted to her and felt uncomfortable.[36]

Demid—later known as Luis Fernández Oña but born Rodulfo Gallart Grau[37]—worked for the Viceministerio Técnico (Technical Vice Ministry)

Beatriz and Salvador Allende, Cuba, 1967. Alejandro Fernández Allende private collection.

at Cuba's Ministerio del Interior (Interior Ministry). Headed by Manuel Piñeiro since its creation in 1961, this entity was responsible for Cuba's political relations with Latin American left-wing movements, parties, and organizations. After the majority of regional countries severed relations with the island and Cuba's suspension from the Organization of American States (OAS) in 1962, the scope of its work had expanded. And, as part of this organization, Demid—or Luis, as he will be referred to henceforth— had been responsible for Chile since late 1963.[38] Because Chile was not a Cuban foreign policy priority, his was not a senior position, but to Chileans he was the gatekeeper to Cuba's government. A Chilean who traveled to the island frequently in the mid-1960s remembered him as the "personification of the revolutionary apparatus."[39] A respectful but generous host who enjoyed Allende's sense of humor and taste for whisky, Luis also knew the senator well when he arrived in 1967, although he had never met Beatriz. And when Allende asked to see Fidel, who was in eastern Cuba, Luis made the necessary arrangements. From Havana, he accompanied them by plane to Holguín and, from there, by helicopter to the Sierra Maestra.[40]

On 30 October Beatriz and her father were thus able to attend Fidel Castro's inauguration of a major land-clearing project led by Cuba's armed forces.[41] And this spectacle of a new revolutionary modernity provided the opportunity for Beatriz's first face-to-face meeting with Cuba's leader. As Beatriz later told a Cuban journalist, "We advanced along a little path.... I suddenly could make out his profile and his hand. I stopped in my tracks, I couldn't go forward or back. I was paralyzed. I couldn't say anything: as if I were stupid. My father, who came from behind, pushed me, saying 'what's happened to you, girl?' But he realized perfectly ... the Comandante has an ability to make you lose your nerves, and soon you are not aware of them and you are talking with him." Beatriz explained that "it is difficult for you to imagine what Fidel represents for a Latin American."[42] On this occasion, however, she did not just meet Castro. After the inauguration had finished, she and her father, together with Luis, stayed overnight in the Sierra Maestra with him, President Osvaldo Dorticós, and Manuel Piñeiro, whom she had first met in Chile as a teenager in 1959. Aged 25, Beatriz thus gained new access to the highest levels of Cuba's revolutionary government and was able to talk to them about Che's death and its implications.[43]

She learned that the Cubans were determined that revolution in Bolivia—and Latin America—would not die with Che. This was also the message the Cubans transmitted to others in subsequent months. New Bolivian recruits, many of them university students in Europe and Cuba, had volunteered to join the ELN prior to Guevara's death, and others now arrived in Havana, ready to follow in his footsteps. With survivors and new recruits, the Cubans insisted all was not lost. Havana's leaders no doubt felt compromised. Latin Americans were simultaneously training in Cuban camps ready to take part in guerrilla operations. To shut down revolutionary activities would not only have created logistical problems but would also have been to admit defeat.[44] So they opted instead for a new offensive. As *Punto Final* reported in early November, surviving guerrillas in Bolivia had "prospects for overcoming their current, difficult situation to take up the offensive again."[45] In truth, they were in hiding, desperately evading the country's armed forces, and unable to contact fragile urban networks for months.⁴⁶ Incredulous as the idea of new offensive was at this stage, however, Beatriz and her father left eastern Cuba optimistic.

From Havana, they flew to Moscow as planned for the fiftieth anniversary of the Bolshevik Revolution. This was an expected and understandable pilgrimage for those on the Left. Leading up to the anniversary, the Chilean Left celebrated vociferously. In Congress, deputies and senators paid homage to the Bolshevik Revolution's significance. The Chilean Communist Party organized a festival along one of Santiago's principal avenues, erecting three stages for artists, musicians, and actors.⁴⁷ And newspaper editorials underlined the 1917 revolution's stimulus for popular movements to rethink their theories and tactics.⁴⁸ Chilean left-wing commentators also underscored the significance of the Soviet Union as a powerful symbol of modernity.⁴⁹

As important and significant as the Soviet Union was to Chile's left-wing leaders, members of the revolutionary Left, like Beatriz, inspired by Cuba and by Che Guevara's example, were not convinced. Moscow's emphasis on peaceful coexistence and gradual revolution in stages seemed tired in comparison with the faster, dynamic Cuban route of armed struggle. Arriving directly from Havana, Moscow must also have seemed cold and alien to her, not least because there were so few Cubans present. Indeed, tensions between the Soviet bloc and Cuba had been growing for some time. As Castro experimented with unorthodox economic planning and moral—as opposed to material—incentives for workers, his Soviet bloc sponsors had grown impatient. Fierce disagreements over Cuba's support for revolutionary insurgencies in Latin America had become more acute when Moscow's leaders learned Che was in Bolivia at the end of 1966.⁵⁰ As one Eastern European observer complained, "Peaceful coexistence ... is considered by Cuba's leaders as a conciliation with imperialism; therefore they favor the idea of having 'the first, second, third ... many Vietnams ...' [as] the driving forces of Latin America's revolution ... the revolution is viewed as the fruitful result of a couple of convinced people's courage and bravery.... The USSR's and the socialist countries' experience in building socialism is denied."⁵¹ For their part, Cuban leaders bemoaned what they saw as the Soviets' tepid support for Third World revolution and publicly blamed the Moscow-aligned PCB for Guevara's death.⁵² When the Soviet press published articles by Latin American communist parties criticizing Cuba, Castro downgraded his delegation to Moscow at the last minute. One Cuban official also told his Czechoslovakian counterpart that Havana was disappointed by the Soviet response to Guevara's death.⁵³

For Beatriz, being fixated on Che in Moscow was therefore complicated. But she was not alone. There, she met a lawyer and Socialist, Arnoldo

Camú, and his wife, Celsa Parrau, both of whom had spent a month in Budapest, Prague, Berlin, and Paris. Now, as compatriots, they gravitated toward each other. As Celsa remembered, they talked at length one evening in Allende's hotel room about socialism and Chile's future. But conversations "fundamentally centered on what was happening in Cuba." Che's legacy and how to follow in his footsteps were at the forefront in their minds.[54]

Havana

When Salvador and Beatriz flew back to Havana en route to Chile, Beatriz decided she wanted to stay in Cuba, where she raised the possibility of guerrilla training.[55] Although she had broached the idea with Fidel directly before she left for Moscow, she had been rebuffed. Now, trying again, the same thing happened, ostensibly because the Cubans feared compromising Allende's position as president of Chile's Senate. Luis was therefore instructed to take her to the Federación de Mujeres Cubanas (Cuban Women's Federation, FMC) run by Vilma Espín. There, he introduced her to Irina Trapote, who worked for the FMC's external relations department.[56]

Quite apart from her father's position, sidelining Beatriz by sending her to the FMC was significant. Women had a complicated place in late 1960s revolutionary Cuba. In many respects, they were celebrated as being "decisive" participants in building a new society.[57] In December 1966, Fidel Castro had gone so far as to proclaim that top-down emancipatory measures for women constituted "a revolution within a revolution."[58] Through state-run child care, communal eating, and laundry facilities, women were able to leave the home and enter the workforce, particularly when it came to teaching and agriculture. The FMC boasted a million members by the late 1960s and was accorded a prominent voice in Cuban society. In early 1968 it would launch a new campaign to bring one hundred thousand women annually into full-time work.[59] For anyone arriving in the late 1960s — Beatriz included — Cuba therefore appeared to be revolutionizing gender relations.[60]

However, behind the scenes, few women had access to power and decision making. Only 5 percent of the Cuban Communist Party's Central Committee were women, while its Political Bureau and Secretariat were exclusively male. At provincial and regional levels, few women became first secretary.[61] And although the FMC held a prominent position, it simultaneously excluded women from the main centers of power. More significantly for Beatriz, women were seldom trained militarily. True, women participated in militias created after the revolution, worked for the police, and led neighborhood defense committees.[62] As one observer in Havana at the end of the 1960s noted, the "tradition of the woman guerrilla" was also "assiduously maintained."[63] Tamara Bunke, for example, otherwise known as "Tania," who fought alongside Che in Bolivia, was romanticized after her death in 1967.[64] Yet, significantly, Tania had never been meant to join Che's column: as most women involved in Cuban-led revolutionary ventures, she had been trained for work in the urban underground and had been forced to abandon the city only when her presence was discovered.[65]

Indeed, women were not considered physically suitable for guerrilla warfare. They were not required to do compulsory military service. Instead, they were encouraged to contribute to the revolution in ways that did not challenge their "health and femininity."[66] And when it came to "femininity," Cuban women's magazines devoted ample space to traditional "female" tastes, tasks, and traits: fashion, motherhood, children, cooking, and sewing.[67] "Beauty care and agricultural work are not at odds," read a caption in *Granma* to pictures of female voluntary agricultural workers.[68] Moreover, in the late 1960s, the Cuban government published a list of 496 jobs that could not "under any circumstances" be done by women because they were "unhealthy, dangerous, or excessively strenuous." Known as Resolution 48, this list—including metallurgy, mining, construction, the handling of machinery or chemicals, and transportation—was accompanied by another (Resolution 47) comprising 430 female jobs men were asked to relinquish unless they had "lost their physical capacities as a result of old age, accident, or illness." Women in revolutionary Cuba were envisaged working as archivists, telephonists, librarians, medics (except X-ray technicians), or in the health and food industry.[69]

As well as Allende's position in Chile, therefore, Beatriz's gender precluded a more receptive response to her request for guerrilla training. For now, Irina took Beatriz to a firing range in Havana where she was offered the "rudiments" of "shooting practice ... a few little shots [*disparitos*]."[70] This was far less than Beatriz had hoped in her quest to be like Che and Tania, but it temporarily appeased her.[71]

It was while she was in Havana that Beatriz began to see Luis socially despite her marriage and his serious relationship. Luis had also been married once before, was already a father, and had a reputation for having affairs with women who visited the island. He was charming and hospitable, someone who enjoyed his contacts with the outside world as well as what they offered (presents, clothing, alcohol, friendships).[72] Yet, as he remembered, the minute Beatriz stepped off the plane, it was "love at first sight." Now, with Beatriz alone in Havana, mutual attraction grew. As a friend of Beatriz's explained, she was drawn to Luis as the Cuban Revolution personified—"a guy who had fought ... been in combat ... who carried a rifle, *la patria o muerte*."[73] Luis and Beatriz enjoyed trips to the cinema in Vedado. But shared political and revolutionary ideas brought them together.[74] In this respect, they conformed to Cuba's atmosphere at the time. As Irina remembered, "All of us ... were in political work ... and [focused on] the defense of the revolution. We did not have time to go out dancing here or there, or to party."[75]

Beatriz's relationship with Luis and her revolutionary attachment to Cuba were serious enough to prompt her to make a long distance call to Chile, break off her relationship with Renato, and tell him she was not coming home. Back in Santiago, the couple's friends rallied around him and helped raise funds so he could go to Cuba and win her back.[76] Yet her decision had a lot to do with problems—both ideological and personal—that already existed. Beatriz found Renato's heavy drinking particularly difficult, for example.[77] And he found her attachment to Cuba "extreme."[78]

Yet, she was not alone in this attachment.[79] "I felt that this was my land," one young Chilean revolutionary who went to Cuba in 1968 to undergo guerrilla training explained.[80] Such were the numbers of Latin Americans going to the island in search of similar instruction that those charged with looking after them often found it hard to keep up. It was accepted that different parties and insurgent groups should be kept apart to protect their operations even when they came from the same country. Yet compartmentalization was difficult, especially when people who knew each other were in Havana at the same time. In some cases, they discovered each other's presence and escaped Cuban minders to meet up secretly; other times, they had no idea acquaintances were in the city.[81]

The Havana Beatriz knew in late 1967 was therefore a melting pot for revolutionaries, but a controlled one, managed primarily by those like Luis working with Piñeiro at the Ministry of the Interior. Her experience in Havana was demarcated by her gender and her father. He opened doors, but his democratic position closed them when it came to revolutionary work. Because she was a woman she was also sidelined to the FMC. There is no evidence to suggest she met with other Chileans in Cuba, nor that she was involved in any specific revolutionary project. What her long-term plans were—or what the Cubans had in mind for her—is hard to determine, for they were cut short in December when Renato arrived in Havana looking for her.[82]

Cuban Guerrillas in Chile

Although Beatriz returned to Chile with Renato, their relationship was over. They would not begin the process of annulling their marriage—

the only possibility in a country where divorce was illegal—until March 1969.[83] However, Beatriz moved back to Guardia Vieja and, for reasons no one fully understood, refused all contact with him.[84] Somewhere between Havana and Santiago, their breakup became deeply acrimonious, making life difficult for their friends, who had to choose sides.[85] Renato was "devastated" and drank heavily. As he told one friend, Beatriz had become "very radical—she thinks she is going to become a revolutionary." When Renato asked his friend to deliver a note to Guardia Vieja hoping Beatriz would talk to him, she begrudgingly opened the door but refused to look at it.[86] After this, in fact, her friendship group changed; as a result of ideological changes and the transition between university and adulthood, as well as the way the relationship ended, she lost contact with many intimate friends from the BUS.[87]

Beatriz's distance from Renato and his friends happened at the same time as they assumed new positions in the Socialist Party and the Chilean far Left advanced onto the national stage. In the months Beatriz had been away, a lot had changed. But because she was now fixated on Cuba and Che's message of revolutionary internationalism, she was relatively distant from domestic party politics. The changes were also complex for her, as her father opposed them and was criticized for his electoral strategies. That he, like Beatriz, supported revolutionary insurgencies abroad did not seem to shield him from opponents. He was not able to convince them that Chile's different circumstances required alternative strategies. The Socialist Party was thus increasingly divided, with Allende, Secretary-General Aniceto Rodríguez, and an older generation on one side and a radical younger wing on the other.

Pivotally, at the Socialist Party's congress in November 1967 in Chillán, while Beatriz was in Cuba, the latter group won increasing representation in the Central Committee. Carlos Altamirano and Rolando Calderón, a young militant who had risen up through the left-wing rural union federation, the Confederación Nacional de Campesinos e Indígenas Ránquil (National Campesino and Indigenous Confederation Ránquil) whom Beatriz had met volunteering with the BUS, received the biggest share of votes. Ricardo and Renato were also elected. The party was now predominantly young, with 78 percent of the conference's delegates having been party members for fewer than seven years.[88] Significantly, despite Allende arguing against it, delegates also approved a resolution accepting the inevitability and legitimacy of armed struggle. That Socialists were meeting in the immediate aftermath of Che's death and the day after repressive action against striking workers killed seven people influenced proceedings.[89] But it also reflected a longer process of radicalization and conviction that peaceful, democratic revolution was ultimately impossible.[90] And, henceforth, the Chillán resolution would provide symbolic approval for military initiatives within the party.

Elsewhere, Beatriz's friends in the MIR had also gained ground. In November 1967, Luciano Cruz had been elected president of the Federación de Estudiantes de la Universidad de Concepción (with BUS support).[91] In December, Miguel Enríquez had also traveled to Cuba, where he had initiated contact with Piñeiro and finally secured a direct link to the island (there is no indication he met Beatriz).[92] Upon his return, Miguel had then been elected secretary-general at the MIR's third congress. His election gave a younger generation control, replacing older Trotskyist leaders. It also signified a decisive alignment to Cuba, about which previous leaders had been lukewarm, dubious of Havana's emphasis on rural focos and relations with other Chilean parties. With Miguel and his cohort in charge, the MIR also resolved to prioritize action and military preparation.[93] How these changes in the Socialist Party (PS) and MIR would affect Chilean politics was still uncertain. Even so, the revolutionary Left was increasingly relevant. This put Beatriz in a good position, although she became increasingly "reticent" and critical of party politics.[94]

When Luis arrived in Chile at the end of January 1968, Beatriz sharpened her focus on Cuba and its clandestine revolutionary operations still further. This was the first time Luis had visited the country. Because Chile had no diplomatic relations with Cuba, he entered as an economist attending a meeting at the UN Economic Commission for Latin America. Luis nevertheless disappeared to meet Chilean left-wing party leaders. During what turned out to be more than a month in the country, the affair he and Beatriz had begun in Cuba a few months earlier also became "much deeper and personal." As he explained, "[An] important factor was the communion of ideas, of revolutionary commitment."[95] One weekend, Beatriz invited Luis to join the Allendes at Algarrobo, even though their relationship was still secret. Luis also grew closer to her family. On 8 March, the international day of women, for example, he went to Guardia Vieja to deliver flowers for women of the house—Beatriz included.[96]

While Luis was in Chile, Beatriz's opportunity to practice revolutionary internationalism also accelerated. On 27 January 1968, Manuel Cabieses, editor of *Punto Final*, opened the door to a Bolivian who brought news that Cuban survivors from Che's column—Harry Villegas Tamayo, Daniel Alarcón Ramírez, and Leonardo Tamayo Núñez, known as "Pombo," "Benigno," and "Urbano"—were escaping into Chile. As Cabieses explained, his magazine was "a kind of Cuban consulate" in the absence of formal diplomatic relations (a student who trained in Cuba in 1967 remembered carrying a suitcase full of money to Chile for *Punto Final*).[97] Cabieses notified Luis and immediately called the Chilean, Elmo Catalán, affiliated to Cuba, who in turn communicated the news to Havana. Catalán also sent a message back to the Cuban guerrillas saying Chileans would be waiting.[98] Elmo and Luis then planned how to protect them when they crossed the border.

Crucially, Elmo was able to mobilize a small clandestine group he had already established in 1966 to support Che Guevara's revolutionary project in Bolivia. A working-class left-wing journalist in northern Chile and a member of the Socialist Party close to Carlos Altamirano, Elmo had probably visited Cuba for the first time in 1962 and received intelligence training. He had then traveled to the island various times and had seen Luis in Mexico City using offices of *Qué Pasa?*, a magazine reporting guerrilla operations and cooperating with Cuban intelligence.[99] Elmo also reportedly met Che in Prague to discuss how Chileans could support his Bolivian venture.[100] Moreover, as one of the Chileans who worked closely with him recalled, aided by his journalistic cover and work for the country's copper federation, Elmo had collaborated with the Cubans to prepare Che's entry into Bolivia.[101]

Events in Chile had conspired to strengthen Elmo's conviction for armed struggle. As with other radicalized Socialists in the mid-1960s, Allende's 1964 defeat and the El Salvador massacre, where he often worked as a journalist, had been decisive. "For all that I speak of revolution, liberation or love for the people," he would write to his family, "I will be [no more than] a conscious slave of the system, an accomplice of oppression or, in many cases, gendarme of its own brothers, if I do not take the only honest road that exists to make our countries independent: that of armed struggle until its ultimate consequences."[102] Accepting that Chile was unsuitable for armed struggle, he had concentrated on helping the Cubans' Latin Americanist revolutionary project—and more specifically Che Guevara, whom he desperately hoped to join. He also recruited Chilean volunteers in 1966–67 and sent some to Havana for training so they could be integrated into Che's column once established.[103]

The recruits Elmo had assembled were an eclectic mix, not all conforming to stereotypical images of bearded middle-class student revolutionaries. Among them, for example, were the brothers Fernando and Carlos Gómez, young working-class Socialists recruited at the El Salvador mine after the massacre. Both had begun working before they were ten years old and knew persecution firsthand. Fernando had also been in the navy but, having been expelled, joined Carlos, a union leader at the El Salvador mine.[104] They knew Elmo through his work for the copper federation, his journalism, and a book he had written in 1965: *La Encrucijada del Cobre*, detailing U.S. private copper companies' exploitation of Chile.[105] As Fernando remembered, "Elmo was training me as a militant and speaking to me a lot in El Salvador.... The Cuban Revolution filled us with joy and militant fervor.... My older brother [Carlos] was invited to a 26th of July [celebration in Havana] ... and he underwent military training.... [I was] invited to Cuba for military training, despite Chile not 'qualifying' for guerrilla struggles.... We didn't choose Bolivia, we committed ourselves to fight in the country under Che's command, this is how it was put to me while I was undergoing military training in Cuba, I would be part of the reserves."[106]

Félix Huerta, a fifth-year medical student at the University of Chile and a militant in the BUS, was another Elmo chose and more typical of the recruits we think of as joining Latin American guerrilla campaigns. Again, personal connections explained his choice (Catalán had met Huerta covering student protests in 1967). Félix was also close to Altamirano. However, the network Elmo used to recruit him was wide enough to approach him via Félix's psychiatry professor in mid-1967.[107] Having been on a student trip to Bolivia in 1965 (he took Fanon's *Wretched of the Earth* and works by Nicolás Guillén and Jean-Paul Sartre), Félix had an impression of the country being "fragile" with "working masses ... such as the miners, the indigenous population ... suffering, resentful." Meanwhile, his experience in the Federación de Estudiantes de la Universidad de Chile (FECH) had persuaded him that the bureaucracy of university politics and the people involved would not change much—"that a different kind of people would be needed to really fight."[108] He therefore said yes when approached. However, aside from receiving intelligence training from Manuel Cabieses, who imparted what he had learned in Cuba, Elmo's group had not yet done anything particularly significant.[109]

It was in this preliminary phase, before her trip to Cuba, that Beatriz had probably begun collaborating with Catalán's network. She had been associated with him since at least 1966, when he had introduced her to Fernando Gómez at a restaurant in Santiago shortly before the latter departed for Cuba.[110] But her role is unclear, and it may be they simply knew each other from Catalán's work for her father's campaign and association with the radicalized wing of the PS. Whatever the case, a little over a year later, when the Cuban guerrillas escaped into Chile, Beatriz's relationship with Elmo became important. At the instigation of Luis—who believed he "introduced" them—the two of them met at a cafeteria on Pedro de Valdivia Avenue in Santiago in early February to discuss how Beatriz might help with rescue efforts. And she jumped at the opportunity.[111]

For all her willingness to assist, however, this was not an auspicious start to internationalism. The rescue operation was a fiasco, demonstrating the improvised nature and lack of preparedness of Catalán's incipient network and the Chilean Left overall. Due to weather conditions, the Cubans did not arrive at the designated entry point, leading to a complex search operation on the border. Elmo, Luis, and, interestingly, given its growing distance from the Cubans' proclivity for armed revolution, the Communist Party tried to disorientate security services with false news in *El Siglo*. Local Communist militants and trade unionists went to find the Cubans. Elmo also dispatched Félix to the border, disguised as an anthropologist, armed with a revolver and fifty bullets, though, having never fired one, Félix had no idea what to do with it.[112] For her part, Beatriz asked her father to intervene on behalf of the fugitives. On 17 February, with their escape reported by the Bolivian press, he petitioned Frei's government, demanding they be treated fairly and not returned to Bolivia.[113] At Beatriz's request, Allende also traveled to Arica three days later to "welcome" them (although when they didn't appear he left to participate in scheduled protests in Santiago against the Vietnam War).[114]

Following Catalán's instructions, Beatriz also went north herself, traversing the Atacama Desert in her own Land Rover jeep, which "an uncle" had bought her when she graduated. The jeep had been an odd choice. It was unnecessary in Santiago, drawing attention and amusement. Beatriz's mother also disapproved, regarding it as unbecoming for a young woman.[115] Yet Fernando always surmised that Elmo had been the one to suggest she ask for it, thinking it might be useful in future Bolivian operations (another indication of her early involvement in this network).[116] Now, in February 1968, according to Benigno, "Beatriz travelled to the Andes mountains ... a young, pretty girl ... there a whole week waiting to see if we would appear ... although not completely alone, for she was armed with a pistol.... She had even brought weapons ... in case we arrived unarmed. She was also carrying quilts, coats, food, cigarettes, and medicine for the altitude, as well as different antibiotics."[117]

Despite all these efforts, the Cubans could not be contacted. As the media and security services closed in, the possibility of finding the guerrillas undetected also diminished.[118] The Cubans and their Bolivian guides thus handed themselves in and asked for asylum. From a small police station near Camiña, they were transferred to a military installation in Iquique and, a day later, by plane to Santiago.[119] Meanwhile, left-wing Chileans mobilized to defend them, which infused daily politics and front-page headlines. Frente de Acción Popular (FRAP) parliamentarians petitioned the government to offer them asylum.[120] More than three thousand demonstrators also gathered in Iquique, some armed with Molotov cocktails and stones.[121] As one unsympathetic international observer reported, "extravagant enthusiasm" greeted the guerrillas.[122]

The Cubans' physical presence in Chile thus brought the region's revolutionary struggle to its population in a new, concrete, visible way, exacerbating fault lines running through the country. Alongside sympathy, they provoked anger. *El Mercurio*, for example, denounced the "the Socialist attorneys of OLAS" acting on their behalf. "The process brings to the fore the most absurd characters," editors wrote, "in favor of those who arrive with weapons in hand to launch subversion in Chile."[123] The paper also argued the escape had demonstrated that subversives, relying on fake passports, money, and networks, threatened state institutions.[124] The Cubans were, meanwhile, unrepentant. As Pombo told the press, "We are convinced armed struggle is the only way to free peoples under imperialism and tyranny." Chile did not have "suitable" conditions, he and his companions conceded. But Benigno insisted "guerrilla struggles have not finished."[125]

Given the domestic political ramifications of the guerrillas' arrival, Frei's government expelled them immediately.[126] Yet determining a route for them was not straightforward. They were reported to have their own money, and Elmo also had Cuban funds.[127] Yet they feared any plane that flew across Latin America could be shot down or detained when refueling. At Guardia Vieja, Allende and a pilot therefore examined alternatives with Luis. Ultimately, they decided on a commercial LAN flight first to Easter Island and then to Havana via Tahiti. To offer the guerrillas added protection, Allende and his sister, the Socialist deputy Laura, accompanied them to Tahiti. Reports at the time said he paid for these flights. However, Beatriz gave him the money to do so, having been given it by Elmo.[128]

For a constitutional president of the senate to guarantee the safety of armed revolutionaries was extraordinary. And, unsurprisingly, Allende faced fierce criticism.[129] Typical of Chile's intra-Left divisions, however, this criticism came not only from the Right; the PCCh was also angry at being excluded from the final arrangement. Beatriz's involvement complicated Allende's position. In a private meeting, Communist Party representatives denounced her as a "Cuban agent," a charge her father denied. Allende was not aware of the extent of his daughter's role, thus Beatriz had to explain herself.[130] For although father and daughter were both working to support Cuba and its revolutionary ventures abroad—and although Allende was willing to risk his political credibility by flying Cuban survivors to safety—the episode reveals they did so separately. Beatriz was now a revolutionary operative in her own right, even if the story of the

Cuban guerrillas demonstrated the risk she ran of implicating her father and the intra-Left tensions this could cause.

With the Cuban guerrillas' escape, Che's campaign spilled into Chile and permeated national politics. For both those who feared Cuba's reach and those inclined to romanticize the region's guerrilla decade, it captured imaginations. Cross-border clandestine revolutionary efforts may have been fragile, but Chilean support networks and coordination with Cuba would improve. Ultimately, transnational guerrilla operations required institutional high-level political support and money. The survivors might never have succeeded in getting home had they not had Cuban funds and had left-wing parties not been willing to jump to their defense. In helping to mobilize her father, Beatriz played an important role in this respect, and the Cubans would never forget her collaboration.

"Che's Heirs"

The Cuban guerrillas' departure did not spell the end of Beatriz's and Luis's connection with Guevara's revolutionary venture or each other. For Luis, whose job revolved around Chile, not Bolivia, this was only by chance. In late January, a Bolivian had appeared at Prensa Latina's Santiago office purporting to have access to a copy of Guevara's diary. A month later, the messenger had returned carrying a vinyl disc of Bolivian folk music with a microfilmed diary inside. It was almost impossible to read as each frame captured multiple pages. Luis thus spent hours under a lamp in the bedroom of Manuel Cabieses's daughters determining its authenticity. On 15 March, they finally sent it to Havana with *Punto Final*'s secretary, hidden in a disc of Chilean folk music, where it was published.[131]

Luis also returned to Havana around this time, although his affair with Beatriz continued. As his friends remembered, he returned "really enthusiastic."[132] Beginning a long-distance relationship was nevertheless complicated. No diplomatic relations or postal services between their countries existed, and Luis still had a Cuban girlfriend. He and Beatriz therefore had to rely on people traveling between Chile and Cuba—often via Spain or Mexico—to deliver secret letters and gifts. Among the presents Beatriz sent Luis were books, Violeta Parra and Quilapayún LPs, and a Chilean artisan knife. He sent her photos of Che and Cuban cigarettes.[133] She addressed her letters affectionately to him using nicknames or terms of endearment (*Amor mío, queridísimo, Papote*). They also devised a code for romantic messages and revolutionary activities. Across the bottom and top of her letters, Beatriz scribbled the numbers "5" and "1000" repeatedly to denote kisses and hugs.[134] She referred to her father as the *cacique* (leader), Bolivia as "Valdivia," and members of the ELN as *los Valdivia-*

nos; those who had trained in Cuba were *becados* (scholarship holders), and miristas were *cafiches* (pimps).[135] In her letters, Beatriz nevertheless described herself as longing for news from Cuba and bemoaned not being able to afford a call to Havana to hear his voice.[136]

Their communication difficulties attest to the veracity of their relationship. Although there were later allegations the Cuban revolutionary regime tasked Luis with beginning the relationship to gain access to Allende, the hurdles they overcame suggest otherwise (his relationship with Allende was also already good). If the Cuban government had been in control it would have at least facilitated communication. Instead, when Luis told Piñeiro about his affair a year after it started, his boss reprimanded him and told him their relationship could not work. And in hindsight, Luis admitted it was "crazy."[137]

For now, with Luis back in Cuba and when not working, Beatriz spent her time collaborating with Catalán's network. This clandestine organization was increasingly targeted, providing specific support for the remnants of Guevara's guerrilla operation by helping more survivors escape Bolivia to Cuba via Chile, recruiting new volunteers, and putting together infrastructure to support a new Bolivian insurgency. This meant mapping out the Chilean-Bolivian border, securing safe houses, and establishing supply stores between Santiago and the Andes. And, in this respect, Beatriz's jeep was essential. On exploratory missions across Atacama Desert and the Andean border region, she drove the car carrying a pistol "in her belt and a grenade in the glove box."[138] As Félix Huerta remembered, she was not averse to taking risks, having once driven fifteen hundred kilometers across Chile in a car packed full of explosives.[139] Her brakes failed on another occasion in Valparaíso, forcing her to maneuver in "pirouettes" to avoid crashing.[140]

Beatriz also called on loyal friends to donate their houses, money, or supplies. As Félix explained, she was vital to the organization as a result of her contacts and ability to resolve problems.[141] Friends did not always know what they were contributing to. Her former teacher, Arturo Jirón, for example, recalled Beatriz asked him for donations for an "orphanage" only later to discover the "orphans" were revolutionaries destined for Bolivia.[142] Pivotally, Beatriz also co-opted "Dina," one of the Allendes' maids, to look after a safe house.[143] In addition to earlier recruits, Catalán's secret network now included Arnoldo Camú and his wife, Celsa, both of whom Beatriz had met in Moscow. As a lawyer for trade unions and the banking sector, Arnoldo's contacts helped secure collaborators and safe houses in well-to-do neighborhoods. In the course of coordinating these clandestine operations, he, Celsa, Beatriz, and Elmo also established a close, secretive, and intimate friendship. Meetings between them were "ad hoc" and "very informal," Celsa remembered.[144]

The group's first major operation took place in May 1968. While students were in Paris carrying Che flags and their Chilean counterparts occupied university buildings, as we shall see in chapter 6, Catalán's network rescued Inti, the ELN's leader, along with Rodolfo Saldaña, or "Saúl," in charge of the remnants of the organization's urban underground in Bolivia.[145] It is unclear whether Inti wanted to be rescued. He had stayed back in Bolivia when the Cuban guerrillas had escaped to help rebuild the ELN within the country. However, Cuba's leaders wanted him in Havana so they could coordinate—and likely control—planning for a new insurgency. In April, the Cubans and Catalán therefore sent Fernando to La Paz to get him. It was a difficult mission. The group ended up lost, crossing the Andes and the vast salt lake near the Chilean border by foot in subzero temperatures. Saúl suffered such severe altitude sickness that he had to be carried most of the way. And because Fernando's toes were frostbitten, Beatriz arranged for Jirón to amputate two of them.[146]

Compared with rescuing the three Cuban guerrillas a few months earlier, this operation was nevertheless a success. Having entered Chile undetected, Beatriz drove Inti and Saúl to Santiago in her jeep. There, in a safe house, she, Arnoldo, Celsa, and Elmo looked after them, providing medical attention and security. It was an important moment for Inti, allowing him to recover and plan for the future.[147] As Fernando remembered, the ELN's leader arrived "very worried about the decimation of his organization, almost without logistics and [with] the urban part of it having received heavy blows and on the run." Thanks to his stay in Chile his "optimism" returned. He received a Chilean passport and ID, allowing him to travel to Cuba. The Chileans also physically changed his appearance, removing a characteristic mole, giving him new teeth (without taking any out), thick-rimmed glasses, and a new hairstyle.[148] With Catalán's help (he probably wrote most of it), Inti also issued a new ELN manifesto published simultaneously in La Paz and Santiago on 19 July 1968 entitled *"Volveremos a las montañas"* (We will return to the mountains).[149]

Elmo meanwhile helped Inti recruit cadres to fight alongside him in Bolivia. This was not always successful. When he and Beatriz organized a special meeting with miristas to ask if they wanted to join, for example, they declined, arguing their "fight was in Chile"—a decision that left Inti and Elmo "both very annoyed." However, Elmo was eager to take part in the new Bolivian insurgency. And, like him, his network jumped at joining the ELN under Inti's leadership. As Fernando remembered, with Che dead, they vowed to "continue his struggle and his example."[150]

No one seems to have questioned Guevara's model in making this decision. Instead, as a result of his death, it was accepted and romanticized. Action rather than theory was prioritized.[151] "The revolution is not made with declarations and conferences," Inti would insist, "the revolution is made by fighting, responding to the enemy's brutal violence with revolutionary violence."[152] Che's call for "two, three, many Vietnams" was also repeated almost verbatim. Because the Vietnamese people were fighting against "Yankee imperialism ... for us," the ELN's new manifesto read, "we must fight for them."[153] In the words of a hymn sung by future ELN recruits, "We are all, Comandante Che / that Vietnam that you dreamed of ... that blood that you shed / will rise like a Phoenix."[154]

Alongside Vietnam, Bolivia was only vaguely discussed as a place ripe for revolution, where "misery, hunger and death" pervaded.[155] The ELN had little connection to mass organizations, and it never articulated goals in terms of seizing power in Bolivia.[156] The Chileans involved also had few personal ties to the country.[157] True, the ELN's members spoke of fighting for socialism, conceived as freedom from capitalist exploitation, a planned economy, industrialization, and free education. During Guevara's campaign in Bolivia, the ELN's first public statement had also referred to rescuing "a country being sold slice by slice to Yankee monopolies" and raising living standards.[158] However, rather than being nationally framed, the ELN's new manifesto embraced Guevara's vision for Bolivia as the center of a *regional* revolution. The ELN's "only and final" goal was the "liberation of Latin America" in keeping with "the Bolivarian dream and Che's dream to unite Latin America."[159] "There are those who want to freeze movements ... within their national borders," Inti would tell a Chilean journalist, echoing OLAS resolutions. "It is absurd. The struggle is everyone's ... the struggle against imperialism is one and the same." The ELN was not "an organization made for Bolivia. This is the era of continental revolution," he explained.[160]

In following Che unhesitatingly, Chilean ELN recruits like Beatriz also embraced armed struggle as "the only dignified, honest, glorious, or irreversible road" for bringing about revolution. "The struggle itself will create its leaders," the new manifesto continued.[161] As Félix remembered, leadership entailed being "ready to work harder, whatever the risks, however ungratifying."[162] And this meant being prepared to die. In his homage to Guevara in October 1967, Castro had celebrated the blood he had spilt.[163] And *Punto Final* had subsequently published a widely circulated poem dedicated to Guevara by the Cuban poet Nicolás Guillén inciting revolutionary hopefuls to follow Che to the grave.

Wait for us. We will leave with you. We yearn
to die to live as you have died,
to live as you live,
Comandante Che,
friend.[164]

It was this sacrifice in the name of continental revolution and association with Che's revolutionary example that Chilean recruits—Beatriz included—signed up for when they agreed to join Inti's insurgency in mid-1968. Few, if any, believed they would survive. But young recruits were imbued with the popular idea of being "consistent" (*consecuente*) with their ideals.[165] And "Volveremos a las montañas" was explicit in this respect: members of the ELN would uphold Che's ideals "until death."[166] As one ELN recruit explained, "We were very young and we lived a passionate adventure, without fear and drunk on the romantic pride of being Che's heirs."[167]

They Love Me There

A day after "Volveremos a las montañas" was published, Inti, Saúl, and two Chilean ELN recruits secretly left for Havana.[168] Around the same time, other Chilean members of the ELN (known as *elenos*) also made their way to Cuba using long, complicated routes. Recruits lied to family and friends, saying they were going to Europe for various reasons.[169] Félix, for example, boarded a boat to Cannes, France—a $300 journey Elmo paid for (presumably with Cuban money). There, he made his way to Paris to meet other Chilean recruits before going to Cuba via Moscow (traveling via Prague was suspended after the Soviet invasion).[170] It is unclear what Beatriz told people. It is possible she simply said she was visiting Cuba. As a frequent visitor to the island, her father would not have been concerned. Some friends remember they knew she was going back and forth to Havana, and she also brought friends gifts (Gilda Gnecco remembered receiving a shell necklace).[171] "They love me there," Beatriz told Elena Gálvez when asked about Cuba.[172]

Whatever friends and family knew, Beatriz arrived in Havana in early August 1968 and would stay until December.[173] This was different from previous visits; now she was a revolutionary insider. Certainly, the Cuban leadership increasingly trusted her. As Juan Carretero, one of the intelligence officers working alongside Piñeiro on Bolivian operations, remembered, she played "a very prominent role," not as a combatant but rather seeding the rear guard in Chile. And, in doing so, she demonstrated "a loyalty to Che's legacy."[174] "She was Latin American, her upbringing, her thinking was 'Our Latin America,'" another Cuban intelligence officer explained, referring to José Martí's idea of a region distinct from the United States. She was "a model woman and a model revolutionary."[175]

But, of course, being a model *female* revolutionary meant conforming to aforementioned Cuban gender norms, different from those associated with the iconic Guevara-style *male* guerrilla. Like other women recruited to revolutionary insurgencies, for example, she was trained for intelligence work needed for the urban underground. This meant learning such covert communications as radio operations and coding.[176] On account of her medical training, Beatriz also received auxiliary (field) medicine training.[177] However, to protect her father's reputation and minimize chances of her involvement being detected, she was told she would be supporting the insurgency from Chile. While in Cuba, Beatriz provided organizational support for the ELN, coordinating preparatory courses for male recruits involving shooting, explosives, and communications techniques. As one of the Cuban special forces who administered this training recalled, Beatriz was in frequent contact.[178]

These "female" tasks of intelligence and coordination were deemed essential but supplementary to the insurgency's success. In Bolivia, women tended to make uniforms for their male counterparts rather than wear fatigues themselves.[179] Even when women assumed leadership positions in the urban underground and got to don them, they were relegated to traditional subservient roles in men's company—serving food and caring for them. A contemporary account of a woman who trained in intelligence with Beatriz in Cuba, for example, praised her as an "an authentic revolutionary" dressed in combat fatigues but focused exclusively on her serving Inti "pots of coffee ... with her revolver at her side," being "worried about sharing out the food."[180] Even Tania, the celebrated female guerrilla who had accidentally joined Che's column, had sewn clothes and organized food for her male counterparts when she was not hiking. Insisting she wanted to be treated as "just one more member," wearing (men's) boots too big that left her in constant pain, she could also not escape being remembered in stereotypically gendered roles by companions. "She was like a mother," one insurgent recalled.[181]

Beatriz, too, was accorded a maternal role with the ELN *in addition to her* communications, intelligence, and logistical work. As an ELN member described, "She was a bit like our mother and our platonic girlfriend, aside from her enormous effectiveness. She took charge of saying goodbye to each compañero that left Chile for the Altiplano, checking his route, passing him through different secure houses, reminding him of codes, giving him a last hug."[182] This caring side was an important part of Beatriz's character. She was "affectionate, kind, loving ... protective," a fellow eleno described her.[183] She also devoted time to looking after relatives (wives and mothers) of elenos when they were in Bolivia.[184] But these extra roles—beyond covert intelligence and the demands of public health work—were expected of her, conforming to constructed ideas about women's inherent virtues. As one newspaper column at the time noted, women could not compete physically with men, but they outshone them in "tactile sensibility."[185]

Even so, Beatriz bitterly resented being regarded as "inferior" when it came to the ELN's insurgency itself. Like her male counterparts, she wanted to fulfill the organization's sacrificial pledge to fight and die in Che's memory. And she hated being left behind when her male comrades departed for training and armed combat in Bolivia. It was "traumatic for her," Luis recalled.[186] As Fernando remembered, "Not going to Bolivia to fight affected her, it hurt her, she didn't understand it, and she suffered a lot, she claimed [decisions were based] on her status as a woman, that it wasn't fair, there was a heated argument with Elmo and she made it clear to me, even to the point of asking me [what I thought,] and I answered her with a clumsy phrase ... 'you are more valuable in Chile!!!' And this made her furious because she thought [I was saying] she was weak."[187]

In her fight against predetermined gender roles, Beatriz managed to gain some concessions. She received training from Cuban special forces in Havana, four or five afternoons a week, learning to use FAL and AK-47 rifles, grenades, and explosives.[188] One weekend, Luis also took her hiking around Punto Cero—a military encampment, thirty kilometers east of Havana where guerrilla recruits also trained.[189] According to Luis, it was not a very demanding excursion—a few "little hills" ("I don't think that she had the strength for [more formal training]," he explained).[190] But it gave her the chance for a brief moment to feel like the kind of guerrilla she had hoped to be. A picture of the excursion shows Beatriz standing proudly with Luis amid foliage, carrying a FAL rifle over her shoulder. As Félix, who saw Beatriz the next day, remembered, she was "very happy." She never seemed to have any doubts about her ability to be a guerrilla, he recalled. Although he worried about his own credentials, she had admirable "willpower."[191]

And yet it was he, not Beatriz, who would undergo an intensive rural guerrilla training program in Baracoa, eastern Cuba, along with sixty to one hundred other male recruits at a camp known as "Bolivia Libre."[192]

Luis and Beatriz, Punto Cero, Cuba, 1968. Luis Fernández Oña private collection.

From August onward, special forces Benigno and Pombo provided a grueling program. The elenos marched 35 to 40 kilometers a day with 25 to 30 kilograms on their backs. They did not bathe for six months.[193] For many, this was the first time they had seen serious combat weapons, let alone used them.[194] Learning lessons from Guevara's venture, during which two Bolivians had drowned, instructors also spent considerable time teaching recruits to swim.[195]

Even with such preparation, there were deficiencies and accidents. A young Bolivian was killed by a bazooka during a training exercise.[196] Arnoldo and Elmo were not deemed up to physical training, with the former destined to work for the rear guard in Chile and the latter designated the ELN's "political commissar" in Bolivia.[197] Although recruits were brought together to study Che and Pombo's Bolivian diaries or analyze Fidel's speeches, Félix would also lament the lack of theoretical military preparation. Recruits used "real explosives, real munitions, mortars, and so it was easy to have accidents. Nobody walked about with the safety catch on their rifles."[198] (Tragically, Huerta would be shot during a bar fight in Havana and paralyzed before he ever got to Bolivia.) Finally, at the end of 1968, elenos were transferred to Punto Cero for additional firing practice (at least two hundred rounds a day), personal defense (karate), the Quechua language, cartography, intelligence, and field medicine.[199]

Chile

A little over a year after Che's death, another Cuban-orchestrated insurgency in Bolivia was therefore in full swing. With training complete, the ELN transferred members to Bolivia, mostly via Chile, in late 1968 and early 1969. The Cubans facilitated journeys, providing disguises, cover stories, and documentation. When he left Cuba in November 1968, Inti also carried a substantial sum of Cuban money, and other ELN members were reportedly given $3,000 each for their journey.[200] In Chile, elenos used the underground network established by Elmo, Beatriz, and Arnoldo. Compared with ad hoc adventures to rescue the Cuban guerrillas, the group's logistics had improved. It now had safe houses throughout northern Chile, as well as supply stores (arms, explosives, military uniforms, boots, and medicines).[201] A friend of Beatriz's also worked from a small house on the outskirts of Santiago changing stamps in passports and preparing false documents.[202] In Santiago again, en route to Bolivia, Inti stayed in a small apartment in the city's Barrio Alto, spending time with his family at the beach (smuggled across the border by Chilean elenos), and going to the Cajón del Maipo on training exercises before leaving for Bolivia in early May 1969.[203]

Like Beatriz, the Chileans who coordinated operations were therefore vital to the Bolivian insurgency. Having returned home in December 1968, Beatriz managed radio communications between Santiago and Havana from her bedroom. This would be the principal means of contact between ELN operatives inside Bolivia and the outside world; only she and select people in the organization's high command, Inti included, knew codes used to decipher messages.[204] It was also exhausting, requiring nighttime work decoding and relaying information back to Bolivia and Cuba.[205] Her younger cousin, Ana María, knowing nothing of the ELN but living with the Allendes at the time, remembered Beatriz constantly falling asleep in the bath. But she never knew why. As she recalled, Beatriz was "the most mysterious person you could imagine.... She was always involved in something you did not know about ... something serious, something dangerous, something complicated." People would appear whom Ana María felt she should recognize, only later to realize these were "super important" revolutionaries. She never received warning, in some cases bumping into them in the corridor in her pajamas. And she never asked questions; Beatriz characteristically kept her affairs private.[206]

Unbeknownst to Ana María, Beatriz was also desperately missing Luis. "I want to see you, to see your smile," she wrote to him in early 1969 just after returning from Cuba. "If I have you close everything seems possible ... everything makes sense."[207] Writing in the evening, lying on her bed, she imagined him knocking on the door and surprising her.[208] "My love ... I love you, I am totally in love with you," she confessed.[209] When she received letters from him, she memorized them. As she told him, "Yesterday and today ... I was happy for a brief moment after receiving your news. ... You can't imagine how happy you make me," although she admitted it came with "a bitter taste ... of inevitable distance."[210] She also had nightmares ("I desperately look for you, I see you.... I ask you not to leave and I wake up startled") and confessed she feared he would forget her.[211] When she drew him a sketch titled "Typical outfits of your average '*pollo*' and '*polla*' [guy and girl]," she tried to normalize and make light of their abnormal affair. She depicted herself smiling, carefree in sandals, and her Cuban lover with cigarettes in his top pocket casually dropping grenades and money out of a suitcase. Seemingly about to pull a pistol from his belt, it is unclear what this "typical" couple was meant to be doing, let alone what world they lived in. But as a glimpse of Beatriz's imagination, it is revealing how happy this caricatured idea of Luis's espionage work apparently made her and how she portrayed their lives as *unextraordinary*.

Beatriz's love letters to Luis were entangled with an intense longing for Havana revealing a complicated existence at home. "It's so difficult to leave Cuba," she wrote, "everything grates and I don't know what to do to begin to adapt."[212] "I am hungry for news from there," she insisted frequently. "Tell me how everything is going, the agricultural work, etc., and about you."[213] She started biting her nails again. "Only you are able to give me the security and peace [to make me stop]," she wrote, "not having you makes me desperate."[214]

Beatriz's sisters thought she was "crazy"; they watched her from a distance but did not dare ask anything directly. As she told Luis, they had been unsure if she was ever going to return from Cuba. It was obviously impossible to tell them about her visit. Although her mother tried to find out about her relationship with Luis, Beatriz deflected questions. She was more candid with her father, even if she was wary about sharing too much. As she wrote to Luis, she told Salvador she could not say more for security reasons and "he understood well," though "he seemed somewhat worried 'about me ... and because it could implicate him' [and] he repeated this 3 times, according to him it wasn't news to him given all your talk about the Valdiviano [Bolivian] matter.... He identifies me with the Valdivianos, although at times he would have thought, though less than before, that the cafiches [MIR] was the thing [I was involved in].... In terms of us ... he repeated that he has an optimal impression of you, I think that for him what we have has always been obvious."[215]

Because she did not want to implicate her father in her revolutionary

Sketch, Beatriz to Luis. "Facha clasica de una polla y de un pollo cualquiera," no date. Luis Fernández Oña private collection.

activities—and it seems Luis was worried about this too—her options for moving from Guardia Vieja were limited. "I can't live with my grandmother now that she is directly looking after my uncle and his family," she wrote, referring to Dina and Arnoldo, known as "tío" on account of being a few years older than most elenos. She also did not feel she could get too close to her mirista friends, who, as we shall see, were engaging in urban guerrilla activities by this point. Fearing her relationship with them could jeopardize her father's reputation, she kept a careful distance.[216]

In many ways, in fact, Beatriz was stuck and alone. Clandestine work, with its emphasis on secrecy and strict compartmentalization, compounded her tendency to be guarded and private. As Fernando Gómez reflected, it was hard: it affected people's emotions, friendships, love lives, work, and personality. You had to learn how to say the bare minimum when you were used to jumping into discussions; you had to be ready with explanations. "You lose your privacy, that is to say, you don't have it, you live behaving as if you were someone normal, but you aren't," he explained. And although Beatriz's relationship with her father did "not deteriorate," she now had to "remain silent" or keep things from him, and this affected her.[217] As Allende's daughter, she had to be especially careful about her clandestine activities. She therefore co-opted others where risks of getting directly involved were too high.[218] Meanwhile, as a woman, she was forbidden from becoming the kind of armed revolutionary she wanted to be. She was desperate be with Luis in Cuba. And when it came to Bolivia, she was confined to a supporting role. Instructed to stay in Chile, she also had limited means of influencing Bolivian events, a source of disillusionment when the ELN's plans went awry.

6 : : : **Revolutionary Upheaval**

While Beatriz had been involved in the ELN in 1968 and 1969, Chile had been changing in ways that would shape its revolutionary future and her own interaction with it. Her professional life shifted directly as a result. Her inclination for armed struggle also had more resonance than ever before, although she sometimes disparaged what she regarded as the contradictory, inconsistent, and careless way left-wing militants explored "the violent road."[1] Revolution now appeared more proximate or threatening, depending on where people stood along Chile's increasingly fraught political spectrum. True, Chile's formal political system rooted in parliamentary democracy, free and frequent elections, consensus building, and legitimate institutions remained in place.[2] Yet radicalization of the country's younger population, the development of new left-wing intellectual and theological currents, university occupations, strikes, land seizures, street clashes, and urban revolutionary attacks meant upheaval permeated society.

Although part of a "global 1968," radical shifts in Chile were related to specific repercussions of Frei's reformist experiment, the energies it unleashed, and its perceived failings. Within the Christian Democrat Party (PDC), radical factions emerged wanting to take reforms further. The Christian Democrat's youth leader, Rodrigo Ambrosio, for example, argued unambiguously for socialist transformation.[3] In mid-1967, the PDC's national council also approved a report titled "Non-Capitalist Road to Development."[4] In May 1969, radical Christian Democrats then formed a breakaway party, the Movimiento de Acción Popular Unitario (Movement of Popular Unitary Action, MAPU), which came to stand on the far left of Chile's political landscape. When the government used armed force in Puerto Montt to quash a land invasion in 1969 resulting in eight dead and over forty injured, widespread protests and land seizures followed. Even young Christian Democrats charged Chile's interior minister with "fascism" and demanded his resignation.[5] Already, two years before the end of his mandate, international observers noted that Frei was involved in a "holding operation."[6] As Beatriz would reflect, despite "reformist language" and "with foreign aid no other government ever had ... he could not fix [Chile's] problems."[7]

Although Chile's political institutions remained robust, many looked to direct action as an alternative. In Santiago alone, between 1967 and 1972, 54,710 families (comprising 10 percent of Santiago's population) received homes through land seizures.[8] Students at the University of Chile occupied the institution's central buildings and facilities in mid-1968, following their contemporaries' example at Catholic University the previous year. Originating in the reformist impulse set forth by the Frei agenda, the occupation succeeded in bringing about decentralization of faculties and co-government, whereby students received 25 percent of decision-making votes.[9] As Inés Pepper, a medical student, recalled, she felt part of a "force able to ... transform the world."[10] And when right-wing critics complained about politicization of higher education, Alejandro Rojas, who was Communist president of the Federación de Estudiantes de la Universidad de Chile (FECH), recalled, they argued that "politicization was inevitable" as it mirrored "a much deeper crisis in Chilean society."[11]

As they had been for some time, in fact, students were directly involved in developments outside the university system. But the reform process reflected and accentuated this trend. And like Beatriz's cohort in the early 1960s, volunteering in poblaciónes and rural areas now radicalized students further. While they used ideological arguments to rationalize their affiliations, one student recalled being driven more by "emotions and feelings ... [by] the poverty, the ravages of winter in extremely precarious poblaciónes, land occupations that gave origin to those fragile poblaciónes, the strikes, the marches."[12] Increasingly, students saw themselves as participants in a revolutionary process made necessary by the failings of state-led services and reforms. When it came to land occupations, for example, they set up tents, built houses, provided health services, organized people, ran literacy courses, and offered "leadership training."[13] In the south, engineering and architecture students at the University of Concepción also helped design settlement communities.[14]

In addition to Frei's perceived failings at a societal level, his links to the United States drew criticism. Anti-imperialism was "the principal logic" underpinning young left-wing Chilean activism; it was "something deep, that came to us from within," a Socialist militant recalled. Frei's government was dedicated to "limited reformist capitalist modernization, pro-American and definitely not ... Latin America's urgencies ... possibilities, and necessities."[15] Dynamic intellectual currents in Santiago added weight to anti-imperialist frameworks and a new way of interpreting Chile's position in the world: not as a "backward" nation, lagging behind in a capitalist world system, but in an exploitative and dependent relationship with the United States. Economic crises and inequality were perceived as symptoms of global problems rather than local failings, the solutions for which would not be solved by Washington-sponsored reformist projects but by an overhaul of the world's economic system. From Andre Gunder Frank's *Capitalismo y subdesarrollo en América Latina* to Fernando Henrique Cardoso and Enzo Faletto's *Dependencia y desarrollo en América Latina*, both the result of work undertaken in Chile during the late 1960s, the emergence of dependency theory precisely at this moment provided a theoretical underpinning for the revolutionary Left.[16]

Beyond the dependency and development issues, the Vietnam War, as a symbol of U.S. imperialism, also mobilized left-wing groups.[17] As well as legitimating internationalist revolutionary ventures such as that of the Ejército de Liberación Nacional (ELN), it galvanized local actors much as U.S. intervention against Cuba's revolution had done a decade earlier. As the Juventud Socialista (JS) leader and medical student Carlos Lorca underlined, Vietnam joined Cuba in playing an "essential role in radicalizing large masses of Chilean youth."[18] In late 1967, young Christian Democrats and Communists had also organized a five-day student protest march from Valparaíso to Santiago involving thousands of young Chileans. As one participant remembered, his shoes broke and he had to walk kilometers with blisters while others fought dehydration to make it to the capital.[19] In March 1969, Beatriz's father had visited Vietnam as part of a tour taking him to North Korea, Cambodia, and Cuba. As he later told Régis Debray, Vietnam, like Cuba, had strengthened his political convictions.[20]

And yet, as with Cuba, interpreting Vietnam's significance exposed and exacerbated Chilean divisions. When North Vietnamese delegates were invited to the XIX National Conference of Juventud Socialista in April 1968, alongside Cuban and North Korean youth representatives, for example, the government refused them entry into the country.[21] The police also fought JS "assault groups" in the streets over Vietnam.[22] Moreover, at the march for Vietnam, there were fierce intra-Left disagreements. While Communists marched for peace with doves as symbols, Socialists, dressed in combat green, carried pictures of Che and called for "two, three, many Vietnams." As a result, Communists denounced their Socialist comrades as "extremists, irresponsible, anarchists."[23] An international war on the other side of the world thus served as a lens through which to interpret domestic realities and fight local battles regarding revolutionary strategy. Indeed, as upheaval unsettled politics and everyday life in Chile, it did so in a confused way. By the late 1960s it was clear Chile was changing, that traditional norms and rules of the game were being challenged, but what would replace them was far from certain.

Campus Oriente

Beatriz lived with these developments, was involved in many of them, and was affected by their ramifications. However, she did so "with one foot here [Chile] and another abroad," mirroring other elenos' experiences.[24] As a clandestine revolutionary on the margins of the Socialist Party (PS) fixated on Cuba and keen not to undermine her father's congressional position, she had already withdrawn from Chilean political life.[25] There are suggestions that she participated in meetings concerning university occupations and reform and that she was close to JS leaders. But she was dislocated from, and frustrated with, the world she lived in.[26] Privately, she described Chile as "a country without an answer for young people. Santiago is very ugly, everything is dry, how I long for Havana."[27] For the revolutionary Left she belonged to, university reform—like the government's reformist agenda—did not address underlying structural problems. Instead, it radicalized those within the institution so they were more inclined to fight "the system" in the socialist revolution ahead.[28]

Even so, the university reform process provided Beatriz a teaching job at the University of Chile's new public health department at its Campus Oriente, created thanks to decentralization. The shift to teaching meant Beatriz had to leave clinical work at the Consultorio Ismael Valdés, although she would continue to visit patients at their homes and do "social work" in poblaciónes ("she was very attached [to helping] the sick," a friend remembered).[29] When Manuel Ipinza, the new director of this department, based at the Hospitals Toráx and Salvador, had asked her to join his staff, she accepted enthusiastically, not least because she was struggling financially with legal costs relating to annulling her marriage.[30] Having worked with Beatriz at San Juan de Dios and at Ismael Valdés, Ipinza already knew her well, regarded her as hard working ("very responsible ... very competent"), and shared a left-wing affinity with her. True, as a Communist, Ipinza disagreed with Beatriz's belief in armed struggle and was against any collaboration with the Movimiento de Izquierda Revolucionaria (MIR). But they respected each other.[31] "He is very nice, not sectarian at all," Beatriz wrote to Luis. That he wanted to visit Cuba and was happy to hear about the island ("I talk to him everyday [about Cuba] and I inundate him with photos and posters from there") also endeared him to her.[32]

Ipinza put together a close-knit left-wing team, meaning Beatriz's politics increasingly fused with her career.[33] He recruited his friend and medical school classmate Eduardo "Coco" Paredes, who, in addition to having worked full-time in public health at the Hospital San Borja, was a member of the PS's Central Committee since Chillán and soon to be recruited to the ELN (quite possibly thanks to Beatriz). Beatriz had also known him since childhood, and as the son of family friends, Eduardo was particularly close to her father. Some even went so far as to describe him as Allende's adoptive son.[34] The two men shared a complicity based on a shared sense of humor and character. Partly because of this and partly because Eduardo spoke French, Allende invited him on his trip to Vietnam, Cambodia, Korea, and Cuba in early 1969. For her part, Beatriz described Eduardo as having an "open and expansive character."[35] And although she had previously regarded him as "politically ... a little disorientated ... unprepared," from mid-1969, when the two began working together at the Campus Oriente, they became increasingly close, with Eduardo finding his orientation within Beatriz's milieu.[36] It was in Ipinza's department that Beatriz also grew to know Patricia Espejo, one of four sociologists employed to teach there. Beatriz had crossed paths with Patricia for years. But they now became friends and political collaborators.[37] Patricia was affiliated with the MIR and married to Eugenio Leyton ("a *cafiche* [mirista] ... at the highest level," Beatriz called him). As she wrote to Luis, their house was "brazenly a base" for the MIR.[38]

Politics unsurprisingly affected this department's relationship with its students. Before the reform process, Campus Oriente had typically attracted elite, upper-class students. And when Ipinza—a professor elected by students, academics, and professional staff—took over, the sixth-year students were overwhelmingly from the right or center-right (only two were left wing, he recalled). In this context, students' parents, many doctors themselves, accused teachers of turning their sons and daughters into communists.[39] However, overall, the relationship between faculty and students was close. At lunchtime, students would congregate in their teachers' offices to debate politics in "an environment of lots of assertiveness but lots of respect."[40] As Cecilia Sepúlveda, one of Beatriz's students in her third year of medicine, remembered, "There were very fierce discussions ... the whole country was arguing ... there was a great amount of polarization." And in this climate the department was "an interesting space for debate." Much as Beatriz had done, only with more urgency and encouragement, students discussed medicine's role in alleviating Chile's problems, and Beatriz "spoke with lots of passion."[41] She had a tendency to be private and "a little introverted," another student recalled, no doubt because of her clandestine affiliations and desire not to compromise her father's position, but she was "very committed."[42]

Students were also given the opportunity to collaborate directly in community-led projects, typical of public health and outreach initiatives at the time. Having been swept up in the reform process, the younger cohort Beatriz taught in 1969–70 formed part of an "exceptional generation," Ipinza remembered.[43] Students took the reform process's emphasis on extending the university to the wider population to heart, collaborating across faculties to launch projects and offer talks, courses, and services to the wider community.[44] And for those studying in Ipinza's department, part of their training involved traveling to poorer neighborhoods to understand their socioeconomic conditions and writing reports.[45] Their experience is impossible to understand without grasping the Chilean medical profession's move toward socialized and integral medicine over the previous decade. But as in other sectors, students now took reformist initiatives forward with urgency and drive.

Specifically, Beatriz, her colleagues, and their students were involved in building a new clinic to replicate Benjamin Viel's Ismael Valdés in the La Reina district of Santiago. There, they joined an innovative construction project championed by Fernando Castillo Velasco, the district's Christian Democratic mayor, the rector of the Catholic University after its reform process, a family friend of the Allendes, and father to Beatriz's friend Carmen. The idea behind "La Villa," as the project was called, was for the area's poorer populations, made up primarily of construction workers, to build a new community themselves, aided by sympathetic volunteers.[46] Within La Villa, Ipinza's team established a polyclinic designed by civil engineering and architecture students. Medical students simultaneously learned both how to treat patients and how to run a polyclinic and link it to the community.[47] It was an ambitious project demanding time outside normal working hours.[48] As Patricia recalled, she and Beatriz were consumed by public health and politics day and night.[49]

As committed as she was, Beatriz was nevertheless distracted. Manuel and Patricia often had to cover for her and Eduardo without knowing precisely why. On one occasion, Beatriz arrived in her jeep and told Ipinza she would be away for a week. He did not ask questions. Luckily, he remembered, university authorities did not ask any either, even if students wondered where "Doctora Allende" was.[50] Beatriz was grateful for Manuel's support. As she would write to Luis, "He has behaved so well with me and with Paredes.... He does everything to make it easy for us to work politically and he doesn't question our schedule or things like that.... He is *my friend* ... *because of his manner and behavior I have been able to do what I do*."[51]

Military Preparations

When Beatriz wrote of Ipinza's support for what she did, she implicitly referred to her work for her father's presidential campaign in 1969–70 (see chapter 7), the ELN, her relations with Latin American armed revolutionary groups, a radicalized PS faction, and the MIR. As well as covering for her at work, Ipinza also allowed his house to become a safe place where Beatriz could meet Miguel Enríquez. For two summers in a row, Ipinza gave her his keys when he was on holiday, and during the first of these, five members of the Movimiento de Liberación Nacional–Tupamaro (Tupamaros National Liberation Movement, MLN-T, or Tupamaros), the Uruguayan urban guerrilla group, moved in.[52] Elsewhere, in 1968–69, Chile's revolutionary Left had turned to focus on covert and semicovert military preparation for armed struggle. No faction promoted an immediate guerrilla insurgency in Chile, but believing violence was an inevitable and necessary part of a revolutionary process, they stepped up organization, training, and, on occasion, isolated armed operations.[53] Two pivotal developments in 1968–69 were important in this regard, contributing to the overall climate of revolutionary upheaval in the country. And in both cases, as much as Beatriz was distracted by Bolivia, she was aware and complicit.

The first was the creation at the end of 1968 of an armed apparatus within the Socialist Party known as the "Organa." Its origins lay in the party's Chillán conference in 1967. But, more immediately, it stemmed from rural mobilization and land seizures, as well as party militants' willingness to help defend rural workers from landowners and government forces. Party declarations and developments in the countryside were nevertheless interconnected, with those advocating armed preparation seeing rural conflict in the late Frei period as "key to implementing the agreed strategic path."[54] After a prolonged strike supported by the PS's National Agrarian Commission and Socialist leaders in the left-wing union federation, and the Confederación Nacional de Campesinos e Indígenas Ránquil, rural workers had occupied the Fundo San Miguel, a large country estate in San Esteban, Los Andes, in July 1968. And when they had, radicalized Socialist students from the University of Chile supported them. The link between students and rural activists was a logical outcome of activism and voluntary work since the mid-1960s. Significantly, some of these students and rural leaders, such as Rolando Calderón from Ránquil, had previously visited Cuba, with a few receiving military training. They also had access to a Bolivian army–owned Czechoslovak machine gun, revolvers, Winchester rifles, explosives, pistols, rudimentary handmade grenades, and Molotov cocktails, which they stockpiled for the occupation.

And when more than five hundred armed carabineros arrived to remove occupiers with six tanks, a violent confrontation ensued before the occupiers surrendered to avert a "massacre." Over one hundred campesinos, union leaders, and Socialist student militants were arrested.[55]

The weapons used by campesinos and students against carabineros had been defensive—protecting those taking the reform process into their own hands against landowners and the state, which opted for violence to contain them. But the occupation and battle for San Miguel was also emblematic of a strategic shift toward armed preparation and practical application of it as a component of revolutionary change within the Socialist Party. And it was precisely following this action that radicalized militants established the Organa, considered by its members to be similar to the ELN faction within the PS but under Chilean, as opposed to Bolivian, leadership and more focused on local concerns.[56] The Organa subsequently sent further militants to Cuba for military training, even if one of those involved recalled it as "guerrilla sport," centered on the idea of a "rural foco," rather than training suited to Chile's circumstances.[57] In 1969–70, as we will see, the Organa also set up training camps in southern Chile.[58]

Beatriz was not at San Miguel or directly involved in establishing the Organa.[59] She also expressed incredulity at the PS's "inconsistent" position, with rank-and-file members talking openly about armed struggle in the buildup to Chile's March 1969 congressional elections while the party remained "caught up in the elections." As she complained to Luis, "They speak of violence and the violent path in electoral tribunals; it is ridiculous."[60] Her objection, as someone trained in covert work, related to strategic contradictions, the lack of concrete preparedness, and carelessness with which such ideas were expressed. Even so, she knew many Organa members and would come to work closely with them. Because the elenos were more established when it came to logistics, training, and revolutionary credentials, they were also able to support the emerging military apparatus inside the party. And there are suggestions that the ELN supplied the Bolivian machine gun used at San Miguel.[61]

Personal ties and friendships, as well as her role as a university teacher, also explain this growing cooperation and exchange between elenos and the Organa, with Beatriz one of the key contacts between groups. As we know, she had first met Rolando in the mid-1960s and knew many of the radicalized students at San Miguel and in the Organa well. Félix Huerta was, meanwhile, very close to his former classmate, Carlos Lorca, a medical student, leader in the FECH, and member of the Organa. And by 1970–71, such ties, together with new Chilean priorities bringing elenos' focus back home, would cause both organizations to merge.[62]

Beyond the Organa, the second significant military development on the revolutionary Left in 1968–69 was the MIR's decision to embark on armed operations. This was partly related to the movement's conception of a "popular war," comprising social and political mobilization and military preparation. But it was also immediately to raise money to survive.[63] Forced to go underground after student militants in Concepción kidnapped a journalist, miristas were unable to work to support themselves. Although a small group embarked on an exploration of the Andes to see if they could establish a guerrilla training camp, it was disastrous: after three days, with feet destroyed and spirits wounded, they had crossed into Argentina and pawned their watches to buy bus tickets home.[64] The MIR's armed actions—mostly comprising bank raids and propaganda—therefore focused on cities, mirroring urban guerrilla groups in the Southern Cone like the Tupamaros, though more rudimentary.[65] As Beatriz wrote to Luis in February 1969 after having spoken to Miguel Enríquez, her friends from Concepción were now involved "in something serious."[66]

Miristas would not have survived had it not been for supporters within established Chilean left-wing parties, particularly the PS. As Eugenia Palieraki has noted, the MIR became "a convenient annex of the PS.... The small left-wing party offered a space in which young militants could experiment [with] their ideals, without constraints." Socialist leaders "could not afford to expose the party [to this kind of behavior *within* the PS] without losing its electoral credibility." And, crucially, among those who supported miristas during this period were Salvador Allende and his sister, Laura (Andrés Pascal's mother), who provided safe houses or, as in the case of Osvaldo Puccio, Allende's secretary, helped hide money.[67]

Beatriz was a particularly significant accomplice in this respect: in regular contact with miristas, hiding their money, and securing safe houses.[68] She was nevertheless worried about their carelessness.[69] As she wrote to Luis in early 1969, "I warn you the *cafiches* are doing things to get $ but they're not looking after themselves at all," and "I'm scared they could drop the ball, they have improved but they're very sloppy and they don't want to learn!"[70] Looking back, Andrés Pascal accepted this judgment, acknowledging that compared with the highly clandestine ELN group, MIR adherents were practically "shouting in the streets." And Beatriz did not try to recruit him to the ELN for this reason.[71] The Cubans appear to have shared Beatriz's preoccupations. When Luis had been in Chile in early 1968, for example, he had a meeting with miristas in a house where they kept arms and had worried about security. "I did not feel good," he remembered, fearing his association with the MIR would be discovered and used against Cuba.[72] In fact, the Cubans kept a relative distance, declining to support the MIR financially as much as the Chilean revolutionary organization would have liked and urging it to raise its own funds, which it did through armed robberies (or "expropriations," as miristas called them).[73]

Meanwhile, in all developments, Beatriz's relationship with the Cubans—and in particular, her love affair with Luis, a key figure in Cuba's intelligence operations in Chile—made her a unique conduit of information. She offered Havana's leaders a new channel of communication with Chilean left-wing factions, ranging from Beatriz's own father, president of the Chilean Senate, to the Organa, and to the MIR.[74] She passed messages between them, and her intimate relationship with Luis meant she could be candid. The tone of her letters also suggests she and Luis agreed on their analysis of developments.[75] And, as such, at least by 1969, her role as a bridge between Cuba and Chile went beyond the specificities of her involvement in Bolivia. She informed him about Chileans traveling to the island and their character and political stance. Simultaneously, the revolutionary Left's growing links with Cuba gave her a way of communicating with Luis, with both of them using militants' trips to the island to send each other letters.

As a result of her training in Cuba and her intimate relationship with the Cuban regime's inner circle, Beatriz also felt empowered to judge others, including her friends in the MIR as the Cubans did themselves. In this sense, she formed part of a particularly divided Left in Chile that spent almost as much time arguing within its own ranks over who best understood the revolutionary path forward as it did forging that path. Assuming a posture of presumed superiority and knowledge of how revolution *should* be pursued—who could interpret and best understand Lenin's significance for Chile's reality, for example—became part and parcel of militating for one of Chile's fractious left-wing parties. Revolutionary fervor was in the air, changes were afoot, and armed confrontations with the state occurred with growing frequency. But the question was to what end. And, ironically, all this was happening while the hopes founded of Latin America's guerrilla decade that inspired local armed groups were progressively undermined.

ELN Difficulties

The ELN had run into serious difficulties almost as soon as recruits arrived in Bolivia after Cuban training. On the one hand, the political context in the country changed when President Barrientos was killed in a helicopter crash on 27 April 1969, leaving Luis Adolfo Salinas, his civilian, social democrat–leaning vice president, in charge. Although this change had little impact on the commitment of ELN recruits (after all, they were focused on fulfilling Che's legacy and bringing about another Vietnam in Latin America rather than the specificities of Bolivia's political context), it appears to have had an effect on Cuba's willingness to support them.[76]

On the other hand, a series of raids in Cochabamba in July 1969 destroyed much of the ELN's work since 1968. The news that Rita Valdivia, known as "Maya," had been killed in a gun battle was particularly difficult for Beatriz given the two of them had trained together and become friends in Cuba less than a year earlier. As the head of the ELN's urban network in the city, Rita's death and the discovery of organizational details found at her house was a serious blow. Having fled the scene, her Chilean partner—recruited by the Cubans rather than Catalán—was found dead. Meanwhile, in La Paz, toward the end of July, security forces seized ELN supplies and propaganda. Henceforth, recriminations and accusations of betrayal began flying within the ELN.[77]

It was in the context of Bolivia's changed circumstances and the ELN's misfortunes that the Cubans began withdrawing assistance. Regional and global developments were also significant. When Castro had committed to a new Bolivian insurgency, rural focos had already failed or were under severe pressure across Latin America. However, the Cubans had subsequently suffered further defeats in Venezuela and Guatemala. Brazil's military dictatorship had also defeated a string of insurgencies, and an attempt to establish a guerrilla foco in Tucumán, Argentina, had failed.[78] These defeats, atop of Che's death, had led the Cubans to rethink strategy. The existing strategy had already substantially weakened their position when it came to their tense relationship with the Soviet Union, which they depended on for economic and military support. Facing ultimatums from Moscow to switch course, Castro had no real alternative other than to pull away from the brink. In August 1968, he had signaled his readiness to work with the Soviets when he did not condemn the invasion of Czechoslovakia. And in 1969 the Cubans began aligning intelligence organizations with their Soviet bloc counterparts, sending a group of Piñeiro's team on an Eastern European tour.[79] In late July or early August 1969, Havana's leaders then recalled all Cuban personnel from the ELN insurgency, including Benigno and Pombo, who were in Rome en route to Bolivia. And although the Cubans let most non-Cuban elenos at Punto Cero depart for Bolivia, others were prevented from leaving the island. Sonia Daza Sepúlveda, a Chilean living in Cuba trained for the urban underground in Bolivia, for example, was told a few days before she was scheduled to leave that she would not be going.[80]

The Cubans never explained their decision, leaving questions unanswered to this day.[81] The radio Beatriz was operating from Chile is reported to have simply gone quiet. And none of her letters to Luis—who dealt primarily with Chile rather than Bolivia—give a reason (that she would visit Cuba in late September and had the opportunity to talk face-to-face with the Cubans probably explains why).[82] Beatriz did manage to smuggle a Soviet pistol to Inti in Bolivia in late August; her father had brought it back from Cuba. As Luis remembered, Piñeiro had ordered him to gift it to Allende, which he did reluctantly. And when he found out it reached Inti, he assumed Beatriz had a role in persuading her father to give it up, although he never asked either of them about it.[83] Awaiting further instructions, ELN recruits in Chile destined for Bolivia meanwhile found themselves stuck.[84] Increasingly fearful of disloyalty, Inti ordered cadres to discipline suspected infiltrators.[85]

Then, on 9 September 1969, Inti was killed in a gun battle when security services raided his safe house in La Paz and found him alone in a back room without an exit. Not only did this strip the ELN of its leader and direct link to Che's guerrilla column, but the way he had been found—without any protection or escape route—seemed to underscore the organization's incompetence.[86] It was a devastating end to almost two years of organization. And in Chile, Beatriz is said to have read to ELN members "Los Heraldos Negros" ("The Black Riders") by the Peruvian Marxist César Vallejo, evoking the messengers of death:

There are blows in life so violent—I can't answer!
Blows as if from the hatred of God; as if before them,
the deep waters of everything lived through
were backed up in the soul ... I can't answer![87]

While elenos mourned, Inti's brother Osvaldo "Chato" Peredo, and those who opposed retreat, took charge. Elmo, who belonged to this group, was more experienced than Chato, but it was decided, possibly learning from Che's experience, that a Bolivian should lead the organization. Chato's familial ties to Inti and, through Inti, to Che were also important. Even so, he was not a natural choice and had lived outside Bolivia for almost a decade. Havana's leaders sent one last donation to the ELN with a Chilean envoy, but ultimately, Chile's elenos were now the insurgency's principal foreign backers.[88]

The ELN was thus left divided, on the run, and struggling financially. As Chato remembered, reassembling elenos was difficult amid widespread demoralization after Inti's death.[89] Some, including Fernando Gómez, left the organization. In late 1969, the ELN then engaged in botched robberies to get money, leaving more members dead. In December, police also attacked Chato's safe house in La Paz, and although Chato managed to escape, David Adriazola Veizaga, or "Dario"—the only remaining Bolivian survivor of Che's column—was killed. Bolivian authorities also seized more money and arms.[90]

Beatriz was notably disheartened in her letters to Luis, longing to be in Havana.[91] "I would do anything to talk [to you] at length," she wrote in January 1970.[92] She also transcribed Pablo Neruda's poems by hand for him. Verses from his poem "Ausencia" (Absence) pointed to the painful separation she felt:

> My love,
> we have found each other
> thirsty and we have
> drunk up all the water and the blood,
> we found each other
> hungry
> and we bit each other
> as fire bites,
> leaving wounds in us.
>
> But wait for me,
> Keep for me your sweetness.
> I will give you too
> a rose.[93]

Much of Beatriz's romanticized attachment to internationalist guerrilla operations meanwhile faded as a result of the ELN's rapid deterioration. As she wrote, her "relatives in Valdivia" were in "poor health and [her] cousin Dario died." "As you can imagine this has affected me a great deal," she admitted.[94]

The ELN's mission had always been dangerous, but the risks had been considered worthwhile: a stepping-stone to continental socialist revolution. However, now, some began to question the rush to action. And perhaps grasping her own deficiencies, Beatriz had a new urge to study. In mid-January 1970, she wrote to Luis asking him to send her "LENIN's works ... I must admit too much ignorance ... I need to overcome that ... I never decided to study the classics of Marxism and now I am doing it ... Also in the hospital, if I have time, I read things on social anthropology which complements sociology well."[95] She looked forward to the university's summer holidays to read further.[96]

Even so, Beatriz and Arnoldo remained committed to the ELN's operations: loyal to Che, to Inti, and to Elmo, now a leading figure in the ELN's high command. The momentum and structures in place throughout Chile to support a Bolivian insurgency as well as reluctance to give up on a revolutionary future explain their decision. To help move it forward, in April 1970, for example, Arnoldo helped smuggle money that the Tupamaros raised to the ELN. And although police at the Chilean-Argentine border seized half of the money, the £9,000 Chato received breathed life into a moribund organization.[97] Beatriz and Arnoldo were also able to recruit new members to the ELN in 1969–70. And, in this respect, Chile's climate of upheaval driven by university reform, land seizures, the PDC's crisis, and its use of force helped. Inti's death, like Che Guevara's before it, also stoked the allure of heroic sacrifice.[98] Víctor Jara, a popular Chilean folk singer and Communist militant, wrote an uplifting song he performed at the University of Valparaíso about finding Inti, taking his manifesto "Volveremos a las montañas" as the inspiration for its title:

> Give me a rifle, captain
> The blood that we shed
> will guide our brothers
> exploding in liberty.
>
> We will return
> to the north, to the south
> to the American Indian
> I and you with a guardian angel,
> with the voice of Che Guevara,
> will fire my rifle.[99]

Indeed, despite revolutionary setbacks throughout Latin America, guerrilla insurgencies and regional revolution were increasingly honored on the pages of *Punto Final* and celebrated in everyday life and culture as well as politics, allowing Chilean elenos to recruit friends, family, and university students with ease. By 1969–70, Chilean elenos could count on almost a hundred militants.[100] Beatriz's childhood friend and Andrés Pascal's wife, Carmen Castillo, was one such recruit. She was asked to receive coded telephone messages twice a week and travel directly to Bolivia as a conduit of information. She recalled Beatriz persuaded her to get involved to secure a brighter regional future. "Thanks to her, Latin America became visible," she remembered. "I was proud to be one of the many anonymous people in the fight to make the continent more just, more beautiful, more powerful.... She told me about Cuba, Che's guerilla campaign, repression in Venezuela, the popular struggle in Chile.... I did not know the name of the group or the guerillas to be helped, I only knew that it was necessary to fight to the death, that there was daily danger and that the enemy was infiltrated everywhere. I liked the secrecy, I did not resent having a double life, it excited me to be and not to be just bourgeois, a university student, Andrés' faithful companion."[101]

In addition to Socialist militants, religious theological shifts throughout Latin America in the late 1960s attracted radicalized Catholic students to the group. Liberation Theology, as it became known after a meeting of Latin American bishops in Medellín, Colombia, in August–September 1968, inspired different groups, not all of whom sanctioned armed struggle. To the far left, however, it provided a framework for Catholics to join revolutionary movements.[102] Fusing theology and revolution, including ideas of sacrifice prevalent in both, Catholic students in Chile and Bolivia depicted Che as "Christ in the mountains"—an idea encouraged in *Punto Final*, which published a verse by the Spanish poet León Felipe, misleadingly attributing it to Che:

Christ, I love you
Not because you came down from a star
but because you revealed to me that man has blood,
tears,
anguish,
keys, to open closed doors to the light.
Yes ... you taught us that man is God,
A poor God crucified like you.[103]

Rather than new recruits spending six months training in Cuba as those recruited in 1966–68 had, new Chilean and Bolivian recruits now received quick ad hoc preparation in the countryside. As one ELN member remembered, recruitment was much less rigorous "with the [ELN's] new militaristic direction ... the only condition was whether you were willing to take up arms, to fight, without any argument."[104]

Dead Ends and Bridge Building

It was in these circumstances, almost three years after Che Guevara's death, that the ELN launched an ill-fated insurgency on 19 July 1970 under Chato's command near Teoponte, 270 kilometers from La Paz. Of the 67 who took part, only 20 to 25 had been part of the original group that received training in Cuba.[105] Although 8 were Chileans, Elmo Catalán was also strikingly absent, having been murdered a month earlier along with his new Bolivian girlfriend, a student leader in Cochabamba recruited to the ELN in 1969 and pregnant with Catalán's child.[106] Their deaths fueled conspiracy theories and yet more division within the ELN after the murderer was identified as an eleno. While some tried to paint him as a CIA operative, others explained the double murder as a part of a love affair gone wrong. Some also privately insinuated Chato orchestrated it to secure his leadership.[107] Whatever the cause—unclear to this day—the discovery of two bodies under a bridge on the outskirts of Cochabamba was a sorry end to Catalán's venture. Pointless and remote, his death stood diametrically opposed to the continental revolution that had brought him to Bolivia. Two more Chileans, Carlos Gómez and Félix Vargas, henceforth left Bolivia and returned to Chile.[108] They were lucky. Only eight of those who launched the insurgency near Teoponte would survive, emerging from the mountains, starving and destitute, in a negotiated amnesty in November 1970. The guerrillas also had no way of communicating with the outside world via Beatriz while they were in the mountains, having decided to abandon their radio equipment for logistical reasons.[109] To this day, many insurgents' remains have not been found.

At the tail end of Latin America's guerrilla decade, the Teoponte insurgency was a tragedy, exposing the ELN's limitations and the broader conceptual flaws of the Guevarista revolutionary project. As Félix remembered, "There was a belief that everything could be solved by killing people.... It was very difficult to take their foot off the accelerator for those who wanted the guerrilla foco."[110] Would the insurgency have turned out any differently at a slower place with more training and theory? Founded on an internationalist project Che himself had failed to realize, its members' enthusiasm could not make a regional revolution out of conditions that were not precipitous. Plagued by infighting, security breaches, a rampant counterinsurgency operation backed by the United States, and the Cubans' abandonment, the ELN's hope of resurrecting Guevara from Bolivian soil and bringing imperialism to its knees was doomed to fail from mid-1969, if not before. As one Chilean eleno retrospectively acknowledged, the Teoponte operation was "madness." But the possibility it would succeed seemed real at the time, buoyed, as it was, by the "spirit of the era."[111] This "spirit" was defined by frustration with the pace of change in Chile counterpoised with the Cuban Revolution's celebrated narrative of a few armed guerrillas sparking a successful revolution. This optimistic, potent, yet inaccurate idea had captivated a young generation impatient for change since the early 1960s, Beatriz included. The Tricontinental and Organización Latinoamericana de Solidaridad (OLAS) Conferences, together with Guevara's and Debray's writings toward the end of the decade, had then promoted it further.

If revolutionary internationalism had once given Beatriz purpose, its frustrations now left her disillusioned. She was devastated by the news of Elmo's murder, despite "arguments, discrepancies" with him in the past. "[My] mood has been very low," she wrote to Luis on 25 June 1970. "I still do not know anything exact." "I can hardly write to you as I would like," she added, although she drew strength from homages for Elmo at universities, in the press, and by unions.[112] Although Beatriz's commitment to the ELN continued, she and other surviving members of Elmo's clandestine network also began withdrawing from it. This was logical, Chato later reasoned, given their commitment had been to Inti and to Elmo, not to him.[113]

They also had growing reasons for shifting their attention back home.[114] As the country geared up for a presidential election in September 1970 and revolutionary upheaval unsettled politics and society, Chile's future hung in the balance. Students on the left, campaigning collectively as the Unidad de la Izquierda (Left-Wing Unit), won control of the FECH in November 1969, defeating the Christian Democrats after 14 years, seemingly signaling the country's future direction. Yet divisions within left-wing student groups also foretold future challenges. True, the Left had been strengthened by MAPU, the radical Christian Democratic breakaway party. But Socialist students had backed the victorious Communist candidate, Alejandro Rojas, only when Aniceto Rodríguez, secretary-general of the PS, issued an ultimatum to unite behind him or leave the party. In doing so, Socialists lost around 400 votes in an election won by a margin of 778.[115] As this episode showed, the Left was on the march, but compromise was problematic, especially when radical tendencies were the alternative.

Intra-Left struggles had also affected nominations for a presidential candidate. It was no secret Salvador Allende was determined to run for a fourth time. But he faced challenges from within the PS. In a runoff against Aniceto Rodríguez, the party sent Central Committee members to consult grassroots constituencies. And when all but two districts voted for Allende, Rodríguez resigned, leaving the former to run against himself. Significantly, however, the party did not rally round him: Allende received thirteen votes, but fourteen members of the Central Committee abstained.[116]

One of Allende's challenges was persuading the party's revolutionary Left factions—and particularly its radicalized youth at the end of the 1960s—of the viability of a peaceful, democratic road to socialism. Although he had been at the Tricontinental and an instigator of OLAS, had visited Vietnam and supported strikes, land seizures, and mobilizations, he was still regarded as being from an older generation of leaders misguidedly wedded to staid electoral strategies and political institutions. "They considered him a social democrat, and in those times that was insulting," a Juventud Socialista militant recalled.[117] As another Socialist reflected, Allende was operating "in a minefield."[118] The Cubans, having shifted their views of the revolutionary situation in Latin America considerably in 1969 and never having believed a guerrilla insurgency would work in Chile, did what they could to encourage those they had inspired to support Allende as the only figure able to unite the Left. But they also doubted his chances.[119]

In this context, Beatriz was in a difficult situation. Ultimately loyal to her father, despite her own pessimism about electoral politics, and closely aligned to the Cubans, she did what she could to support Allende's candidacy. Her legitimacy and credibility as a member of the revolutionary Left proved an asset for her father, ensuring not more voted against him. Although she was not there, for example, when Allende went to see Rolando Calderón, in hiding due to his role in land seizures, to ask for his support, the latter urged him to talk more to his daughter. And Allende had agreed he would.[120] Beatriz had also met with students involved in San Miguel and in the Organa at Guardia Vieja at the end of 1969 to persuade them to support her father.[121] And she, Félix Huerta, and Carlos Lorca had also spent hours successfully convincing Carlos Altamirano, on the PS's revolutionary Left, not to run as a candidate. "What were we, a bunch of dumb kids [*pendejos*], doing there in the middle?" Félix wondered decades later. "We had the capacity to believe we could get involved in everything." He also remembered Beatriz as a crucial intermediary for her father. "She could assemble a lot of [people], she was very loved by Allende ... by Altamirano.... She was a hinge in many things and for many people." But, as he acknowledged, it was "paradoxical" that this group, with "such leftist positions," were Allende's "most fervent supporters," despite his being a moderate figure in favor of a peaceful, democratic road to socialism.[122]

At the end of 1969, Beatriz also organized a special clandestine gathering between her father, the MIR's leaders, and their families. It was an "incredible party," one participant remembered. Beatriz secured them a safe house over the Christmas period, where Miguel, Bautista, and Andrés, in hiding at the time, had the opportunity to spend time with their wives and babies.[123] In subsequent months, having been asked directly by Allende, the MIR agreed to suspend its armed actions until after the election. As

Andrés Pascal recalled, the fact Beatriz's father was able to provide the MIR with funds, in part from Cuba, allowed it to concede (rather than having to rely on "expropriating" banks). Henceforth, the MIR also agreed not to officially ask its followers to boycott the election.[124]

Despite all her efforts, Beatriz was nevertheless conflicted.[125] As her father's campaign got under way, melancholy infused her letters. "I'm very depressed, a bit fucked [*jodida*]," she wrote in March 1970.[126] At least for the first half of 1970, Cuba, rather than Chile, remained her source of strength. "I think of you all and your people's campaigns in the battle of the sugar harvest," she explained to Luis, referring to the drive for a record-breaking ten-million-ton harvest in 1970. "This has helped me a lot."[127] When news broke that this harvest had failed to reach its target a couple of months later, she admitted to being personally affected. She craved news from the island (she begged Luis to send her Castro's full speech on the harvest) and feared "imperialism could exploit" the news as a pretext for invading the island. She applauded Castro's acknowledgment of failure as "revolutionary frankness." And she reassured herself Cuba had still achieved its biggest ever sugar harvest thanks to widespread mobilization. Appropriating a Cuban identity, she celebrated "our [*sic*] Cuban people's degree of consciousness ... [and] capacity for sacrifice."[128]

As she had done for a decade, in fact, Beatriz had come to internalize and view Cuba's experience as her own. "I plan to spend 26 July like you all," she wrote to Luis, referring to her plans for celebrating the anniversary of the 1953 attack of the Moncada barracks that gave Fidel Castro's movement its name. Revealing her adoption of Cuban tastes, rituals, and cultural practices, she told him she would eat "white rice, black beans, pork etc. of course with the joy of knowing that it is one more anniversary and with the sadness of not being together this day."[129] She also chain-smoked "Popular" Cuban cigarettes that Luis had sent her. Indeed, the cigarettes were a common currency in Cuba's dealings with Chile's revolutionary Left, chosen by revolutionary hopefuls as a symbol of Cuban authenticity and identification with "the people" despite Piñeiro's intelligence team preferring and trying unsuccessfully to encourage Beatriz and the MIR's leaders to smoke better, more expensive, refined Cuban brands.[130] What had started as a political affinity a decade earlier had translated into a new, personalized loyalty, heaped with emotional significance by 1970. This loyalty had gone so far as to surpass her interest in Chile and its future. However, as Allende's campaign heated up, Chile came back into focus, forcing her to recenter her attention.

7 : : : Working for the Revolution

Beatriz became heavily involved in her father's fourth presidential campaign in mid-1970. Earlier that year, Salvador Allende had been nominated as the candidate for the Unidad Popular (UP)—a coalition forged in 1969 comprising six parties, including the Socialist Party (PS), the Communist Party (PCCh), the Movimiento de Acción Popular Unitario (MAPU), and the Radical Party. As with his PS nomination, his selection had been riven with intra-Left divisions. Beatriz, consumed by her work at the university and her involvement in the Ejército de Liberación Nacional (ELN), had been disdainful of party machinations. True, she had been involved in persuading PS radical sectors to support Allende. But, as she had written to Luis, the nomination process had been "slow, traumatic, and not easy"—"a spectacle ... of disunity ... a very negative image." She also worried about implications for her father. And she was skeptical of an electoral victory: "I do NOT have faith in this," she had written at the beginning of the year. "I do NOT see any possibility at all in it."[1] Beatriz dreaded the return of political campaigning to Guardia Vieja and the rhythm of yet another election. Waiting for her family to return from Algarrobo in January, she relished the calm before a new political storm. Everything was about to "change completely," she predicted. The house would become a "madhouse"—an "inferno of people, letters, telephone calls, meetings etc."[2] At least when his campaign started, she had therefore, for various reasons, not been a key player.

It was Beatriz's emotional attachment to her father—rather than sudden faith in peaceful democratic change—that altered this. Pivotally, Salvador Allende had a minor heart attack. Potentially devastating in the midst of campaigning, this health scare needed careful management. Beatriz immediately contacted Oscar "Cacho" Soto, a young cardiologist and Eduardo Paredes's best friend, who recommended anticoagulants and rest (publicly, the candidate was said to be suffering from flu and bronchitis). Oscar had never treated Allende before but was deemed trustworthy and became his private doctor henceforth.[3]

Beatriz was nevertheless shaken by what had happened. Although Allende recovered quickly, she decided it was her "duty" to "look after him."[4] She told her father he had to "delegate work and responsibility to others because [campaign work] was too much for him" and tried "modestly to help him as a doctor, as a daughter, avoiding displeasures, dislikes, playing the role of companion and secretary and replacing him at a few small events."[5] On 3 May, for example, Beatriz spoke on his behalf at a not-so-small rally of seven thousand in La Cisterna.[6] Joining Allende's campaign team more actively than before, she also accompanied her father to interviews and helped him prepare for a televised presidential debate. This was to be doubly challenging given Allende's health. Beatriz therefore assembled a team of trusted friends at Guardia Vieja, including Jorge Arrate, a young economist she had known from the Brigada Universitaria Socialista (BUS).[7] These efforts paid off; the debate went well, helping quash rumors he was seriously ill.[8]

Beatriz's sudden resolution to take a more active role in supporting her father led to her sacrificing the most important thing to her at the time: visiting Cuba. "It pisses me off, it hurts me," she wrote to Luis. In mid-1970 it appeared everyone was "packing bags" to go to Cuba, leaving her in "a deep depression ... I envy them," she confessed.[9] Significantly, however, her father's heart attack also forced Beatriz to engage more with what was happening around her. In March she had admitted "little Chile is beginning to get interesting." But little else.[10] Now, mobilized by her love for her father, she began reflecting more on his campaign. As she wrote to Luis at the end of May, "I think the current moment Chile is living through has great political importance, and I concede ... the importance of the UP as a process.... Even though it is difficult, I do not exclude the possibility of an electoral triumph. This country has become very polarized, the political level has risen, as has anti-imperialist consciousness and in general. The Unidad Popular is doing well.... I love my father very much and I respect him more every day.... He has made me sign up [for the campaign] and collaborate."[11]

What Beatriz found when she joined in mid-1970 was an ideologically charged electoral race, echoing past presidential campaigns but building on them. As in 1964, women and youth groups mobilized, supporters volunteered in disadvantaged neighborhoods, thousands attended rallies and marched in the streets; workers lobbied their colleagues, and young Allendistas painted walls with the UP's insignia (one propaganda group called itself the Elmo Catalán brigade).[12] At a grassroots level, Beatriz also campaigned in poorer communities, talking to women, in particular, persuading them to vote for the UP.[13] Electioneering, working at the university, and maintaining her ELN commitments meant she was exhausted. But this had advantages: "There are so many things [happening] that days are flying by," she wrote to Luis in June. "At night I get back so wrecked that I don't have much time to think and feel lonely."[14]

In many respects, the Left stood a better chance than in 1958 and 1964. This is not because its percentage of voters had risen drastically. As it turned out, a slightly lower percentage of people voted for the UP in 1970 than had voted for the Frente de Acción Popular (FRAP) in 1964. For all the enthusiasm of those who did campaign, there were some on the left—particularly those radicalized after 1964—who were pessimistic about the UP's chances. Many miristas who had voted for the FRAP now simply refused to participate in the electoral system they scorned.[15] Those under twenty-one and illiterate Chileans remained disenfranchised, meaning official voter registers did not accurately reflect the much broader mobilization in favor of the UP. However, rather than the electorate being split two ways, with the Right conclusively backing the Christian Democrats against the Left, it was now divided three ways, between the Right, the center, and the Left, giving the latter a greater chance of securing the most votes. Moreover, the Christian Democrat's candidate, Radomiro Tomic, was a progressive within the Christian Democrat Party (PDC), believing a future alliance with the Left was inevitable. Arguing Frei's Revolution in Liberty needed accelerating, his followers essentially backed a program for transformation akin to Allende's. The combination of his supporters and the UP's thus gave overwhelming weight to proposals for radical change. Against this agenda and the PDC's record, former president Jorge Alessandri stood for a resurgent right wing, grouped since 1966 under a new party, the Partido Nacional (National Party, PN).

Allende's position, similar to his previous campaigns, now focused on Frei's failings, his subservience to "national and foreign capitalism," and his use of "violent repression." The UP's Basic Program declared that the country needed a "people's government" to "put an end to imperialist domination ... and initiate socialist construction." Supporting the UP meant proclaiming oneself "in favor of the urgent replacement of current society" through nationalizations, a new constitution and People's Assembly, investment in education and culture, incorporation of the armed forces into development, suffrage from age eighteen irrespective of literacy, and diversification of Chile's foreign relations. Significantly, the UP promised that change would take place through existing political institutions, while guaranteeing individual and social rights and respecting opponents operating within the law. *La vía chilena al socialismo*—the Chilean way to socialism—would initiate a new form of socialist transition grounded in "democracy, pluralism, and freedom."[16] As a means of giving practical meaning to this vision, Allende announced forty measures underpinning a Unidad Popular government. A reference to Chile's short-lived 1932 Socialist Republic, which had also promulgated forty measures, these included milk programs, house building, free medicine, and the dismantling of Frei's mobile police units involved in recent repression.[17] It was an ambitious to-do list. Despite the early June cold Santiago weather, thousands heard Allende deliver pledges, marching in four separate columns to Avenida Bulnes accompanied by musical bands and a giant mechanical dinosaur to represent Chile's right wing with a model Uncle Sam holding its reins.[18]

Having proven he was campaign fit, Allende resumed an intensive schedule, touring the country with Beatriz accompanying him when she could. On 8 June, for example, they traveled north of Santiago, visiting poblaciónes and industrial sectors and greeting large crowds. Mirroring rallies in Santiago, different columns marched on town squares, with Beatriz and her father accompanying a youth column and provincial party leaders in La Serena. Beatriz then stood next to her father on stage as he announced the UP's forty measures to eighteen thousand supporters.[19] Beatriz was pleased to see evidence of Cuba's influence around the country. Even in desolate areas, consisting of "3 or 4 houses of miners and peasants," private spaces were adorned with the revolution's images. "I have found with surprise that when entering these houses you find a portrait of Fidel or Che cut out from a newspaper and stuck on the walls," she reported; she felt emotionally touched to see Cuba's "sacrifice and teachings ... lighting up places like these."[20] She and her father also had fun campaigning. Visiting poblaciónes, local men flirted with her by calling him "father-in-law." "I die laughing," Beatriz wrote to Luis. She also confessed she was surprised by what she witnessed. "I think everything is going well. ... Chile is changing." Contrary to her internationalist ventures, she now also acknowledged she could have a bigger impact in Chile than abroad. And yet, for someone who had long since doubted the prospects for peaceful revolution, mobilization scared her. "I am screwed ... after seeing the faith and hope so many people have," she confessed. "I don't know what all this means if [hope] comes to nothing.... Something bigger than the campaign has to happen because I have seen people's cravings for governmental power and ... a thousand images pass through my mind.... I don't know if we are prepared for all the possibilities and alternatives that can come ahead."[21]

Ultimately, she was pessimistic about winning and worried what would happen if Allende lost or was blocked from assuming power.[22] Although a sizable sector of the PDC was sympathetic to or at least willing to accept the Left, the government's propensity to use repression against opponents and the Right's resurgence were threatening. From 1965, rumors existed of a military coup to counter the growing strength of left-wing parties, of strikes, and of Christian Democratic reformism.[23] A frustrated army mutiny in October 1969—the so-called Tacnazo—had then rung alarm bells regarding the restlessness of Chile's traditionally constitutional military. And regardless of the Organa and the ELN, the Socialist Party clearly had no real policy toward the military.[24] Elsewhere, right-wing paramilitary violence mounted. In May, a rural governmental engineer had been murdered in Linares province and landowners were blamed, prompting the first combined national strike by rural workers' unions.[25] Reports of contraband Belgian machine guns arriving from Argentina for extreme right-wing groups fueled fears.[26] The Left accused Frei's government of systemic violence, pointing to San Miguel, Puerto Montt, and carabineros beating students "with impunity."[27] As Allende warned, there seemed to be "a clear intention to create a climate of violence in anticipation of the Unidad Popular's victory and as a way to create conditions to oppose it."[28]

In this context, Beatriz and others close to the president were worried about Allende's security.[29] Campaign staff had previously haphazardly guaranteed his safety. In 1964, for example, two campaign staffers, armed with pistols, had taken turns accompanying the candidate and had employed a third to gather intelligence.[30] Yet, by early 1970, Allende's team concluded such arrangements were unsustainable. In April 1970, the Socialist Party and the Organa—increasingly linked to the Chilean elenos—reached a similar conclusion. Because of his links to the president and the ELN, the PS's Central Committee thus chose Eduardo Paredes to reinforce security.[31]

Out of sight, Beatriz worked closely with Eduardo, her ELN background and Cuban training making her indispensable. On a basic level, she had already persuaded her father they should take karate lessons for self-defense (she joked she would become "a dangerous woman").[32] More important, she and Félix Huerta, recently returned from hospital in Havana after being accidentally shot and paralyzed, began recruiting others to form an armed escort. Félix's brother, Enrique, who had recently bought a large U.S.-made taxi, became Allende's driver.[33] And Beatriz also begged Fernando Gómez, back in Chile after leaving the ELN, to help: "I want to ask you a huge personal favor," she told him in late June. "I trust you completely and I fear for my father's life, he walks [around] alone, those that accompany him are party comrades almost his own age, no one looks after him, nor does he accept protection, I am worried, tell me that you will stay and you will be with him, at his side." With Enrique, Fernando therefore formed the beginning of Allende's new security detail, soon to be known as the GAP—the president's Grupo de Amigos Personales (group of personal friends).[34]

However, Allende did not immediately welcome the prototype GAP. As Fernando recalled, his first day was a "disaster." Allende was resistant to having armed guards, demanded he drive, and refused to eat with *pistoleros* in the house, insisting he was not in danger. When Fernando decided establishing an escort would not work and told Beatriz, she, Fernando, and Allende had a tense meeting. According to Gómez, she spoke softly but sternly, threatening her withdrawal from the campaign if Fernando left. And Allende relented.[35] Even so, this episode is revealing for what it tells us about the tensions between Beatriz's militarized perspective of threats and his optimism regarding peaceful democratic change. It is unsurprising that her main contribution to his campaign drew on her ELN experience and was grounded in her belief confrontation lay on the horizon. For all his sympathy toward his daughter and the far Left, Allende was simultaneously uncomfortable. But the formation of the GAP in the context of mounting fears of right-wing violence marked a convergence of two revolutionary groups trained in different worlds: Cuba's guerrilla training camps and Chile's Congress.

In subsequent weeks, the GAP was fortified. By the election, its members had eight pistols and four safe houses. Three other elenos also joined, organizing logistics for campaign tours.[36] That elenos played such a prominent role is partly thanks to Beatriz, who facilitated collaboration. Elenos had previously focused abroad because they, in line with the Cubans, had not believed Chile was suited to immediate armed revolution. They had therefore insisted on defensive preparation for future confrontation, concentrating their energies on Bolivia. But military organization now went beyond the ELN. Indeed, precisely at this moment, members of the BUS and the Organa had embarked on establishing a guerrilla training camp near Chaihuín, in southern Chile, preparing preemptively for what they saw as inevitable conflict. It was a disaster, with one student killed when the military found the camp. It also created a scandal in the country, playing into right-wing threats of a violent revolutionary future should Allende be elected.[37] There is no evidence to suggest he or Beatriz was directly involved, although Beatriz knew some who took part and would serve as an interlocutor between them and her father at various points during the campaign. But the episode underpinned an uneasy relationship—and vulnerability—between the UP's stated democratic ambitions, these military tendencies, whether they would be coopted into Chile's socialist future, and how they could be explained to opponents.

For now, Allende relied on a small group of volunteers for his safety and his daughter to help bridge the divide between the UP and the far Left, including the MIR. Predicting he would win or lose by twenty thousand votes at a meeting Beatriz convened with Félix and other young socialists just before election day, he asked what forces the Left had to defend itself if needed. As Félix remembered, they had "people who had experience, training" but mostly "good intentions and speeches ... very little."[38] Beatriz was among those who feared the worst. On election day, she, Eduardo, and Patricia Espejo, her colleague from Campus Oriente, thus decided there should be loyal militants stationed at the Hospital Salvador, to treat the injured in the event of violence.[39] Hernán Coloma, who had been at Chaihuín, similarly assumed a secret position with other militants on the city's outskirts, in preparation for a potential coup.[40] Preoccupied with the prospect of a violent backlash, the revolutionary Left—Beatriz included—thus missed much of the campaign's celebratory atmosphere. But, in fearing the worst, they were not entirely wrong.

Victory and Fear

Allende's narrow victory on 4 September 1970 was greeted with shock and euphoria. As Beatriz recalled, her father was so overwhelmed he couldn't speak.[41] Having composed himself, he called Alejandro Rojas, Communist leader of the Federación de Estudiantes de la Universidad de Chile (FECH), to ask if he could use the students' building on Santiago's principal avenue to address supporters. It seemed fitting given young peoples' role in pushing for change.[42] Hearing the news on the radio, Hernán and other members of the Organa couldn't resist celebrating. Rather than stay on guard like "imbeciles," he recalled, they joined a group of miners at the last minute, advancing down Providencia.[43]

Beatriz and Patricia also headed downtown.[44] As Gilda Gnecco, Beatriz's former supervisor, remembered, crowds carried marchers along, their feet hardly touching the ground.[45] "It is hard to define what we felt," Beatriz would tell a Cuban journalist. "Thousands and thousands of images, different emotions, came to mind. It was a struggle of years, a dream that we saw coming and that we suddenly could not believe to be true. I remembered the man from the pampa, the man from the saltpeter, copper, and coalmines. Chilean women and children ... Chilean youth, who in recent times had suffered a lot of repression. One had the feeling that all the doors were opening and, at the same time, this sense of responsibility came down on us. It was a feeling between euphoria and anguish: everything together."[46]

In fact, Allende's narrow victory over Alessandri—by less than forty thousand votes—was far from secure. Alessandri refused to concede, and according to Chile's constitution, Congress had the final say where no overall majority existed. Moreover, the congressional vote on 24 October gave the opposition six weeks to mobilize and block the president-elect. As Beatriz remembered, her father anticipated conspiratorial action, warning "comrades ... to be alert and organized."[47] Meeting with young Socialists at Guardia Vieja the day after the election, he warned they had to reinforce security, that there would possibly be "attacks" against him. With Beatriz by his side, Allende predicted that the UP would gain ground in municipal elections in April 1971 while the Right recovered, but he acknowledged that the longer-term future was harder to foresee. "Hold on Catalina, we are going to gallop," he told these young Socialists, employing a colloquial phrase to denote a roller coaster ride on the horizon.[48] That Beatriz's friend and close ELN collaborator Celsa Parrau accompanied Inti Peredo's wife and children to Cuba from Chile for safety is indicative of the threat those closest to her predicted.[49]

Beatriz also traveled to Havana in mid-September on her father's behalf. Allende had asked his mistress, Miria Contreras de Ropert, known as Paya, a key member of his campaign team, to accompany Beatriz. And they got on remarkably well.[50] In Cuba Beatriz confided to a Chilean living there that she had never had any faith in elections but now understood her father had been "right" and was committed to being at his side.[51] Barely two weeks after his election, Beatriz was pivotal in mediating a new Cuban role in Chile. Had she not been involved, Allende's relationship with the island's leaders would probably have ensured the Cuban-Chilean relationship was strengthened anyway. But given Beatriz's role as her father's personal envoy and her close contact with Piñeiro's intelligence team through her work for the ELN and her relationship with Luis, ties were immediate and intimate. Over the course of four nights of meetings, Beatriz briefed Fidel on the situation in Chile and requested his help in reinforcing her father's bodyguard.[52]

For his part, Castro transmitted advice via Beatriz reflecting lessons learned from Cuba's experience and a shift in Cuba's foreign policy since 1968. After years of revolutionary losses in Latin America, the Cubans were opting for pragmatism and consolidation. In contrast to the Cuban revolutionary zeal Beatriz had admired in the 1960s, Castro thus advised Allende to be cautious: to prevent experts and technicians from leaving Chile, avoid acting "too revolutionary" so as not to provoke opponents, sell copper on the dollar market, and maintain good relations with the military.[53] As Juan Carretero, a senior member of Piñeiro's team, remembered, Beatriz became a "bridge of great value" between her father and Cuba's leaders.[54] Returning to Santiago, utilizing her communications

Fidel Castro and Beatriz, Havana, no date. Archivo Fundación Salvador Allende.

training and a new Radio "Zenith" the Cubans provided, she also managed coded communications from Cuba to Chile. To protect Allende, the radio was installed in Paya's home rather than Guardia Vieja, and Beatriz used her ELN code name, Marcela, for security.⁵⁵

On a personal note, Beatriz's relationship with Luis also now took a leap forward. Assuming Luis, as the person responsible for dealing with the country since 1963, would go to Chile, Beatriz married him on 16 September. As Luis remembered, the decision was automatic and mutual: "We reached the conclusion it was the right time." Even more so than her first marriage, it was a simple event, involving signing a marriage certificate.⁵⁶ Whether Beatriz knew Luis was simultaneously in a relationship he had continued during their long-distance affair is unclear. Her love letters suggest otherwise, but given her relaxed attitude toward her father's affairs and friendship with Paya, it may be that she knew and accepted this situation, waiting for the opportunity for them to be together. Either way, given the opportunity to formalize their relationship, Luis did not hesitate in leaving his Cuban girlfriend.⁵⁷

As predicted, Luis also followed Beatriz to Chile, arriving in Santiago shortly after her on 26 September. During Beatriz's stay in Havana, one of her key discussions with Castro had centered on Cuba's ability to train and arm the GAP. Castro had subsequently sent Beatriz and Paya home with a

Carl Gustaf portable antitank recoilless rifle each, which they managed to take into Chile undetected via Madrid.[58] He had also agreed to send three Cubans to Chile representing different branches of Cuba's intelligence and security apparatus—Tropas Especiales (Special Forces), Interior Ministry, and Piñiero's Departmento General de Liberación Nacional (General Department of National Liberation)—to assess the situation. And, as one of these three Cubans, Luis entered the country covertly as part of a delegation of veterinary scientists attending a Pan-American congress. He also managed to smuggle ten additional pistols into the country for the GAP. Beatriz was in Concepción with her father when he arrived, so Luis handed the pistols directly to Paya. He then moved into a safe house for the next month.[59]

Beatriz and Luis were nevertheless soon able to see each other regularly. In addition to meeting in the Cubans' safe house, Carmen Castillo lent them hers so they could spend time alone. With her Radio Zenith, Beatriz was meanwhile able to transmit messages from Havana to the Cubans and help coordinate their movements. The Cubans had to be very careful of being identified by their accents and generally went out only after dark. A group of trusted Chileans, including Paya and Eduardo's wife, Eva, looked after them. They were cooked for and driven around the city, cautiously coordinating meetings with left-wing parties and with Allende's nascent bodyguard.[60]

In the months that followed, in fact, the Cubans became the GAP's "professors."[61] Allende's security had already been strengthened immediately after his victory. Six new recruits had joined from the ELN and Organa. At her instigation, Beatriz had also organized a meeting on 5 September between the president and Miguel Enríquez to ask for his collaboration. Ten miristas had subsequently joined its ranks. A former member of Chile's armed forces, Mario Melo, expelled from military service for left-wing views and linked to the Movimiento de Izquierda Revolucionaria (MIR), was also brought in to help. Not only was this a way for miristas to use the skills honed in military training and urban guerrilla actions, but it was also a way for Allende to incorporate them and neutralize their potential opposition.[62] One of those who joined, Max Marambio, had close links to Havana and became one of the guard's leaders. The GAP also began to draw on foreign (East German and Mexican) and local left-wing parties' intelligence.[63] Preparations were made for more Cuban arms transfers after November 1970. Members of the island's intelligence services and Tropas Especiales—including members of Castro's bodyguard—would arrive in future months to offer training. And the GAP's recruits traveled to Cuba for additional instruction, usually lasting two weeks. Organizationally, from its rudimentary origins, the GAP eventually consisted of four branches: garrison (to protect the president's residences and La Moneda); bodyguard; operations (intelligence); and services (logistics, arms, medical supplies).[64]

All the while, Beatriz presided over the political dynamics of GAP as well as managing relations between her father and the Cubans.[65] And she and her collaborators were astute in predicting some sort of backlash against Allende's victory. True, there is no evidence to suggest plans to assassinate the president-elect existed within the armed forces. But plotting began apace across Chilean society, and Allende faced sporadic attacks (some armed) in subsequent years.[66] In the United States, meanwhile, the Nixon administration initiated a series of covert actions to block Allende's confirmation as president. These operated along two "tracks," which increasingly focused on an "in-house" coup: military intervention to force new elections. When General René Schneider, Chile's constitutionally minded commander in chief of the army, refused to countenance any move against Allende, Nixon's ultrasecret Track II gave the CIA permission to remove him, sending arms and at least $50,000 to help. Yet, in pursuing these desperate strategies, U.S. officials responded to, and worked with, Chileans. There was no shortage of anti-Allende collaborators. Among them, Frei and Augustín Edwards, a right-wing businessman and *El Mercurio*'s owner, appealed directly to U.S. officials, while Track II dealt with retired military officials and right-wing paramilitaries.[67]

Ultimately, Schneider was assassinated in a botched kidnapping operation on 22 October 1970 that was supposed to have triggered a military coup. Although the group responsible was not in direct contact with the CIA by this point, U.S. officials had provided a green light and encouragement. But in doing so, they paradoxically confirmed Allende's inauguration. With the shock of Schneider's assassination reverberating around the country and an agreement between the UP and the PDC on constitutional guarantees secured, Congress confirmed Allende's victory on 24 October by 153 to 42 votes.

Meanwhile, Schneider's assassination had a profound effect on left-wing strategic planning. On one level, it removed Allende's doubts about an armed escort. The next day, he instructed the GAP to be doubled to defend his mandate and Chile's revolutionary process.[68] Wanting as much information as possible about the Schneider case, Allende asked Frei to allow Eduardo Paredes to shadow the director general of investigations, a position the latter assumed after Allende's inauguration.[69] Preoccupied, Fidel also dispatched Juan Carretero to Chile clandestinely with instructions to help ensure Allende assumed office.[70] On another level, Schneider's assassination reinforced the revolutionary Left's ideas about the inevitability of confrontation. As the MIR reasoned, conflict between imperialism, its local allies, and popular forces had "merely been delayed" by Allende's election but would henceforth "be more legitimate and ... take on a more massive dimension."[71] Ricardo Núñez, a member of the PS Central Committee, already inclined toward seeing armed struggle as unavoidable, similarly reflected that Schneider's murder provided corroboration of this fact. The bourgeoisie would not give up their privileges, concluded radical PS members, who therefore had to be ready to defend Chile's revolutionary process. Yet there was little agreement on how to do this. The Communist Party, inclined to working through Chile's political institutions and consolidating the UP's electoral victory, was wary of antagonizing enemies through military preparation.[72] And, in many respects, Allende and many of the people he would choose as advisers and ministers—particularly when it came to foreign policy—also held this position.[73]

On the eve of Allende's inauguration, his closest confidants and the UP coalition were thus divided. While these differences would matter less in the honeymoon period following his assumption of power, they became serious under pressure. For now, Allende, with Beatriz's help vis-à-vis the far Left, and his own long-time contacts in Chile's diplomatic and political world, managed to straddle divisions between factions, incorporating different groups into his administration and using their distinctive strengths to bolster chances of forging a revolutionary path. But long-term unification of forces and advancement along a coherent path to socialism would not be easy.

La Moneda

Following Allende's inauguration, Beatriz left her job to work full time at La Moneda, her commitment to revolutionary change and loyalty to her father surpassing seven years of medical training and a career in public health.[74] Having helped coordinate her father's armed escort and serving as liaison with Cuba, she was now formally named as one of his private secretaries. Although Osvaldo Puccio stayed on as Allende's long-term secretary, with his own staff down the hall, a "private secretariat" was established next to the president's office.[75] This was a gendered and personalized office, occupied by women tied to Beatriz or her father. And characteristically for many contemporary archetypal female roles, it was offstage. But it was also highly influential. Beatriz helped assemble an administration, determined access to the president, and delegated jobs to trusted contacts. "She knew how to command," a friend explained.[76]

Paya officially ran the private secretariat. Although not previously po-

Beatriz and Salvador Allende, Santiago, no date. Archivo Fundación Salvador Allende.

litically active beyond her role during Allende's campaign, a close friend remembered "she radicalized at high speed," because of both her relationship with Allende and her sons' militancy for the MIR. She also had secretarial and management experience and was adept at handling accounts.[77] Paya therefore controlled the president's diary and finances, being responsible for buying the GAP's twenty-five cars with presidential funds, signing off on salaries, and paying expenses. And, as such, she was known as "the GAP's mother."[78] Alongside Beatriz, one of the GAP's members recalled, Paya was also the person Allende trusted most.[79] Beatriz meanwhile dealt with political relations between her father and Chilean left-wing parties (including the MIR), Cuba, and, as we shall see below, Latin American revolutionary movements. As Isabel Jaramillo, a young journalist with links to Cuba and secretarial training, who joined the secretariat in early 1971, explained, Beatriz dealt with "sensitive" cases. It was not a traditional secretarial role; she often arrived late or was away from her desk, but the access she had to her father and the bridge she offered to the revolutionary Left was vitally important as her father sought to walk a fine line between different left-wing sectors.[80] In addition to Isabel, Beatriz asked her Campus Oriente colleague, Patricia Espejo, to join the secretariat. Both were committed revolutionaries, although they relinquished formal militancy for political parties to serve Allende directly.[81] They were also romantically attached to the far Left, with Patricia married to mirista Eugenio Leyton and Isabel soon to be in a relationship with William Whitelaw, a leader in Uruguay's Tupamaros, whom she met when he arrived at La Moneda for a meeting with Beatriz in early 1971. Patricia helped manage the president's diary and his contacts, while Isabel worked for Beatriz on matters relating to Cuba, Latin American revolutionary movements, and analysis of the international and domestic press. However, these roles could change with exigencies of the moment.[82]

All accounts suggest La Moneda was a particularly convivial place to work for Allende's team. As Frida Modak, Allende's press secretary who worked in an office adjacent to Beatriz, remembered, there was a special atmosphere, underpinned by friendships established over years.[83] Although the president ate in a formal dining room, such younger staff as Beatriz, Frida, members of the GAP, and invited friends congregated in a small kitchen down the hall.[84] Allende treated La Moneda staff well. His sense of humor and practical jokes allowed them to deal with the stress of government.[85] As Beatriz would describe, the president was "so generous, so cordial, so apparently calm.... He had this capacity to always see the positive side of things."[86] Every evening around eight o'clock, the president would also invite staff into his office for a whisky to discuss the day's events. And although Beatriz preferred a glass of water, she was always there. As his daughter, she was able to speak frankly, to question and challenge him.[87] Allende's routine was nevertheless demanding. He was a "work machine," Beatriz explained, "he leaves us all behind.... Sometimes they ask him why he works so hard, and he responds that the responsibility [of government] is of such magnitude, he cannot rest a single minute."[88] Beatriz shared this sense of duty: "her commitment was total," friends remembered.[89]

The process of moving into La Moneda and setting up a government was nevertheless tricky. The outgoing Frei administration stripped everything from government offices, desks, telephones, and pens included. Allende's private secretaries therefore equipped them from scratch.[90] More problematic, Beatriz was among those closest to Allende who feared the CIA had installed bugs in La Moneda. The first two days of Allende's presidency were thus spent scanning the building for surveillance devices. And, in this respect, the Cubans were important.[91] As one of the GAP's members remembered, they reviewed the whole building. Cuban systems and technology were not particularly advanced, but microphones were removed on several occasions during Allende's administration. Beatriz and Luis were key to these arrangements. Yet, similar to his initial response to armed protection, Allende was not convinced such measures were needed.

Scanning for microphones therefore took place after he left La Moneda at night.[92]

Beyond liaising with the Cubans and helping to set up the GAP and Allende's secretariat, Beatriz was also instrumental in helping her father assemble other collaborators. Working with Félix Huerta again, she helped coordinate two advisory groups. The first, the Centro de Estudios Nacionales de Opinión Pública (Center for the National Studies of Public Opinion, CENOP), became what Allende called his "intellectual GAP." It was initially proposed by Claudio Jimeno, a sociologist with a doctorate from the United Kingdom who had worked with Eduardo at the Hospital San Borja's Centre for Preventative Medicine. Its goal was to use "modern methods of sociological intelligence"—including opinion polls, surveys, and media analysis—to assist the president. Comprising representatives from the Communist and Socialist Parties' political commissions and Félix, whose bedroom was often where they met, CENOP produced short reports read by Allende every morning. The group's members were disdainful of the president's older collaborators, viewing them as "outdated." CENOP's reports were also read by Carlos Prats, Chile's new constitutionalist commander in chief of the army; the Cubans; the Soviets; Allende's political adviser, Joan Garcés; and his speechwriter, Augusto Olivares.[93]

The second group Beatriz helped assemble was more informal and changeable, comprising young Socialist militants and invited representatives of other left-wing parties, such as the MIR. Aside from Beatriz, this group consisted of Félix and Eduardo, JS leaders like Carlos Lorca, and those, as we shall see below, in charge of the PS's evolving military apparatus, such as Rolando Calderón, Arnoldo Camú, and Félix's former medical school classmate Ricardo Pincheira. This group had been meeting since before the election, but Beatriz now assembled it regularly. As Félix remembered, Allende was "thoughtful ... he listened a lot and he liked to listen to young people" and different perspectives.[94] For young militants with no parliamentary experience or formal political roles, to have such links to the president was striking and cannot be understood without grasping Beatriz's role and personal ties. Beyond formal party structures, it gave them direct access to the president, whom its members hoped to influence, and it gave Allende insight into Chile's complex left-wing scene. Although the president had other advisers—for example, old friends like the diplomat Ramon Huidobro and the Inter-American Development Bank functionary Felipe Herrera, the lawyer Hernán Santa Cruz, or Víctor Pey—and despite his interaction with party and congressional leaders, this group was also a way of incorporating a younger generation of revolutionary leaders into his administration. As Beatriz would later reflect, Allende "always maintained a dialogue with youth organizations, which he gave special importance to.... He saw in young people freshness, generosity, healthy motivations."[95] Meeting in private, intimate spaces, in an informal atmosphere of trust, they also felt they could convey opinions that might not otherwise have been voiced.

Beatriz was always present at such meetings. Although not a named CENOP analyst, she helped devise strategies for gauging public opinion, such as monitoring cinema audiences' responses to newsreels.[96] She did not take notes but, in Félix words, she had an "impressive memory" and could relay three-hour meetings verbatim. If Allende wanted to convene an encounter, it was also Beatriz he asked to organize it. She visited Félix almost daily, arriving late in the evening and throwing stones at his window. She chain-smoked Cuban cigarettes with him, drank a coffee, and debated politics. She liked bouncing ideas off him because they tended to disagree. Despite having been in the ELN, he was generally closer to the PCCh's positions, whereas she was more aligned with the MIR's; Beatriz had a good impression of Miguel Enríquez and he did not, Félix remembered, believing Miguel invented and exaggerated certain things, like the MIR's forces. However, he shared Beatriz's profound loyalty to Allende.[97]

Elsewhere, Beatriz used her position to secure jobs for friends and ensure her father had trustworthy collaborators. Arturo Jirón, her former teacher, was invited to join Allende's medical team and, in 1972, would, somewhat unconventionally for a young surgeon, be appointed minister of health thanks to her recommendation.[98] She also suggested her father appoint her former boss, the pediatric and public health specialist Manuel Ipinza, to the position of vice president of Chile's National Board of Kindergartens.[99] Elsewhere, Beatriz did not completely forget her medical training and vocation for public health initiatives in poor districts. As minister, Jirón recalled she would help him deal with the politics of health care. She would also join him to have lunch with pobladores outside Santiago "to get to know their problems." "That was her way of working," he remembered, "always close to where problems were."[100] Her medical contacts also allowed her to resolve health crises. When a right-wing smear campaign suggested young volunteers working in poblaciónes were contracting sexually transmitted diseases from one another, for example, Beatriz rang up a former course mate to ask him to investigate (he found the allegations to be false).[101]

Revolutionary Solidarity

When it came to international relations, Allende had a diplomatic team that proceeded somewhat cautiously. Chile's new foreign minister, Clodomiro Almeyda, was one of those who supported this position and recalled Allende resisted the far Left's "primitive battle instinct" toward the United States. Chile remained within the Organization of American States and reached out to Argentina's military government to neutralize its threat. Overall, in fact, the UP advocated "healthy realism."[102] This was contrary to Beatriz's inclination, which was far more belligerent. Indeed, against Castro's advice and a general acceptance of the need to operate cautiously in other areas, she is known to have criticized her father for not explicitly and publicly denouncing the United States more. She also favored a punitive approach to private U.S. copper companies—denying them any compensation when nationalized.[103]

Although he resisted Beatriz's influence when it came to the United States and formal diplomacy, Allende nevertheless relied on her as a parallel and unofficial foreign minister when it came to Cuba and revolutionary movements.[104] As Beatriz had written to Luis months before Allende's election, along with establishing relations with Vietnam and North Korea, reestablishing diplomatic relations with Havana was one of the "first measures" he wanted to adopt as president. And, as a conduit of information for her father, she relayed his wishes that the Cubans prepare for this.[105] The topic had also come up when Beatriz visited Cuba in mid-September. Then, via Beatriz, Castro had reportedly advised Allende to wait—"six months, a year, or two"—so as not to antagonize enemies.[106] But, for the president—as for his daughter, who had been an activist for Cuba since her teenage years—relations with Cuba were a long-standing unconditional commitment. Allende sealed the deal privately at his inaugural reception, taking advantage of the Cuban delegation's presence in Santiago. A week later, on 12 November, he announced the resumption of relations, ending Cuba's diplomatic isolation in Latin America, with the exception of Mexico, since 1964.[107]

For Beatriz, the reestablishment of relations was both a private and a political cause for celebration. Luis was immediately named chargé d'affaires, and although, as someone who rose up through the police force and intelligence, he had no diplomatic training, he embraced the position. It is possible Allende, requested by Beatriz, had asked that his new son-in-law and longtime Cuban contact take up this post. But it was also a logical decision, given Luis's years of service as Piñeiro's Chile specialist.[108] In the months that followed, eight or nine intelligence officers, including Juan Carretero, would handle relations with Chile's political parties, and Luis would join this team, focusing primarily on relations with the president. Mario García Incháustegui, a friend of Castro's and former Cuban diplomat at the UN, would take over as ambassador, and Irina Trapote,

Beatriz's friend from the Federación de Mujeres Cubanas, assumed work for the embassy's new cultural attaché, Lisandro Otero.[109] In the space of a year, Beatriz's life—as with others on the far left—therefore dramatically changed. In December 1970, Allende would declare an amnesty for thirty miristas, as well as thirteen other far Left militants.[110] And having been depressed by the ELN's fortunes, her longing for Luis, and her distance from Cuba at the end of 1969, Beatriz now found herself in a position of power, working directly with the Cubans she had so often dreamed of seeing. Through her relationship with Luis, Cuba's revolutionary regime also had a direct channel to the presidency.

The resumption of Chilean-Cuban diplomatic relations recalibrated the inter-American Cold War power balance. Alongside nationalist military regimes in Peru and Bolivia that had come to power over the previous two years, anti-imperialist forces appeared to be gaining ground. To be sure, these were relative gains. Right-wing dictatorships still ruled Brazil, Paraguay, and Argentina. But in Washington, Nixon and Kissinger were worried enough to refocus attention on the region, reaching out to military allies to bolster counterinsurgency operations and isolate Chile.[111] For those targeted by such forces, Chile offered a pressure valve and escape— as democratic countries throughout the region had before—but more so now that a left-wing government was in charge. Already, hundreds of Brazilians, among them intellectuals and guerrilla groups, had arrived in Chile during the Frei administration fleeing repressive practices. By 1973, 1,200 Brazilian exiles were living in Chile, including 70 Brazilians released in a hostage exchange. Other groups, including far Left revolutionaries, began seeking refuge in Chile. Within the first few weeks of the Allende presidency, Chile offered asylum to 17 Bolivians, 9 Uruguayans, and 12 Mexicans.[112]

The day of his inauguration, thanks to Beatriz's prior intervention and involvement, Allende had also welcomed eight Teoponte survivors into Chile, including the ELN's leader, Chato Peredo, in a negotiated settlement with Bolivia's nationalist president, Juan José Torres.[113] Beatriz and other Chilean elenos had subsequently met Chato in early 1971 and decoupled themselves from the ELN's command structure. They did not feel Teoponte's failings had been sufficiently addressed and now saw Chile, not Bolivia, as the place where imperialism could be best challenged.[114] This focus on Chile was "understandable," Chato recalled; after a meeting with Allende organized by Beatriz, he also agreed that ELN operations in Chile would be strictly clandestine so as not to compromise the new Chilean president's democratic mandate. Beatriz's involvement with the group also diminished significantly; she did not want to undermine her father, and Chato supposed anything relayed to her would get back to the president.[115] Even so, she did not give up the association entirely. She was friends with the German-Bolivian member of the ELN, Monika Ertl (or "Imilla"), for example, who spent time in Chile in early 1971 before leaving for Hamburg. There, on 1 April, Monika walked into Bolivian colonel Roberto Quintanilla Pereira's office and killed him. Conceived as "popular justice," given Quintanilla's order to amputate Che Guevara's hands and his role in Inti's murder, the ELN hailed the operation as a victory.[116]

When it came to Latin American revolutionary exiles arriving in Chile, Beatriz meanwhile used her father's position—and her own within his team—to offer solidarity. As a member of the Uruguayan revolutionary movement, the Movimiento de Liberación Nacional–Tupamaro (MLN-T), who arrived legally and openly in Santiago in December 1970 remembered, Beatriz and a group of her associates found them places to stay with sympathetic PS militants, as well as arranging food, clothes, medicines, and documentation.[117] It was the same work she and other Chilean elenos had undertaken for Bolivia, and it was also a way of returning the Tupamaros's internationalist solidarity for the ELN.[118] The relationship between La Moneda and the Tupamaros in Chile was "wonderful," Patricia remembered.[119] Beatriz coordinated this support, providing the "political link from La Moneda," working predominantly with other women like Patricia and Isabel in the Secretariat; her ELN comrade, Celsa Parrau; and from December 1970 onward, her childhood friend, Carmen Castillo, whom she hired to work with them on matters relating to Latin American revolutionary groups.[120] Money for this work came from "everywhere," Celsa remembered: from the Cubans, from La Moneda, from individuals involved. Luckily, the Tupamaros did not ask for much; they "lived humbly."[121]

In return for the solidarity they received, the Tupamaros in Chile—numbering around twenty by the end of 1970, but set to rise steeply over the next two years—offered to support the UP. Their collaboration with Allende's government was complicated by the president's request, as with the ELN, to avoid open involvement in domestic politics—and association with the MIR in particular—so as not to provoke criticism of foreign intervention. In early 1971, the leadership of the MLN-T thus temporarily suspended nine militants in Chile who wanted to support the new government (it seemed "absurd" not to cooperate with Chile's revolutionary process, one of them explained).[122] Months later, these same Tupamaros were asked to help the president's security team by sharing their expertise. Responding to Enrique Huerta's request, for example, three went to work in a garage set up by the GAP in the Independencia district of Santiago which prepared cars, equipping them with bigger tires, radio systems, and hidden trunks, allowing them to carry arms. Although Enrique was their contact, Beatriz was aware of, if not overseeing, arrangements and would attend meetings regularly.[123] As a result of her relationship with William Whitelaw, one of these nine MLN-T militants, Isabel also helped coordinate security relations from the Private Secretariat.[124]

The close relationships between the Tupamaros and Allende also meant they worked with Chile's president when the British government asked him to help negotiate the release of Britain's ambassador in Montevideo, Geoffrey Jackson. Having kidnapped Jackson in January 1971, the Tupamaros wanted a ransom. Over more than a month, in highly secret meetings managed by the president's private secretaries, Allende reportedly and privately offered the Tupamaros $20,000 to release him. When this was refused, he sent an emissary to Montevideo to ask them for direct talks with the British and assigned Carmen—hired by Beatriz—to facilitate secret meetings between British diplomats and Tupamaro leaders.[125] Unsurprisingly, given what we know about existing links, with Beatriz as the Uruguayan revolutionaries' primary interlocutor in La Moneda, the British were suspicious of Allende's position. He "wants the best of both worlds," the British ambassador reported, noting "suspicious aspects" of his dealings with the presidency. "The contact I saw in the dark room at the President's house did not talk with a Uruguayan accent. It is possible that the whole thing was a put-up job; that the contacts are extremely close and that Allende really plays it as the Tupamaros wish," he surmised. "He may think that if we and the Tupamaros can reach agreement so much the better for him; but that if we cannot, both sides will, with luck, consider that he has done the best for them."[126]

Ultimately, Allende played his hand well, and although Jackson was released via another channel in Montevideo, the Foreign Office was grateful.[127] As the ambassador surmised, the president's approach to Latin American revolutionary movements helped compensate for an otherwise relatively conservative foreign policy agenda when it came to far Left critics. And Beatriz was grateful of the opportunity to put her internationalist solidarity into action. But it would be a mistake to regard Allende's actions as merely cynical calculations given his prior support for guerrilla insurgencies abroad, not to mention his co-option of the MIR and elenos into his inner circle. As Beatriz would explain, "He showed practical solidarity toward a great number of Latin America liberation movements,... even with compañeros who chose certain roads in Chile ... [that he] did not agree with. He always had a gesture of solidarity.... He observed critically, but at the same time taking some lessons from what was, for example, the Tupamaro movement's struggle."[128]

The refuge that Allende's Chile offered to revolutionaries was important in establishing the country as a fulcrum for revolution in the region, even if it espoused an alternative model for socialist transformation. As if to confirm its status at the forefront of revolutionary change, as well as a seemingly new chapter in Latin America's revolutionary struggle, Régis Debray, author of *Revolution in the Revolution?* and a prominent intellectual collaborator with Cuba and Che Guevara, arrived in Chile in early 1971. In Santiago, Beatriz asked Carmen to look after him.[129] Beatriz, Luis, Juan Carretero and Max Marambio also accompanied him on a day trip to Valparaíso, where they stood smiling for an official commemorative tourist portrait. And yet, as with other aspects of Chile's democratic revolutionary process, the warm welcome someone who had so prominently espoused violent revolutionary change received in Chile was awkward. Sitting down with Allende, Debray asked how exactly the president defined "revolution." To him, he challenged, it was about "replacing power of one class with another. Revolution is destruction of the bourgeois state's apparatus and its replacement by another, and none of that has happened here." Was it possible to have a "revolution without arms," Debray demanded. Allende's response was yes. He underlined the specificity of Chile's circumstances, its long history of left-wing organization and party structures, and opportunities the constitution offered to "open the way" to change. He also stressed the number of transformations his government had already instituted. Ultimately, he believed the UP's legalism would protect his government (even when it came to U.S. intervention, Allende stated his *electoral* triumph had tied Washington's hands), and he advocated a large-scale consciousness-raising program to boost support for revolutionary changes. But he admitted the path ahead would be difficult, that the government had already faced serious provocations—including Schneider's assassination—and reactionary conspiracies. The future depended on whether his opponents would opt for direct confrontation, and he accepted that the Left had to be vigilant and prepared, if necessary, to oppose reactionary violence with revolutionary violence (he did not specify how). Pushed on differences between left-wing sectors, Allende also acknowledged only tactics separated them: "The end goal is the same," he insisted.[130] To a large extent, this was true. His solidarity with Latin American revolutionary movements, with Cuba, and with Chilean far Left groups showed he did not reject them but sought to integrate and ally with them in pursuit of a common objective. The GAP and the president's advisory groups also show he was already exploring defensive military options for protecting his presidency. Indeed, after six months, his administration—uniting to forge a common path ahead, drawing on different strengths from Chile's kaleidoscopic Left, and resisting opposition attacks—still looked relatively promising.

Family Life

If Allende's first six months in government was a honeymoon period, it was also one for Beatriz and Luis. With his position in Chile public, but with neither yet earning a formal salary, Luis had moved into Guardia Vieja. But they soon found a small house to rent on Calle Martín Alonso Pinzón. It was somewhere they could finally build a life, and Allende, who had always given them his blessing, bought them a washing machine and television.[131] By coincidence, their new house was also ten blocks from the new presidential residence, Tomás Moro, so when Allende moved in February 1971, they were able to visit easily.[132] Beatriz and Luis meanwhile bought two dogs—a sheep dog and a collie—from the same family that bred the dogs Beatriz had grown up with.[133] Testimony to their sympathy for armed revolution and to the revolutionary Left's romanticized obsession with weapons, she and Luis named the dogs after rifles used in guerrilla combat: "FAL" and "AK." The couple's social life also revolved around politics. Colleagues came to their house to eat, or they were invited to other people's houses. With work absorbing their time, reading books and going to the cinema or plays was rare, although Beatriz's love of folkloric music continued. Generally, though, they arrived home late from work and, exhausted, went straight to bed.[134] In this respect, they were not alone. Unidad Popular supporters expended enormous energy for their government. As Carmen remembered, days "prolonged for a long time after sunset."[135] Left-wing health care professionals volunteered to serve on medical trains touring Chile.[136] Volunteers spent holidays working on infrastructure projects.[137] Women ran political campaigns to explain government programs, offering "popular education" in mothers' centers.[138] Militants did not feel they could waste time socializing for the sake of socializing; social lives were political.[139]

Meanwhile, the Allendes' family circumstances were as complicated as ever. Although Beatriz was multitasking for her father, Isabel and Carmen Paz were conspicuously absent from Allende's inner circle. Isabel worked at the National Library, and as had been the case in Frei's administration, Hortensia—as First Lady—was in charge of running the Coordina-

Beatriz and Luis, Havana, 1972. Biblioteca Virtual Salvador Allende Gossens.

dora de Centros de Madres (Coordinator of Mothers' Centres). But with an office on the other side of La Moneda, she was rarely seen in the president's wing.[140] Indeed, neither Beatriz's sisters nor her mother were similarly enmeshed in the fabric of the presidency. And, for her part, Beatriz was increasingly distant from them. Her relationship with her mother, in particular, was dreadful. Beatriz despaired of Hortensia's tastes and concerns—her precious ivory collection, for example.[141] Her mother had also initially been disapproving of Beatriz's relationship with Luis when he moved to Santiago. As Luis remembered, things were tense, and though nothing was ever said openly, he understood Beatriz's mother worried about the effect her relationship with a Cuban could have on Allende's standing.[142] That Beatriz worked closely with Paya cannot have helped. But Beatriz was also openly contemptuous of her mother. When, on occasion, Allende would invite his presidential staffers for dinner at Tomás Moro after work, Hortensia sometimes joined them. When Hortensia gave her political opinions, these nevertheless caused offense. Her views, generally more in line with those of Christian Democrats, were "a burden" for Allende, Patricia remembered, but Beatriz considered them "worse" and would leave the room.[143]

While her sisters kept a distance, Beatriz's relationship with Paya blossomed.[144] Twenty years younger than her father and therefore closer in age to Beatriz, the two embraced their joint role in looking after the president, in handling the day-to-day running of La Moneda, and in sympathy for the MIR. Moreover, Allende's happiness with Paya was important to Beatriz, standing in stark contrast to the increasingly bitter and frequent arguments he had with his wife.[145]

To escape Hortensia, who tended to go to Cerro Castillo, the presidential residence in Viña del Mar, accompanied by her two other daughters and their children, Allende—accompanied by Beatriz and Luis—spent virtually every weekend at Paya's country house.[146] Just outside Santiago, at the foothills of the Andes, "El Cañaveral," as it was known, was a tranquil, spacious house with a pool and enough room to host intimate friends. Leaving late on Friday after work, Allende, Paya, Beatriz, and Luis—and invited guests—would not return to the city until Sunday evening. Salvador and Paya had separate bedrooms, and they were careful not to show any physical affection in front of Beatriz but were obviously intimate. Paya always made sure she had Beatriz's favorite foods (sea urchins, for example), and she enjoyed cooking for her guests, of which there were many: Allende's private secretaries and their partners, his press secretary, Augusto Olivares, his young Socialist advisers, Cuban embassy personnel, doctors, and members of the GAP. And those who spent weekends at Cañaveral recalled it as idyllic. It was a safe space where the president could relax among trusted confidants, where he could swim, play chess, enjoy food and wine, and watch cowboy films, his favorite entertainment.[147]

Interestingly, Chile's other left-wing political parties were rarely invited to El Cañaveral. Luis Corvalán, secretary-general of the Communist Party, worried about being excluded: "In El Cañaveral, many things are decided and the Communists do not have anyone there," he complained privately.[148] The Socialist Party's secretary-general from January 1971, Carlos Altamirano, visited often but was not invited when his relationship with Allende soured later on. Friends in government who had known the Allendes for decades—particularly those who knew Hortensia—either were not invited or chose to stay away, declining complicity in Salvador's relationship with Paya.[149] The situation was thus a case where personal and intimate relations affected national politics and foreign relations. Like CENOP meetings in Félix's bedroom, Cañaveral also tells us something about Allende's chosen inner circle. While he had close advisers at various different levels of government and the UP functioned as a collective of political parties, his administration is impossible to understand purely by examining the ministers he appointed or institutional party histories. Groups on the margins of formal government were just as, if not more, significant. Certainly, it was at Cañaveral that Allende had the opportunity to talk through the previous week and the challenges that lay ahead with his closest confidants.

By mid-1971, however, the honeymoon period he had enjoyed was coming to an end. The UP's parties had done better than hoped in the country's April municipal elections, securing 49.7 percent of the vote, despite covert U.S. funding for opponents. As Beatriz later conceded, there had been "great nervousness" about the government's "first exam."[150] In July, Congress also voted unanimously for the nationalization of copper, the flagship policy of Allende's political career and the signature achievement of his administration. When her father announced compensation would be subtracted from "excess profits" companies had reaped—later determined more than the compensation itself—Beatriz congratulated her father, gifting him a painting by Cuban artist René Portocarrero that he had admired in her house.[151] The UP was also able to count on an enthusiastic following among grassroots supporters who felt their quality of life had improved thanks to rising wages, increased public spending, and state-led programs in education and public health. The UP built ninety thousand houses in 1971, almost double the number built in 1969 and four times 1970's figure.[152] As Beatriz reflected in mid-1971, Chileans supported the government because "they know there is no repression, that there is a profound agrarian reform, that natural resources are being transferred into state hands. They even know about the most simple and quotidian facts, so vital for Chilean families such as ... [receiving] half a liter of milk daily."[153]

Yet, by mid-1971, challenges loomed, exacerbated by intra-Left disagreements over the pace and priority of socialist transformation. At a basic level, divisions obstructed government projects. Assigning a representative from every coalition party to run such projects collectively meant "not one head, but many," a state employee remembered.[154] While Allende called workers to launch a "battle for production" in May 1971, championed by the Communist Party, the more radical wing of the UP argued that this campaign diverted attention from seizing control of the means of production. As with Frei's administration, rising expectations also put pressure on the government. In the second half of 1971, the government would confront the first of many strikes in state-owned enterprises by workers demanding more money.[155] Elsewhere, land seizures increased. In Santiago, pobladores constructed new communities, the most prominent being Nuevo La Habana, established just after Allende's inauguration in November 1970, with the MIR's active involvement.[156] The UP's parties were generally sympathetic, having supported similar moves for over a decade, but as Allende explained, his government now wanted to avoid "anarchic" solutions to housing problems.[157] Freely admitting she had helped twelve tomas in six years of Frei's administration, Laura Allende now told *Eva*, the high-society woman's magazine, that rural land seizures were "understandable" but "not justifiable because they affect production." She called on Chileans to "have confidence the Government can resolve their problems."[158]

Although the UP accelerated land reform, taking over almost as many farms in eight months as the PDC had done in six years, occupations nevertheless continued, and the demand for faster revolutionary change grew.[159] While the MIR and left-wing sectors of the PS supported such moves, the government was increasingly in the uncomfortable position of having to assert control and manage revolutionary impulses. In May 1971, for example, the government used police for the first time to deal with an illegal occupation. At the end of May, in his first message to Congress, Allende then outlined his ideas on the construction of socialism *without* destroying the bourgeois state, angering those on the far left who insisted that the two were incompatible.[160] Beatriz did not hide her displeasure in private, berating her father when she disagreed with him but ultimately remaining loyal. And although he listened, he did not necessarily follow her advice.[161] Indeed, divisions on the left, between the government and grassroots supporters as well as between parties, caused growing problems. While the president asked his daughter to assemble advisory groups of different viewpoints, resolving these differences was more difficult.

At a strategic level, they also affected how the Left dealt with mounting opposition. The Communist Party's leaders, like Allende, favored tactical alliances, shying away from any use or talk of armed struggle, fearing provocation and believing state institutions could bring about change. Socialists, predicting they would need to resist counterrevolutionary violence at some stage—and that it was necessary to prepare militarily—came together at the party's congress in La Serena in January 1971. In this respect, the fusion of the ELN, the Organa, and Juventud Socialista militants, along with their combined election to more than half of the Central Committee's seats, was important. Carlos Altamirano—sympathetic to this line of thinking—was elected secretary-general. Recognizing that the Unidad Popular was in government but did not yet have power to embark on a transition toward socialism or the ability to defend the government, the PS created a new defensive organization superseding the Organa, known as the "Frente Interno," consisting of a military apparatus and intelligence structure. The GAP would become part of this organization. And Rolando Calderón would be decisive in establishing it. This went beyond Beatriz's responsibility as her father's private secretary and initial coordinator of the GAP, but it was significant that at least two of those in charge of the Internal Front's organizations were longtime friends: Ariel Ulloa, a former member of the Sierra Maestra BUS nucleus from Concepción, would be in charge of the so-called Organization within the Internal Front, and her close ELN collaborator Arnoldo Camú would head its military apparatus. Beatriz also knew those heading the Frente Interno, Exequiel Ponce and Ricardo Pincheira, who was now in charge of its intelligence unit, from the ELN (she had encouraged Luis to get to know the latter when he visited Cuba in May 1970).[162] From early 1971 onward, this new structure began preparing for a potential coup.[163] And although Allende had remained silent about the Internal Front at La Serena, Beatriz—fully supportive and connected with the party's new structures—was key to helping him convene regularly with its leaders, whom he, at least in part, increasingly depended on for intelligence and physical protection.[164]

Even so, the question of defense was—and would remain—difficult. Chile's Cold War struggles in the early 1970s differed from the majority of those in Latin America. It pitted a left-wing government already in power against those trying to turn back a state-led revolutionary project rather than left-wing insurgents against a U.S.-backed regime. Unlike the cases of Cuba and Nicaragua after 1959 and 1979, respectively, the UP did not have its own military force capable of withstanding attacks from opponents or sufficient trust in the state's preexisting intelligence and security apparatus. The combination of Cuban arms and training, the PS's Internal Front, the MIR's experience in urban guerrilla operations and grassroots mobilization, and the Communist Party's own highly secret, defensive military apparatus did not provide the basis of a coherent defensive strategy. To the contrary, even at their peak, these uncoordinated defensive measures at a party or presidential level were no match for the combined weight of Chile's professional armed forces backed by a united civilian opposition and the U.S. government. As Debray succinctly summarized in early 1971, Chile faced an "unstable equilibrium," but "power came from the barrel of a gun, and the popular government does not have its own armed apparatus."[165]

Meanwhile, the UP's commitment to peaceful democratic change meant opponents remained resilient and powerful. If anything, the shock of Allende's victory and the UP's success in municipal elections led to a right-wing resurgence and reassertion of power by Chile's old establishment. Now, however, a sector of the traditional Right, aided by powerful sponsors abroad, readjusted its tactics and increasingly embraced violence, sabotage, and destabilization. The PDC's position also moved decisively against the UP in early June 1971 after Edmundo Pérez Zujovic, Frei's former minister of the interior, was assassinated by the Vanguardia Organizada del Pueblo (Organized Vanguard of the People, VOP), a small extremist left-wing organization formed in 1968–69 by individuals who had been expelled as "provocateurs" from the Juventudes Comunistas de Chile (Communist Youth, JJCC) and the MIR.[166] Targeted for his responsibility for the Puerto Montt massacre, Zujovic's murder was the kind of disaster Allende had been desperate to avoid. In early 1971, in fact, following armed raids and robberies, he and his closest associates—Beatriz included—had asked Tupamaros based in Chile to persuade VOP's members to lay down arms, but to no avail. Allende's team saw the VOP as an "extremely serious problem," one of those close to negotiators remembered, but the VOP's leaders were "fanatical and intransigent" (many suspected but never proved CIA collusion).[167] That Eduardo Paredes led police operations against the VOP's leaders, resulting in three of them and three policemen being killed, did not lessen charges.[168]

The episode exacerbated fears the UP was merely a cover for imminent violent revolution and blocked incipient negotiation between the UP and left-leaning sectors of the PDC. It also tipped the correlation of forces in Chile toward the government's opponents. Immediately after Zujovic's murder, the UP narrowly lost to Christian Democrats in ideologically charged elections for the position of rector of the University of Chile and a congressional seat in Valparaíso. In both cases, the right-wing PN backed the PDC candidate, uniting opposition to Allende in a pattern that would characterize Chile's political balance henceforth.[169] While two-thirds of Chile's electorate had voted for far-reaching change in 1970 by backing Tomic or Allende, the scales now tilted away from the UP as the PDC moved right. More ominously, Socialist Party sources reported that representatives of the PDC, PN, and armed forces began meeting up with each other after Zujovic's death.[170] As Beatriz told a journalist in mid-1971, "There is permanent political opposition that deforms facts and is fundamentally expressed through newspapers.... [Opponents] also try to obstruct all government measures. They carry out sabotage against production. In industry [they initiate] inflation.... Landowners ... kill cattle or send it to Argentina. They hinder all government plans.... Sometimes, [critics] reproach us with issues that in six months cannot be changed, that are part of the inheritance we received from the capitalist system. ... A huge lack of housing and a whole series of problems that cannot be solved in the time that the Unidad Popular has been in power."[171]

When she gave this interview, Beatriz was in Cuba ostensibly delivering a copy of Salvador Allende's first message to Congress. But, with Luis accompanying her, they were able to take a few days off to visit Varadero. Beatriz had also arranged for Patricia, who traveled with them, to stay on to receive defensive military training. It was "hard," Patricia recalled; she wore army fatigues and learned how to use weapons. In retrospect, knowing how ineffective such training would be, she remembered it was also "absurd ... like a dream." And knowing Allende would disapprove, Patricia simply said she was going on holiday.[172] As well as being revealing for what Beatriz (and Patricia) kept from Allende, this training is indicative of the Cubans' willingness to help Beatriz in security matters without consulting him. And yet, for the most part, the Cubans' role in Chile during the UP was requested, welcomed and sanctioned by the president, who used Beatriz as his interlocutor.[173]

Now, in Cuba, as her father's confidant, Beatriz also had the opportunity to talk with Fidel Castro about the UP's performance. By mid-1971, the Cuban leader regarded Beatriz as a trusted and personal acquaintance. Although this was partly because she was Allende's daughter, those who witnessed the relationship firsthand testified that Castro came to admire Beatriz as a revolutionary in her own right. When she was in Varadero with Luis, Castro stopped by to visit her and took her fishing. On one of at least four trips to Cuba during her father's presidency, he also taught her to fire a bazooka. And he would listen carefully to her assessment of Chile's situation. The prognosis she delivered by mid-1971 came as little surprise. As Luis remembered, Beatriz mostly focused on the UP's growing challenges.[174]

8 : : : The Battle for Chile

The battle for Chile intensified from mid-1971, playing out across society. As the government strove to implement its program, it encountered growing resistance from opponents and criticism from frustrated supporters. The lack of food supplies caused friction, while university campuses rocked with political clashes.[1] Characteristic of the crisis unfolding was a growing disinterest in negotiation, if not refusal to countenance it. When the Unidad Popular (UP) candidate for the University of Chile's rector in early 1972 stood for "coexistence," for example, he lost, at least in part because the Movimiento de Izquierda Revolucionaria (MIR) fielded its own nominee, campaigning against "conciliation."[2] True, Allende and the government—impelled by the Communists within it—continued to reach out to the Christian Democrats (PDC). But given a lack of compromise on core aspects of each other's programs, exacerbated by the left wing and the right wing of the UP and the PDC, respectively, efforts failed. As in other parts of Latin America, the perception actors were involved in an urgent zero-sum game proved pervasive.[3] Language employed in Chile certainly constructed politics in confrontational terms, alienating those the UP needed to persuade to join its program for radical change.[4] As Francisca Espinosa Muñoz noted, "Words such as 'conflict,' 'struggle,' 'resistance'" gave the impression of a "permanent 'battle field.'"[5] In this respect, governmental campaigns—the "battles" for production, copper, and hake—and Allende's message to Congress in May 1972 referring to "two worlds ... in confrontation, two concepts of social order and human existence," clashed with the idea of a peaceful road to socialism.[6] Having remained robust, Chile's democratic political system founded on decades of consensus building and institutional legitimacy now entered into definitive crisis.[7]

Of course, in the struggle to determine Chile's future, the Left faced a belligerent opposition. Chile's professional middle classes, which the UP needed to win over to secure majority support for socialist revolutionary change, turned against the government at the end of 1971.[8] Fidel Castro's twenty-five-day visit in November–December 1971 also provided the context for a decisive new phase of oppositional mobilization. On 1 December, two days before he was supposed to leave Chile, female opponents of the UP took part in the first so-called March of the Empty Pots. Banging pans, women protested food scarcity before it was a significant problem.[9] Women's charges that extreme left-wing groups physically attacked them amplified their rebuke. Ignoring the participation of the right-wing paramilitary group, Patria y Libertad, in the women's march, the PDC launched impeachment proceedings against Minister of the Interior José Tohá for failing to guarantee citizens' security. Allende was forced to call a state of emergency.[10]

The women's explicit suggestion they faced a *foreign* and un-Chilean threat resonated particularly loudly in the context of Castro's visit. "We don't want foreigners/in our offices . . . we don't want Marxism," a poem written by one of the marchers stated.[11] Although branded as an apolitical cross-class protest in defense of Chile and the family, opposition parties also backed the march as an answer to Fidel's presence in the country.[12] And although Beatriz stood offstage, avoiding direct attacks, the relationships she mediated between her father, Cuba, and Latin American revolutionary movements, as well as her efforts to escape the confines of domestic life and motherhood, were among the opposition's main targets.

Gender and Revolution

Women's mobilization against Allende was significant. In the escalating battle for Chile, gender—specifically, ideas of what it meant to be a woman or a man—was fiercely contested. More than the left, Allende's opponents zoomed in effectively on what they understood to be "the nexus between gender change and broader socioeconomic change." Intermingled with the fear the UP would upend traditional hierarchies, opponents warned of a systematic—even violent—left-wing threat to families and women's roles within them.[13] One male commentator for the Chilean magazine *Paula*, for example, depicted the burgeoning women's liberation movement abroad as bringing foreign insurgency into Chilean's most intimate spaces: "we, the men," he wrote, "risk waking up one fine morning to find an activist in our office, a Tupamara in the kitchen, a White Panther in the marriage bed; someone who will make us pay dearly for what they call 'millennia of patriarchal domination.'"[14] Indeed, the idea of an armed woman—the "guerrilla-woman" Beatriz herself had aspired to be—was an anathema to the Right. It was the worst possible example of power being seized, subverting ideas of femininity and entrenched ideas regarding men's monopoly on the right to bear arms.[15]

In truth, however, Chilean women's participation in armed preparation took place only sporadically and exceptionally in the early 1970s. As Beatriz's own experience testifies, even in exceptional circumstances, the

Left's own embedded conservatism determined the roles women played within revolutionary circles. There is evidence male party members mocked left-wing women who formed defensive militias.[16] Indeed, only after 1973 would women take a more consistent part in left-wing military activities.[17] But the idea of armed revolutionary women, bolstered by images of female Cuban militias, was still deemed threatening. Taking away any sense of empowerment from Chilean women, a male *Paula* reader wrote to editors about his fears that "external agents" had created "confusion regarding the duties at society's core ... [in its] families."[18]

Indeed, in fighting against radical change in Chile, Allende's opponents, like the Right elsewhere in Latin America's Cold War, increasingly equated fighting Marxism-Leninism and "foreign" revolutionary influences with an urgent reassertion of traditional gendered norms.[19] Certainly, the significant mobilization of anti-Allende women from late 1971 onward was not about women demanding political representation and power. Rather, female opponents of the government argued they were getting involved to put pressure on men — particularly, men in the armed forces — to fulfill the masculine role of defending the country so women could return to the home, look after their children, and provide meals.[20]

Beatriz was one of many women resisting such views of womanhood. Through her request for armed training, her security and defense work in government, and her role within the inner circle of presidential power, she consistently challenged gendered ideas regarding power and residual societal attitudes about what being a woman meant. When she gave birth to her first child on 27 September 1971, she embraced motherhood as complementary rather than contradictory to her work and politics. As friends remembered, she had always wanted to have children before she was thirty, so was "very happy" when her daughter was born. For her family, also, this was a moment of celebration amid mounting political tension. Luis and her father had gone shopping enthusiastically for the baby in the weeks before her birth. And Beatriz's hospital room had filled with flowers and visitors.[21]

But, for Beatriz, revolution took priority. And while women's magazines counseled expectant mothers to rest and pamper themselves, Beatriz refused to let motherhood slow her down.[22] She was at her desk when her first contractions started and would take only two weeks off after her daughter's birth.[23] In this regard, like her mother and countless other Chileans of her social milieu, she was able to rely on domestic workers: one, who did the cooking and cleaning, and another, Carlota or "Loti," who looked after Maya.[24] The name she gave her daughter was meanwhile unmistakably a homage to her revolutionary ideals: Maya, the code name for

Beatriz and Maya, no date. Archivo Fundación Salvador Allende.

Rita Valdivia, a member of the ELN who had died in Bolivia in 1969, and Alejandra, after Fidel Castro's middle name, Alejandro.

In juggling motherhood, work, and politics, Beatriz was not alone. Many of her colleagues and militants were also mothers, combining parenthood with revolutionary commitments. This admittedly involved sacrifices. Patricia would later reflect how little she saw her children while working for Allende.[25] The UP years were "madness," Edith Benado, Beatriz's university friend, similarly remembered, involving juggling young children, work, and political activism; "we gave everything we had."[26]

Beatriz's views on gender were also complex. There is no evidence to suggest she considered herself a feminist or fought explicitly for women's equality. Like many on the left who believed feminism was a distraction, she prioritized *the* socialist revolution over the fight for women's equality.[27] As a prominent woman in the UP told *Eva*, "happily" the women's liberation struggle had not reached Chile; "women got what they wanted without the need to fight ... by right"—presumably through gaining the vote and electing Allende, who would eradicate discrimination through socialism.[28] There were certainly many aspects of the UP's Basic Program underlining the Left's commitment to improving women's position in Chile. Testimony to growing pressures for improved women's rights, in fact, *all* 1970 campaigns had promised equal pay and legal rights for married women. But the UP had also vowed to introduce divorce and protect illegitimate children's rights.[29] In government, the Left raised the number of university scholarships for women from poorer backgrounds, extended maternity leave rights from four to six weeks, gave widows access to workers' pensions, and established kindergartens and communal kitchens for working mothers.[30] Women's participation in politics also rocketed.[31] And in March 1971, Allende had proposed creating a Family Ministry, designating Carmen Gloria Aguayo to run it (his second female minister if appointed). As Aguayo explained, the ministry would help women into the workforce and promote the rethinking of family roles, breaking "the *machista* concept" that women were responsible for domestic work.[32]

However, even among constituencies sympathetic to the UP, Chilean women's proclivity to vote for centrist and right-wing parties continued. Although Allende had received the largest share of women's votes in working-class districts in Santiago in 1970's three-way presidential race, for example, more than 50 percent of working-class women backed his opponents and would vote for the opposition in Chile's 1973 congressional elections. And, of course, in middle- and upper-class districts, women's support for opposition parties was far higher. Nationally, despite marked success in raising the UP's share of women's votes from 31 percent to 39 percent between 1970 and 1973 (see appendix), 61 percent of women voted for the opposition parties that campaigned together as the Confederación Democrática (Democratic Confederation, CODE) in March 1973.[33] It did not help that progressive promises fell short when faced with mounting opposition and traditionalist assumptions on the left.[34] "The revolution stopped at the home," one female left-wing militant explained, despite revolutionary intentions to address domestic gendered inequalities.[35] Opponents also blocked UP bills on women's equality, which, when combined with a lack of left-wing initiative amid escalating priorities, hampered progress. Congress rejected the Family Ministry, which was surpassed by a Secretaría Nacional de la Mujer (National Women's Secretariat), a secondary-level institution, separating what were regarded as *women's* issues—food supplies, family health, and child care—from national politics.[36]

In spite of women's growing political participation, women were therefore still distinctly playing a supporting role in the male job of government, working at the grassroots level, carrying out administrative and communications tasks, education, social work, and food distribution rather than making decisions.[37] Although the UP would put forward nineteen female candidates in Chile's March 1973 congressional elections compared with the opposition's five (one senator and ten deputies were elected), very rarely did women hold prominent positions within left-wing parties or government.[38] This was not questioned at the time, female militants remembered, it was just the way it was: women were the "rearguard" and *ayudistas* (helpers).[39] Where there was a powerful left-wing message on protecting women or improving their positions, as Javier Maravall Yáguez argues, these often "reproduced patriarchal stereotypes" regarding women's spheres and family roles in the home.[40] As Allende put it in late 1972, a woman's "biological imperative to perpetuate her species" meant she was destined to fight to improve children's rights.[41] Securing children's prosperity and "happiness" had been core promises of his campaign.[42] Significantly, however, *women* were expected to deliver these programs.[43]

In this context, for all the barriers Beatriz surmounted when it came to politics, security, and intelligence at the center of government, she was still a coordinator, observer, and facilitator; within the president's inner circle, she was often the only woman, but never a named participant. Like other women, she also assumed additional tasks that routinely fell on women, such as hosting, caring for, and catering to visitors. When it came to Fidel Castro's visit, for example, Beatriz was responsible for assembling a group of women to look after him.[44] Alerted to an unexpected visit from Fidel to La Moneda, it was Allende's private secretaries who rushed out to buy cake.[45] Allende also co-opted women to cook special meals for his guest. His former mistress, the singer and Communist Inés Moreno, organized a barbeque in the countryside, while Paya hosted a farewell dinner for him at Cañaveral, both of which Beatriz attended.[46] At Fidel's request, Beatriz also arranged for Mireya Baltra, the Communist deputy and soon to be minister of labor, to host a meal at her house.[47]

Organizing food for Fidel was not trivial. To the contrary, food became a routine test of the intimate relationship between both heads of state (Castro sent Cuban ice cream to Allende weekly) that women made possible.[48] Nor was food the only basis of Beatriz's interaction with the Cuban leader during his stay. As the conduit between her father and Fidel, Beatriz helped convene, and was present during, meetings with different political groups in Chile. She was thus involved in tense discussions on the Left's situation outlined below. However, her catering revealed residual societal attitudes to women's positions prevailed during a moment of revolutionary change. Far more significant and contrary to the opposition's fears of armed feminist women, prominent ideas on the left about protecting women from armed conflict would also ultimately determine Beatriz's experience of the battle for Chile, excluding her from playing a part in the inevitable revolutionary confrontation she had long since anticipated and prepared for.

Violence and Solidarity

The day after the women's march, Castro and Allende spoke to thousands of supporters at Santiago's National Stadium. Reflecting on his visit, the Cuban leader warned of confrontation. No social system in history had voluntarily resigned itself to revolutionary change without a fight, he proclaimed. Would *la vía chilena* disprove "the historical law of resistance and violence"? Claiming to have seen "fascism" in the streets represented by the opposition's violence and disregard for constitutional order they purported to be defending, he thought not. He also warned opponents were preparing more effectively for confrontation than were revolutionary forces.[49] He had been shocked to see prominent UP women at a reception the night of the empty pots march rather than challenging opponents in the streets.[50] Chiding that it would take ten minutes for thousands of Cubans to assemble, as Chilean supporters had done that evening, and that in twenty-four hours six hundred thousand armed Cuban men could be mobilized, he implicitly underscored the Chilean Left's unpreparedness. "In combat, man is decisive; in combat, moral factors are decisive; in combat, man's morale is what decides," he proclaimed. Responding to Allende's promise that evening to defend his government with his life—that, only by riddling him with bullets could his enemies depose him—Fidel also insisted others should follow his example and prepare to die for Chile's revolutionary process.[51] These proclamations mirrored Fidel's private advice to UP leaders to get ready to confront oppositional violence with revolutionary violence, albeit carefully, not in contravention of each other and, pivotally, not in opposition to the president. During his visit, Cuban military specialists had also explained which arms Cuba could procure for them.[52]

Before leaving Chile, Castro gave his hosts gifts accentuating this message. After his speech at the stadium, for example, he visited Tupamaros working in the Grupo de Amigos Personales (GAP) garage and gave the group a Colt-45 pistol.[53] He also gave Salvador Allende an AK-47 with the inscription "To Salvador, from his comrade in arms, Fidel." And he

Shooting practice. Beatriz and Juan Carretero, Cajón del Maipo, no date. Archivo Fundación Salvador Allende.

gave Beatriz an Uzi machine gun for person-to-person combat.[54] In a world where arms were precious beyond their monetary value—where their symbolism was paramount and prized for the decisive revolutionary future they purported to offer rather than the destructive capacity they contained—these gifts were significant.[55] For Beatriz, the Uzi was a valuable reward for loyalty, an apparent gift of legitimacy to a woman who had craved acceptance and inclusion into a hypermasculine world of armed revolution. And she would cherish it. Henceforth, Juan Carretero and Luis took her to the Cajón del Maipo to learn how to use it.[56]

Fidel's gifts nevertheless fitted awkwardly within the Chilean context of a peaceful road to socialism. Rather than heeding advice to unite behind Allende, the UP also proceeded in an uncoordinated and uncertain way as it dealt with successive crises. As Joan Garcés, a political adviser to Allende during his presidency, would recount, differences between and within left-wing parties on military strategy meant the UP as a whole avoided discussing the topic, leaving different factions to pursue their own course of action.[57] When they did address it, Beatriz invariably acted as a mediator, simultaneously shielding her far Left friends and protecting her father from intra-Left disputes. But this was complex, and resolutions were rarely conclusive.

Predicting confrontation, Beatriz believed the government should focus on mobilizing supporters, preparing militarily, and covertly stockpiling weapons so the Left might overcome a coup and prevail in an armed conflict. Her position mirrored the Cubans' stance and that of the MIR, radical sectors of the Socialist Party (PS), and the Movimiento de Acción Popular Unitario (MAPU). For his part, Allende trod a fine line between left-wing factions. On the one hand, he shared the belief of Communists and more moderate Socialists in prioritizing a resolution to the economic situation, working through state institutions, attempting to negotiate with the PDC and, if necessary, with the United States, to try and gain time to consolidate *la vía chilena*. On the other hand, he increasingly accepted the need for defensive plans for La Moneda, as the bastion of presidential power, and relied on Beatriz, the PS's Internal Front, and the Cubans to help draw them up. But, for him, these were last resorts and as far as he would go in preparing for conflict. Contrary to Beatriz's instincts, he made it repeatedly clear he wanted to avoid civil war and would not countenance leading broader armed resistance to a coup.[58]

In their different approaches, Beatriz and her father thus embodied a strategic fault line running through the Chilean Left's DNA that increasingly came to the fore as the UP's opponents mobilized. Father and daughter continued to work intimately and to respect each other's positions. They were interdependent collaborators. They also essentially wanted the same thing: the continuation of Chile's left-wing government and a chance to usher the country on the path to socialist transformation. But they disagreed over how to achieve this. Their differences reflected an "internal crisis" at the heart of *la vía chilena*'s experience, explained Allende's friend Víctor Pey.[59] And the crisis would never be resolved. Indeed, left-wing leaders' failure to agree on a coherent answer to gathering opposition—let alone a precise vision for socialist transformation—would prove fatal when faced with the opposition's overwhelming political, economic, and military power.

The relationship between the MIR and the government caused particularly serious problems. By 1973, the organization numbered ten thousand militants and thirty thousand activists, split between a vanguard party structure in Santiago and a grassroots social movement in southern Chile.[60] It also had considerable sympathy within the PS, MAPU, and another small left-wing Catholic party, the Izquierda Cristiana.[61] However, the Communist Party opposed its belief in the need for extraconstitutional change, and the UP's opponents used its willingness to support land seizures and solidarity with foreign revolutionaries to attack the government. Ignoring Castro's advice to unite behind Allende, *miristas* increasingly criticized the UP for not going far or fast enough, not supporting mass mobilization and preparing for confrontation. In March 1972, for example, the MIR called for extraconstitutional measures that included dissolution of Congress and strengthening *poder popular* (people's power).⁶² In July 1972, its supporters set up the People's Assembly in Concepción, admonishing the government for not completing its manifesto pledges. Significantly, this split the UP, with the Communist Party (PCCh) condemning, and the PS and the MAPU leaders supporting, the move. The Communist Party henceforth persuaded Allende to break off formal talks with the MIR, while the PS, under Altamirano's leadership, called militants to "advance without compromise."⁶³

The MIR's collaboration with Allende on matters of security, organized by Beatriz and agreed as a means of co-opting them, also broke down. In late 1971, miristas had been expelled from the GAP after stealing arms for their own purposes with a Cuban instructor's help. And, in May 1972, amid rising, sometimes violent, intra-Left tensions, Allende instructed the Cubans to cease all training and arming of miristas. Ulises Estrada, Cuba's intelligence officer in charge of Chile in Havana, flew to Santiago for talks. Insisting the MIR's military preparations could help the government's defense, the Cubans threatened to withdraw training and arms for *all* left-wing parties. Ultimately, the compromise reached allowed the Cubans to keep training miristas but forbade them from transferring weapons to the organization unless a confrontation occurred. The Cubans meanwhile reiterated warnings to Miguel Enríquez to avoid openly opposing the government.⁶⁴

Beatriz was in the middle of such crises.⁶⁵ She frequently dealt with the MIR's opposition and its transgressions, trying to avoid ruptures. She helped smooth over the MIR's departure from the GAP, for example, and after a serious dispute between Max Marambio and Fernando Gómez, she agreed to the latter's demand that the former not be given access to Tomás Moro or La Moneda. In return she asked Fernando to promise that Allende would never learn the details of Marambio's disloyalty. And yet it was clear Beatriz "sympathized" with the MIR and was something of a spokesperson for its positions within Allende's inner circle.⁶⁶ As the "link" between the party and Allende, as she described herself, she also ensured dialogue continued. Because of this, Beatriz would remember her father had a "special relationship" with Enríquez: "Many times they disagreed. ... However, there was a relationship of affection, of consideration and important political dialogue."⁶⁷

Meanwhile, Communists became increasingly disdainful of what they saw as the MIR's reckless provocation. Contrary to Beatriz's positive gloss on the relationship her father had with miristas, there is evidence Allende also privately shared this view.⁶⁸ On one occasion, for example, when

Beatriz asked Radio Portales to broadcast a speech by Miguel Enríquez, her father overrode her, much to her disdain.⁶⁹ By mid-1972, the president was also expending energy in curbing the extreme Left. On 5 August, Eduardo Paredes's Investigaciones unit raided settlements in Lo Hermida district pursuing an armed group known as "16 de Julio de Liberación Nacional." In the process, a young *poblador* died, 11 were wounded, and 160 were arrested. The group's commander was later unmasked as a military provocateur, which was not known at the time. For now, Allende was deeply affected, refusing to believe a violent government-led raid could occur under his government.⁷⁰ The event also had a profound impact on the president's inner circle. Having asked Eduardo to resign, Allende worried about him, fearing he might hurt himself. At one point, Beatriz and her father even locked him in a house with a psychiatrist. This episode "really hurt Tati," Félix remembered.⁷¹ It also reverberated as an example of violence accompanying Chile's peaceful road to socialism.

The intensification of an inter-American Cold War in the Southern Cone exacerbated this impression as growing numbers of revolutionaries sought refuge in Chile. Fleeing a crackdown and military defeats, for example, hundreds of Tupamaros arrived in Santiago in mid- to late 1972. Combined with those already in the country and those not in the Movimiento de Liberación Nacional–Tupamaro (MLN-T), a total of fifteen hundred to three thousand Uruguayans would pass through Chile during the UP years.⁷² As explained by one Tupamaro, who was trained by the Cubans in intelligence, he assisted many MLN-T militants by providing false documentation, allowing them to travel to Havana. Chile thus became an oasis: a rear guard and route to safety amid a growing counterrevolutionary offensive.⁷³ And, as in the past, Beatriz was central to the reception exiles received. Together with others who had been involved in internationalist operations before, like her ELN comrade Celsa Parrau, she provided housing, food, jobs, and documentation. It was solidarity to ensure the "possibility of tactical retreat ... of survival," Celsa reasoned.⁷⁴

Yet Chile's position as a friendly revolutionary state directly entangled Allende in armed revolutionary maneuvers and international crises. On 15–16 August 1972, for example, members of three Argentinean armed revolutionary groups, the Fuerzas Armadas Revolucionarias (FAR), the Montoneros, and the Partido Revolucionario de los Trabajadores–Ejército Revolucionario del Pueblo (Workers' Revolutionary Party–Revolutionary Army of the People, PRT-ERP), escaped from Rawson jail in Chubut, hijacked a plane at Trelew airport, and forced its pilot to fly to Santiago. With the Argentine government demanding Chile return the prisoners and the revolutionaries asking to fly to Cuba, Allende was in a difficult position. That he had established good working relations with Argentina's military government complicated matters further. Moreover, the revolutionaries' escape had not gone well. A military guard had been killed, and only six militants, including ERP leader Mario Roberto Santucho, made it to the plane, leaving nineteen prisoners with no choice but to surrender.[75]

In Santiago, Beatriz unsurprisingly sided with the revolutionaries and lobbied her father to meet their demands.[76] (On a practical level, she also insisted they needed "parka" coats to withstand Chile's winter, sending Patricia to various shops in central Santiago to buy them.[77]) Beatriz thus played a key role in a crisis that had national and international ramifications. As Allende had commented at a Cuban embassy reception, he could not stand Beatriz looking at him with displeasure.[78] True, he did not immediately relent. But when the prisoners in Argentina were executed, Allende announced the hijackers could fly to Cuba. Prior to their departure, Beatriz reportedly visited Santucho and gave him a gun, which she said was from her father.[79] And in retrospect, she was adamant Allende had never doubted what he would do.[80]

Beatriz's active solidarity with Latin American revolutionary groups on this occasion was representative of a broader phase of coordination. For some time, in fact, former Chilean elenos like Beatriz and Celsa Parrau had been providing ad hoc assistance to armed groups in the region. As Celsa remembered, the thinking was that, together, "something much stronger, powerful," could be done. The Cubans, from their embassy in Santiago, had supported coordination between revolutionary groups, although keeping their distance.[81] And as a strategic refuge, Chile provided space for exchanges and collaboration.[82] Chileans' ability to travel freely also allowed them to drive weapons belonging to allied revolutionary groups across borders using vehicles with concealed compartments put together in the GAP's Santiago garage.[83]

In late 1972, however, collaboration was formalized. Building on transnational relationships Beatriz and others in the PS had developed since the late 1960s, the MIR spearheaded the operation. Specifically, in November 1972, Miguel Enríquez called a meeting with the Tupamaros and members of the PRT-ERP, who, having made it to Cuba after their hijacking operation, returned clandestinely to Chile a couple of months later. The result was the formation of what would become the Junta Coordinadora Revolucionaria (Coordinating Revolutionary Junta, JCR)—one of the few regional revolutionary organizations established in Cold War Latin America. While its goal was to fight against imperialism for socialism, immediate tasks included forming a training school and assessing military and logistical operations. It also assembled workshops, using access to factory machines, where members crafted grenades and developed a machine gun ready for testing less than a year later. In June 1973, Bolivia's ELN also joined the JCR.[84] The MIR, and not Beatriz's group of ex-elenos, were part of this organization because it had a clear organizational structure and hierarchy compared with the more informal ELN network within the PS. And according to Chato Peredo, Beatriz was not involved.[85] However, others remembered her at least knowing about the JCR and mixing with those who were.[86]

Beatriz's association with such groups, however distant, is another indication of a complex coexistence between left-wing factions in Allende's Chile. She and those she collaborated with increasingly believed democracy would take them only so far and that together they would be stronger and resistant to counterrevolutionary onslaught on the horizon. As we know, Allende's own position was distinct, but it was also lenient. When, in 1972, he found out Carmen Castillo, in the role of looking after regional revolutionary groups, had been photocopying an urban guerrilla manual in La Moneda, for example, the president asked her to resign. But he did so "with humor and tenderness."[87] And Juan Carretero remembered Allende being proud of his daughter's relations with the Tupamaros and Montoneros.[88] He certainly did nothing to stop her supporting militants arriving in Chile. And, years later, Beatriz—constructing an image of her father reflecting her own sympathies—would describe Allende as a "conspirator."[89]

However, rumors and suppositions about such links were a source of vulnerability for the president in an escalating battle waged against his democratic credibility by the opposition and its international sponsors. The idea of fifteen thousand foreign extremists in Chile by 1973 proved particularly potent.[90] Counterrevolutionary victories forcing armed groups to seek refuge in Chile was not of his choosing. He had also asked revolutionary groups in Chile to avoid intervening in domestic politics or openly associating with the MIR. Even so, transnational ties—with and without his knowledge—internationalized the struggle to determine Chile's future and made the opposition's claim that the Left was somehow un-Chilean more potent. It is difficult to conceive how Allende—or Beatriz—could have stopped this happening without significantly changing course. But, in retrospect, Patricia reflected she and Beatriz probably shared too much with non-Chileans in Santiago during these years.[91]

Perhaps more significant, the far Left's actions in 1972, with or without the president's solidarity, demonstrated that Allende and the UP coalition were increasingly unable to control revolutionary forces and momentum in Chile. The president could not persuade the MIR to follow his line, he reacted to guerrilla movements' initiatives, and he was seemingly irrelevant to transnational networks consolidated in Chile during years in office. That they were pessimistic about peaceful democratic revolution's potential and were making alternative plans demonstrates Chile's constitutional road struggled to be credible. And as the bridge between her father and these groups, Beatriz was at least partly responsible for this dislocation, shielding the far Left and willing her father to keep them on his side. As Allende's inner circle of young Socialist advisers met in the intimate confines of Cañaveral or Félix's bedroom, they struggled to resolve disputes consuming their followers. And, as leaders of different factions talked to one another, debated, engaged in theoretical discussions, and discussed prognoses, the instructions they offered rank-and-file militants regarding defense of the revolutionary process were contradictory.

All the while, the opposition was strong and united. Indeed, the Left's defensive measures—the GAP, mass mobilization under the banner of *poder popular*, and the JCR included—paled in comparison with the Right's organization, resources, and propensity for violence. As much as the Left's relationship with violence was scrutinized and criticized, its preparatory measures therefore need contextualizing. When Chileans in local neighborhoods around the country began discussing self-defense measures, forming militias, and preparing to take control of factories, they did so in response to sabotage and paramilitary attacks, frustrated with ambiguous government advice.[92]

Contingency Plans

Sitting with Allende for national military parades to mark Chile's independence celebrations on 18 September, Beatriz and Patricia clutched pistols while the GAP stood edgily nearby. In retrospect, given the imbalance of forces, Patricia reflected that she and Beatriz were crazy.[93] However, their stance was indicative of opposition the UP faced by September 1972. Congressional investigations and obtrusiveness, sabotage, food hoarding, demonstrations, and media campaigns were, by now, commonplace. In national elections for the CUT, the Christian Democrats won the biggest share of white-collar votes (41 percent), underlining the government's failure to win over the middle class, many of whom were state employees.[94] Right-wing paramilitary groups, such as Patria y Libertad, attacked UP supporters and the country's infrastructure, derailing trains and undermining businesses. Rural "white guards" financed by landowners resisted land reform.[95] The *Washington Post*'s publication of International Telephone and Telegraph (ITT) documents detailing the Nixon administration's efforts to bloc Allende's inauguration had confirmed fears of U.S. intervention. And the government was locked in international debt negotiations to reschedule payments it could no longer make. Having discovered a plot within the army led by General Alfredo Canales, UP parties acknowledged a coup was a decided possibility.[96] In October, truckers unions, shopkeepers, and professional associations then launched a prolonged strike designed to bring the country to its knees.[97]

While the Left's response to the strike was remarkably successful, it exacerbated existing tensions when it came to longer-term strategies for forging ahead with the government's program. Combined state-led efforts and popular mobilization, coordinated using advanced communications networks, had kept the country moving.[98] But grassroots sectors' mobilization gave weight to *poder popular*, separate to the government rather than under its control. As a worker involved in the *cordones industriales*—or industrial belts organized to keep factories moving—explained, this "parallel power" was "the result of the government's inability to face the enemy."[99] With the strike over, the desire to use this power persisted. And while the MIR and sectors of the PS encouraged such efforts, the Communist Party and the CUT criticized them for a lack of discipline and coordination.[100] The result was disconnect between the government and its supporters, some of whom believed in moving beyond institutional frameworks and taking matters into their own hands.[101]

On another level, those within the president's inner circle began concretely addressing contingencies for a coup. Allende faced two options: go underground and lead resistance to a future military dictatorship, or face a coup and try to defeat it from the presidential palace, knowing this would almost certainly fail. By this point, Tupamaros resident in Chile had been instrumental in helping to build hideouts (*berretines*) equipped with arms, false identity documents, and sensitive information.[102] However, in conversations in September 1972, Allende rejected using them in the event of a coup. Instead, contrary to advice from the Cubans and from his own security team, he insisted on the second option. Defensive plans drawn up after September 1972 therefore focused on securing La Moneda and creating concentric circles around it—including cordones industriales—to stop military forces reaching downtown. The Cubans and Allende's security team all agreed that defending La Moneda for more than a few hours was almost impossible given the building's position in central Santiago, surrounded by tall buildings, the Ministry of Defense included. However, the president was adamant. And so, as with so many other UP policies and programs, "Plan Santiago," as the defensive plan was called, was an awkward blend of defense for a constitutional mandate using a Cuban-trained, but limited, personal security detail and spontaneous support from below.[103]

The plan also heavily relied on the assumption that loyal members of Chile's armed forces would resist plotters' advance. From October 1972 onward, when commanders of the three branches of Chile's military were brought into government to restore order after the strike, Allende considered constitutional military leaders key to defense. But a "constitutionalist" stance did not necessarily equate with enthusiasm for the government's program for socialist revolution. To the contrary, although General Prats, commander in chief of the army, expressed sympathy for the UP, an antirevolutionary sentiment and disdain for civilian politicians pervaded the armed forces. Certainly, Rear Admiral Ismael Huerta Díaz, appointed minister of public works in October 1972, resented the military being used by the UP to further its political agenda and would accordingly resign from government three months later. Despite some evidence that the PS and PCCh were cultivating left-wing sectors within the armed forces, such work also fell short, and estimates of loyal groups were wildly exaggerated.[104] Incorporating military commanders into government meanwhile caused controversy on the Left, with radical sectors, Beatriz included, simply distrusting the armed forces.[105]

For now, Allende focused on securing additional support for his government internationally. A month after the strike's resolution, he went on an international tour to Mexico, the UN, Algeria, the Soviet Union, and Cuba. Mostly, he aimed to deter further U.S. intervention and secure credits. In Moscow, Allende appealed for help on the basis that his country had become a "silent Vietnam." But he left disappointed.[106] The Soviets, pessimistic about the UP's future, had been rather incredulous at Chilean requests, which they considered excessive and out of step with support it normally offered developing countries.[107] The trip nevertheless brought moments of acclaim. In Mexico and at the UN, Allende received resounding sympathy. And the president was awarded the Premio Lenin de la Paz and the José Marti medal in Moscow and Havana, respectively. As Beatriz would recall, "He felt a certain pride in having received them."[108] Not having accompanied Allende to Mexico, New York, and Moscow, Beatriz and Luis then flew to Cuba at the start of December to meet him, where Fidel promised a "gigantic wave of solidarity" and forty tons of sugar.[109]

In private, however, the Cubans, much like the Soviets, were frustrated with Chilean delays in trade agreements and Allende's indecisiveness when it came to Chile's revolutionary process.[110] "No obstacle is invincible," Fidel had written privately to Salvador earlier that year. "In a revolution, one moves forward with 'audacity, audacity, and more audacity.'"[111] On 6 September, he had sent another letter to Allende, reiterating Cuba's "willingness to collaborate in any way. . . . Although we understand the

Meeting in Havana, no date. *Clockwise from front, left*: Fidel Castro, Rolando Calderón (*out of shot*), Arnoldo Camú, Ulises Estrada, Manuel Piñeiro, Beatriz, Luis, Carlos Altamirano. Luis Fernández Oña private collection.

Chilean process's current difficulties, we are confident that you will find a way to overcome them." "The points raised by you through Beatriz are already being fulfilled," Castro had also informed Allende, indicating Beatriz had made an earlier trip to Cuba as her father's envoy (details remain unknown). "You can count entirely on our cooperation."[112] Yet, because the Chileans had not agreed how to proceed, exactly how the Cubans could help was unclear.

Back in Santiago, Allende began preparing for the worst. At the end of 1972, he asked Luis to visit him at Tomás Moro. Reiterating his decision to resist a coup with his life, he spoke about his family's future. Primarily, he expressed fears about Beatriz and urged Luis to take her to the Cuban embassy in the event of a coup. Allende was "very worried" about Beatriz, Luis reported to Havana, given she "had always expressed her willingness to participate in confrontation for which she had prepared." And illustrative of the president's conviction that he would ultimately die in a battle defending the UP, he gave Luis money for Hortensia, his daughters, and Paya in the event of his death.[113]

Fearful information could fall into enemy hands, Allende also asked Luis to look after his personal archives and burn them in the event of a coup. A few days later, Beatriz arrived at the Cuban embassy with Paya, Augusto Olivares, Carlos Jorquera, and Víctor Pey to deliver boxes of documents. In subsequent months, Luis asked Allende at least twice whether he should send these to Cuba, but the president wanted them in Chile and destroyed if a coup struck.[114] With or without Allende's knowledge, Beatriz and Patricia also began taking important documents to the Cuban embassy at night so they could be sent to Havana.[115]

That these preparations happened so early is striking for what it tells us about the doom and isolation pervading the presidency as 1973 started. Making plans to secure his records and his and his family's future, Allende relied on the Cubans rather than members of his own party or cabinet to help, indicating the growing distance between the presidency and Chile's left-wing parties. Plans also reveal the president's fatalism that he could not surmount an attack.

The Left won a certain degree of reprieve when, despite odds, it received 43.9 percent of the vote in congressional elections in March 1973. The result put a stop to the opposition's constitutional hopes of unseating Allende by winning a decisive two-thirds majority. Despite the economic crisis in Chile (inflation had reached 300 percent by 1973), the election also demonstrated that ideology and class rather than economic factors shaped political loyalties.[116] And Beatriz had actively campaigned, supporting the candidacy of Carlos Lorca, the JS leader, for deputy in Valparaíso, accompanying him to the countryside.[117]

However, the UP's victory did not stop the opposition. In subsequent months, there were armed street clashes, pro-government journalists were assaulted, and Patria y Libertad's sabotage soared.[118] In response, the Left, and particularly those inclined toward *poder popular*, fought back. In April, the MIR, supported by the PS and the MAPU, launched an agitation campaign, which Allende denounced as provocation, underlining strategic divisions within the government.[119] As they had done since the beginning of the year, strikes in Chile's copper mines also halted production as workers demanded higher wages.[120] When a column of miners marched on Santiago, breaking through police cordons, sympathetic protestors clashed with them, leaving one dead and seventy-six injured.[121] Then, on 29 June, the government withstood a coup attempt, led by the army's second armed division advancing on La Moneda (the Tanquetazo).

The Left's success in defeating this attack was a pyrrhic victory. Inside the military, the coup attempt revealed support for intervention among intermediate-level members of the armed forces, with many voicing solidarity for the plotters and calling on their superiors to "do something." Senior members of the armed forces increasingly feared an "anarchic situation," striving to control the situation, with discussions about intervention increasing henceforth. By this point, those sympathetic to the

UP in the military were also operating clandestinely.[122] In August, pro-government sailors found to be warning left-wing parties of coup plotting were then imprisoned and tortured for indiscipline.[123]

On the government's side, Plan Santiago had essentially worked. Loyal commanders of the armed forces—led by Generals Carlos Prats, Mario Sepúlveda, and Guillermo Pickering, as well as Allende's naval attaché, Captain Arturo Araya—defended the government. Workers and students occupied factories, offices, and universities.[124] And yet, because Plan Santiago functioned so obviously, it precluded chances of it working again because contingency plans were revealed to plotters. And having seen weapons brandished, the armed forces had the pretext to launch devastating raids across Chile in search of arms from 2 July onward. Using a PDC-sponsored arms control law and monitored by a military committee bringing the three branches of the armed forces together in a new coordinated way, these raids employed hundreds of uniformed soldiers, including parachute regiments, as well as buses, jeeps, and helicopters. While the Right framed raids as a means of "guaranteeing ... democratic normality," arms were rarely found. Workers and campesinos nevertheless were rounded up, arrested at random, injured, and killed, leading the Left to accuse the Right and the military of provoking confrontation.[125]

In many ways, in fact, the military's decisive intervention in Chilean politics and the UP's inability to prevent it began with these arms searches.[126] Notably, the armed forces did not target the opposition, providing a permissive environment for right-wing paramilitaries.[127] In August 1973 alone, Patria y Libertad launched 316 attacks on Chilean infrastructure, leaving five dead and one hundred injured.[128] Late on 26 July 1973, a member of Patria y Libertad had also assassinated Captain Araya on the balcony of his home. However, the press pointed the finger at Luis and one of the GAP's leaders as a way of putting Cuba's involvement in Chile under the spotlight and accusing Allende of violence.[129] Even Araya's wife blamed the president, arriving distraught at La Moneda, where Beatriz looked after her.[130]

The Left responded to this offensive haphazardly.[131] The division between Allende, who still, somehow, hoped to save his constitutional road to socialism, and grassroots supporters had been laid bare the day after the Tanquetazo when crowds outside La Moneda demanded he close Congress.[132] Elsewhere, feeling constrained by the CUT and its talk of negotiation in the midst of arms raids, factory workers—with support from the MIR, the MAPU, and sectors of the PS—began autonomously organizing defensive militias.[133] The Communist Party and Allende meanwhile focused on negotiations with the PDC as the solution to Chile's crisis. With analogies drawn to the Spanish Civil War, a PCCh-inspired government slogan proclaimed, "No to civil war!"[134] But saying no to civil war was not necessarily enough to prevent one. And by the winter of 1973, the far Left, including Socialists in government, was openly calling for civil war to stop the opposition's offensive.[135] On 9 September, Carlos Altamirano would proclaim there was no space left for dialogue. "The Right's plot," he proclaimed, "can only be crushed with the invincible strength of the people."[136]

Although Allende's inner circle and left-wing parties unquestionably had arms, military apparatuses, and trained cadres, and while grassroots supporters had mobilized into defensive militias, their collective strength was far weaker than some claimed and the opposition charged. Cultural allusions to arms and romanticization of what they could achieve—particularly when framed in reference to Cuba—boosted the sense of an overwhelming force, quite different from what existed.[137] The GAP had been depleted, losing various members the previous year. In late 1972, for example, Beatriz's ELN comrade Fernando, along with ten others, relocated north to defend Chuquicamata mine and stop arms for Patria y Libertad crossing the Bolivian border. (After a conflict with PS recruits under Rolando Calderón's control, it was Beatriz who helped negotiate Fernando's departure.)[138] In March 1973, a further GAP contingent had also left, feeling trapped by Allende's "political institutional" road. A breakaway faction of recruits, forming independent structures, meanwhile accused the PS of right-wing deviation, while others in the party asked for Allende's resignation in mid-1973.[139] The remaining GAP had two armed escorts, numbering 28 people, a further 20 recruits stationed at Tomás Moro, and 20 new recruits in training by September.

The PS, meanwhile, had around a hundred cadres trained in irregular combat, which could last two hours in a battle against the armed forces, and around one thousand to fifteen hundred men with basic preparation. And the Cubans stationed in Cuba—numbering less than 150 by September—could possibly help.[140] Elsewhere, Luis Corvalán, the Communist Party's secretary-general, informed the East German embassy on 8 July 1973 that it had begun making contingency plans for confrontation having previously believed one could be averted. The party had a thousand militants who knew how to use automatic arms and two thousand who knew how to use "short-range weapons," but there was no coordination between this highly covert military apparatus and other left-wing forces.[141]

Chile's professional armed forces, numbering fifty thousand in 1973, combined with more than twenty-five thousand carabineros, dwarfed such disparate forces.[142] When it came to arms, too, the Left could not compete. According to Patricio Quiroga, the PS had received three arms deliveries since 1970, which it had divided between its own military apparatus and the GAP, totaling just under 100 machine guns, 500 AK-47s, 8 Uzis, 6 RPG-7 (with 9 grenade launchers), 36 P-38 pistols, and 36 Colt revolvers.[143] The Tupamaros' radio-communications team also increased production of *captacanos* (listening devices to detect military and police signals).[144]

With these incongruent forces and arms raids continuing apace, a sense of impending disaster pervaded Allende's inner circle. The GAP's remaining members were exasperated, knowing they could not resist an attack.[145] And, in anticipation of a coup, all nonessential Cuban personnel, children, and most women were sent back to Havana.[146] Believing foreigners would be targeted, the MLN-T also ordered an exodus of militants either to Cuba or Argentina.[147] Foreign revolutionary groups in Chile simultaneously began destroying documents.[148] And the Communist Party prepared to go underground and preserve its leadership structures.[149]

For Beatriz and Luis, these were desperately tense and dangerous months. As the president's close confidants, they were vulnerable to attacks.[150] Patricia was followed daily.[151] And Eduardo Paredes only just survived an attack on his car the day of the Tanquetazo.[152] With both Luis and Beatriz involved in trying to shore up armed preparedness, they were also particularly exposed. As Beatriz told her friend Elena, while driving in Santiago with guns hidden under a blanket in the backseat, she had narrowly avoided being searched by smiling sweetly to the police officer who stopped her.[153] Luis, targeted individually and personally by the press as the embodiment of Cuba's presence in Chile, also feared for his safety.[154] That he was involved in risky operations, such as the delivery of weapons to the Communist Party's military apparatus, only to have the PCCh cancel the operation at the last minute amid arms raids, made his position—and that of other Cuban embassy staff—precarious.[155] Beatriz and Luis, along with many of Allende's closest associates, rarely slept at home, moving between different safe houses.[156] When Allende traveled to Chillán by helicopter on 20 August to attend annual military commemorations for Bernardo O'Higgins, Chile's national independence hero, a tense argument ensued between the GAP and military personnel over his security, with neither trusting the other. The same afternoon, hearing military wives were gathered outside the Ministry of Defense demanding that General Prats resign, Allende returned to Tomás Moro, where he met close advisers, Beatriz included.[157]

The targeted attack on Prats was important. As commander in chief of the army and minister of defense, he had been a constitutionalist block to coup plotting. To remove threats within the army's high command, he had advised Allende, twelve to fifteen generals would have to be sacked, which would spark a civil war.[158] Now, faced with Prats's potential resignation, the question was who would succeed him. Based on information Beatriz had, presumably from the Cubans, PS intelligence, and the MIR, she argued her father should appoint General Óscar Bonilla rather than General Augusto Pinochet, the next in command. As a witness vividly remembered, "Tati was suspicious of all military personnel ... [but was sure] if you had to pick one, it was Bonilla."[159] However, in arguing against Pinochet she was in a minority, given indications he would follow Prats's position. Not only would Allende reject Beatriz's advice, appointing Pinochet on 23 August when Prats resigned, but Pinochet would also be invited to Cañaveral and engage in target practice with Allende and GAP members, illustrating how little was known about him. And Pinochet's promotion, combined with the resignation under pressure of General César Ruiz and Admiral Raúl Montero, constitutionally minded commanders in chief of the air force and Navy, respectively, cleared the way for coup plotters General Gustavo Leigh and Admiral José Merino to take charge. It is impossible to know what would have happened had Bonilla been appointed; after all, he would become a member of Chile's military junta, although he opposed the dictatorship's violent repression and died mysteriously in a plane crash. However, Beatriz's role in this meeting is testimony to her position behind the scenes as a presidential interlocutor and conduit of information when it came to defensive strategy.

Preparing for the Worst

Two weeks later, on 8 September, Beatriz celebrated her thirty-first birthday at Cañaveral. The mood was somber. Around midnight, Ángel Parra arrived to sing and lighten the mood. Allende's newest minister of defense and former ambassador in Washington, Orlando Letelier, also sang tangos.[160] It was "very, very, very, very tense," Luis remembered. While the military stood alert on the road below, no one knew if they were "protecting or threatening."[161] Everyone knew a coup was "imminent," Celsa remembered. Leaving Cañaveral with the Cubans, who were all armed to defend themselves, she and her husband, Arnoldo Camú, traveled back to Santiago down side streets.[162]

With rank-and-file militants awaiting instructions for confronting a coup, Allende and his inner circle meanwhile made concrete arrangements. The president expended considerable effort trying to safeguard his family—and Beatriz in particular.[163] When the Cubans Manuel Piñeiro and Carlos Rafael Rodríguez had been dispatched to Chile in early July after the Tanquetazo to reiterate their country's readiness to help, the president had requested Luis and Beatriz, by then five months pregnant with her second child, be allowed to leave immediately for Cuba. But both Luis and Beatriz refused to go. Without Beatriz's knowledge, Luis had nevertheless started sending personal belongings—photos, household ornaments—to Cuba so they could build a home there if needed (Beatriz was angry when she found out).[164]

Beatriz had also been making contingency plans for Maya, asking her friend Elena to look after her as she had done during the Tanquetazo.[165] But with tensions mounting, Beatriz and Patricia decided it safest to send their children to Cuba as soon as possible (they were booked to leave on 13 September).[166] Beatriz warned Carmen Paz's husband a coup was imminent, urging him to hide his family and not get involved. With her father's knowledge, she also gave him a small pistol.[167]

At the same time, the president planned his own moves and considered his legacy. In early September, he had met with his young Socialist advisers, including Beatriz, Félix, Ricardo Pincheira, Carlos Lorca, Rolando Calderón, Arnoldo Camú, Jorge Klein, Claudio Jimeno, and Eduardo Paredes. With their combined intelligence and Soviet Committee for State Security (KGB) sources, they believed a coup would most likely take place during the first week of September or the week Chile celebrated its independence on 18 September. And, at this meeting, Allende indicated he would ultimately shoot himself when the moment came, placing two fingers under his chin. "The only thing I regret is that people like you who are so young are going to die," Félix remembered him saying. "I have already lived my life."[168]

Allende's resignation to death was probably helped by the fact he believed he would soon have a male heir to succeed him. For six months, he had been romantically involved with Gloria Gaitán, daughter of the progressive Colombian politician Jorge Eliécer Gaitán, who had arrived in Chile at the beginning of 1973.[169] And he reportedly became obsessed with the idea of having a son with her. It was a "way of compensating for his farewell to life," Gloria remembered.[170] If her account of their conversations is true, they are testimony of Allende's gendered ideas about power—shared widely at the time—that his three daughters could not fulfill this role. Beatriz would not know about her father's relationship until Gloria published an account in December 1973, and she was "furious" because her father had kept it a secret from her and because of her loyalty to Paya. (Because Gloria had a miscarriage, she never knew about the pregnancy.)[171]

Back in Santiago, on 10 September 1973, the immediate focus was on when, not if, the military would strike, with the right-wing media calling openly for a coup.[172] Allende's last option was to call a plebiscite, which, having finally received backing from the UP's parties, he spent Monday 10 September organizing. But with reluctant support from the PS, the MIR openly opposed to this move, and the PDC adamant it would not enter negotiations, it is unclear what it would achieve. That night, as Allende's speechwriters worked on an announcement, Paya stayed at La Moneda, where she received news of troop movements. But informed these were mobilizations to deal with expected protests the next day and a strong sense a coup attempt would be launched the following week, Allende told her to get some rest.[173]

11 September

Beatriz and Luis awoke on 11 September when a member of the GAP called to alert them a coup was under way. They were at home—not at a safe house—because Maya was sick. Concerned that it was colder at El Cañaveral, they had not taken her to Beatriz's birthday celebration, and on Sunday, 9 September, they had returned to Santiago to be with her. Despite predictions of an imminent coup, they had also resisted sending Maya to Elena's house in the foothills of the Andes for safety. Pincheira, head of PS intelligence, had reassured them this would be okay. Now, Luis's Cuban chauffeur and security guard left immediately to drive Maya to Elena's. Beatriz also sent Elena a shoebox with photos, a handwritten note describing the Fiat car she owned, instructions to sell it, and $600. With these things, Elena recalled, Beatriz believed she was saying good-bye. Because the chauffeur took Beatriz's car keys to Elena's, however, she and Luis were initially stuck. Around this time, Paya, under instructions from Allende, tried calling Luis to ensure that he stopped Beatriz from leaving, but for unknown reasons she could not get through. And when Luis's chauffeur returned, Beatriz set off for La Moneda. "It was obvious she was going to go," Luis recalled. "Stopping her was impossible."[174]

She arrived at the presidential palace just before 9:00 A.M., not knowing what situation she would encounter. Getting there had been difficult. "I had to pass several barriers," she later explained, "one of soldiers, another of carabineros, both of which I drove the car through."[175] She carried a black briefcase in which were the Uzi that Castro had given her and a Colt Cobra pistol.[176] As one of those in La Moneda would later describe, she seemed "calm," despite the circumstances and being seven months pregnant.[177] She was also lucky to have gotten to the palace at all. Paya, who set off from Cañaveral with eleven armed members of the GAP, only narrowly avoided detention when their truck was stopped by military patrols. Though she escaped, none of her companions survived, her son Enrique included.[178]

Inside La Moneda, Beatriz found her father resigned to the situation. Despite initial hopes, it was already clear the coup was serious. When military leaders had offered him a plane for exile around 8:00 A.M., "he had told them to go to hell."[179] Shortly after Beatriz arrived, he then delivered what would be his last radio address stating his sacrifice would not be "in vain," imploring workers not to "sacrifice themselves," and pointing to a brighter Chilean "destiny" ahead.[180]

It was a strange group of fifty-five people with Allende in La Moneda: his private medical team; Centro de Estudios Nacionales de Opinión Pública (CENOP) analysts; press secretaries and speech writers; loyal ministers and Jaime Barrios, director of Chile's Central Bank; around twenty members of the GAP; Pincheira; and close advisers such as Eduardo, Paya, and Beatriz. Surprising many, Beatriz's younger sister, Isabel, was the last to reach the building. As Eduardo Labarca described, those gathered in La Moneda personified the UP's "contrast of two worlds ... One: Beatriz, el Coco [Eduardo Paredes], the GAP, armed revolution, those who go to die. The other: Isabel, who has never held a pistol, the least bellicose politicians, ministers."[181] Left-wing party leaders were conspicuous by their absence. When a group of Socialist militants a block away called to offer to join them, Beatriz encouraged them, but they never reached the palace.[182]

Meanwhile, Beatriz was burning sensitive documents.[183] And Allende entrusted her to communicate his wishes to the MIR and the Cubans that they not go to La Moneda. As Beatriz told Miguel, Allende believed it was time to act on his proclamations about confronting reactionary violence.[184] Beatriz called the Cuban embassy to say that no Cubans were to leave the embassy. Castro's orders to Cuban personnel had been clear. As Mario García Incháustegui, Cuba's ambassador, recounted, they were not to "fight unless it was the President's explicit request." Without it, they were to concentrate on defending Cuba's embassy: "what he called Quang Tri" (an allusion to Vietnamese resistance against U.S.-backed forces). If Allende *did* ask for assistance, the Cubans could participate, *as long as* the president and the embassy were not surrounded, "there was popular participation," *and* "there were some units loyal to the government." Yet Cuban embassy staff had been prepared to overlook such prerequisites and were "ready ... to leave" when Beatriz called. Reaching La Moneda would have involved "a loss of men," Luis admitted, but they would have gone if Allende had asked. Now, following Beatriz's instructions, they focused on avoiding provocations. As Castro had insisted, he did not want Cubans to act as "detonators ... that could give the impression that an army of foreign mercenaries ... were taking over Chile's civil war for themselves."[185] As the Cubans reasoned, Allende's decision, relayed by Beatriz, was based not just on similar calculations but also on his "humanitarian" desire to save lives.[186]

In La Moneda, this same preoccupation underpinned Allende's determination to save the seven women in the building (Beatriz, Isabel, and Paya; the journalists Frida Modak, Verónica Ahumada, and Cecilia Tormo; and Nancy Julien, Jaime Barrios's Cuban wife). In the basement, sheltering from imminent air force bombing, Allende begged his daughters to think of their families and their mother and to leave. He also insisted that Beatriz tell Fidel what had happened. But she was intransigent, believing it was her "duty" to be with her father; "I tried to hide," she would admit, "but my father insisted strongly, with a military tone."[187] "Pushed," as she later told Luis, Beatriz found herself led to the door, handing Oscar Soto her pistol on the way. The women—without Paya, who did hide—then stepped out onto the street where the military had promised to escort them to safety. And the door shut behind them.[188]

When they discovered the jeep that was supposed to be waiting for them was not there, Beatriz turned back, banging on the door. But she was refused reentry. Caught between snipers firing on the palace and those inside returning fire, Isabel persuaded her to leave.[189] As Beatriz would remember, "I had a deep feeling of guilt, although I understood it was useless. I knew I would never see my father again."[190] The women spotted the offices of the PDC newspaper, *La Prensa*, where Frida had contacts, and they sheltered for over an hour in the building's basement during intense bombing of the palace. But unable to stay indefinitely, Beatriz, Isabel, Frida, and Nancy ventured outside, encountering the destruction of La Moneda.[191]

The following hours involved an improvised search for safety. Its haphazardness is striking given the preparations for a confrontation, who Beatriz was, and her contacts. But it is indicative of Beatriz's assumption she would stay with her father (and her father's that she could be stopped from joining him in the first place). It is also emblematic of the overall state of the Left's uncoordinated resistance to a coup that so many had expected for months. The fighting that did occur took place in isolated pockets around the city in industrial cordons or poblaciónes. Members of the PS's military apparatus, meeting that morning and distributing arms, joined workers at the Indumet factory in leading a resistance. Among the three hundred people gathered, Beatriz's friends Arnoldo, Exequiel, and Rolando took up positions, ready to put to use their military preparation, while Celsa, a nurse, prepared to treat the wounded. But this was about it.

The Communists ordered their cadres to seek cover and go underground, while the MIR, meeting at 11:00 A.M., said it could gather four hundred people, but not until 4:00 P.M. Meanwhile, Altamirano was forced into hiding.[192] Far from the safe haven Allende had thought it would be, Tomás Moro was also bombed and raided, leading Hortensia to flee under fire. And Beatriz did not yet know that, from midday, two infantry companies and carabineros in trucks, carrying mortars and machine guns, had begun to encircle the Cuban embassy.[193]

For now, walking east, Beatriz, Isabel, Nancy, and Frida sheltered in a luxury hotel lobby, trying to look inconspicuous. But with guests popping champagne corks and celebrating the coup, they could not help standing out.[194] It was there, deciding what to do, that Beatriz would overhear news of her father's death.[195] Leaving the hotel, the three women then walked toward the river Mapocho, stopping for Beatriz, heavily pregnant, to sit down, before hitching a lift with a young couple. But when the car reached Plaza Italia, they were stopped by the military and asked to show their bags. Instinctively, since she was carrying a weapon, Beatriz feigned contractions. It probably saved their lives; police told them to drive straight to the hospital. Then, on a side road near Providencia, Isabel asked the driver to stop the car, realizing a friend lived nearby. Finally, from the house of Isabel's friend, Beatriz contacted Luis at the Cuban embassy.[196]

It was then she learned for certain her father was dead and those with him in La Moneda had been detained. Beatriz's worst fears were confirmed. Via the Cuban embassy, the military offered her, her mother, and her sisters the opportunity to attend her father's burial. But when Luis, accompanied by the ambassador, left to collect her around midnight as negotiated, a fierce gun battle ensued. "Miraculously," as the Cubans would report, Luis and Mario survived, but plans were aborted, leaving Beatriz's mother, members of her extended family, and Allende's air force attaché to go alone. In the following twenty-four hours, the challenge for Beatriz was then to collect her daughter, reach the Cuban embassy, and leave the country with the Cubans, who decided in the early hours of 12 September that this was their only option. (Isabel did not wish to go to Havana but rather sought asylum in the Mexican embassy with Hortensia, Carmen Paz, and their families.)[197]

Quang Tri

Beatriz's decision to seek asylum in Cuba was logical. But before sending Luis to collect her, the Cuban embassy had to confirm she would be allowed to leave. In negotiations early on Wednesday, the armed forces had agreed to the Cubans taking Patricia, Isabel, and their children. But

Beatriz was different. As Mario García Incháustegui recalled, coup leaders could use Beatriz, "who, after all, is spiritually Cuban," as "blackmail." Ultimately, however, her gender and the idea that women and children should escape violence meant no such problems arose; they were not regarded important (Max Marambio, who reached the Cuban embassy early on 11 September, was not allowed to leave).[198]

Even so, the job of picking up Maya and Beatriz was difficult. En route, the car Luis was traveling in, accompanied by Chilean military personnel, was attacked. Luis's chaperones also searched Elena's husband at gunpoint before he handed Maya over. Only with his daughter safely at the embassy did Luis then go to pick up Beatriz, who said a quick good-bye to her sister at the door of their refuge. "I remember her face," Luis recalled, "she was very downhearted" due to her advanced pregnancy and "wounded by her father's death."[199]

Arriving at the embassy, they encountered frenetic activity. Having been there since the previous day, staff had been involved in preparing to evacuate. They burned all secret correspondence not already destroyed prior to the coup. From 7:30 A.M., Patricio de la Guardia, a member of Cuba's Tropas Especiales, also oversaw construction of makeshift wooden crates to transport the embassy's arsenal: 395 AKs, 10 RPG-7, 35 or 40 rocket launchers, 50,000 AK cartridges, and 40 hand grenades (including 85 AKs the Communist Party had not taken but excluding individuals' personal weapons). With prospects for defending Allende's government dashed, the Cubans planned to smuggle all weapons out of Chile. With not enough wooden crates to transport them, sacks, suitcases, and wine boxes were also being considered when a Chilean military general arrived and unknowingly stopped the operation (120 weapons and six or seven RPGs would be left behind). The alternative, embassy staff later explained to Cuba's Politburo, would have been to sacrifice 147 Cubans in the embassy to save the weapons.[200]

Embassy staff simultaneously collected Patricia, Isabel, and their children, sheltered at the ambassador's residence; Prensa Latina staff; and money from Cuba's commercial office and fought to secure the release of two Cuban medical students detained and tortured the day before. Meanwhile, the Cubans waited all day to hear if the Soviet embassy would offer them an Aeroflot plane at Pudahuel Airport to leave. And Mario made arrangements for the Swedish ambassador—the most willing, and not a socialist bloc diplomat, which may have been a provocation—to take over the embassy's interests and arsenal, as well as asylee Max. Finally, the ambassador negotiated to have his Mexican, Peruvian, and Soviet counterparts accompany them to the airport.[201]

But the evening journey to Pudahuel was tense, with the Chilean military warning of possible sniper fire en route and La Moneda shrouded in darkness when they passed it. Beatriz, Luis, Maya, and Loti went ahead in one of the convoy's cars, while the ambassador, accompanied by his Swedish and Peruvian counterparts, rode in a bus at the back hoping to deter an attack on the thirty-three wooden crates containing arms behind them.[202] Once at the airport, there were further complications with bag searches. In addition, ground staff would not allow the airplane to be serviced, and complaining of the weight of the Cubans' cargo—more than four tons (in addition to excess passengers on the plane)—they refused to load it. Ten embassy staff therefore lifted their makeshift crates into the hold (a few began to come apart). The ambassador waited until everyone was on the plane before boarding himself.[203]

On the way to the airport, the Mexican ambassador had handed Beatriz a letter her mother had hastily written at Mexico's embassy, telling her about Salvador Allende's burial under armed guard at Santa Inés Cemetery in Viña del Mar. For all her arguments with Salvador and disagreements with Beatriz, she was distraught. "I don't know when I will see you.... I write to you crying because I would have liked to kiss you and hug you." Significantly, although she had not been able to see his body, Hortensia believed unequivocally that Allende had taken his own life. "He always said I will not die either sick or in exile," she wrote to her daughter.[204] Indeed, those closest to Allende accepted and understood he had died by suicide.[205]

The Cubans were nonetheless dubious. They were also unsure what resistance to the coup amounted to as they left Chile. Taking off from Pudahuel, they saw isolated flares, suggesting pockets of activity around Santiago. They had also heard unverified reports on open phone lines that PS leaders were fighting but received no contact from the Communist Party. Some grassroots Communist militants were said to have been firing at troops from buildings close to La Moneda, but Samuel Riquelme, one of those responsible for the party's military apparatus, had been in his office on the day of the coup, waiting for Allende's instructions, before going underground around midday. Overall, as they left Santiago, the Cubans surmised that resistance was "sporadic" with "lots of foci [of resistance] but ... uncoordinated ... everyone acting for themselves." And they presciently estimated the military would kill between one and seven thousand.[206]

Resistance was thus obviously weaker than the Left had hoped and military leaders feared. As Patricia remembered, Beatriz was among those who had been "naive" when it came to military preparations. The story of the left wing's plentiful arms caches that the armed forces reacted to so brutally—and the far Left boasted about—was quickly revealed to have been "a fairytale."[207] The image of Beatriz carrying a Colt pistol in La Moneda as if this were going to save her was also "risible" in hindsight, according to one of her companions, given their "bombing with cannons and bazookas."[208] The MIR's haphazard efforts to retrieve weapons from the Cubans that they had been promised in the event of a coup had also fallen apart: at around 10.30 A.M. on 11 September three miristas had arrived at the embassy unarmed. As Ulises Estrada would explain, embassy staff had made the difficult decision to give miristas only four small pistols rather than the more than one hundred AKs they were expecting. It had been too late and too risky, Estrada remembered. It would also have been precisely the type of provocation Castro had warned against, and the weapons would have been seized. Now, leaving Chile, they presumed the three miristas were dead.[209]

Unlike many seemingly ad hoc decisions made on 11 September, Allende seems to have been clearest about his own moves. His order for Beatriz to leave La Moneda was predictable. For almost a year, he had been trying to keep her from getting caught up in a confrontation. Given her predilection for armed struggle and her training, it was obvious she would want to join her father when the time came. And so Allende tried to curtail her freedom of action, co-opting trusted collaborators behind her back. It was an understandable move from a father desperate to protect his daughter. But Allende's efforts also amounted to an act of betrayal from the person Beatriz loved most. For in ordering her to leave the presidential palace, Allende effectively prevented her doing what she believed was her revolutionary duty. And he did so because she was a woman. Eduardo Paredes was allowed to stay and was killed by the military. As Félix reflected, Beatriz had reason to be jealous of the relationship Eduardo had with her father.[210] In later years, she tried to reason that Allende's decision was made simply because, for humanitarian reasons, he did not want women to die rather than because he believed that women were incapable of fighting.[211] Either way, as with the Cubans' refusal to train her to become a guerrilla insurgent and go to Bolivia, her gender—and men's views of what this meant—determined her choices. As Fernando Gómez reflected, if being refused guerrilla training in 1968 had been a first "death" for Beatriz, being forced to leave La Moneda was a second.[212] The latter may have saved her, as well as her unborn child, but it left a deep scar that would eat away at her henceforth.

9 : : : **Another Life**

Beatriz arrived in exile in Cuba on 13 September 1973. It had been a tense journey. Taking off from Pudahuel, the Aeroflot IL-62 plane flew unusually close to the Andes. The Soviet pilot—trained during World War II—also switched off lights, radios, and signaling devices to avoid detection. Passengers sat in the dark, collectively holding their breath.¹ As Patricia remembered, she did not speak to Beatriz until the plane stopped in Lima just after 4:00 A.M. And then it was difficult to know what to say. Looking at each other, they saw the "pain and the anguish and the death and all that it signified." "This is when our lives ended," Patricia explained, and "another life began."²

What this new life would look like and how those on board would make sense of the past was still to be determined. Reeling from defeat, Beatriz would be one of millions of left-wing Chileans—including more than two hundred thousand exiles—forced to take stock of what had happened, pick up the pieces, and, somehow, forge a new path ahead.³ Beatriz's close circle of friends—already on edge, having lived through the tense UP years—were now dispersed, on the run in Chile or around the world, adjusting to a violent, unsettling new reality, and fighting their own personal battles. A revolutionary era had come crashing down. "It is impossible to describe how, what you have built in a lifetime and in three years, is lost in a day," Beatriz would reflect.⁴ "One day we were all celebrating life," the Chilean left-wing intellectual Ariel Dorfman explained, "and the next day we were all, all of us, every last one, being hunted down."⁵ As well as losing her father and becoming an exile, Beatriz had to deal with the "the brutal destruction of her entire existence's achievements and dreams," Arturo Jirón reflected.⁶ True, she and others on the left clung to revolutionary convictions and the hope that circumstances would change so that they could overturn events. But for now, they confronted a jarring reality. "The time for reflection after the massacre begins," Beatriz's friend wrote to her.⁷

Beatriz touched down in Havana in this context. Cuba had been her second home since the late 1960s—a place she dreamed of. Yet arriving as an exile was different. With Fidel in Vietnam, Raúl Castro, President Osvaldo Dorticós, and other senior government officials were on the tarmac to greet her, Isabel, Patricia, their children, and Loti as the first Chilean exiles to arrive in Cuba.[8] But there was little time to talk. As Raúl reasoned, Beatriz was in a fragile state and needed rest.[9] Vilma Espín, the Federation of Cuban Women's president, who had first met a young sixteen-year-old Beatriz in Santiago when she arrived as a triumphant revolutionary in August 1959, took her directly to hospital. There, having been assured that the contractions she felt since the coup were not signs of premature labor, Beatriz was driven to a large house on the outskirts of Havana where the Cuban government housed state guests. She, Luis, Patricia and Isabel and their children, with Loti, would then live here in the months that followed.[10]

Simultaneously, across town, Luis and other Cuban embassy staff were debriefing Raúl, Piñeiro, Dorticós, and members of Cuba's Politburo at the Consejo de Estado. After three days of no sleep, Luis remembered the "tiredness and tension" of this five-hour meeting.[11] However, they had to reckon with important questions relating to Cuba's reputation as a revolutionary power, Chilean left-wing parties' future, and the global Left: had it been the right decision to negotiate departure from Chile, or should they have stayed and fought alongside Chilean left-wing parties? Why had Chile's road to socialism failed, and what ramifications did its defeat have for revolutionary strategy? Ultimately, Raúl and members of the Politburo told embassy staff they had done "the right thing" in leaving, that they had had little choice in the circumstances but that they would have to wait for Fidel's verdict when he returned.[12]

Arriving back in Cuba on 18 September, having cut his Vietnam visit short, Fidel refrained from delivering a decision. Instead, he focused on converting a scheduled anniversary event for neighborhood revolutionary committees on 28 September into a mass solidarity rally for Chile. And with Beatriz agreeing to speak at the event, he coordinated how she—and he—would frame their speeches. Letting Maya and Patricia's children play at his feet, his questions sometimes felt like an "interrogation," Patricia remembered, as he repeatedly asked details of phone calls, personnel, and movements during the coup.[13] But getting the story of what happened right mattered. Fidel had always had an acute understanding of the role of history. Since his struggle against Batista, he had appealed to history as a source of legitimacy, depicting his 1959 triumph as the fulfillment of Cuba's struggle for independence. When Che had died, he had also explicitly framed his death as underlining revolution's continued potential. In the onward march of history, revolutionary defeats—this time in Chile—could not be understood as reversals but as temporary obstacles in a forward struggle for socialism. "There may be setbacks, retreats," Fidel proclaimed in Prague en route back to Cuba, "but strategically Latin America's liberation movement advances."[14]

To confirm this, the coup's history had to be carefully constructed. How Beatriz portrayed her father's last movements and words had the potential to deliver instructions to the Chilean Left. How both dealt with the Chilean experience could also affect Cuba's international relations and its population's faith in revolutionary progress. Fidel's decision to distance Cuba from Chile's failed revolutionary process on 28 September needs to be read in this wider context. Underlining the "different roads" Chilean and Cuban revolutionary processes had taken, Castro noted that socialist goals were not in question but rather the Chileans' methods and particular circumstances. As Fidel explained, the coup had to be understood in the context of deeply embedded forces: the "bourgeois state apparatus," the armed forces' ambiguous role, a judicial system and media in "reactionary" hands, "landowners and the agrarian bourgeoisie" who "sabotaged" production, an "economy ... at breaking point" burdened by external debt, and U.S. imperialist aggression. The UP had been forced to operate with "hands tied," meaning Allende's years in power were "years of struggle, of difficulties, of agony."[15] As a diplomat in Havana reported, Castro was unmistakably trying to limit Chile's impact, treating it as "a self-contained issue."[16]

On another level, Fidel spent considerable time constructing a narrative of Allende's death. Contrary to agreement among Chileans who knew him best, Castro insisted he had been murdered—or at least this was how to present his death. Revolutionaries were expected to fight to the death, not resign themselves to defeat. As Castro and Dorticós had previously proclaimed, suicide was "unjustifiable and improper" revolutionary behavior. Yet battlefield martyrs, sacrificing themselves for the cause, were models to follow.[17] And it was this latter interpretation of Allende's death Cuban leaders preferred. As Carlos Rafael Rodríguez wrote to Beatriz, "The pride of knowing Salvador died as a hero" helped deal with the "immense pain" of what had happened.[18] Unsurprisingly, the most frequent image disseminated of Allende in Cuba henceforth depicted him firing an AK-47.[19]

Beatriz told Fidel she believed her father had died of suicide, but he was not swayed. Instead, he convinced *her* to portray Allende's death as an assassination.[20] In this respect, she—and the speech she delivered on 28 September—played a key role in constructing history. There was one witness to corroborate Fidel's story: Luis Renato González Córdoba, known as "Eladio," a young PS militant who had joined the GAP earlier that year, at age nineteen.[21] Yet Patricia and Beatriz were suspicious of him. They knew the GAP's members well but hardly knew him. His escape was also unclear, although he explained he feigned illness, and Mexican embassy records show he flew to Mexico City on 16 September.[22] As Patricia recalled, "The guy started telling his version of the coup," but details did not add up.[23]

While preparations for 28 September were under way, Luis had meanwhile been dispatched to Mexico City to meet Beatriz's mother, her sisters, and their families, arriving in exile. At the airport on 16 September, he joined President Luis Echeverría and three hundred government functionaries and journalists while twelve hundred gathered outside. In a brief press conference, Hortensia thanked Mexico effusively and asked journalists to report events in Chile.[24] Her decision to seek exile in Mexico was logical. She had good relations with Mexico's first lady, Maria Esther Zuna de Echeverría. From 11 September onward, Mexicans had shown widespread solidarity with Chile. As in Cuba, they observed three days of mourning for Allende.[25] Mexico was also receptive to asylees. Having already granted exile to more than 150 Chileans in the first two weeks after the coup, Mexico's Santiago embassy would lobby the Junta to take a further 200 Chileans and 100 foreign nationals by 28 September.[26] And in following years, approximately 3,000 exiles arrived in the country.[27]

However, in the coup's immediate aftermath, who inherited Allende's legacy—embodied by his immediate descendants—was deeply symbolic, and Havana's leaders were anxious to assume primary responsibility. Luis thus traveled to Mexico to persuade Hortensia to join Beatriz in Cuba. But she refused. She had never had a particularly sympathetic view of Cuba, and because the Cubans had worked closely with Paya, this compounded her distance.[28] On 24 September 1973, she nevertheless arrived in Cuba for a visit and, four days later, sat next to Fidel, alongside Beatriz, on the podium at the Plaza de la Revolución in front of a million Cubans.[29] Mexico's ambassador in Havana reported that it was the "most extraordinary" rally he had ever seen in Cuba.[30] And Hortensia's presence was a Cuban triumph for a carefully stage-managed event officially laying the Chilean president to rest in a unified way.

Although Hortensia did not speak at the event, this was the start of a major public role for her as the "face" of solidarity. As the Chilean Junta's representatives would fume, "The image of a woman inconsolable due to the loss of her saintly and adored husband attracts like a magnet, and she is used to focus points of attack against the Junta. Abroad, the customary and permanent Tencha-Salvador disagreements are not known. Nor is the Allende-Payita extramarital life."[31] However, the Junta's efforts to dis-

Beatriz Allende, Havana, 28 September 1973. Prensa Latina.

credit her in subsequent years were largely ineffective.³² Beatriz's relationship with her mother would also improve as she took on a protective role, often writing Hortensia's speeches and coaching her on speaking engagements.³³ And her mother rose to the occasion. "We may have disagreed often," she confided to Beatriz, "but I knew how to appreciate his greatness and his humanity."³⁴ Conveying this respect worldwide, she also changed her version of Allende's death: disavowing comments immediately after the coup, she now said her husband had been murdered.³⁵

As planned, Beatriz's speech on 28 September, delivered immediately before Fidel's three-and-a-half-hour eulogy, also added legitimacy to this story. "I come to confirm that the president of Chile fought to the end with a gun in his hand," she told crowds; "enemy bullets" killed him. She also attested to her father's loyalty to Cuba.³⁶ Even so, despite her long history of left-wing militancy, Beatriz was not used to public speaking. Footage of the 28 September event captures a heavily pregnant woman in mourning, with dark-rimmed eyes reading a previously prepared speech, barely able to see over four large microphones. The delivery was difficult but measured, straight, and stoic.³⁷

Crucially, as Allende's heir apparent, Beatriz was able to deliver a posthumous, final message to the Chilean Left, calling for continued revolutionary commitment. "I would like to tell you what [President Allende] asked me to transmit to you," she proclaimed: "He signaled that a long resistance began that day [11 September] and that Cuba and revolutionaries would have to help us fight it." Citing her father, she called for left-wing unity. And, addressing Allende's memory, she promised Chileans would "not give up": "Your people will not fold the flag of revolution; the struggle to death against fascism has begun and it will finish the day we have a free, sovereign, socialist Chile."[38] As she had written days earlier to Ramón Huidobro, a friend of her father's and a former ambassador in Buenos Aires, "One of his last phrases was 'this is how the first page [of history] is written, my people and America will write the rest.' Everything he said at the end was [with regard] to all honest and non-fascist men's responsibility to participate and help in future resistance to the greatest extent they could.... The task is everyone's and we all have a place in it."[39]

"We will win," Beatriz promised. Receiving a standing ovation, she stepped down from the podium, walked past Fidel, briefly held her mother's outstretched hand, and joined prolonged applause for her father's memory. She also took a deep breath and, with the cameras fixed on her, stared into the distance, wiping away the few tears she could not hold back.[40] From an early age, Beatriz had feared having to say good-bye to her father at a public funeral. As she had commented to a university friend when they had watched coverage of a state funeral in the early 1960s, this was one thing she did not like about Allende being a public figure: the idea that he would have a big funeral rather than something "intimate."[41] But, of course, such a private good-bye was impossible. And with her call for action in her father's name, Beatriz's new life as a leader of the resistance to Chile's dictatorship formally began.

Solidarity with the Resistance

Two weeks after speaking at the Plaza de la Revolución, Beatriz established the Comité Chileno de Solidaridad con la Resistencia Antifascista (Chilean Committee of Solidarity with the Antifascist Resistance) in Havana. She chose the anniversary of Che Guevara's death to inaugurate the committee: a date resonating with revolutionaries as a call to arms.[42] Henceforth, "eighty percent of her attention, day in day out, was centered on the struggle," a colleague remembered.[43] In this respect, Beatriz was not alone. As a friend wrote to her from exile in Paris, the key was to find something to do to "kill time and the imagination"—to alleviate "anguish of feeling far away and impotent."[44]

Beatriz's commitment nonetheless meant putting family life on hold. Already racked with guilt for being pregnant on 11 September and therefore unable to fight alongside her father, she worked full-time until giving birth on 5 November 1973.[45] As Luis remembered, Beatriz acted as her own midwife, managing the process. And they named their son Alejandro

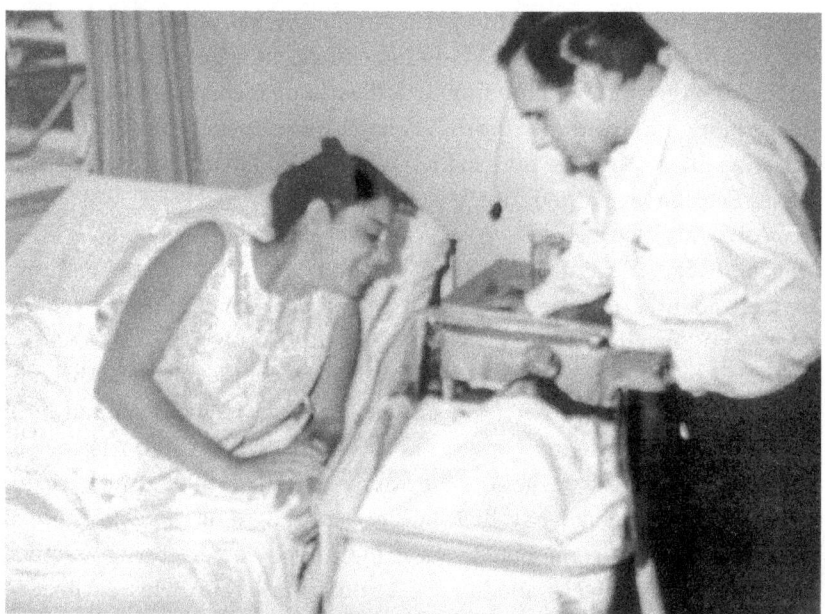

Beatriz, Alejandro, and Luis. Sagrado Corazón de Jesús Hospital, Havana, 5 November 1973. Alejandro Fernández Allende private collection.

Salvador—Alejandro being Fidel's middle name and Salvador to honor his grandfather. It was not like Maya's birth, surrounded by family and well-wishers. It was private. Beatriz received three bunches of flowers: one from Castro, one from Piñeiro, and one from the Federació de Mujeres Cubanas. And when Fidel visited her, he proposed Alejandro's surnames be swapped to Allende Fernández. The association between Beatriz's father and son was therefore compounded, adding to a sense she had abandoned one for the other.[46]

As if to compensate, Beatriz left her children with Loti and threw herself into solidarity work, honing her organizational skills and capacity for long hours learned as a medic, an Ejército de Liberación Nacional member, and her father's secretary. With Beatriz as the Comité Chileno's executive secretary, it grew rapidly. Housed in what had been the Chilean embassy in Havana in Vedado, the committee came to employ twenty people full-time over the next year. The Instituto Cubano de Amistad con los Pueblos (Cuban Institute of Friendship with Peoples, ICAP), which managed the island's relations with nongovernmental groups worldwide, paid staff salaries and travel expenses.[47] Cuba also funded printing costs and dissemination of information through the comité's bulletin, *Chile Informativo*, and special published reports, which became vital for solidarity work in international forums. Quite simply, like other Chilean exile-led organizations around the world dependent on state support, the Comité Chileno would not have functioned without such assistance. Indeed, the Cuban authorities developed "a very close relationship" with Chilean left-wing efforts. "All the information we had," Cuba's intelligence official, Ulises Estrada, explained, "we gave to her."[48]

Beatriz also worked closely with a dedicated Chilean team.[49] Writer Gonzalo Rojas, the embassy's chargé d'affaires, was named the committee's president, and Francisco Fernández Fredes, the embassy's first secretary and Socialist militant, took over when Rojas resigned to focus on writing. As part of the same generation, Beatriz worked well with Francisco. They had known each other since their late teens. Both had been members of the Brigada Universitaria Socialista (BUS), and Francisco had also grown close to the Allende family as a result of his wife's friendship with Isabel. Having studied law, he had taught at the University of Chile and worked in the Senate, assisting Allende before being assigned to Chile's embassy in Havana in 1971. As Beatriz told him, she now needed his diplomatic expertise to run the committee.[50] With his experience and her legitimacy as Salvador's heir, they represented the committee's executive leadership, which worked with a secretariat representing seven Chilean left-wing parties. The comité also established the Information Department, whose staff included the Chilean sociologist Marta Harnecker, soon to be Manuel Piñeiro's wife—another direct link to the Cuban government's highest echelons.[51]

The Comité Chileno's wider significance—and Beatriz's role in it—was speaking for La Izquierda Chilena en el Exterior (the Chilean Left Abroad). Established by exiles meeting in Havana between October and November 1973, responding to the Comité Chileno's direct call, this collective aimed to unify the Left and coordinate resistance efforts.[52] Crucially, with Beatriz acting as a bridge again, it brought the Movimiento de Izquierda Revolucionaria (MIR) and constitutive parties of the Unidad Popular (UP) together. As explained by Juan Carretero, Cuba's senior intelligence officer, the Chilean Left's sectarianism caused difficulties, but Beatriz dealt with divisions with "natural ease ... she was a point of unity."[53] That she had never held a formal position within the Socialist Party (PS) hierarchy helped. True, this "unity" was relative, tense, and short lived. But in asserting an international presence, it was symbolically and logistically important. The Izquierda Chilena directed its activities from two offices: the Comité Chileno in Havana and one in Rome called Chile Democrático. Officially, Rome was its headquarters, but in practice international work was divided, with Havana responsible for the Americas and Chile Democrático concentrating on Western Europe.[54]

Within this framework, the Comité Chileno's explicit goal was to "promote and develop solidarity" by raising awareness of Chilean developments worldwide, putting pressure on the dictatorship, and channeling support garnered from such campaigning to "the resistance" back home.[55] The notion of "resistance" was never defined nor could left-wing parties agree on the form it would take. And in future years it would be bitterly contested. But, for now, it was broad enough to encompass strategies ranging from preserving party structures and maintaining networks between militants and civil society (as in the case of the Communist Party [PCCh]) to campaigning to release political prisoners and supporting families of the dead or disappeared and armed resistance (as in the case of the MIR). As a Chilean left-wing declaration issued in Paris in February 1974 vaguely stated: "The choice between each method of struggle, and the initiation of each stage of the fight, will be the product of the correlation of forces and of the organization the people and revolutionaries reach at each moment." All parties also agreed on the need for defiance. "Brutal and massive repression has not only not been able to break workers' combat spirit and organization," the declaration underlined, "but it has not achieved the purpose of erasing the parties that express and lead mass combat from the map."[56]

From December 1973 on, Beatriz's most important role in resistance efforts was managing the Left's finances by distributing solidarity funds to Chile via a bank account she controlled in Cuba (CUBALSE-12).[57] By mid-1974, money collected in Europe was transferred to Cuba from an account in Luxembourg, while U.S. and Latin American solidarity campaigns routed funds through Mexico.[58] Beatriz then shared CUBALSE-12 funds between the Chilean Left's different parties. By August 1974, the CIA understood this arrangement, observing the Cubans and the PCCh had proposed it in February 1974 and calculated shares based on pre-coup trade union elections. The PS, the PCCh, and, after Cuban intervention, the MIR were all allocated 30 percent, with the Radical Party and two of the other small UP parties receiving the rest.[59] Using money allocated to the PS, Beatriz then followed party instructions and sent at least $200,000 to Chile between 1974 and 1977.[60] Meanwhile, total funds in the CUBALSE-12 account amounted to $350,000 in March 1975, $507,494 in July 1975, $80,000 in February 1976, and $106,060 in October 1977.[61] Precisely what happened to this money is hard to verify. Some was shared out in small amounts between families of clandestine party members or the detained for food, medical bills, and lawyers.[62] Money also covered living costs, transport, and false documentation for underground cadres.[63] It reached Chile mostly via Peru and Argentina, with help from Cuban embassies and sympathetic collaborators.[64] As Mónica Echeverría, Carmen Castillo's mother, recalled, she recruited various middle-age female friends and ex-diplomats to travel to Buenos Aires on "shopping trips," where they met contacts in cafes or bars and, among purchases, smuggled money into Chile hidden in secret compartments of suitcases.[65]

Even so, Beatriz never considered the money she distributed enough; it felt like "a drop of water."[66] Limited communication between clandestine party structures and the Chilean Left abroad also hampered coordination and targeting this money strategically.[67] On a trip to Rome in October, Hortensia had professed being in "daily contact with Chile," a claim the U.S. embassy picked up.[68] Yet the reality was very different. Getting information to and from underground parties in Chile relied on coded letters posted around the world and secret intelligence services (East German and Czechoslovak intelligence, for example, helped exiled PCCh leaders contact underground cadres in Chile).[69] However, the PS had no contingencies for maintaining clandestine contact within Chile let alone with the outside world, something Beatriz urged the party to address in early 1974 by selecting trusted cadres and training them in intelligence. Communication had to use "extreme security measures," she insisted to Carlos Altamirano, PS secretary-general.[70] But for the most part, communication was sporadic. Patricia Espejo had smuggled the address book she had kept as Allende's private secretary out of Chile in her bra, which allowed her and Beatriz in Havana to try and track down comrades in Santiago.[71] The Cubans also provided telephone lines passed through other countries. However, as Patricia remembered, "nobody was there."[72] They had either sought asylum and gone into exile, disappeared underground, or been captured.

Indeed, the news coming from Chile was devastating. Among those Beatriz had collaborated closely with in the past, Eduardo Paredes and all advisers to Allende in La Moneda had been detained and tortured or killed. Arnoldo Camú was murdered on 24 September. Those in charge of left-wing parties' military apparatus, such as Ariel Ulloa for the PS and Samuel Riquelme for the PCCh, had sought asylum.[73] And Bautista van Schouwen, MIR leader and Beatriz's friend from Concepción, had been detained at the end of November. As Miguel Enríquez wrote to Beatriz in a letter smuggled out of Chile in January 1974, "He fell accidently fulfilling his tasks ... unarmed.... The information is still confusing, but the most serious [sources] say he is in the military hospital.... Others say that they shot him."[74] Very quickly, Beatriz and Patricia also realized coup leaders had gained access to the secretaries' records when military pronouncements calling for Allende's associates to hand themselves in listed them in the precise order they had appeared on Patricia's contact sheet in her desk drawer at La Moneda. And with this realization came self-recrimination about naïveté and inadequate security.[75] "From Chile we know little," Beatriz admitted to another exile on the eve of the coup's first anniversary. "The news from the PS is contradictory and not very encouraging.... The PCCh, it seems, has recuperated and is finishing its reorganization.... The MIR has also received hard blows and I know little about the rest."[76]

Meanwhile, Beatriz's Chile, the world she had inhabited, was quickly turned upside down. The dictatorship targeted anybody who had any contact with Allende or Cuba. Her former tutor from Concepción, Jorge Peña, and her former supervisor, Manuel Ipinza, were detained in concentration camps, their offices ransacked.[77] A medic in southern Chile, the father of Marcela Contreras, Beatriz's friend from Dunalistair, was detained for his professional links to Allende.[78] In fact, medical doctors and health care professionals linked to the UP were especially persecuted—either killed, "disappeared," or fired—resulting in a "dire ... loss of human capital."[79] With approximately eight hundred doctors lost from the Servicio Nacional de Salud (SNS) and universities by 1975, solidarity groups noted a "sinister" pattern. The Junta and its supporters in Chile's Medical College also moved against the SNS, promoting privatized medicine as a substitute for Chilean health care's "socialist structure."[80]

Indeed, it was soon clear that the dictatorship's repression went far beyond targeting key individuals in Chile's left-wing parties. Twelve thousand were killed in the first few months, 80,000 were arrested within six months, 160,000 lost their jobs for political reasons, more than a thousand university lecturers were laid off at the University of Chile and the Catholic University, while murals were painted grey. In total, approximately one in ten families would suffer arrest, torture and/or exile.[81] Soldiers raided homes and burned books. Chileans who had Cuban publications therefore preemptively ripped out copyright pages, burned collections, or buried them, living in fear. As she waited for a clandestine eleno to help her seek asylum, Sonia Daza Sepúlveda also had to coach her six-year-old daughter, born in Havana, never to mention Cuba.[82] As Hernán Sandoval wrote to Beatriz from exile, "It appears our imagination does not enable us to understand.... The degree of psychological deterioration that some of our compañeros have shown when they arrived [in exile] leads you to think that fear is a force of extraordinary paralyzing and disintegrating power."[83]

Closer to home in Beatriz's case, family albums Hortensia had assiduously kept were also burned.[84] FAL and AK, Beatriz and Luis's two dogs, found at Tomás Moro, were also reclaimed by their previous owner and renamed "Nixon" and "Kissinger."[85] At the most mundane level, romantic attachment to revolutionary struggles or interest in Cuba and Third World causes were stamped out and erased in favor of pro-U.S. associations and anticommunist regulations.

Indeed, the dictatorship did not assume power to restore Chile to its pre-1970 or even pre-1964 position. Very quickly it became clear that military leaders, working with civilian advisers and intellectuals, wanted to erase vast swathes of Chile's past and revolutionary impulses enmeshed in society since at least the late 1950s and to exorcise ideas, identifications, and culture underpinning citizens' conception of the world. In doing so, the Junta constructed an exclusionary nationalism, expelling thousands, stripping them of their legitimacy, and redefining what being Chilean meant. Who was allowed to claim this identity and who was excommunicated now depended on disavowal of the Left in the broadest possible sense. It also meant conforming to conservative social norms, moral codes, and political behavior. Long hair was shorn, beards shaved, women returned to their traditional place in the home, and legal abortion was forbidden. Democratic rituals relating to election campaigning and militancy, so central to Chilean politics for decades, also disappeared. If these changes were telling of a Cold War conflict won by the forces of anticommunism, this was a particular form of it, bearing no resemblance to U.S. liberal democracy. A particularly vehement and violent Cold War ideological, cultural, and societal battle to determine Chile's future ensued. And among the many different groups it targeted were people like Beatriz, her world, and everything it stood for.

Highs and Lows of Solidarity

Chilean exiles internationalized their efforts to fight back. Millions would be receptive worldwide, projecting their own circumstances and ideals onto Chile's situation. And exiles like Beatriz, supporting, mobilizing, and crafting opposition to the dictatorship, were dexterous in tapping into these various meanings, ranging from the cause of radical socialist revolution to social democracy and, increasingly, human rights. As the Chilean former Socialist senator María Elena Carrera reflected, the Chilean Left waged "a battle on all fronts ... a political battle, an organizational battle, a battle of all types, and if possible, even military.... One of the fronts was the diplomatic front, the front of world public opinion, and that front was the one most accessible to those of us in exile."[86]

Indeed, aside from distributing solidarity funds, Beatriz's efforts to affect life in Chile required extensive travel to lobby governments to divest from and put pressure on the dictatorship. Within two months of its establishment, the Comité Chileno defined four priorities: stopping murder and torture, freeing political prisoners, guaranteeing asylum seekers' right to leave Chile, and preventing UP supporters from losing their jobs.[87] With these goals in mind, Beatriz's first major trips in December 1973 and January 1974 were to Western Europe. Leaving Maya and Alejandro in Havana, she and Luis visited Sweden and Italy, before returning to Cuba at New Year and then crossing the Atlantic a month later to visit France and West Germany. In Stockholm, Beatriz had publicly received approximately $100,000 from the Swedish prime minister, Olaf Palme. Everywhere she went, she gave speeches, held press conferences, gave interviews, and met with governmental and nongovernmental groups.[88] In Rome, over Christmas, she had also met other Chilean exiles staying at a small hostel run by Italian communists.[89] Returning to Europe in late January, she met with other members of the Chilean Left in Paris.[90] Western Europe's social democrats and left-wing parties provided a particularly receptive environment. As one exile, who had studied in Paris in the 1960s, wrote to Beatriz, French mobilization for Chile appeared to surpass the pro-Vietnam movement he had witnessed the decade before.[91] In Munich, at a rally at the end of January, Beatriz thanked solidarity activists and asked them to continue campaigning against dictatorial repression.[92]

However, Beatriz's trips abroad were tense. Cuban embassies in Europe had intelligence to suggest Chileans sympathetic to the Junta were arriving in countries Beatriz visited with the intention of "doing harm." Although nothing happened, Luis remembered constantly fearing something might.[93] The Chilean junta certainly recorded the Allende family's travels and public engagements, noting Beatriz's "importance" for the "resistance" and Havana's significance for "subversion" in Chile.[94] And they were not alone. Brazilian intelligence recorded Beatriz's and Hortensia's interventions.[95] And Mexican intelligence kept close tabs on Hortensia's daily movements, while receiving reports from other foreign intelligence agencies on her activities abroad.[96] Moreover, the dictatorship unsurprisingly identified Beatriz personally as an enemy. Following her trip to Stockholm in December 1973, it thus moved to strip her of her nationality. Citing Law No. 175, decreed a week before Beatriz had arrived in Sweden, the military began proceedings against her, arguing collecting money for the "resistance" exemplified what it meant to "seriously threaten the essen-

Beatriz, Stockholm, December 1973. Biblioteca Virtual Salvador Allende Gossens.

tial interests of the state from abroad." A simple report from the Chilean embassy in Stockholm recording dates of her visit and public engagements was deemed sufficient grounds.[97]

Of course, Beatriz's travels were examples of what the Chilean Junta perceived as a broader threat. Following the Pan-European Conference of Solidarity with Chile for four hundred participants that Beatriz and other exiled left-wing leaders attended in Paris in early July 1974, Chile's ambassador in France insisted the dictatorship "worry in a primordial way." These kinds of meetings had symbolic importance, he argued, being used to disseminate left-wing accords and give a false "impression of unity" among "extremist fronts." That they could count on professional politicians and "abundant international funding" made them particularly dangerous.[98] To counter "anti-Chilean" sentiment and what they regarded as an "international Marxist offensive," the Junta's diplomats reactively asked for money, resources, and guidance, suggesting new publications to answer the Left's "bulletins." "Modern advertising is an indispensable but complex and expensive weapon," Chile's ambassador in Paris argued.[99] A week after Beatriz's visit to Stockholm, for example, the Junta thus sent $5,000 and a new cultural attaché to Stockholm.[100] In under a year, Chilean left-wing exiles' organizing and activism therefore had a tangible and costly impact on the Junta's reputation. "Foreign and domestic policy is one and indivisible," noted the Chilean Foreign Ministry in October 1974.[101] "The battlefront" to determine Chile's future, the Junta's ambassador in Paris warned, had moved "outside Chile's borders."[102]

In this "battle," Beatriz's personal involvement was significant.[103] Local campaigners in the United States, for example, valued her visit to Washington, deeming it "eminently useful" for lobbying congressional figures to cut off aid to the dictatorship, especially because coming face-to-face with Beatriz's "personal loss" moved interlocutors. Her visit had served to "reconfirm and re-enthuse our friends to take particular note of Chile," her Washington hosts concluded.[104] Through her communication with the National Coordinating Center in Solidarity with Chile (NCCSC) in the United States, Beatriz was also able to set specific campaigning goals, including boycotts and pickets on Chilean copper imports, demonstrations against businesses operating in Chile or Chilean companies with U.S. offices, pressuring banks to stop loans to the dictatorship, and mass mobilization for coup anniversaries.[105] In September 1974, Beatriz also led large-scale tributes to her father in Venezuela and Colombia, where she joined Angela Davis and her mother, just arrived from Berlin.[106] In subsequent months she then traveled to Algeria, London, Paris, Brussels, and Finland.[107]

A year after the coup, the Chilean Left's biggest success was UN Resolution 3219, condemning the dictatorship's human rights violations by 90 votes to 8 with 26 abstentions.[108] Cuba's UN delegation helped prepare this resolution, which was supported by Non-Aligned states, Socialist bloc countries, and Western European delegations. As Ricardo Alarcón, Cuba's representative in New York, noted, the vote was widely considered "the hardest blow to the Junta so far."[109] And Beatriz acknowledged the strategy of reaching out to a "broad front" of international supporters had been important.[110] The Comité Chileno's preparation of materials for dissemination at the United Nations was also effective and replicated in other international forums.[111] By August 1974, five hundred copies of *Chile Informativo* were being distributed to solidarity committees, embassies, political parties, organizations, and governments.[112] And local solidarity committees petitioned the Chilean Left for further materials. "Especially useful are communiqués expressing the unity of the Chilean left and people against the military government," a member of the NCCSC wrote, asking for "new posters ... records or literature" to distribute in the United States, considering them "vital ... [for] propaganda and fund-raising."[113]

Left-wing Chileans back home and in exile clearly appreciated global solidarity work.[114] Writing from Berlin, Guaraní Pereda, a member of the PS Central Committee, applauded Beatriz's efforts as "beautiful and instructive"—of "great value."[115] In January 1974, Miguel Enríquez had also written that he had been able to follow her work from Chile via brief reports published by newspapers and long-wave radio. He urged her to continue calling for liberation of political prisoners by publicizing names of those detained and disappeared. "Everything you have done has been excellent and an enormous help to the resistance here," he informed her.[116] Materials produced by exiles also reached Chile. As a woman in the armed opposition to Pinochet in the 1980s recalled, she first understood the dictatorship's repression in 1975, at age sixteen, reading a clandestine report produced abroad and distributed secretly, held together with scotch tape.[117] Similarly, the PCCh's clandestine leadership in Chile conveyed thanks for solidarity efforts, describing them as "vital" and a "mighty stimulus."[118]

Solidarity work thus mattered a great deal for symbolic, if not practical, reasons. Whether this defiance could bring the Junta down—let alone salvage the revolutionary project Beatriz had been part of—was still to be determined. But when it came to a global battle of ideas, it effectively demarcated the way the conflict would be fought and constructed an enduring narrative of the dictatorship.[119] Transcending ideological labels by taking ownership of the language of human rights and democracy proved particularly useful in reaching wider audiences than a focus on revolutionary socialism might have done. And the Chilean military's brutal repression, its incompetence, and intransigence on the world stage provided ample evidence to work with. Another message exiles underlined was imperialism's responsibility for the coup.[120] This was actually not how parties generally understood the reasons for the UP's failure internally, with self-criticism focusing on their own—or each other's—failings. But in solidarity activism, Chileans pointed to U.S. intervention as the primary cause of conflict, delegitimizing coup supporters as imperialist puppets. As Beatriz told *Exprés Español*, the Right had been "organized, orchestrated, helped, and financed by North American imperialism."[121]

A year after the coup, Chilean-led solidarity efforts could therefore celebrate various successes. This did not mean exiles faced no challenges. Particularly detrimental, as we shall see, was the corrosion of the Chilean Left's semblance of unity. Compared with the straightforward task of stating what they were against, constructing a collective narrative of future priorities was far more difficult. But spearheaded by such people as Beatriz, the global solidarity campaign that was launched immediately after the coup brought left-wing factions together, helping ensure its fragile survival against all odds.

Daily Life in Cuba

Exile meanwhile meant adjusting to daily life in Cuba, building a home, and adapting to new circumstances. Cuba was not unfamiliar to Beatriz. Unlike many exiles, she did not have to learn a language. She also had friends on the island and a Cuban husband. But Havana was no longer the city of Beatriz's first visit or her years of guerrilla internationalism. By the mid-1970s, the island felt different. For more than a thousand exiles arriving in the first year after the coup, it was also a forced refuge rather than the stepping-stone to an imagined revolutionary future it had once appeared to be.[122]

As a figurehead for the Chilean community in Cuba, Beatriz was in an awkward position between her compatriots and the Cuban state. As Francisco Fernández would write to a fellow exile in Costa Rica, "refugees" were the Comité Chileno's second priority after solidarity, involving "solving their various problems."[123] This was not easy. Arriving with little, Chilean exiles needed housing, food, and work. But Cuba did not have ample resources to offer them. To the contrary, in a speech at the Thirteenth Congress of the Confederación de Trabajadores de Cuba (Cuban Workers Confederation) in Havana in mid-November 1973, Fidel Castro acknowledged Cuba's economic challenges. As the British chargé d'affaires reported, the speech was "shot through with anxiety, both explicit and implicit." Just as Chilean left-wing exiles were arriving in the country that had inspired them when it came to building a revolutionary state, Castro was admitting how much was left to do. As he had told more than two thousand delegates from sixty countries, "Cuba was not yet qualified to 'live in communism.' Cuba still lacked a developed economy, wealth derived from the workers' efforts, and the right 'culture' and was thus at a 'socialist stage.'" Castro also talked of "new sacrifices," introducing water meters, and worsening electricity problems. Perhaps more significant, Castro's speech put an end to Che Guevara's "new man" ideal of socialist development. The old Cuba that had captivated Beatriz was making way for one in which material rewards drove the economy. Emphasis was also placed on efficiency and steadfast adherence to Soviet-style planned development.[124] Late 1973 was therefore a difficult time for exiles in Cuba. The Workers' Congress had elected Salvador Allende as its "honorary president," Hortensia was invited to give a speech, and Cuba's solidarity with Chile was repeatedly proclaimed. At the event, Fidel Castro had also asked five hundred Cuban construction workers' "micro-*brigadistas*" to donate one apartment each to a Chilean family within a year. How Cuba would accommodate twice as many exiles as those already in Havana was unclear.[125]

For over a year after the coup, most Chileans lived in Havana's hotels, with the Hotel Presidente taken over completely. Arriving in December 1973, Sonia stayed with her children in the Habana Libre for almost two years.[126] As well as living in cramped conditions with no certainty of the future, exiles were also dealing with trauma. As Francisco recalled, helping them was "very hard ... because there were people who were in a state of profound shock."[127]

In this context, the Cuban government and civil society expended considerable efforts to make exiles feel at home. As one young Chilean remembered, she encountered "love on the street."[128] Exiled children were enrolled in schools and received Christmas presents, despite Cubans not celebrating Christmas themselves. Having been asked by his party to serve as a coordinator for Chilean residents at the Hotel Presidente, Enrique San Martín González, who had run the culture and publications department at Chile's Ministry of Education during Allende's presidency, was given tickets to plays and musicals to distribute. He also organized a cinema group, and Cuban personalities gave talks "to help [Chileans] integrate." Some exiles also engaged in "voluntary jobs" to repay solidarity.[129]

However, not all exiles integrated well, and as months passed, the situation grew tense. As the CIA noted, many were "unhappy about their lot in Cuba" and felt "isolated and cut off from meaningful political activity."[130] Finding employment was particularly problematic, especially as some were uninterested in work, believing exile would be short lived. Many also demanded armed training so they could return quickly to Chile and fight the dictatorship.[131] They were "very impatient," Francisco explained, "there were people who childishly ... believed it was a case of being in Cuba 3 or 4 months to receive military preparation and then returning to incorporate themselves into the struggle ... without establishing whether there was infrastructure ... if there was an organization that could welcome them."[132] "There was a lot of fantasy," Manuel Cabieses, a mirista who arrived in Cuba in 1975 after being in prison, similarly reflected.[133]

Beatriz and Francisco spent considerable time dealing with such "fantasies," especially as the Cubans were reticent to coordinate an armed insurgency in Chile immediately after the coup.[134] As the CIA observed in mid-1974, Havana's leaders were "not sanguine about the prospects of converting ... Chilean exiles into guerrilla fighters." Although they accepted armed revolution against the dictatorship was ultimately necessary and trained "some exiles ... for eventual infiltration into Chile," they were "cautious about the time and place. They feel the Chilean people must first tire of the Junta and its policies."[135] As Ulises Estrada explained, "The internal movement was very fragile.... It was very hard, and if they had gone they would have had to fight against the junta without the [right] conditions. Morale would have fallen ... practically everyone was operating alone." In these early years, those with training were therefore stuck in Havana waiting for things to improve. "They did not know how to create the conditions," he added. Even if they had known, he continued, doing so "could take your life." "Later the fight was more organized," he explained, "but at the beginning it was crazy."[136]

Beatriz and Francisco mediated between exiles and Cuban authorities in this context. At a meeting in early 1974 in one of Havana's hotels, things became heated, with exiles berating Beatriz and Francisco for not doing enough to persuade the Cubans to train more of them militarily.[137] Beatriz also found dealing with complaints about living arrangements difficult and was "sharp" with exiles' demands.[138] When some of the Hotel Presidente's residents issued a formal "complaint" in 1974 regarding conditions, Beatriz got "very angry." At a long meeting on the hotel's terrace, she criticized the Chileans' "lack of consideration" for Cuba's position, facing a blockade and receiving so many exiles. Instead of being critical, she argued, exiles should be grateful.[139]

With it becoming clear that the Chilean dictatorship would last years, the Cuban state nevertheless had to find longer-term solutions to exiles' housing and employment. Relocating exiles to other parts of Cuba predictably met resistance, not least because Chileans feared being unable to communicate with anyone beyond the island. The Comité Chileno therefore became a central postal service, distributing letters to and from exiles via people who traveled to Mexico, Panama, Canada, and beyond. Ultimately, Beatriz and Francisco were also tasked with validating decisions and persuading exiles to accept them. Chilean left-wing parties were allowed to name a few militants for priority housing in Havana. Otherwise, ICAP assigned Havana's apartments to families, sending couples and single adults elsewhere.[140] Those who received housing in Havana rarely got accommodation in the center, with the majority destined for Alamar, a large community east of the city that micro-brigades had constructed since 1971. And it was not unusual to wait for two hours for a bus to Alamar, one exile remembered.[141] Chilean exile groups of fifteen to twenty had also joined micro-brigades to construct two of these apartment blocks.[142]

Even so, once built, the Cuban state was eager to show it could provide a modern home. As one exile remembered, his family received a "TV, bed, kitchen ... refrigerator, everything, even what all Cubans did not have." Families also received food rations, including six kilograms of rice a month, one kilogram of meat or chicken a week, milk for children, bread, and vegetables. These rations nevertheless required readjustment. Even

Isabel, Beatriz, unidentified, and Patricia, Havana, ca. 1975.
Isabel Jaramillo private collection.

during UP years of scarcity, exiles had tended to earn professional salaries and enjoy more comfortable lives. "The truth [is] that we were not used to it," one recalled. "We learned that to make empanadas when there wasn't any meat to put in them, we could make them without ... with fried onions.... We became inventors."[143]

Beatriz found the exiles' situation especially uncomfortable as their circumstances contrasted sharply with hers. She, Patricia, Isabel, and their children had everything they needed in their large government-owned house from day one. Their children ate meat every day, and drivers were on hand to take them where they wanted to go. Feeling awkward she was treated so differently, Beatriz would therefore ask her driver to drop her two or three blocks away when she went to talk to Chileans in the Hotel Presidente.[144]

In early 1974, Beatriz and Luis had then been assigned their own apartment in Vedado and would subsequently receive a house with a garden in Miramar. As Luis remembered, Celia Sánchez, Fidel's confidant and secretary to the Cuban Council of Ministers, had personally furnished it with furniture, sheets, towels, and everything the family needed.[145] As well as an apartment, the Cubans also gave Beatriz a car, a cook, and a cleaner. Although both were from Cuba's Tropas Especiales, who could provide the Cuban regime with information on her daily life, Beatriz welcomed them. For someone who had never done domestic chores or fried an egg, they were indispensable.[146] In addition to Loti looking after the children, they freed up time for committee work and travel. And Beatriz could also count on the funds her father had given Luis before the coup. In agreement with Fidel Castro and in accordance with Allende's wishes, Beatriz took responsibility of the large briefcase of money Luis had been given in late 1972, distributing its contents between herself, Hortensia, her sisters, and Paya.[147] On one visit to Mexico, possibly using these funds, Beatriz also subsequently helped Carmen Paz buy a car and an apartment. Exile "would be long," she told her sister, concerned that she should be comfortable.[148]

As if to make up for her and her family's own privileged position, Beatriz actively tried to ease her friends' lives.[149] For many, she quickly became someone they depended on for money, guidance, and a link to Allende's legacy. Her militant resistance gave exiles hope. Foreigners depended on her to channel support to the right people, to travel to solidarity events, and to talk about her father. Those resisting the dictatorship in Chile may not have known she was personally responsible for bank accounts, but they also relied on funds she managed from abroad to survive. And exiles around the world wrote to her for instructions and assistance in securing visas or providing materials.

Beatriz juggled these requests as best she could. Yet she never believed she was doing enough.[150] "She always demanded more and more of herself," a friend who saw her at the end of 1974 remembered.[151] But how much more could she do? There were warnings from friends and family that she needed to slow down. Already, in early 1974, for example, Chile's former Socialist senator, Maria Elena Carrera, wrote to her from Peru: "Rest a little, take care of the child ... do not believe that life is eternal.... We have the right to be happy once in a while. This also helps at work. Take every moment of personal happiness and enjoy it.... I have not done what I recommend and I regret it."[152] But Beatriz seems not to have taken this advice. As she would write to a fellow exile, "Not to rest a minute and to maximize initiatives that contribute to making the Junta's life difficult is our basic duty."[153] And in prioritizing politics—as she had done her whole adult life—she was not alone. As a former member of the GAP wrote to her from exile, "The ghosts of comrades from the GAP, of your father, of so many people with so much hope that believed in us and that live, suffer, and fight in Chile make it a moral obligation."[154]

The problem was that as time passed, Beatriz grew increasingly frustrated with what this maximum effort was achieving. She found Miguel Enríquez's death on 5 October 1974, as well as the fate of her longtime friend Carmen Castillo, who was pregnant with Miguel's child and had been wounded at the time of his murder, particularly difficult. "I never thought we would have to attend such an event," she wrote shortly after a memorial service for Miguel in Havana; it is "still difficult to get used to." She campaigned tirelessly for Carmen's release from prison and flew immediately to meet her in Cambridge, England, when she arrived in exile.[155] "She took me in her arms, for a long time. She listened to me," Carmen remembered.[156] Working for Cuba as well as the Chilean Left, Beatriz also accompanied Carmen to the Cuban embassy in London, where she recorded an account of Miguel's final moments for Beatriz to take back to Havana.[157]

What Miguel's death meant and how the MIR's conduct in Chile before and after the coup was interpreted nevertheless became deeply contested. As always, Beatriz clearly sympathized with her friends from Concepción. In a eulogy, Cuban leader Armando Hart celebrated Miguel's "heroic death" and "unquestionable talent" and called for a "close alliance" between the PCCh, PS, and the MIR, underlining the legitimacy of responding to reactionary violence with revolutionary violence. Hearing it, Beatriz wrote of her "happiness." As she privately confessed, this was "at last" what many needed to hear: "Something that satisfies us completely. It was what we were missing." Yet she also confessed that the speech left "a bitter taste" because she "would have liked some party of the Chilean Left or some leader, during this year, to have raised something similar."[158]

The problem, of course, was not everyone shared Beatriz's view of the MIR. Just as the MIR had divided the Left before the coup, its call for armed resistance to the dictatorship—as part of a broader, regional "revolutionary war" akin to Vietnam's struggle against the United States—was also challenged.[159] And now, at the level of exile-led solidarity campaigns, disagreements broke out over how to remember Enríquez. In Rome, for example, a "fierce" discussion ("verbally violent") ensued between Communist and Socialist Party militants about whether to highlight the UN's condemnation of the Junta or Miguel in publications. Arguing the MIR had worked "against Allende" during the UP and had been proven wrong, Communists accused the Socialists of continuing to give the MIR "oxygen" despite negative consequences. Socialists, for their part, insisted on trying to build unity between different left-wing factions, arguing that Miguel had been a "consistent antifascist fighter, who died heroically." When it came to how the Chilean Left presented itself to the outside world and how its constituent parties viewed resistance priorities, different groups thus appeared to be pulling in opposite directions.[160] To Beatriz, solidarity work at the UN and armed resistance were not contradictory. She embraced the former to support the latter. But, to others, Chileans and non-Chileans included, the MIR's position was divisive.

Indeed, as we shall see, the facade of left-wing unity declared immediately after the coup with the establishment of the Izquierda Chilena quickly gave way to the reassertion of preexisting divisions and new disputes. At stake was not only whether Chilean left-wing parties could bring down the dictatorship but also what would replace it. And when it came to defining a future, the Junta's opponents disagreed. If deciding on a revolutionary path had proved difficult before 1973, the UP's overthrow, repression, and dispersal of left-wing forces around the globe now made the task even harder.

10 : : : **Disillusionment**

In August 1975, Beatriz resigned from her role as the Chilean Left's coordinator of solidarity funds. She told Carlos Altamirano, secretary-general of the Socialist Party, her decision resulted from problems affecting solidarity on the eve of the coup's second anniversary. Two years after the Unidad Popular's overthrow, left-wing parties had helped grow a global campaign against the dictatorship comprising diplomatic isolation and sanctions, international condemnation of human rights violations, written reports, and fundraising. However, these achievements masked difficulties. Beatriz's resignation letter warned of a crisis of leadership and coordination threatening the relationship between Chilean and non-Chilean solidarity activists. The Socialist Party's divisions inside Chile and in exile, not to mention tensions existing between these interior and exterior wings, exacerbated problems. With initial sympathy ebbing since 1973, it was now more important than ever to maintain momentum and faith among supporters worldwide, to keep up pressure against the dictatorship. Concerned that trust was breaking down and fearing her association with the Chilean Left's increasingly problematic management of funds would bring the Allende name into disrepute, Beatriz described her decision as definite. A flyer printed by the U.S. National Coordinating Center in Solidarity with Chile (NCCSC) publicly naming Beatriz as being in charge of a European bank account appears to have been the final straw. The Rome office was in charge of the Luxembourg account from which funds were transferred to the Cuban account she managed. But with her counterparts in Rome refusing to answer questions about donations and transfers, she was unable to thank solidarity organizations or answer questions, thus creating a "climate of distrust." It was both "just" and "essential" that Chilean left-wing parties communicate their gratitude, she complained, and yet despite her "repeated requests," such messages were not forthcoming.[1]

Beatriz's decision to stop managing the Chilean Left's funds from Cuba did not imply resignation from solidarity activism or the Socialist Party (PS). Her life continued to revolve around her work at the Comité Chileno, frequent trips abroad to mobilize support, mediation between different left-wing factions, or coordination of international campaigns. She also remained in charge of the PS's account in Cuba. But the tone of her communication with colleagues grew more critical. After receiving a "painful" letter from a Dutch solidarity organization that had not been thanked for its donation, she demanded "serious" work "to create a climate of efficiency and trust, in order not to harm [our] compañeros in Chile." When it came to the Socialist Party's finances, she also insisted Altamirano take better control, given the party needed "money to fight." With "all trends or factions" asking for support, she urged him to move beyond the "abstract" and make this his priority.[2] Months later she was still demanding resolutions: Who was going to replace her and respond to solidarity organizations? she asked the Rome office. Who was going to thank people for money that arrived (like the 300,000 kronas from Sweden or the $1,000 from the Vancouver Chilean Association)? Who was going to share out nearly $80,000 in the CUBALSE-12 account?[3] When her resignation and the measures she asked the PS to enact still appeared pending after a further six months, Beatriz's frustration grew. The solidarity account was "going to hell," she complained.[4] And although he urged her to rescind her decision, Hernán del Canto, a member of the PS leadership in exile, acknowledged she had good reason to be "tired and angry." Parties had not treated her and those supporting the resistance seriously enough.[5]

When colleagues belittled Beatriz as being a bit *depre* (depressed), she hit back, asserting she was "*critical* which is something different."[6] As she admitted, she found it hard not to express annoyance.[7] And yet Beatriz's confidence and room for maneuver were diminishing. As the toll of the dictatorship's repression grew in 1975–77 and Chile's left-wing parties were consumed by defeat and self-criticism, exiles' ability to affect change diminished. For all the Cubans' logistical support, it was also increasingly clear that Beatriz's position in Havana had drawbacks when it came to resources and communication. And although solidarity campaigns for Chile brought new attention to human rights during these years, Chileans involved in day-to-day activism faced a painful reality: the rise of a global human rights discourse by 1977, epitomized, but not exclusively represented by, President Jimmy Carter's new foreign policy agenda, which put pressure on the Junta but did little to advance the goals of Chilean left-wing parties.

Indeed, more and more, what the Chilean Left was fighting for was ambiguous and diffuse, with the exigencies of solidarity campaigning compromising long-held commitments to revolutionary socialism. Certainly, Pinochet's regime remained firmly entrenched in power, stronger than in 1973 regardless of international pressure. Outside Chile, counterrevolutionary victories, such as the coup in Argentina in March 1976, bringing a virulent anticommunist dictatorship to power, added to a pessimistic landscape. After initial years of defiance, the Left acknowledged that there were no quick solutions on the horizon. Revolutionary projects and parties that had been built over the course of previous decades were under siege. The socialist future that people like Beatriz had once envisaged as proximate now also faded from view. It was therefore unsurprising that Beatriz grew disillusioned with the world around her and her inability to change it. And she was by no means the only exile to suffer depression as the dictatorship's intransigence and longevity sunk in.

Priorities

Beatriz continued to be driven by the need to support people inside Chile. "You are right," her friend wrote to her in late 1975, "[we must] not lose patience or our 'compass'.... The most important thing is to make things better and less difficult for those who are fighting inside Chile."[8] As a declaration by the Chilean Left issued in Paris after the coup had emphasized, "Those of us who are currently outside the country dedicate all our efforts to contributing to the common struggle directed from within."[9] But two years after the coup, the situation was dire. A report on human rights in Chile compiled by the Comité Chileno in 1975 listed 6,000 Chileans being detained at the time (with a cumulative total of 95,000 having been detained since 1973), systematic torture, involving sexualized violence, mock executions, and intimidation of family members. Added to this were almost 1,000 counted disappearances in Santiago alone.[10] As U.S. policymakers observed, the dictatorship was in "complete control of the internal situation," and although the Junta suggested Chile remained under siege, U.S. observers concluded it was "unlikely that any significant 'guerrilla' effort could be mounted" in the foreseeable future.[11] Socialist leaders in Chile drew similar conclusions. Meeting a young militant clandestinely in Santiago in June 1975, one described the party's leadership as "dead men walking." "As a generation we made many mistakes," he acknowledged, arguing resistance had meaning only because a younger generation would replace them.[12]

In this context, the help Chilean exiles offered was important but insufficient. "If something worries me," Beatriz had written to her aunt Laura, in a letter delivered by Cuban intelligence agents in early 1975, "it is hearing that 'money doesn't arrive,' 'that inside [Chile] comrades are dying of hunger,' 'that there are still no secure channels to send money,' that 'no one receives anything' and to know that the Party has money in its account *although it is not much*."[13] When Beatriz received communications from Chile regarding the dictatorship's repressive apparatus, she found them difficult. "I confess that I find it hard to remain calm ... to think that behind these forms there is a story of a revolutionary prisoner in the hands of these sons of a b ...!"[14]

The Left claimed some success when Unidad Popular (UP) ministers imprisoned on Dawson Island, such as Clodomiro Almeyda and Orlando Letelier, were released in early 1975. When Laura Allende arrived in Cuba, having also been detained, she was warmly greeted.[15] In April 1975, the Socialist Party had subsequently held its first full plenum in Havana since the coup, agreeing to restructuring and priorities. It had also acknowledged the lack of a cohesive "military policy" prior to the coup and "the consequential need to adapt the revolutionary movement organically, ideologically, and militarily."[16] Initially, Beatriz hoped this plenum would strengthen the party and the collective Left.[17] In mid-1975, in Oaxtepec, Mexico, and Berlin, the UP's parties had then met for the first time since the coup to reconstitute their alliance.[18]

However, the process had not been easy, with factions disagreeing bitterly, not least about the UP's relationship with the Movimiento de Izquierda Revolucionaria (MIR) and the Christian Democratic Party.[19] The existence of two different underground Socialist factions in Chile since early 1974—the Dirección Interna and the Coordinadora Nacional de Regionales—complicated the picture. At the PS's Havana plenum, in fact, the party's secretariat had been split over which to support, with Altamirano vacilating and effectively supporting both until at least 1976.[20] Then, in June 1975, leaders of the PS's Dirección Interna in Chile, Carlos Lorca, Exequiel Ponce, and Ricardo Lagos Salinas, were detained and disappeared. Friends of Beatriz's, key figures in Chile's revolutionary generation coming of age in the 1960s, and close collaborators of her father's during the UP years, their presumed deaths were big defeats. Writing to Altamirano, Beatriz preferred not to dwell on her feelings but focus instead on responding: "Accumulated hatred should make us more efficient in all areas. I am now very concerned about the cohesion and unity of the PS; the significance of this blow and the even greater responsibility that now rests on your shoulders." She urged him to authorize sending money from the PS's Cuban account to Chile.[21]

Yet, as she complained, her pleas went unanswered. She also believed the Dirección Interna had been betrayed. In March 1974, it had issued a critical account of the party's conduct prior to the coup, underlining its failure to establish a "leading force capable of successfully directing the process," noting errors of "insurrectionist verbalism" and describing communication between the party and working-class masses as "dramatically impotent." Divisions between the party's interior and exterior wings had subsequently grown.²² As CIA analysts had concluded in August 1974, "the exiles seem to make their own decisions, frequently to the disgust of those at home." Noting the Socialist Party was "badly fragmented," they identified divisions between moderates inclined to abandon Marxism-Leninism and those advocating mass revolutionary violence. While Altamirano seemed to shift toward the former, intelligence sources indicated "the Cubans, the MIR, the ERP, and Beatriz Allende" were opposed, supporting "PS radicals [in Chile], led by Exequiel Ponce."²³ Communist Party leaders similarly informed East German leader Erich Honecker that the PS's situation was "very difficult," with Altamirano quite simply arguing that the Dirección Interna was "wrong."²⁴ Now, less than a year later, with the Dirección Interna's leadership captured, Beatriz criticized the inadequate support internal leaders had received. "It angers me to say the least," she would write to Gustavo Ruz, a member of the Dirección Interna who had escaped into exile; "nobody moved a finger," she complained, arguing the PS had been guilty of "bad solidarity work" and had lacked "orientations and instructions" after the coup.²⁵

The lack of clear guidance and coordination amid such divisions became increasingly problematic in 1975. By the end of the year, with further disagreements among leaders in exile, in addition to the appearance of a third internal faction of the PS in Chile, Beatriz was among those who regarded the "PS's weaknesses" as reaching "a tragic level."²⁶ Divisions between the Communist Party and the MIR had also sharpened, particularly when the PCCh published a document in September 1975 criticizing the MIR's armed actions for playing into the Junta's hands. It also called miristas petite bourgeois ultra-leftists who had deviated toward *revolucionarismo*, deserted the proletariat, and sparked working-class division. Socialists also viewed this document as an attack on their positions before the coup and those recently agreed on at the Havana plenum.²⁷

Beatriz's perspective and that of her collaborators reveal the impact of these splits. On one level, PS internal wrangling consumed leaders' attention, engendering strategic paralysis. In this context, requests for greater leadership and coordination increasingly reached Beatriz. Writing from Bogotá, for example, Edgardo Condeza, a Socialist militant, friend, and fellow medical student from Concepción, urged her to pass on requests for guidance to Altamirano and Adonis Sepúlveda. Among other things, he asked for instructions, for one of them to visit Colombia, and to explore financing options. With thirty-two exiled Chilean Socialists engaged in political education and work within mass organizations, he wanted the party's support. He also asked for military preparation for militants in Colombia.²⁸

From Washington, Orlando Letelier also wrote to Beatriz of his frustrations with the lack of leadership from both the PS and the UP. "There are many compañeros who end up distancing themselves from the tasks of the Resistance because they are not assigned specific tasks, because they lack direction, because they feel, with or without reason—more with than without—that leaders do not care to help them and direct them [when it comes to] their basic problems," Letelier wrote to Beatriz in October 1975. "When they are assigned tasks, they go to work and they do it with enthusiasm," he continued, meaning "less time for ... fights within the Left, all of which favors fascism." Orlando also felt he was alone when it came to his work at the UN. As he wrote to Beatriz, he had received no "guidance or support, from Rome or wherever." Working with Beatriz when it came to campaigning materials, as well as a small team in the United States, he was largely operating on his "own inspiration."[29]

As she had done so often before, Beatriz acted self-consciously as a "bridge" between factions to resolve such issues.[30] Increasingly critical of Altamirano's leadership of PS funds and the Rome office, Beatriz had lobbied Clodomiro Almeyda, executive secretary of the reconstituted UP after his release from Dawson Island, to better support Letelier.[31] She was also asked to step in to resolve acrid disputes between UP parties and the MIR, finding herself stuck in the middle. From one side, her cousin, Andrés Pascal, urged her to persuade other Chilean left-wing parties to abandon what he called a "sterile and mistaken policy": "the stupid and harmful illusion of establishing a subordinate alliance" with the Christian Democrats rather than getting behind the MIR. As he had written to her at the end of 1974, "I urge you to make the greatest efforts to promote and hasten the unity of the left behind the policies of the revolutionary Resistance. That you use all your influence and moral weight to hit the insensitive consciences, that you are hard and aggressive against those who impede unity, and that you also use your charm to push the hesitant. The sacrifice of so many heroic men, as well as [that of] your father, Miguel, and the thousands of dead and imprisoned combatants must bear fruit in unity that will lead us to victory."[32] His entreaties also chimed with the MIR's public proclamations as part of the regional Junta Coordinadora Revolucionaria (JCR) against "reformism" and in favor of "just and necessary revolutionary violence." Repression in Chile, a joint JCR declaration insisted, had overwhelmingly proved pacifist formulas wrong.[33]

On the other side, Letelier complained to Beatriz that miristas were causing difficulties with PCCh and PS representatives, accusing him of being sectarian and, in so doing, damaging the Chilean Left's cause (Beatriz asked the MIR's representative in Cuba, *Punto Final*'s former director, Manuel Cabieses, to investigate).[34] By early 1976, the Cubans were also complaining to Beatriz of the "inexcusable" news that two rival solidarity committees were operating in the United States: one linked to the U.S. Communist Party and another linked to the MIR. Laura Allende's trips to the United States and her advocacy of the MIR's positions also caused tension with the National Coordinating Center in Solidarity with Chile, run by U.S. Communist Party leaders.[35] In his trips to Stockholm, Moscow, Canada, the United States, and Mexico, Almeyda reported on productive solidarity work but acknowledged that "united and centralized direction is missing."[36]

Yet, aside from being a conduit of information, what could Beatriz do to resolve these problems? People wrote to her for advice, for support, asking her to solve disputes and problems. But these requests seemed to emphasize her powerlessness rather than her authority. If mediation between Chile's left-wing parties had been deeply problematic during the UP years when all sides were in the same country, if not its capital, mediating across the globe and between factions of parties divided geographically and ideologically proved impossible. Where once, as her father's daughter, she had been a pivot at the center of government, with no center of gravity among the Chilean Left she was now increasingly isolated. Lacking a formal position with the PS's party structures, and with many of the leaders she had worked closest with now dead, her influence diminished further. She also had to deal with a member of the Chilean community in Havana breaking into the Comité Chileno and stealing solidarity funds. As Jaime Faivovich, a lawyer and former journalist for *Punto Final*, who had served as governor of Santiago and undersecretary of transport during Allende's administration, wrote to her, the episode left a bitter taste.[37]

On the Barricades of Solidarity

By late 1975 and early 1976, when not embroiled in political infighting, Beatriz's concerns primarily revolved around preparing materials for targeted international campaigns such as those at the United Nations and the Organization of American States to secure resolutions condemning the Junta. The United Nation's conference in Mexico to mark its International Year of the Woman in 1975, yearly meetings of the International Commission of Enquiry into the Crimes of the Military Junta in Chile, and the Non-Aligned Movement's meetings provided additional platforms for the Chilean Left to mobilize support. At the women's meeting in Mexico, for example, thirteen hundred delegates, including those from Congo-Brazzaville, Mongolia, Vietnam, the United States, the Soviet Union, and Cuba, participated at a special solidarity event for Chile.[38] The Comité

Chileno prepared reports for these occasions, providing names of those detained and disappeared and details of torture practices, describing detention centers and security service apparatuses involved in human rights violations.[39]

Increasingly, in fact, Chile's status around the world, at least in part thanks to Chilean left-wing activists, rested on the issue of human rights. More than the battle for socialism, the dictatorship's violent repression garnered support from an array of governments and nongovernmental groups worldwide. It was also a cause all left-wing Chilean parties could agree on. Yet once Chilean opponents of the dictatorship had drawn attention to human rights violations and secured international condemnatory resolutions against the Junta's practices, the question was how to translate these into concrete sanctions. As leaders representing the UP at a Non-Aligned Movement meeting in 1976 noted, the key was moving toward "effective measures."[40]

Keeping up pressure against the dictatorship also meant maintaining the intensity of activism initiated immediately after the coup. A Chilean report on U.S. support noted that by mid-1975 solidarity was "of a spontaneous type ... that fluctuates in its intensity and its characteristics, mainly due to the influence of external events." The Chilean Left therefore had to push for a permanent "stream of solidarity tasks."[41] As Beatriz had written to Almeyda, it needed "constant work," and she urged him to travel widely to mobilize support for UN campaigns: "We need you ... on the barricades of solidarity."[42] Beatriz followed her own advice. Between 1975 and 1977, her travels included separate trips to Finland, the Hague, Brussels, Berlin (at least twice), Stockholm, Guinea (twice), Angola (twice), Mexico (at least twice), and the Caribbean. Trips were challenging, and as we shall see below, they also had ramifications for her home life. Although she found Angola "extraordinary," it is also worth questioning whether this trip was driven by solidarity or by Cuba's commitment since late 1975 to supporting its newly independent left-wing government.[43] Even so, the two dovetailed in some respects (proceeds from the Comité Chileno publication of a small book on Angola funded Chilean operations).[44]

Back in Havana, Beatriz's day-to-day efforts to sustain support involved compiling the comité's bulletin, *Chile Informativo*. To improve distribution, however, its publication and printing had moved to Mexico in 1975.[45] Another Comité Chileno innovation beginning in 1976 was the production of a monthly radio program. Dealing with issues such as the U.S. congressional Church Report regarding covert intervention in Chile prior to the coup, it was recorded by Chileans with the collaboration of Radio Havana broadcast to Chile via Algeria. The program had a double purpose, Beatriz explained, as it was vital for transmitting "other voices ... to Chile" and as "collective work" by all left-wing Chilean parties, bridging party political divisions. Chilean exiles around the world and local communities in Europe and Algeria also appreciated programs.[46] The Chilean Left's global links with the Cuban and Algerian governments, assiduously maintained by exiles, thus provided the means of communicating directly with local groups within Chile as well as in exile. In Chile, listening secretly to these programs was an act of private resistance, but it also buoyed exiles' spirits.

Even so, keeping solidarity moving was hard work. As Beatriz's correspondence attests, difficulties existed in disseminating publications. She lambasted counterparts publishing *Chile Informativo* in Mexico for delays. "The most important thing for any publication is its aspiration to be regular," she wrote in March 1976, "so that ... *information has validity.*"[47] In the United States, meanwhile, exiles faced the language barrier, although Orlando was able to reproduce and disseminate English-language materials to more than four hundred U.S. solidarity committees.[48] The bulletin also did not always reach subscribers, forcing the Chileans to pay the Cuban embassy in New York to dispatch further copies by airmail.[49] When, on rare occasions, Beatriz expressed joy or satisfaction in her correspondence during 1975 and 1976, it was related to overcoming such hurdles.[50] Generally, however, she judged efforts to keep solidarity moving as falling short. And as the Junta's staying power grew, Beatriz's morale fell.

Setbacks

The Chilean Left then faced two significant setbacks in 1976. The first was a military coup in Argentina in March 1976, definitively shutting off a refuge for Chilean exiles and an important cross-border transition point for funds and people. Prior to this, Argentinean military intelligence had already detected and undermined Chilean operations in the country. In December 1975, for example, police had seized $20,000 Beatriz had sent to a contact in Buenos Aires for transfer to Chile. Not only was the money lost, but it also became apparent that the Argentine security services had been monitoring the Chilean Left's network via its phone calls and travels since April of that year and had passed this information on to the Junta.[51] Weeks after the Argentine coup, Edgardo Enríquez, Miguel's brother and the MIR's leader in exile whom Beatriz had known since Concepción, was then captured in Buenos Aires, handed over to Chilean security services, and killed.[52] A month later, in May 1976, William Whitelaw, Isabel Jaramillo's former partner, a regular contact of Beatriz's during the UP years, and a founder of the JCR representing the Tupamaros, was also killed in

Buenos Aires.[53] As John Dinges noted, infrastructures of the MIR and the JCR were "eradicated" following the Argentine coup.[54]

Moreover, in strengthening the counterrevolutionary offensive in Latin America by the mid-1970s, the Argentine coup gave weight to a regional anticommunist ideological crusade. Similar to the Brazilian, Paraguayan, Uruguayan, and Chilean military regimes preceding it, but even more so, Argentina defined "communist" in the broadest possible terms. Like the Chilean Junta's violent exclusionary nationalist project determining who could be considered Chilean, the Argentine military dictatorship constructed a narrow version of citizenship. For exiles like Beatriz and all those who had been wedded to a regionalist revolutionary project in the 1960s, a new antithetical reality now shattered any lingering hopes of rescuing that project and excommunicated them from the very region they had not so long ago aspired to transform.

The regional dimension of the Left's defeat was compounded by the Southern Cone dictatorships' formal collaboration from November 1975 under the "Condor System" or "Organization," known to U.S. intelligence as "Operation Condor."[55] By coordinating intelligence gathering and security operations against perceived enemies in the Southern Cone, Europe, and the United States, the military regimes targeted remnants of armed revolutionary groups as well as democrats and human rights campaigners. Indeed, Condor's founders made explicit connections between the Tricontinental Conference, the JCR, and what Chile's intelligence chief, Manuel Contreras, called the "pleasing face" these groups were given through "solidarity committees, congresses, Tribunals, Meetings, Festivals and conferences, etc."[56] The connection made between such groups was not entirely unfounded, of course, with links existing between different left-wing groups and strategies in exile, but with armed movements mostly wiped out, the principal targets of Condor were, as Dinges argues, "dangerous democrat[s]," not "violent terrorist[s]."[57]

A direct consequence was the Chilean Left's second pivotal blow of 1976: the assassination of Orlando Letelier in Washington, D.C., on 21 September 1976. In killing him, the dictatorship took away one of its most effective opponents—"one of the Party's best men," as Beatriz called him. It also crippled the Chilean Left's international operations and reputation. Letelier's work at the UN, OAS, and U.S. Congress had relied on his personal contacts and drive, using his ambassadorial and ministerial experience, and working with others like Beatriz in preparing materials against the dictatorship. His unique contribution was therefore not easily replaced. "The void Letelier leaves is tremendous," Beatriz lamented in early 1977, noting this was even greater given the "lack of direction and more systematic support from higher levels."[58] And for months after his death it remained unclear if he would be replaced.

There were also wider ramifications of Letelier's death, both for the Chilean Left and for Beatriz. For one, security became a bigger issue than before. Although the FBI had warned Letelier nearly a year before his death that he was being followed, he had brushed the news aside. As he had written to Beatriz in October 1975, "I have not given it much importance."[59] Now, in the aftermath of his death—in addition to the assassination of Carlos Prats, former commander in chief of the Chilean army, in Argentina and a bomb attack on left-leaning Christian Democrat Bernardo Leighton in Rome—Beatriz was angry, demanding improvements to safety. As she wrote to Almeyda a month after Orlando's death, "We have asked ourselves a thousand questions, but I also wish we could take concrete steps.... It takes so much to transform ideas into actions." She urged him and other Chilean left-wing leaders to take precautions and worried increasingly about her mother as a figurehead of Chile's solidarity campaign.[60]

Security concerns were also driven by fears of infiltration and surveillance.[61] If anything, however, the Chilean Left probably *underestimated* security threats, being successively and rudely awakened to them. By 1977, the dictatorship's Dirección de Inteligencia Nacional (National Intelligence Directorate) had ten thousand people working for it and at least double that many paid informants, including left-wing militants.[62] On one occasion, a member of the Socialist Party who agreed under torture to help the Junta was caught at the airport in Havana stealing documents for the dictatorship.[63] From early 1974 onward, Chilean embassies abroad could also count on high-level informants, who relayed details of exiles' meetings and arrangements for fund transfers to Cuba and Chile.[64] And the CIA had detailed knowledge of the Chilean Left's finances.[65] Despite the warm welcome Mexico's government gave Chilean exiles, its intelligence agents also reported extensively on Chilean left-wing personalities. (Hortensia was even followed to Zihuatanejo beach resort over Christmas, with her daily excursions logged by the Director of Federal Security.)[66]

As well as individuals' physical security, Beatriz admitted to becoming "obsessive" about the Chilean Left's records (she confided the Cubans and her father had taught her to take this concern seriously).[67] "I beg you ... burn the letter," she instructed those she wrote to, even when dealing with routine matters.[68] By early 1977, if interlocutors were not taking serious precautions with their personal files—for example, keeping them at a friendly country's embassy—she deemed it "impossible" to write seriously to them.[69] "We cannot continue being such idiots [*huevones*] ... and go down the route of repeating errors, irreparable losses, and handing over information that is too valuable for our precarious situation," she wrote to Luis Maira, head of the UP's Secretariat for Solidarity in the Americas. "Forgive the sermon, I don't have a priest's mentality, but one has to take care of one's friends."[70]

Beatriz's obsession was partly a direct consequence of Letelier's assassination. Orlando had Beatriz's letters to him in his briefcase at his death; when the FBI leaked these to reporters, they were used effectively to call her, the Chilean Left, and global solidarity into question by linking them to Cuba. Specifically, one letter from May 1975 and another from August 1976 revealed Beatriz had been sending Orlando money from Havana and detailed U.S. campaign activities.[71] With news of the "Havana connection" made public by journalists Jack Anderson and Les Whitten, U.S. intelligence agents began following Orlando's assistant, Juan Gabriel Valdés, in New York, monitoring his interaction with Cuban embassy staff. And now, previously sympathetic collaborators warned the Chilean Left to stay away from "dangerous Cuban agents." When Juan Gabriel contacted Whitten to explain that such money came from international solidarity rather than the Cuban state, the journalist was unconvinced, retorting that the Cuban embassy official he had met was a sinister figure. Beatriz meanwhile refused to comment when Whitten called her and found herself having to explain the "lamentable" episode to the Cuban Communist Party's Americas Department.[72] Letelier's so-called hush-hush papers also revealed that Chilean funds had helped the democratic deputy, Michael Harrington, travel to Mexico to attend the third session of the International Commission of Enquiry into the Crimes of the Military Junta in Chile. "Chileans buy support from liberals in Congress," an article in the *Democrat and Chronicle* announced, referring to a "secret money drop" and "well-meaning liberals" hoodwinked by Marxist revolutionaries.[73]

Unsurprisingly, the conservative Chilean newspaper, *El Mercurio*, amply reported on Letelier's "Cuban connection." Given Havana's links to the KGB, it argued "the Kremlin's hand was behind Letelier's campaign." Harrington's sponsorship of an amendment to suspend aid to Chile on human rights grounds appeared to confirm the dictatorship's claims that he had been "manipulated" in a communist-inspired plot. For at least a year, the Junta had complained that the Cuban ambassador to the United Nations "organized Chilean exiles."[74] Now, citing a letter from Orlando to Beatriz at length, *El Mercurio* argued that Letelier's papers were "embarrassing" proof.[75]

Letelier and Beatriz had been fully aware that connections to Cuba might have undercut their cause in the United States and that human rights, rather than left-wing political appeals, offered an effective way to boost it.[76] Following Orlando's death, Beatriz's correspondence reveals a further degree of pragmatism and resignation to the problems Cuba's involvement could generate for the Chilean cause. When eighty members of UNESCO voted for a moderate resolution against the Junta rather than a more condemnatory one—a "bitter victory," as she called it—Beatriz recommended "another country, in Latin America take the defense of Chile ... not always Cuba."[77]

Beatriz faced other problems working in Cuba. In late 1976, the Chileans' ability to distribute materials through Cuban embassies suddenly became more difficult. Rather than sending a print run of a hundred books about the latest meeting of the International Commission of Enquiry into the Crimes of the Military Junta via one of Cuba's embassies, for example, Luis Maira had to carry them personally to Europe. From Havana, Beatriz lamented simply, "we cannot send them."[78] Elsewhere, to resolve problems, materials crisscrossed the Atlantic going from Havana to New York via Berlin rather than directly from Cuba to the United States.[79] Being in Cuba also entailed shortages of materials and equipment needed for running the Comité Chileno and its information center, and these pressures mounted in late 1976 and 1977. Meeting with members of the Americas Department in Havana in early 1977, Beatriz asked for additional backing but was not optimistic given Cuba's focus on saving; "everything that is extra-plan or of big expense, at this time is very difficult, not because they do not want to give us the minimum possible, but because of the situation [here]," she wrote to Luis Maira (Lucho) in Mexico.[80] When visitors came to the island, she asked them to bring vital materials for the committee, such as pen cartridges, "writing materials," a typewriter, ink, stencils (for the bulletin), a mimeograph, and a tape recorder that did not rely on batteries, which were hard to come by in Cuba. As she confessed, "I have a beggar's mentality, in order to secure our work."[81]

In spite of these problems, Beatriz remained steadfastly defensive about Cuba. "When Cuba is questioned, I become intolerant," she admitted. "I have often seen stupid attitudes toward it ... and whenever I am provoked on this point I fall into the trap, because it is something I will never negotiate."[82] Indeed, for her, we must remember human rights did not replace previous socialist utopian projects or loyalty to Cuba's revolutionary regime. Rather than human rights being the "last utopia," as Samuel Moyn has suggested, it was merely one way Beatriz conceived of fighting for the utopian revolutionary future she had set her sights on almost two decades before and still upheld.[83] However, not all Chilean leftists felt the same. By the late 1970s, some former militants were already turning toward social democracy, away from revolutionary Marxism and armed struggle, forging the basis of what would be a "renovation" of Chilean Socialist thought. While Beatriz continued to believe fiercely in Cuba and in the idea of socialist revolution, she was no longer riding a wave of optimism but attempting to shore up a receding dream.

Internal Front

By early 1977, Beatriz was also dealing with personal difficulties. In March, Luis asked Loti, the woman who had looked after Maya since she was born, to leave their house. Cuban authorities then forcibly relocated her to the eastern city of Holguin. Having found out Loti was a lesbian, Luis claimed to have been worried about her influence on Maya.[84] Although he would regret this later in life, his views at the time reflected the Cuban Revolution's reprehensible attitude toward homosexuality. Homophobia in the 1960s and 1970s was primarily targeted at gay men, who were thought to challenge the revolution by undermining notions of masculinity associated with it. For much of the 1960s, in fact, homosexuals had been rounded up in police raids, and as many as sixty thousand were sent to reeducation and hard labor camps.[85] By contrast, lesbians were relatively ignored as they were not perceived as threatening revolutionary masculinity.[86] But life on the island as a gay woman was not easy, with women being known to have taken their lives after Cuban political commissars confronted them regarding their sexuality.[87]

What made Loti's persecution inevitable was the Cuban state's institutionalized belief that homosexuality was learned behavior, and as a result, children risked being "infected." At Cuba's First National Congress on Education and Culture in 1971, homosexuals (both male and female) had been banned from participating in education. Three years later, Law 1267, published in May 1974, prohibited gay people from working in jobs where they could influence children.[88] Already in the 1960s, Fidel had made his position clear in this respect: "We must inculcate our youth" against "learning" to be gay, he proclaimed.[89] Loti's banishment was thus in keeping with the state's societal norms, formalized in the mid-1970s and persisting into the 1980s.[90] As friends remember, Beatriz was devastated.[91] But there is no evidence to suggest either that she did anything to protect the woman who had looked after Maya since birth or that she could have made a difference if she had. That Chilean homophobia was virulent across society, including among the revolutionary Left, meant she had no reason to be surprised about intolerance.[92] A devout supporter of the Cuban Revolution, she also tended to side with its leaders and its laws.

As Hernán Sandoval remembered, he asked her around this time how "Padrecito Fidel" was—an allusion to the way they used to refer to "Padrecito Stalin" as university students. And Beatriz got angry, asking why he had become so critical; Cuba might have its problems, she insisted, but it had to be viewed in its own context, which in her eyes absolved it of sins.[93]

Even so, Beatriz lamented Loti's departure for what it meant for her own life—namely, taking on domestic and child care duties she had never had to consider before. As she admitted shortly after Loti left, "I don't know how to do anything, and this has me exhausted ... improvising and for the first time in my life doing domestic chores that infuriate me. I lose time and, finally, it screws me [*me jode*]." The shock was evident in the way she described her situation melodramatically in private letters. "Long live the weaker sex!!!! And its liberation. I almost feel in the feudal era, servant of the glade and surrounded by 'feudal gentlemen.' The best gift that everyone can give me is a book on 'How to learn to cook' *for idiots*," she wrote.[94]

Beatriz's call for help and the allusion to her gendered responsibilities was telling of broader issues affecting her home life. At the same time as Loti left, and partly as a result of tensions resulting from her banishment, Luis and Beatriz also separated. For Maya and Alejandro's sake they decided he should not leave their house so soon after Loti's departure. But Luis would move out in June. As Beatriz wrote to Osvaldo Puccio in May, their relationship had improved as a result: "The situation is finally defined and ... it occurred the Chilean way, that is, in friendly terms, which does not normally happen here."[95] It was no surprise to many who knew them that they had been having difficulties. Luis was drinking heavily, and although it is unclear whether Beatriz knew, he had also had at least two affairs since they arrived in Cuba. As Luis would remember, he and Beatriz were suffering separately from what had happened in Chile. Neither was able to help the other, so they sought solace elsewhere.[96] Indeed, their son, Alejandro, would later reflect that both of them probably suffered from what we now recognize as post-traumatic stress disorder.[97] Their marriage difficulties were also not uncommon among exiles who had experienced the coup and its aftermath. "The crisis between couples is a regular and constant fact of exile life," two Chilean psychologists concluded. "It speaks to the transformations ... disunions ... conflicts and difficult situations experienced."[98]

Within this context, a key source of tension for some time had been Beatriz's work and travel. Although she and Luis had initially traveled together after the coup, leaving Maya and Alejandro in Havana, she had increasingly gone alone. As Luis would explain, he resented being left at home raising their children, believing Beatriz should spend more time with them.[99] Thus Beatriz tried to reduce her travels in 1976, asking Francisco to replace her. When he pointed out that people wanted Allende's daughter, not him, she admitted she had no option; Luis was increasingly uncomfortable, and she had problems on her "internal front."[100]

Like his attitude toward Loti, Luis's expectation that Beatriz should be at home more to look after their children was by no means unique in Cuba (or beyond). The Cuban government had actually instigated a widespread discussion of women's place in society and families in late 1974. In November 1973, Resolutions 47 and 48 that had delineated jobs as male or female back in the 1968 were revoked. The following year, the Cuban state had increased the number of state nurseries and extended maternity leave to four months to help women in the workforce.[101] Ahead of the UN-inspired International Year of the Woman in 1975, and responding to the global women's liberation movement of the 1960s and 1970s, Cuban leaders also appear to have strategically wanted to do something new when it came to gender equality in the home. A key part of this program was a "Código de la Familia" (Family Code) introduced in 1975, which, in addition to establishing equal legal rights for women, stressed that men should get involved in household chores and child care. The proposal, revolutionary in many respects, sparked intense discussions throughout Cuba. As the U.S. feminist Margaret Randall observed, machismo in Cuba was being challenged, and men tended to use "historic" or "biological" reasons to object. During a five-day national Federació de Mujeres Cubanas (FMC) congress in late 1974, household labor was a "frequent topic of discussions," with women expressing frustrations that domestic responsibilities prevented them from acting politically.[102] And the "tension between tradition and change" persisted. As Lois Smith and Alfredo Padula found, men tended to be "uneasy" with household responsibilities enshrined in the Family Code "and feared being ridiculed by their male peers."[103]

Indeed, Luis faced precisely this kind of pressure, being mocked by colleagues and friends for having to support Beatriz and stay at home to look after the children. That invitations to attend Cuban receptions and congresses were addressed to Beatriz and her partner rather than the other way round compounded his discomfort (Beatriz reportedly asked for this to be changed, or at least for invitations to include Luis's surname, but was told this was not possible).[104] He became "Beatriz's husband" in a patriarchal society where men were supposed to be the head of the family. Because of who she was and her role in the global solidarity campaign, therefore, Beatriz unintentionally challenged persistent ideas of masculinity and the family still prevalent in society despite top-down, state-led reform efforts to change them.

Beatriz participated directly in events like the second FMC congress that addressed the Family Code.[105] And she had also been there when at a ceremony on International Women's Day in 1975 male Cuban leaders presented the Family Code to Vilma Espín—a gift bestowed on women by the island's male leadership.[106] Available evidence suggests Beatriz's participation was limited to expressions of solidarity between Cuban women and their Chilean counterparts rather than discussing gender roles. Ultimately, Beatriz focused primarily on using women's events in Cuba and abroad to publicize Chile's plight. Privately, she was also deeply cynical of such events. "How awful these types of commemorations are," she confessed following women's day celebrations on 8 March 1977. "I would only like it, if this day men cooked delicious things and took care of the children, and we could have a full holiday," she added, underlining her recent frustrations with assuming expected female tasks she had previously avoided.[107] The Cubans assigned two new women from the country's special forces to come and help Beatriz around the home and to look after Maya and Alejandro, but she found them cold and unloving—like "refrigerators," she told a Cuban friend.[108] Edith Benado, Beatriz's friend from the Brigada Universitaria Socialista (BUS), now in exile in Havana and working with Beatriz at the Comité Chileno, remembered asking her why she did not take advantage of the specialist state boarding school designed to look after exiled children. But Beatriz, already guilty about her privilege, felt uncomfortable about using spaces for children with greater needs.[109]

Whether it was stress or coincidence, Beatriz and Luis were then both hospitalized in mid-1977. Luis suffered from hepatitis caused by alcoholism, although he had also had pneumonia, bronchitis, asthma, and hypertension in previous years.[110] Why Beatriz was admitted to hospital is less clear. A probable cause was thyroid problems, which Edith remembered she struggled with. These also explain her weight fluctuations, tiredness, and, at least in part, depression. Indeed, back in March she had described her "mind" and "pen" as being tired, remarking "the first is odd!," which may have led her as a trained doctor to seek medical help.[111] However, she also had a car accident around this time that damaged her spine. As she described herself candidly to Osvaldo in early May 1977, her "soul and life" were "fragile."[112] And to those she corresponded with, she explained her hospitalization as the result of back problems, of being "damned because of my bloody spine." "I'm wearing a neck brace, the pain continues and maybe I'll need surgery," she wrote in June. "I think it will be the fastest route to uproot the evil."[113] Yet doctors in Cuba preferred to postpone a risky operation, recommending she swim to improve her mobility and pain, which she began doing every morning. She also began working from home.[114]

Beatriz was nevertheless lonely. She wrote covertly to Elena Gálvez in Chile, whom she had first met during her internship at the Hospital San Juan de Dios, pretending to be living in the United States and asking her to visit. It was only later Elena realized this plea was for both their sakes — a way of getting Elena out of dictatorial Chile and having a friend close by.[115] She also asked Hernán Sandoval and his family, living in Guinea, to visit her in Cuba, and she requested Osvaldo Puccio find photos of her father and send her copies of the memoirs he was writing: "emotionally, it will be good to read them," she explained.[116] Indeed, Beatriz took personal solace in things that reminded her of her father and her childhood. In her garden, she planted a Framboyan — a red flowering tree her father had always admired.[117] She also enjoyed receiving Chilean comics featuring the cartoon characters Condorito and Lulú, which were shared out among those working at the Comité Chileno. "You make us all happy," she wrote to Carlos Antonio, who sent them from Mexico.[118] As she confessed, "I need ... things like that ... urgently and letters with a sense of humor."[119] And she wrote about a small music box — the size of a matchbox — she had been given: "When I feel that shit reaches the level of my neck, I play it and the Internationale comes out sweetly," she confessed in July 1977.[120]

But in searching for remedies she admitted she was struggling. She started seeing a psychotherapist in Cuba based on her self-diagnosis of depression. And yet she told Isabel Jaramillo she did not feel it was working.[121] She also asked Francisco to help her when it came to paying utility bills and home repairs, saying Luis had always done this before.[122] And walking the length of the Malecón with Patricia, she confessed to being lost. "What do you do on Sundays?" she asked in search of inspiration. Having grown up in a house full of guests and family lunches and having enjoyed weekends at Cañaveral during the UP years, she could not adapt to being on her own with her children at weekends.[123] She had a "deep melancholy," Patricia remembered. On this walk, the two of them cried, remembering their shared commitment to revolution and talked about moving on from solidarity activism, potentially returning to public health. It was a relatively common pattern among exiles: the first few years being devoted solely to fighting the Junta and the hope of returning to Chile before a "second stage" began, in which exiles began living in "real time," facing up to an indeterminate life abroad, and adapting to their new circumstances.[124] Before leaving Cuba for Europe shortly after this conversation, Patricia went to see Elena Pedraza, a Chilean sociologist exiled in Cuba and a family friend of the Allendes. She asked her to look after Beatriz, about whom she was worried.[125]

Moving On

Four years after the Chilean coup, Cuba's attention on Chile had diminished. Rather than days of buildup on the front page of *Granma*, with emblematic images of Allende sporting a rifle, news of commemoration events were now mostly reported in smaller columns of inside pages.[126] As the paper noted, Chileans resident in Cuba participated in a "simple remembrance service" the Sunday prior to 11 September 1977 in Parque Lenin, over which Paya presided.[127] A formal Cuban event also took place attended by members of the Communist Party's Central Committee and the Department of the Americas, Laura Allende, Andrés Pascal, Paya, and Comité Chileno staff. But Beatriz was conspicuously absent from reports of these events. As her friend, Sonia, who had accompanied her to a small commemoration at the Comité Chileno on 11 September, remembered, Beatriz turned to her after one speech proclaiming imminent victory against the Junta, saying simply, "There is nothing that can be done for Chile."[128]

For some time, in fact, Beatriz had been increasingly pessimistic. "Everything is slower than one would like," she lamented, as she worked on putting together extensive lists of those detained and disappeared by the dictatorship.[129] Her concerns regarding left-wing unity, efficiency, and security persisted. She remained highly critical of the Rome office ("they are a bunch of unproductive *huevones*").[130] And she was increasingly forthright about rethinking resistance efforts. Having returned from a trip to Mexico in late June 1977, she wrote of a "bittersweet taste" because the visit proved how much still needed to be done. She now believed civilian resistance within Chile was the best way to challenge the Junta.[131] As she wrote in July 1977 to Jaime Tohá, Socialist militant and former minister of agriculture under Allende now living in Mexico after release from Dawson Island, exiles had to concentrate on "the important aspects of the Resistance that exist within Chile." Their "duty" was to mobilize solidarity "using the imagination, not conforming to the habitual, superstructure communications to organisms, movements, personalities etc.... I think that the trigger must always be the interior, and we [should] have the ability to respond coherently ... in escalation, at a world level. Measuring ourselves so as not to destroy everything, and changing the targets, because ultimately the enemy always learns faster than us."[132]

Beatriz's frustration had much to do with the ongoing left-wing splits.

In May 1976, the dictatorship had destroyed the Communist Party's clandestine leadership and disappeared one of the Movimiento de Acción Popular Unitario's surviving leaders in the country.[133] Although communication with those operating underground in Chile for a reconstituted PS Dirección Interna improved in late 1976—"a note of encouragement," Beatriz called it—divisions remained acute.[134] To address the "political 'impasse'" resulting from "indiscipline" and a "lack of decision," in August 1976 Almeyda and Rolando Calderón had demanded Altamirano support only *one* PS faction inside Chile (the Dirección Interna) and that he fight against "factionalism and divisionism," decisively support the struggle inside Chile, strengthen ties with socialist countries (while maintaining independence), and improve ties with the Communist Party as part of a broad antifascist front. They had insisted on an "ideological struggle against right and 'left' deviations." And they implored him to act before the party disintegrated further into "sterile and demoralizing struggles."[135]

Informing Beatriz of their decision to challenge Altamirano, Rolando had written that they were "engaged in an ideological struggle" and acting "against a lack of definition and dispersion." As a result of her own frustrations with Altamirano and what she saw as his lack of support for the Dirección Interna, Beatriz was clearly seen as an ally Almeyda and Calderón needed to keep informed. Calderón's emphasis on resuming flows of money to Chile would also have pleased Beatriz, though his request to have party funds transferred to Berlin to help distribute them through routes that were "less burnt" spoke to the crisis affecting financial aid to Chile. "There is still a long way to go," Rolando acknowledged; "perhaps what is most important ... is to reach just positions that reach out to the militant masses, that they understand these, and make them their own, and this is undoubtedly not the job for a few leaders but for all of us."[136] Although Altamirano had essentially accepted Almeyda and Calderón's points, issuing a declaration to this effect in September 1976, and although talks between the interior and exterior wings of the party were held in mid-1977, establishing a coherent apparatus with a clear strategy or ideology proved impossible.[137] At the end of November 1976, Beatriz had still felt Altamirano did not sufficiently grasp the situation in Chile or respond adequately to it, complaining of a "lack of political orientation."[138] That she took her frustrations with the pace of change inside Chile out on the PS leadership may or may not have been justified. After all, repression inside the country made it desperately difficult for resistance efforts to get off the ground. And yet, in her complaints, as Almeyda and Calderón's correspondence suggests, she was not alone.

In an effort to breathe more life into the Comité Chileno in Havana in early 1977, Beatriz and Francisco had been restructuring the organization, which included adding a Caribbean section and a new officer responsible for establishing a data bank of the Junta's repression within the Comité's information center.[139] In September 1977, in what was to be her last trip abroad, Beatriz, along with Francisco, Luis Maira, and the former Communist senator Julieta Campusano, went to Jamaica to build up their work in the Caribbean, primarily focused on mobilizing support for anti-Junta campaigns at the United Nations and other international organizations.[140]

A few weeks later, on 4 October 1977, Beatriz wrote to Carlos Altamirano stating she had decided to leave the Comité Chileno. "Recently, I realize we have a reduced workload, that we have become routine, that I lack, or we lack, initiatives.... The level of solidarity also depends to a large extent on events in Chile; ... from outside it is impossible to force things."[141] Her complaint that solidarity had become ineffective was not unique. As one Chilean exile active in anti-Junta campaigns remembered, he "began to realize the mechanical and repetitive routine of international organization, the perfect uselessness of so many of their activities, the bureaucratic coldness of their officials."[142] Other Chileans in Cuba similarly remembered the boredom of repetitive printing jobs and frequent embassy receptions with the same people.[143]

Indeed, Beatriz felt that she had little power to effect change. As Anselmo Sule, a Radical Party representative of UP, had told a member of East Germany's Politburo on the event of the coup's fourth anniversary, no significant counterweight against Pinochet existed inside Chile, and opponents had been unable to form an active domestic political front against the regime from within the country. Clandestine work carried out by UP parties was "barely visible."[144] Pinochet's speech at Chacarillas in July 1977, in which he set out a long-term plan for the institutionalization of the dictatorship, had also underlined the Junta's determination to stay in power.[145]

It was in this context that those Beatriz spoke to in late 1977 remember her despairing. As Hernán Coloma, former member of the BUS and the Organa, remembered, Beatriz spoke with "a lot of pain" about left-wing divisions, the lack of respect different sectors had for one another, and the problems this was causing the resistance. She also cried, which surprised him, because he had never seen her cry before.[146] Other friends remember her as being disdainful of party politics more generally. She asked her friend Sonia if she was still an active member of the PS. And when Sonia replied she had not been since 1973, Beatriz replied she was not either. By this point, "she didn't believe in the party at all," Sonia explained.[147]

Ideally, Beatriz wanted to leave solidarity to fight clandestinely for the resistance in Chile. Visiting Ariel Ulloa, her friend from Concepción and a member of the PS's Frente Interno during her father's administration, now in exile in Santa Clara, she spoke about this wish. Her desire was "romantic" and "did not make sense," he reflected; her role as a figurehead for global solidarity was far more important than "going to Chile to die."[148] And yet she was desperate to put the idea of *patria o muerte* into practice. "She wanted to be Tania."[149] Whenever Juan Carretero and his wife, Nancy, visited her at home, Beatriz would show them the picture of Juan teaching her how to fire her Uzi in the Cajón del Maipo, which was displayed prominently in her house.[150] And although she privately admitted guerrilla insurgency was probably not the answer to Latin America anymore, she was not convinced enough to abandon this route for herself.[151] In late September, visiting Ulises Estrada, she got on her knees and begged to be able to go back to Chile to "fight."[152]

But the Cubans said no. "It was not our fault," Ulises explained. "There was no way of helping her do this. We ourselves did not have the conditions to do it and the Chileans did not have the conditions to receive her.... She tried many times [to persuade us]."[153] That Beatriz was Allende's daughter made the Cubans even more reluctant to help her, not wishing to be responsible for her death or detention. The Socialist Party's representative in Cuba, Julio Benítez, echoed these concerns.[154] However, the verdict was especially hard for Beatriz, who was in contact with Chileans beginning their military training to return in a not-too-distant future. In 1976 and 1977, in fact, Altamirano had authorized two groups of PS militants to receive training in the USSR and Cuba.[155] And when Carlos Gómez, one of Elmo Catalán's initial recruits for Bolivia, had passed through Havana on his way to the Soviet Union, he visited Beatriz. Talking until dawn, he was another of those surprised to see her cry. On this occasion she was also insistent that Luis, who was there, give Carlos his Browning pistol as a donation to the resistance. When he refused, she got angry and Luis relented.[156]

Unable to return to Chile, Beatriz's options were limited. Her mother and Isabel, increasingly worried about her, asked her to move to Mexico. By June, Hortensia was also urging her to look after herself, not to work too hard. "Do not feel defeated," she counseled, "go on."[157] And yet, as Beatriz confided in Patricia, she was unsure how she would adapt to Mexico. Her relationship with Hortensia and Isabel had never been very good, even if it had improved in exile. More important, she feared leaving Cuba would be "a betrayal of the revolution" and thus refused to consider it.[158]

Remaining in Cuba, Beatriz essentially had two career options. In Mexico in June 1977, she had met Frida Modak and told her how proud—

and jealous—she was seeing her working full-time in her old profession as a journalist. As she told Frida, she now wanted to return to medicine.[159] This was also what she told her former mentor, Arturo Jirón, when she phoned him from Mexico.[160] The other option she had was to study Marxism, as she had been doing at the Cuban Communist Party's Escuela Superior, Ñico López. For two years, in fact, she, Patricia, and Paya had been attending evening and weekend classes. Although it was something that occupied her time, the three of them did not take it particularly seriously. Beatriz would make a point of asking difficult questions, probing the relevance of Trotsky's thought, for example, while safe in the knowledge that, as Allende's daughter, she could not be criticized.[161] In 1977, she was on the point of graduating and considering further, full-time study. But she preferred the idea of returning to medicine.

Because it had been ten years since Beatriz practiced medicine, however, Cuba's public health minister advised she would have to do an internship to retrain before working as a pediatrician. When Ulises told her the news, it hit her hard. "I am useless even as a doctor," he remembered her responding; her "mood" was "terrible, terrible."[162] "I'm useless," she told Sonia around this time, berating herself for her inability to help her father more on the day of the coup and what she could not now do either in Chile or in exile.[163]

Decided

It is difficult to determine precisely when Beatriz made the decision to take her own life. Before Luis left, she once brought up the idea of them committing suicide together, a comment he rebuffed as a strange joke. But he had worried about her depression and tried to speak to Ulises and Carlos Rafael Rodríguez about his fears in the months before her death.[164] Beatriz's letters suggest her decision was not definitive until perhaps a week before. Why else would she have asked Osvaldo and Miriam for spare parts for her car and to keep writing to her on 27 September? On 4 October, when informing Altamirano she was leaving solidarity work, she stated she would be enrolling full time at Ñico López. "I think ... we need to return to Chile with a higher level [of preparation] and with everything in order," she explained. However, it is possible she used this excuse—which she also gave to others—so as not to raise suspicions of how desperate she was. She told Altamirano she had passed the PS account to Francisco, noting the balance as $106,960.07, and reassured him her absence would not affect the Comité Chileno's information work.[165] The same day she wrote to Dr. Pérez Carballas at the Public Health Ministry's

Beatriz, Havana, 1977. Archivo Fundación Salvador Allende.

postgraduate institute to say she would not be taking up the opportunity to restart her medical career due to "political responsibilities."[166]

In late September and early October, her friends remember her mostly talking about Maya and Alejandro and struggling as a mother.[167] In late September she wrote to Osvaldo and Miriam of "a great sense of failure that I cannot help." She worried about six-year-old Maya's "insecurity," in particular.[168] On Saturday, 8 October, when she attended a formal ceremony to commemorate the tenth anniversary of Che Guevara's death, she appeared distracted, remaining standing when everyone else had sat down. In a long conversation that evening, she asked how Nancy Carretero managed to juggle work, housework, with looking after her children, admitting she was unable to.[169]

By this point, however, she had decided she could not go on. On Saturday, she had also visited Luis, who was in hospital again, and they talked vaguely about trying to make their marriage work again, but when she returned to see him on Sunday he was asleep and she did not wake him.[170] On Monday, 10 October, a national holiday in Cuba, she went to Santa María del Mar, a beach east of Havana, with Francisco, his partner Irina, and Irina's children. Watching them playing with Maya in the waves, Beatriz told Irina she wished she could see Maya grow up, a comment Irina thought strange but brushed away, not realizing its significance.[171] At the beach, Beatriz also bumped into Ruben, a former member of the GAP and a Comité Chileno colleague. When he asked how she was, she told him she was going to return to studying, but she also spoke at length about her disillusionment with her life in exile. "I don't want to be 'Allende's daughter' anymore," she told him, explaining she no longer wanted to be sent around the world, that she wanted to live as other exiles, build an ordinary life, and be free to decide her future.[172]

But, of course, Beatriz could not stop being "Allende's daughter." It was who she was and what had shaped her political, personal, and social life. It had been both liberating and confining to exist in relation to her father. She had been devoutly loyal to him. But in being so, she prevented herself following what might otherwise have been different paths, such as militancy for the MIR or armed action and resistance in Chile. That she was his daughter had partly ensured she was not sent to Bolivia to work for the ELN's underground, and her father had stopped her fighting against the coup.

The night of Monday, 10 October, Beatriz visited Cuban friends Neida and Sergio Guerra, talking and watching TV with them for hours. Because Luis was living in a room above their apartment, it had become usual for her to drop by, but this time she stayed an unusually long time. As was common, she talked politics with Sergio, who had worked at the Cuban embassy in Chile before the coup. But this time, she also talked at length to Neida, asking her repeatedly to look after her children, imploring her as a loving mother, using the excuse she was going to board at Ñico López. (Neida told her she couldn't; she already had two children and worked full-time at the Interior Ministry.) At 1:00 A.M., Beatriz drove home.[173] Her friends later heard Maya slept with her that night.[174]

The next morning, Tuesday, 11 October, Beatriz took her children to school and returned home, fixing a note to the door telling the Cuban woman who came to clean to call Isabel Jaramillo before entering the house. She wrote a farewell letter to Fidel Castro justifying her decision by blaming her mother and Luis for not looking after Maya and Alejandro more and informing the Cuban authorities she wanted to leave her children to Isabel "Mitzi" Contreras, Paya's sister. She also expressed her thanks to the revolution and her despair at not being able to perform even the most basic tasks anymore.[175] And she sat down at her desk with the Uzi that Castro had given her six years earlier.

Onward March

On 11 October 1977, senior members of Cuba's intelligence service arrived at Beatriz's house in Miramar, Havana. Seeing an ambulance, shoppers also began to congregate outside La Copa commercial center opposite. Before long, police moved spectators on, and classes at a nearby primary school were suspended. Two intelligence officials then drove to the airport, where they boarded an airplane to Santiago de Cuba to see Fidel Castro. When they finally got a chance to talk to him that night, they told him Beatriz was dead.[1] As Ulises Estrada remembered, Fidel was "really tormented." Standing by the swimming pool at the house where he was staying, he repeatedly said her name and asked why she had done it. Because there had been so many witnesses, he also had to decide what to do. It was obvious the government had to control the news, and quickly. But suicide was deeply problematic in a country where living for the revolution was a moral duty—where revolutionaries were expected to devote their "last atom of energy" to its cause.[2] And it was even more so when it came to a high-profile exile, a surviving heir to Chile's revolutionary process and a celebrated Cuban ally.

Flying back to Havana, Ulises and his companion, Juan Carretero, had the difficult task of drafting a statement. On 12 October 1977, Prensa Latina reported Beatriz had shot herself as a result of depression and "psychological wounds" from 11 September 1973.[3] Then, on 13 October, following meetings between senior Cuban government officials, the Communist Party's newspaper, *Granma*, publicized the news. "Comrade Beatriz Allende took her own life," a small bottom, right-hand, front-page column read. In accordance with Fidel's guidance, the announcement blamed the Chilean dictatorship for her death. Beatriz may have killed herself, having taken the "erroneous" decision that her opportunities for fighting it were shrinking, the article read, but this did not strip away her revolutionary virtues. She was simply "a new victim of fascism," unable to overcome the tragedy of Chile's coup and dictatorship.[4]

Beatriz undoubtedly suffered the effects of the military dictatorship that crushed Chile's revolutionary past. Historiographical focus on repression has tended to eclipse wider ramifications of its violence and extreme political change. Her suicide is thus a reminder to count those scarred psychologically in addition to the official numbers of murdered, disappeared, and tortured. There were millions whose lives were never the same but whose stories remain untold, not least those who fought against the dictatorship as part of a clandestine resistance (armed or otherwise). As Sofia Tupper writes, official narratives "leave out ... those who died metaphorically."[5] And Carmen Castillo would reflect that she "was lucky ... not to kill [herself] out of sorrow, or ... nostalgia."[6]

Beatriz was obviously not so fortunate. A decade after she had arrived in Cuba following Che's death, her revolutionary certitude had been hit from every angle. And her self-perceived impotence—as a revolutionary, medic, and mother—was painful. The challenges of everyday life, such as learning to cook or raising a family, seemed insurmountable and alien compared with the idea of taking up arms to spark regional revolution, something she had been so confident about doing a decade earlier. For the majority of us, this will be difficult to understand. But grasping the world she came from, the times she lived through, and the peculiarities of her own life's circumstances helps get to the heart of her predicament. When the revolutionary project she had worked toward came crashing down and showed no signs of being resurrected and when even taking part in a sacrificial insurgency against the dictatorship was denied to her, she felt trapped. As Allende's daughter, as a militant who had lost faith in party politics, as a disillusioned solidarity activist, as a doctor who could not practice medicine, and as a woman, expected to fulfill roles she had never envisaged doing, she faced a prolonged life in exile unable to effect what she regarded as meaningful change. She had never been a Marxist intellectual or—as part of a revolutionary generation who privileged action over theory—been particularly interested in studying Marxist thought. The death of her father and of so many friends, the breakdown of her marriage, her guilt at not being able—or perhaps more precisely, not being able to want—to be a mother to her two children also contributed to her decision. And her letters reveal her to have been both mentally and physically ill, depressed, and in pain. If she had had self-diagnosed depressive tendencies in the late 1960s that she had been able to fight off by thinking of Cuba and Luis, these lifelines were gone by 1977. Even if she refused to criticize it, Cuba had lost its earlier romance and promise and was in the midst of institutionalizing a Sovietized system she had once disparaged. She fought constantly to run a solidarity bulletin and had to explain herself to Cuba's leaders when solidarity work proved disappointing. In loyally wedding herself to the Cubans, in fact, she was able to rely on the legitimacy and continuity of her revolutionary ideals as the bedrock of her identity. But doing so also stripped her flexibility to determine how to live her life. Luis had left her, was in a relationship with someone else, and was constantly ill. He had also been sidelined by Manuel Piñeiro after the coup, having been vaunted by Cuba's intelligence as an invaluable channel to Allende and the Chilean Left but no longer of use after 1973.

And yet, for all the damage the coup, the dictatorship, and exile did to her, one of the principal arguments of this book is that Beatriz cannot be reduced to merely having been a victim or, as the dictatorship's press argued in the aftermath of her death, a passive woman subject to "inhuman political utilization" by the Cubans.[7] To the contrary, she was first and foremost a protagonist and historical actor: one of the many women who held such roles but who have been forgotten amid historians' predilection to focus on male leaders of political parties and their institutional histories. That societal structures and revolutionary culture determined men held the keys to power and leadership did not mean women had no influence or stood on the margins as mere victims with "virtues." The male-as-protagonist and female-as-victim narrative is just too simplistic, as is the public versus private dichotomy that tends to separate "male-driven" and "female-driven" histories. Yes, violence and repression were heavily gendered, with women suffering the effects of brutal sexualized violence during the dictatorship.[8] But for all they may have suffered the dictatorship's effects or been unable to break through patriarchal systems of power, Beatriz and countless other women were also central participants in resisting the dictatorship.[9] And they were also key players in momentous revolutionary upheavals and defeats of the past. Beatriz chose and embraced a revolutionary project, captivating many of her generation in the long 1960s. Less than a decade before her death, in fact, it had seemed victory was on the horizon, and she had played a key role in striving to make it a reality. Before being "victims," she and her milieu lived, loved, thought, and dreamed. And when Beatriz's surviving friends and family told me her memory needed rescuing, they were also referring to the years she, they, Chile, and Latin America lived through before their worlds changed irrevocably.

Understanding what underpinned the revolutionary aspirations held by Beatriz and others of her generation, where they came from, and why they had increasing resonance in Chile over the course of the long 1960s is not a question of narrating one specific event or idea or of choosing between external influences and the peculiarities of domestic circumstances. As we have seen, it requires grasping changes in Chilean politics and society over the course of more than a decade, the complex interaction of various actors and their environment, and the intersection between different local and international factors. It is impossible to understand the UP's victory in 1970 without comprehending the experience of Frei's presidency, with its raised expectations, mobilization, disappointment, and anger. Similarly, the crisis of legitimacy faced by Chile's socioeconomic model in the early 1960s—aggravated by the clash between frustrated development at home and a promise of modernity abroad—helps explain a widespread impulse for change conditioning the decade that followed.

While attributing the reasons for failure of the Unidad Popular (UP) to Beatriz individually would be absurd, we also cannot ignore her centrality in Allende's team as it sought a solution to the crisis and opposition his government faced in 1973. His inner circle, of which she was a member— along with Chile's left-wing parties, their grassroots supporters, and social movements of the time—faced terrible odds: powerful, foreign-backed opponents who helped bring about economic paralysis, launched armed attacks against the government, and worked explicitly to bring it down. Within these circumstances, winning over middle sectors and persuading them to support Chile's transition toward socialism—already a problematic challenge—proved impossible. The question of violence, which Beatriz spent much of her time worrying about, also posed a particularly difficult conundrum. Operating within a nominally constitutional democratic system, its use by the Left was provocative but its negation naïve. Landowning elites, industry, members of the armed forces, and right-wing paramilitaries were not averse to using it to repress workers and left-wing sectors or to attack the state, its supporters, and even army generals directly. And there was copious evidence an attack of some sort lay on the horizon. But how the collective Left should respond was bitterly contested and unresolved. While some sectors of the UP refused to address the issue, believing that the country's traditional consensual politics and political institutions would withstand such an assault, Beatriz was one of those who knew they would not. She was thus intricately involved in trying to find some way of bridging divides on the issue, recruiting revolutionary groups from abroad to share their expertise, attempting to persuade her father to accept armed conflict as means of saving Chile's revolutionary process, and assembling what she could of a security detail to protect him. But, as it turned out, these were desperately insufficient measures in dealing with the defense of the revolutionary project and its millions of adherents, spanning the length and breadth of Chile. And doubly so, when confronting Chile's combined professional armed forces. As Allende's adviser Joan Garcés reflected in a posthumous account of the UP years, objective internal conditions and the international context also "irredeemably condemned" insurrectionist tactics to "immediate failure."[10] And the last year of Allende's presidency shows those on the revolutionary Left closest to the president understood this predicament but were unsure of how to resolve it.

Could Beatriz personally have done anything different that would have saved the situation? Probably not. Could the revolutionary Left to which she was so loyal have been more cautious and careful, at least rhetorically? Almost certainly. Would this have changed the past? It is impossible to know. There is good reason to argue that the fixation of the Communist Party (PCCh) on a negotiated solution to Chile's crisis, which Allende shared, was "doomed to fail" as long as the UP's opposition refused to compromise, obstructed democratic government, and opted for nonconstitutional violence as a response to revolutionary change.[11] After all, it was these opposition forces that wielded the violence that definitively ruptured Chile's constitutional democratic system, rather than the Left. And it was precisely the prediction they would that made the revolutionary Left focus on military preparation. As the Right and the military understood it, only *they* could legitimately use violence. And use it they did. As Chile's post-coup history reveals, while the Left argued over its justification, opponents had no qualms about employing violence indiscriminately to control Chilean society, politics, and culture.

In the wake of the coup, Beatriz was then one of the Chilean Left's leaders who dedicated her life to fighting the dictatorship. At the forefront of such efforts in the immediate, desperate period after the coup, she was a protagonist of global solidarity. True, within the Socialist Party (PS), it was ultimately male left-wing leaders like Altamirano and Almeyda who called the shots, with Beatriz asked to manage finances and ferry messages between them, acting as a bridge, secretary, and organizer. But she was an essential and respected figure, privy to internal party arguments and regarded as an ally that different factions wanted to have on their side. In handling bank accounts and mobilizing international support, she was also pivotal to the most difficult phase of the resistance focused primarily on survival.

Because of the way Beatriz died, however, her place in histories of resistance is complicated. As her friend Carmen Castillo remembered, among Chileans, her death provoked an agitated debate: "'Militants die fighting,' the great majority exclaimed. I responded, 'Does this mean suicide, for you, is not a good death?'"[12] Had Beatriz been a man, she would almost certainly have died on 11 September or, before that, in Bolivia. And had this been the case, her history and memory would have been far more prominent and less contested. Beatriz's death, in contrast, required coming to terms with the defeat and tragedy of the revolutionary Left in a way that Che Guevara's and Miguel Enríquez's martyrdom did not. It epitomized failure and despair at a difficult time. Her readiness to confront the problems of post-coup mobilization and resistance strategies also proved uncomfortable. Clashing with celebratory histories of global solidarity campaigns, her story reveals the costs, inefficiencies, complications, and everyday challenges of those on the front lines of solidarity organizing. And, at least as far as Beatriz's correspondence suggests, while undoubtedly important for morale, the concrete financial and logistical support solidarity exiles managed to transfer to Chile fell short. Ultimately, in fact, Beatriz's decision to kill herself was at least in part because of a profound sense of disillusionment with four years of efforts to overturn the coup on top of the effects of the coup itself.

One of the many tragedies of Beatriz's death is that had she lived, she would have seen a new phase of resistance take shape, building on the work she had felt so depressed about. With the onset of economic crisis, mass protests in Chile broke out in 1983–86, which left-wing parties within Chile and abroad were able to support far more effectively than they might have done a decade earlier.[13] This was the internal, bottom-up resistance Beatriz had regarded as so necessary to antidictatorial action just before her death. And following the initial "reactive" response to the coup and the dictatorship, what Manuel Antonio Garretón called a "reorganizing phase" began in 1978, meaning the Left was in a much better position to respond.[14] Efforts Beatriz was directly involved in contributed to the Left's ability to survive and then regroup in this way. Her history also reminds us not to treat solidarity and resistance as automatic and teleological. As it shows, opposition to the dictatorship was built as a result of individuals' immense effort, perseverance, and determination, Beatriz's included. To call her a victim therefore obscures the roles she played as a protagonist and driver of history.

Aftermath

In the wake of Beatriz's death, the Cuban authorities visited Luis in hospital and gave him two options: leave Cuba to serve either in Angola or in Ethiopia, where Cuban forces were engaged in supporting Marxist governments at war. With many blaming him for Beatriz's suicide, he chose the latter, believing, as Ethiopia's conflict with Somalia had only just started, he stood a better chance of dying. But he survived and came back to build a life in Cuba, outside government and intelligence work. Although Beatriz had left their children to the care of Paya's sister Isabel Contreras, or "Mitzi," he saw them regularly. And because there was no communication between Hortensia and Mitzi, Luis became Hortensia's principal link to her grandchildren, whom she visited and invited to Mexico regularly.[15]

Elsewhere, Beatriz's friends and colleagues were scattered around the world when they heard about her death. Patricia deciphered it from a Belgian newsstand a few weeks after leaving Beatriz in Cuba.[16] Hernán, the student who had accompanied her to Cuba in 1960, was at a World Health Organization reception in Brazzaville, Republic of the Congo. "Allende's daughter has killed herself!" an aristocratic British representative cheerfully announced as drinks were served, not realizing the friendship she and Hernán had shared.[17] Her former tutor and political mentor at the University of Concepción, Jorge Peña, had just arrived in exile in Panama following detention in Chilean concentration camps.[18] In Berlin, Celsa Parrau, her close friend from the Ejército de Liberación Nacional (ELN), received the news by telephone. Widowed after the coup and exiled in East Germany with her two children, she remembered being unable to breathe.[19] In Boston, studying for a postgraduate degree, Beatriz's student from the University of Chile read about her death sitting in a booth at an Italian restaurant.[20] Hernán Coloma, a founding member of the Organa, was in Moscow receiving military training, while Jorge Arrate was in Rotterdam, heading the Institute for a New Chile, an initiative spearheaded by Orlando Letelier just before his death.[21]

In fact, even a glimpse of where Beatriz's friends, family, and colleagues were when she died gives us an indication of the centrifugal force the coup, and the Cold War violence it was part of, had to disrupt individuals' lives and communities. For as much as the conflict was about nuclear strategies and superpower summits, it was also about the way ideological conflicts affected human lives and experiences. From work in nongovernmental organizations to armed resistance and human rights organizing, her friends' experiences also spoke to the particular complexities of the late 1970s. Militants' contrasting trajectories reflected, and responded to, a reconfiguring of global politics that radically altered the logics and certainties of the past, the long sixties' revolutionary ferment included. Quite simply, Beatriz died at a moment of global transition. In 1977, Amnesty International won the Nobel Peace Prize, and Jimmy Carter was inaugurated as president, putting human rights at the center of his foreign policy. In Samuel Moyn's words, the "moral world ... changed," ushering forth human rights as "last utopia," replacing "other utopias, both state-based and internationalist" that had ended in "dark tragedies," with revolutionary socialism being one of them. Beatriz herself may not have moved on to embrace this new utopia, but for the international system as a whole, human rights, Moyn writes, provided "a pure alternative in an age of ideological betrayal and political collapse."[22] Indeed, by this point, a pervading sense of political, economic, and social crisis had pushed people to rethink the past and the future. Richard Nixon's resignation, 135 coups, at least 35 wars, and the assassination of 11 heads of state worldwide had challenged established political authority by the end of the decade. Restrictive certainties when it came to gender, race, and sexuality were also beginning to be dismantled.[23]

If, in retrospect, a perceived sense of upheaval was exaggerated compared with later events, what emerged in its wake revolutionized world history for at least four decades.[24] The problem for Beatriz and her cohort of revolutionaries was that the path followed henceforth moved inexorably in an antithetical direction to the one that they had envisaged. Economic and financial liberalization underpinned the rise of neoliberalism on a global scale. The Third World project that had emerged in the late 1950s unraveled as postcolonial states turned inward, struggling to deal with rising oil prices and finding solutions elsewhere.[25] China turned to the market from 1978, and Chile's dictatorship was one of the first countries to spearhead totalizing neoliberal reforms from the mid-1970s. In the Soviet bloc, with Cuba more entrenched than ever, stability, restraint, and pragmatism were embraced. True, Central America's revolutionary upheaval and armed gains appeared to suggest socialist transformation of the kind Beatriz had once envisaged was still a possibility. The Sandinista victory in Nicaragua also welcomed many Chileans to fight or participate in the country's revolutionary process, including Beatriz's first husband, Renato.[26] But Central America's revolutionary trajectory—for all its apparent promise—was an outlier, ultimately besieged by a counterrevolutionary offensive. It also stood in stark contrast to repressive military regimes in South America, which slammed shut old impetuses for change and forcibly instituted a radically new authoritarianism by the end of the 1970s.

Struggling to respond, Chile's fragmented Left split even further. One branch of the Socialist Party and Movimiento de Acción Popular Unitario militants began "renovating" their ideology and strategy. Following self-critical appraisals of the past and inspired by foreign models, primarily European social democracy and Eurocommunism, they emphasized democracy and institutional legitimacy, discarded Marxism-Leninism, at least in terms of a practical guide, and rejected violence from the late 1970s onward.[27] The Institute for a New Chile in Rotterdam, where Jorge Arrate was based from 1977, would become one of the headquarters of this *renovación*.[28]

Other left-wing sectors focused on armed resistance within Chile.

In 1978, the remnants of the Movimiento de Izquierda Revolucionaria (MIR) began Operation Retorno—a political military strategy involving the transfer of militants back to Chile for this purpose.[29] From 1980, the PCCh's new emphasis on "popular rebellion" meant it also provided military opposition to the dictatorship. Internal conclusions regarding the past, combined with inspiration from abroad—primarily, the revolutionary victory of the Sandinistas in Nicaragua in 1979—led to this strategy and, with it, to the creation of a new military wing of the PCCh, the Frente Patriotico Manuel Rodríguez (Manuel Rodríguez Patriotic Front, FPMR). Launching armed attacks on Chilean infrastructure in the 1980s, it worked in collaboration with the MIR and was supported by members of the PS who rejected renovation known as the "Almeyda Socialists."[30] And it was these sectors that had the presence on the ground in Chile to offer support to civil protests there in the early 1980s.[31]

Although, as Victor Figueroa Clark has argued, both left-wing tendencies were instrumental in ending the dictatorship, this is not how history has remembered the process of transition.[32] In 1986–88, following a new wave of dictatorial repression, the "renovated" Left, working with the Christian Democratic Party, opted to work within the dictatorship's institutional system to oppose it, definitively rejecting armed resistance as counterproductive and focusing on winning a plebiscite regarding the dictatorship's future.[33] This strategy worked, leading to Chile's first presidential elections since 1970. Although Pinochet lost, democratization was nevertheless a managed process rather than a radical rupture. The military regime's 1980 constitution was never revoked. Meanwhile, "democratic consolidation" and economic stability were prioritized over mobilization in favor of political or social change.[34] There were good reasons for this: the fear the military would intervene again or the country would return to the ideological conflicts of the past. But in tandem, Chile's revolutionary legacy was reshaped, leaving those associated with revolutionary socialism, armed revolution, and militarized resistance in what Cherie Zalaquett called a "liminal state marked by an unbreakable silence."[35]

Of course, Beatriz was long dead when democratization occurred, unable to influence the transitional process or the way Chile's revolutionary past was remembered. When interviewed in 1977 and asked to define her father's legacy, she had equivocated before underlining his internationalist solidarity with revolutionary movements abroad, his anti-imperialism, his refusal to negotiate, and his military preparation. "Allende was one of the few, although perhaps not sufficiently, who had a military concept," she stressed. "He was fundamentally a man who always fought with ideas and a pen, but in the moment when he had to take up a rifle, he knew how to. And he had the courage to do so." For Beatriz, her father provided an important lesson. "In the future," she insisted, "we will be capable of constructing a true revolution only if we know not just how to conserve and consolidate but also how to defend. I think this is Allende's message: defend revolution with all forms of struggle."[36] She also spoke about the Left's insufficient "class hatred"—a reference to Che Guevara's suggestion, in his 1967 message to the Tricontinental, that this was an indispensable feature of a people's ability to triumph over a "brutal enemy."[37]

And yet, as an apocalyptic vision of escalating carnage in pursuit of a brighter, distant, socialist utopia, Guevara's message—and left-wing identification with it—would increasingly be disavowed as anachronistic in postdictatorial Chile. The ELN and the revolutionary Left may have embraced the idea of mass sacrifice in the name of future victories. But seventeen years of violent dictatorship led many militants to different conclusions. Certainly, Beatriz's perspective on Allende's life and revolutionary struggle would not fare well. Her father's complexities, his ambiguous and permissive stance when it came to the revolutionary Left and Latin American guerrilla movements, would be eclipsed by a portrait more associated with a social democracy and related to the Left's renovation. Her reference to class hatred was also out of step with emphasis on avoiding conflict, on reconciliation, and on consensus building. As Brian Loveman argued, in postdictatorial Chile, "piecemeal reform had become respectable, democracy essential, pragmatism desirable, and moderation a virtue."[38]

Indeed, in many ways, Beatriz's Chile was gone; the world she came from and the revolutionary project she had espoused was replaced by a remarkably durable, neoliberal capitalist model that had little to do with Chilean politics, society, and culture of the long sixties. Quite apart from guerrilla insurgencies, the very idea of state-led public health, to which Beatriz had devoted her career before moving to politics full-time, was superseded in the 1980s by state insurance and private health care, while state spending on health dramatically declined.[39] Where once the state had been responsible for 75 percent of investment in Chile, the private sector now replaced it.[40] In postdictatorial Chile, successive center-left coalition governments also distanced politics—and who was in charge—from civil society. Especially within the PS, what Kenneth Roberts calls the "professionalization of the political class" created divisions with grassroots activists leaving political initiative in the hands of a "technocratic elite." And, of course, this stood in sharp contrast to the kind of direct participation that party leaders and militants had had in social struggles that forged Beatriz's revolutionary generation.[41]

It is impossible to know what Beatriz would have made of this process, the question of insurrectionary tactics, or negotiated transition and democratic consolidation had she lived. Like others who felt out of step with the way Chile's postdictatorial era unfolded and felt "forgotten" by it, Beatriz may well have resented the direction history took. This was certainly not the future she had imagined or fought for. Given her unbending loyalty to Cuba, her links to Almeyda, and her emphasis on military preparation, it is difficult to imagine her being enthusiastic or pleased by the transition that occurred. As a woman in arms, or at least someone who craved to be allowed to use them, and who desperately wanted to return to Chile to fight covertly for the resistance, she would have found adjusting to Chile's new society hard. As Sofía Tupper observed, women in the FPMR—and even more so, those who took up arms at the expense of domestic responsibilities—struggled after 1990 in a Chile that was unprepared to recognize women as "historical protagonists."[42] Many female militants simply returned to their family roles in the decades that followed and were forgotten.[43] For them, and many who maintained a revolutionary left-wing identity, the nature of a negotiated transition to democracy was thus not so much a victory as a solution that kept them on the margins.[44] As one Socialist woman explained, "Transition had to occur as it did, but it clearly isn't what I most wanted. I had old dreams of arriving at La Moneda in jeeps and wearing olive green and unfurling a banner like the Sandinistas."[45]

Of course, like her father, one of Beatriz's strengths was in straddling differences and moving between factions, serving as a bridge and problem solver. She employed flexibility during her period as her father's private secretary and then as solidarity campaigner. She never chose between his democratic convictions and the MIR's positions, between armed resistance and human rights campaigning, because she didn't believe a choice had to be made. To her, all forms of struggle were necessary, legitimate, and inevitable in pursuit of revolutionary change.[46] Yet her belief in "all forms of struggle" marked her for a long time as a historical actor from Chile's revolutionary past rather than its democratic future.

Although the vast majority of left-wing Latin Americans still reject revolutionary violence today, and despite a revolutionary socialist future of the kind dreamed of by Beatriz being hard to imagine, a new wave of civil mobilization two decades after the transition to democracy has reminded many of the long sixties that her generation helped shape. The Chilean student movements that erupted in 2006 and 2011 spearheaded a new atmosphere of rebelliousness and activism for the twenty-first century. Violeta Parra's song "Me gustan los estudiantes [I love the students]," written in the 1960s, became an anthem once again as Chile's historic *juventud revo-*

lucionaria acquired a new symbolic resonance in the country. Campaigning for free education and social welfare, the reasons young people spilled onto the streets, echoed the causes that had once driven Beatriz into politics, albeit in a very different context. An urgency for change also brought forth a new generation of leaders and political groups, many of whom, at the time of this writing, are embedded in Chilean political life. And, then, in October 2019 a new, much bigger wave of protests for democracy and against austerity and the cost of living brought Chile to a standstill. Over a million Chileans took to the streets demanding an end to inequality and a new constitution to replace the dictatorship's neoliberal legacy. In response to the government's recourse to violent repression to quell civil unrest, Victor Jara's song "El derecho de vivir in paz [The right to live in peace]" was re-recorded and sung anew, albeit now without reference to Vietnam and Ho Chi Minh. Indeed, with Third World solidarity and guerrilla insurgencies in the distant past, protesters' references and methods were now rooted in mass mobilization and civil disobedience. But in 2019, as in 2006 and 2011, there was no mistaking the revolutionary initiative that youth seemed to have seized.

Like her contemporaries who survived her and welcomed such activism, Beatriz would have found much of her past in the present. Like those I spoke with, she would probably have been enthused and comforted that repertoires of protest had returned to challenge the status quo and demand change. She would also have been alarmed, but unsurprised, at the repressive force used to resist such demands. What she would probably not have recognized, however, is the growth of Chile's feminist movement and the prominence of women as public figures and leaders. As a woman who challenged gendered norms of her time and who was consistently constrained but tried as hard as she could to be *consecuente*, or true to her ideas in action as well as thought, she was not alone. But her access to, and participation in, high-level revolutionary groups, her position in Allende's inner circle, for example, was exceptional. Today, it would be less so. For example, despite her sister's distance from politics prior to the coup and espousing the cause of "renovación," which Beatriz is unlikely to have embraced, Isabel certainly assumed a prominent political role in Chile after the return to democracy. Beatriz's daughter, Maya, has also represented Santiago's Providencia and Núñoa districts in Congress since 2014, serving as president of Chile's Chamber of Deputies between 2018 and 2019. And, of course, Michelle Bachelet was the first woman to serve as Chile's defense minister before being elected twice as president of the country. Indeed, it is conceivable that had she been born today, Beatriz would have been a politician herself—on stage out of choice rather than necessity, as she was after the coup, and with a starring role rather than one off-stage, where she was for much of the long sixties.

In spite of women's central participation in Chilean political life today, there remains a lot to do when it comes to gender equality. In the midst of the country's 2019 protests and the state's violence toward women who took part in them, the feminist collective Las Tesis performed their song "Un violador en tu camino [A rapist in your path]," a searing call to end gender violence, on the streets of Valparaíso. Their performance subsequently went viral worldwide, bringing attention to Chilean women's fight for change. In the era of #MeToo, Chilean female students occupied universities across the country in April 2018 to demand an end to violence against women and that they be recognized in academic curricula.[47] On 8 March 2019, International Women's Day, four hundred thousand women had also marched through Santiago's streets—the biggest women's march to take place in Chile up to that point.[48] Four days earlier, the city had awoken to find that activists had replaced forty-four metro signs with the names of Chilean women, calling attention to the exclusive commemoration of men as the architects of modern Chile. Demanding that women's roles in building the country be recognized, activists pointed to the importance of history's representation in forging today's world and our future.[49] And, although, as a contested, complex figure in Chile's revolutionary past, Beatriz Allende was not among the names, her story reminds us to count women as historical actors and protagonists—as revolutionaries and activists who fought for change and helped shape the way the past unfolded as it did.

Acknowledgments

I am lucky to have had ample support and encouragement while working on this book. Luis Fernández Oña inspired me to write about Beatriz, opened doors to her friends and family, and shared his private document collection with me. He felt an enormous debt to Beatriz and was unwavering in helping me understand her life in what turned out to be the final years of his own. I am only sorry he—and many others who shared their stories—did not live to see the final book. To Luis, then, and to his widow, Rita, who showed me kindness in Cuba and Chile, my sincere thanks. I am also immensely grateful to all those who agreed to be interviewed despite it often meaning reliving painful memories. This is in many ways their story as well as Beatriz's, and without their generosity, the book would have been impossible to write.

My gratitude also goes to the many who helped me track down sources and Beatriz's contemporaries, including Fernando Barreiro, Cristóbal Bywaters, Claudia Fedora Rojas, Victor Figueroa Clark, Miguel Gasic, Alberto Martín Álvarez, Danny Monsálvez, Gustavo Rodríguez Ostría, Miguel Soto, Marian Schlotterbeck, Olga Ulianova, and Cesar Vera Medrano.

At the London School of Economics and Political Science (LSE), I have been blessed with loyal colleagues, inspiring students, and a stimulating intellectual environment. For their encouragement, motivation, and advice, I particularly thank Roham Alvandi, Nigel Ashton, Molly Avery, Mathew Betts, Nayna Bhatti, Megan Black, Anna Cant, Demetra Frini, Matthew Jones, Paul Keenan, Piers Ludlow, Andrea Mason, Anita Prazmowska, Taylor Sherman, Paul Stock, Imaobong Umoren, and Eline van Ommen.

In Chile, I am indebted to Marcelo Casals, Joaquín Fermandois, Fernando Purcell, Alfredo Riquelme, Alfonso Salgado, Alessandro Santoni, and Olga Ulianova for their advice and friendship. Additional thanks to Sergio Benavides and Carla Hernández at the Fundación Salvador Allende and to staff at the Museo Nacional de Medicina at the Universidad de Chile for their assistance. Felipe Henríquez Ordenes and Marco Álvarez also shared their photo collections with me, for which I am grateful.

For their guidance on research in Mexico City, I thank Luis Herrán,

Alberto Martín, and Vanni Pettina. In Cuba, I am grateful to staff at the Casa Memorial Salvador Allende, in particular Ulises Mitodio Fritz. My thanks to Antoni Kapcia and Isabel Story for their assistance in accessing Cuban sources at the University of Nottingham's Hennessy Collection. For their encouragement and conversations on different themes related to the book, additional thanks go to Ingunn Bjornson, Maricela Gonzalez Moya, Heather Jones, Artemy Kalinovsky, Patrick Kelly, David Milne, Gloria Miqueles, Mario del Pero, Padraic Scanlon, Erica Wald, and Arne Westad.

I am also profoundly grateful to Alan Angell, Margaret Power, and Alfredo Riquelme for their close reading of the final manuscript and for their constructive suggestions. Jeffrey Bryne, Andrew Kirkendall, Victor Figueroa Clark, Aldo Marchesi, Vanni Pettina, Fernando Purcell, Imaobong Umoren, and Arne Westad all read parts of the manuscript in draft form and offered me invaluable feedback.

Transnational history requires transnational research, and following a person's life has involved considerable travel and assistance. I regard myself immensely fortunate to have been able to draw on the LSE International History Department's staff research funds over the past decade. In 2010 and 2013, the Pontificia Universidad Católica de Chile hosted me as a guest teacher, affording me the opportunity to spend longer periods in Santiago and exchange views with staff and students at the institution. I am also thankful to the Department of History at Columbia University for hosting me as a visiting assistant professor in 2012–13, when I began thinking through the project in more detail. In London, my eternal thanks to the British Library, the Institute of Historical Research, and the LSE Library for their global collections and refuge. I have also had research and translation assistance from Jonathan Jeutner, Javiera Soto, Sam Plumb, Hanna Szymborska, Elisa Quiroz, and Roberto Velázquez. I am particularly indebted to Roberto for his assistance with locating sources and translation in the project's final years and for his friendship, insight, and enthusiasm.

At the University of North Carolina Press, my thanks to Elaine Maisner, who believed in this project from the outset, to Dino Battista, Mary Caviness, Cate Hodorowicz, Stephanie Wenzel, and Andrew Winters. For her patience and meticulous copyediting, I am also sincerely grateful to Nancy Raynor.

Outside academia, I am forever thankful to my family and friends. My parents, Anita and Jeremy, my sister, Jessy, and her husband, Jock, have been amazingly supportive. My life has also changed immeasurably for the better since I began writing this book. I fell in love, married, gained a stepson, Spike, and a wider family. I now also have two daughters, Freya and

Alessia, who have made me smile and dance in ridiculous, sleep-deprived ways. Through them, in Harringay, I have also met supportive friends who offered words of encouragement when I most needed them. The staff at Orange Nursery who have cared for Freya and Alessia so well also deserve my heartfelt thanks.

Last but by no means least, I want to thank Tom, my best friend and my husband. The focus writing demands often means being distracted and absent, but he has never ceased to be positive and understanding. More important, he has taught me how to live and enjoy life in ways I never dreamed possible. Thank you, Tom. This book is for you.

Appendix Chilean Election Results by Gender of Voter

	Women's votes (%)	Men's votes (%)
1958		
Jorge Alessandri (Conservative and Liberal Parties)	34.1	30.2
Salvador Allende (FRAP)	22.3	32.4
Eduardo Frei (PDC)	23.9	19
Luis Bossay (PR)	16.1	15.2
Antonio Zamorano (Independent)	3.6	3.2
1964		
Eduardo Frei (PDC)	62.8	49.2
Salvador Allende (FRAP)	31.9	44.8
Julio Durán (PR)	4.7	5.1
Null and blank	<1	<1
1970		
Salvador Allende (UP)	30.9	42.0
Jorge Alessandri (PN)	38.9	32.9
Radomiro Tomic (PDC)	30.2	26.1
1973		
Unidad Popular	39.4	49.1
Confederación Democrática (Democratic Confederation, CODE)	60.6	50.9

Source: Power, *Right-Wing Women*, 73, 95, 138, 217–18.

Notes

Abbreviations Used in the Notes

ABA	Archivo Beatriz Allende, Havana
AFSA	Archivo Fundación Salvador Allende, Santiago, Chile
AGN	Archivo General de la Nación, Mexico City
AHGE/SRE	Archivo Histórico Genero Estrada, Secretaría de Relaciones Exteriores, Mexico City
AMRE	Archivo General Histórico, Ministerio de Relaciones Exteriores, Santiago, Chile
AN	Archivo Nacional, Santiago, Chile
CCA	Casa de Chile Archive, Mexico City
CeDInCI	Centro de Documentación e Investigación de la Cultura de Izquierdas, Buenos Aires, Argentina
CFP/DOS	State Department Central Foreign Policy Files (1973–77), National Archives and Records Administration, Access to Archival Databases, United States
CIEX	Centro de Informações do Exterior, Ministerio, Ministerio de Relações Exteriores, Brazil
CMSA	Casa Memorial Salvador Allende, Havana, Cuba
CSD	Castro Speech Database
FCO	Foreign and Commonwealth Office
FO	Foreign Office
LHA/PHM	Labour History Archive, People's History Museum, Manchester, United Kingdom
LNUH	*Las Noticias de Última Hora*, Chile
NARA	National Archives and Records Administration, College Park, Maryland, USA
TL	Tamiment Library and Robert F. Wagner Labor Archives, New York University, New York
TNA	The National Archives, London
VP/IPS/DFS	Versiones Públicas, Dirección General de Investigaciones Políticas y Sociales, Fondo Dirección Federal de Seguridad, Archivo General de la Nación, Mexico City
WCDA	Wilson Center Digital Archive

Introduction

1. Guterl, "Comment"; Scott, "Gender," 1068.

2. Colley, *Elizabeth Marsh*, xix, 300–301.

3. Kessler-Harris, "Why Biography?," 626; Lepore, "Historians Who Love," 133.

4. See Fermandois, *La Guerra Fría*, 7; Riquelme Segovia, "La Guerra Fría," 11; and *LNUH*, 1 April 1959.

5. Ulianova, "Algunas reflexiones," 236–37; Westad, *The Cold War*, 1–2.

6. Grandin as quoted in Joseph, "What We Now Know," 4.

7. See, for example, Lambe, "Drug Wars"; Lindo-Fuentes, "Educational Television"; Tinsman, *Partners in Conflict*; Manzano, "Sex, Gender and the Making of the 'Enemy Within'"; and Cowan, *Securing Sex*.

8. Zolov, "Introduction," 354; Marchesi, "Escribiendo la Guerra Fría Latinoamericana"; Kelly, *Sovereign Emergencies*; Power, *Right-Wing Women*; Power, "Who but a Woman?"; Chase, *Revolution within the Revolution*.

9. Lepore, "Historians Who Love," 129.

10. Kirkwood, *Ser política*, 82. On archival sources pertaining to women, see Gordon, Buhle, and Schrom Dye, "The Problem of Women's History," 79.

11. See, for example, Amorós, *Miguel Enríquez*; Huerta and Chávez, *El trabajo*; Núñez, Abra, Escobedo, and Claval, *Ricardo Núñez*; and Puccio, *Cuarto de siglo*.

12. Álvarez, *Tati*, 11.

13. Espuña, *Tati*.

14. Labarca, *Allende*.

15. See, for example, Hendrix (International Telephone and Telegraph, ITT) to R. Berrellez (ITT), "Chileans," 6 November 1970, in *Subversion in Chile*, 101-2; Espuña, *Tati*, 146; Cabrera Infante, *Mea Cuba*, 158.

16. See, for example, Espuña, *Tati*.

17. Unfortunately, Luis's letters to Beatriz have not survived.

18. Regarding the same problem, see del Pozo, *Rebeldes, Reformistas y Revolucionarios*, 13n10.

19. Leavy, *Oral History*, 3; Thomson, "Making the Most of Memories," 291.

20. Leavy, *Oral History*, 7, 12.

21. Thomson, "Making the Most of Memories," 292, 296.

22. See, for example, Fermandois, *La revolución inconclusa*; Garcés, *Allende y la experiencia chilena*; Garretón and Moulian, *La Unidad Popular*; and Gil, Lagos, and Landsberger, *Chile at the Turning Point*.

23. See, for example, Schlotterbeck, *Beyond the Vanguard*, and Power, *Right-Wing Women*.

24. Hite, *When the Romance Ended*; Weld, "Spanish Civil War."

25. Sorensen, *Turbulent Decade*, 2-4; Zolov, "Expanding Our Conceptual Horizons," 48; Pensado, *Rebel Mexico*, 4; Casals, *El alba de una revolución*; Salgado, "Making Friends," 300.

26. Gould, "Solidarity under Siege," 352.

27. Gil, Lagos, and Landsberger, *Chile at the Turning Point*, 1.

28. Bermeo, *Ordinary People*, 139; Navia and Osorio, "'Make the Economy Scream,'" 775, 787; Navia and Osorio, "Las encuestas," 118, 126-27.

29. Bermeo, *Ordinary People*, 139, 150-51.

30. Gil, Lagos, and Landsberger, *Chile at the Turning Point*, 1.

31. Manzano, *Age of Youth*, 6-8.

32. Valle and Díaz, *Federación de la Juventud Socialista*, 13.

33. Manzano, *Age of Youth*, 2; Barr-Melej, *Psychedelic Chile*, 48-49.

34. Collier and Sater, *Chile*, 291; López and Menke, *Informativo Estadístico... 1957 a 1960*, 75. For regional and global comparisons, see Castañeda, *Utopia Unarmed*, 191; Labbens, "Las universidades latinoamericanas," 113; Manzano, *Age of Youth*, 54; and Suri, *Power and Protest*, 269.

35. Barr-Melej, *Psychedelic Chile*, 4.

36. Palieraki, *¡La revolución ya viene!*, 149-53. On youth being "significant as an idea" in Chile's long 1960s, see also Salgado, "Making Friends," 305.

37. For transnational influences on revolutionary politics across the Southern Cone, see Marchesi, *Latin America's Radical Left*.

38. Suri, *Power and Protest*, 3.

39. Purcell and Casals, "Espacions en disputa," 2.

40. See, for example, Angell, "The Left in Latin America"; Ameringer, *The Socialist Impulse*; Carr, *Marxism and Communism*; Carr and Ellner, *The Latin American Left*; Castañeda, *Utopia Unarmed*; Castro, *Revolution and Revolutionaries*; Gould, "Solidarity under Siege"; Leibner, *Camaradas y compañeros*; Liss, *Marxist Thought*; Löwy, *Marxism in Latin America*; Marchesi, *Latin America's Radical Left*; Markarian, *Uruguay, 1968*; and Zolov, "Expanding Our Conceptual Horizons."

41. See, for example, Arrate and Rojas, *Memoria (I and II)*; Casals, *El alba de una revolución*; Corvalán, *El gobierno de Salvador Allende*; Jobet, *El Partido Socialista*; Furci, *The Chilean Communist Party*; Naranjo et al., *Miguel Enríquez*; Núñez, *El gran desencuentro*; Palieraki, *¡La revolución ya viene!*; and Salazar, *Conversaciones con Carlos Altamirano*.

42. See, for example, Winn, *Weavers of Revolution*; del Pozo, *Rebeldes, Reformistas y Revolucionarios*; Trumper, *Ephemeral Histories*; Schlotterbeck, *Beyond the Vanguard*; and Salgado, "Exemplary Comrades." For a helpful discussion of the relationship between Chile's lefts, see also Riquelme, "La vía chilena."

43. See, for example, Brown, *Cuba's Revolutionary World*, and Kruijt, *Cuba and Revolutionary Latin America*.

44. Iber, *Neither Peace nor Freedom*, 16.

45. Riquelme, "La vía chilena," 211.

46. See, for example, Palieraki, *¡La revolución ya viene!*; Leibner, "The Italian Communist Party"; Gould, "Solidarity under Siege"; and Markarian, *Uruguay, 1968*, 74–101.

47. López, "Ubicar urgente a Señora Hortensia."

48. *El Siglo*, 8 May 1964.

49. Quiroga, *Compañeros*, 34.

50. On the importance of affective relationships, see Leibner, "The Italian Communist Party," and Salgado, "Making Friends."

51. Zolov, "Expanding Our Conceptual Horizons," 49–55.

52. Barr-Melej, *Psychedelic Chile*.

53. Deutsch, "Gender and Sociopolitical Change."

54. On PCCh female leaders, see Lecourt-Kendall, "Relaciones de género."

55. Zalaquett, *Chilenas en armas*, 137.

56. Power, *Right-Wing Women*. Beyond Chile, see, for example, Manzano, "Sex, Gender, and the Making of the 'Enemy Within,'" and Cowan, *Securing Sex*.

57. Maravall, *Las mujeres*, 44–45, 60–61; Zalaquett, *Chilenas en armas*, 179, 199; Barr-Melej, *Psychedelic Chile*, 71–85.

58. Maravall, *Las mujeres*, 55; Zalaquett, *Chilenas en armas*, 137; Salgado, "Making Friends," 303.

59. Leibner, "Women in Uruguayan Communism," 5–6.

60. Deutsch, "Gender and Sociopolitical Change"; Green, "'Who Is the Macho Who Wants to Kill Me?'"; Lumsden, *Machos, Maricones, and Gays*.

61. Power, *Right-Wing Women*, 252.

62. Gould, "Solidarity under Siege," 364.

63. Scott, "Gender," 1054, 1067–68.

64. Fernández Allende, "Emotivo homenaje."

65. Zalaquett, *Chilenas en armas*, 326.

66. Carmen Castillo as quoted in Zalaquett, 151.

67. For recent studies challenging the societal taboo of writing about women in

arms, see Zalaquett, *Chilenas en armas*; Robles, "Memorias de la clandestinidad"; and Miqueles, "Women in Arms."

68. Robles, "Memorias de la clandestinidad; Tupper, *Historias de clandestinidad*, 41; Salgado, "Making Friends," 303.

69. See, for example, Chase, *Revolution within the Revolution*; Power, *Right-Wing Women*; and Tinsman, *Partners in Conflict*. On avoiding separate histories, see Scott, "Gender," 1055–57.

70. See, for example, Baltra, *Mireya Baltra*; Laza and Cea, *La Negra Lazo*; Lecourt-Kendall, "Relaciones de género"; Maravall, *Las mujeres*; Marín, *La Vida es hoy*; Rosemblatt, *Gendered Compromises*; Schlotterbeck, *Beyond the Vanguard*; Stuven and Fermandois, *Historia de las mujeres*; and Tinsman, *Partners in Conflict*.

71. Scott, *Gender and the Politics of History*, 17, 27.

72. *LNUH*, 26 January 1961.

Chapter 1

1. Beatriz quoted in Baez, *Preguntas*, 237; López, "Ubicar urgente a Señora Hortensia"; Beatriz interview, *Verde Olivo*, 12 September 1976, as quoted in Álvarez, *Tati*, 26.

2. Puccio, *Cuarto de siglo*, 24; Amorós, *Allende*, 82, 113; Figueroa Clark, *Allende*, 22, 49; Allende Gossens, *Realidad médico-social*.

3. Allende, 1952, as quoted in Amorós, *Allende*, 125; Arrate and Rojas, *Memoria (I)*, 165–66, 170–71.

4. Gálvez, with Parrau, interview; Baez, *Preguntas*, 237.

5. Amorós, *Allende*, 115; Álvarez, *Tati*, 26.

6. Labarca, *Allende*, 100, 121–23.

7. Tambutti Allende, *Allende, mi abuelo*.

8. Carmen Paz, Viel, and Gnecco, interview; Álvarez, *Tati*, 44–45.

9. Álvarez, *Tati*, 30.

10. Amorós, *Allende*, 117; Tambutti Allende, *Allende, mi abuelo*; Jeannette Gallo, "Cuatro mujeres retratan a Allende," *El Siglo*, 12 October 1963; Álvarez, *Tati*, 35–36.

11. Álvarez, *Tati*, 32–33.

12. Álvarez, 46; Carmen Paz, Viel, and Gnecco, interview.

13. Rojas, *Historia de la infancia*, 333; Schell, "Beauty and Bounty," 66; Amorós, *Allende*, 114.

14. Figueroa Clark, *Allende*, 15.

15. Carmen Paz, Viel, and Gnecco, interview; Isabel as quoted in Hite, *When the Romance Ended*, 71; Echeverría and Castillo, *Santiago-Paris*, 36–37; Pascal Allende, interview.

16. Pascal Allende, interview.

17. Carmen Paz, Viel and Gnecco, interview.

18. Amorós, *Allende*, 114, 117.

19. Amorós, 81, 118; Figueroa Clark, *Allende*, 53.

20. Tambutti Allende, *Allende, mi abuelo*.

21. Other signed photos were Arturo Alessandri Palma, Raúl Castro, and the Chilean author Manuel Rojas. Erica Vexler, "Pulso familiar del Dr. Allende," *Ercilla*, 20 May 1964.

22. Rojas, *Historia de la infancia*, 490; Álvarez, *Tati*, 38.

23. Carmen Paz, Viel, and Gnecco, interview.

24. Carter, interview, and Contreras, interview; Boza, correspondence.

25. Contreras, interview. On handwriting, see Carmen Paz, Viel, and Gnecco, interview; and "Características del 60A. BEATRIZ ALLENDE," 1959, in Álvarez, *Tati*, 52.
26. Collier and Sater, *Chile*, 286; Schell, "Beauty and Bounty," 61–64.
27. Trapote, interview.
28. Contreras, interview.
29. Pey, interview; Gálvez, with Parrau, interview.
30. Labarca, *Allende*, 107, 121–22.
31. Carter, interview, and Contreras, interview.
32. Isabel and Carmen Paz as quoted in Amorós, *Allende*, 115–16; Beatriz, *Verde Olivo*, 12 September 1976, as quoted in Álvarez, *Tati*, 35.
33. Beatriz, *Verde Olivo*, 12 September 1976, as quoted in Álvarez, *Tati*, 38.
34. Beatriz, *Verde Olivo*, 12 September 1976, and *Mujeres*, February 1977, as quoted in Álvarez, *Tati*, 34–35.
35. Gallo, "Cuatro mujeres."
36. Isabel as quoted in Amorós, *Allende*, 115.
37. Labarca, *Allende*, 107, 118.
38. Carmen Paz, Viel, and Gnecco, interview.
39. Lorca Robles, interview.
40. Amorós, *Allende*, 190.
41. See, for example, Gálvez, with Parrau, interview; Carretero, interview; Salazar, *Conversaciones con Carlos Altamirano*, 231; and *El Mercurio*, 14 October 1977.
42. Álvarez, *Tati*, 39–40.
43. Gallo, "Cuatro mujeres."
44. Gallo.
45. Boza, correspondence; Lorca Robles, Oyarzún, and Peña and Funke, interviews.
46. Schell, "Beauty and Bounty," 79.
47. López and Menke, *Informativo Estadístico ... 1957 a 1960*, 75; Garretón and Martínez, *Biblioteca del movimiento estudiantil (I)*, 52.
48. Schell, "Beauty and Bounty," 67.
49. Collier and Sater, *Chile*, 287.
50. López and Menke, *Informativo Estadístico ... 1957 a 1960*, 80–97; Rosemblatt, *Gendered Compromises*, 131, 137.
51. Benado, interview. See also Contreras, interview.
52. López and Menke, *Informativo Estadístico ... 1957 a 1960*, 96.
53. Boza, correspondence; Lorca Robles, interview.
54. Lorca Robles, interview.
55. Pey, interview. On men's common desire for a son in 1940s Chile, see also Echeverría and Castillo, *Santiago-París*, 69.
56. Falabella, "Gabriela Mistral y Winétt de Rokha," 289–90.
57. Collier and Sater, *Chile*, 286; Schell, "Beauty and Bounty," 66.
58. Antezana-Pernet, "Peace in the World," 168.
59. Collier and Sater, *Chile*, 287.
60. Kirkwood, *Ser política*, 76.
61. Lecourt-Kendall, "Relaciones de género," 49.
62. Rosemblatt, *Gendered Compromises*, 95, 98, 122.
63. Kirkwood, *Ser política*, 81–82.
64. Huerta and Veneros, "Mujeres, democracia y participación social," 390, 392, 394.

65. "The Movement for Emancipation of Chilean Women: Interview with Elena Caffarena," in *Chile Reader*, 318.

66. Contreras, interview.

67. Isabel as quoted in Hite, *When the Romance Ended*, 72.

68. Schell, "Beauty and Bounty," 68; Rosemblatt, *Gendered Compromises*, 51, 149, 167.

69. Allende Gossens, *Realidad médico-social*, 77.

70. *Eva*, 25 June 1943, 6 August 1943.

71. Huerta and Veneros, "Mujeres, democracia y participación social," 397–98.

72. Parrau, interview.

73. Adriana Santa Cruz as quoted in Álvarez, *Tati*, 44.

74. Isabel as quoted in Álvarez, *Tati*, 26.

75. Isabel as quoted in Hite, *When the Romance Ended*, 71.

76. *LNUH*, 28 March 1957, 30 March 1957, 31 March 1957.

77. Arrate and Rojas, *Memoria (I)*, 316–17; Gazmuri, *Frei*, 432. According to Gazmuri, more than hundred people were rumored to have died.

78. Arrate and Rojas, *Memoria (I)*, 234; Amorós, *Allende*, 147.

79. *LNUH*, 28 March 1957.

80. *LNUH*, 9 April 1957, 29 March 1957, 30 March 1957; Collier and Sater, *Chile*, 280.

81. Navia and Osorio, "Las encuestas," 132.

82. Loveman, *Chile*, 223; Arrate and Rojas, *Memoria (I)*, 302.

83. *LNUH*, 23 March 1957; Collier and Sater, *Chile*, 276–78; "Chile: Annual Review for 1957," 27 January 1958, FO 371/132021/TNA.

84. Amorós, *Allende*, 146; Gazmuri, *Frei*, 402; Arrate and Rojas, *Memoria (I)*, 301–3.

85. Jan Lemuñir, "The Birth of a Shantytown," in *Chile Reader*, 335–37; on Socialist Party and Communist Party involvement, see Arrate and Rojas, *Memoria (I)*, 325.

86. Arrate and Rojas, *Memoria (I)*, 323.

87. Puccio, *Cuarto de siglo*, 72; *LNUH*, 3 July 1959.

88. Loveman, *Chile*, 165.

89. Allende Gossens, *Realidad médico-social*, 22, 83, 195–96.

90. *Ercilla*, 16 September 1942.

91. Frank, *South American Journey*, 138–44.

92. Huneeus, *Guerra fría*, 16.

93. Casals, "Estado, contrarrevolución y autoritarismo," 96; Barr-Melej, *Reforming Chile*, 2–3, 10–11; Rosemblatt, *Gendered Compromises*, 6, 21.

94. Collier and Sater, *Chile*, 289; Rojas, *Historia de la infancia*, 431.

95. Casals, "Estado, contrarrevolución y autoritarismo," 97; Barr-Melej, *Reforming Chile*, 3; Amorós, *Allende*, 128; Figueroa Clark, *Allende*, 58–59; "Servicio Nacional de Salúd," *Revista Médica de Chile* 87, no. 1 (1959): 58–61; Cueto and Palmer, *Medicine and Public Health*, 202.

96. Allende Gossens, *Realidad médico-social*, 8; Collier and Sater, *Chile*, 264.

97. Loveman, *Chile*, 215; Drake, "International Crises," 120; Antezana-Pernet, "Peace in the World," 166–67.

98. Amorós, *Allende*, 94, 102.

99. Loveman, *Chile*, 221–22.

100. Collier and Sater, *Chile*, 289–90.

101. Mattelart, *Atlas social*, 123–24.

102. *Eva*, 15 October 1943, 4 July 1952.
103. Aníbal Pinto, "A Case of Frustrated Development," in *Chile Reader*, 309–14; Loveman, *Chile*, 200.
104. Figueroa Clark, *Allende*, 57.
105. Loveman, *Chile*, 212, 215; Huneeus, *Guerra fría*, 35.
106. Loveman, *Chile*, 201.
107. Loveman, 199; Navia and Osorio, "'Make the Economy Scream,'" 787.
108. Loveman, *Chile*, 182, 206; Amorós, *Allende*, 146; Arrate and Rojas, *Memoria (I)*, 182, 249, 313.
109. Casals, *La creación de la amenaza roja*; Loveman, *Chile*, 188, 214; Huneeus, *Guerra fría*, 62.
110. Amorós, *Allende*, 110.
111. Arrate and Rojas, *Memoria (I)*, 245.
112. Huneeus, *Guerra fría*, 27, 225, 262.
113. Antezana-Pernet, "Peace in the World," 167, 181–82; Huerta and Veneros, "Mujeres, democracia y participación social," 389–99; Arrate and Rojas, *Memoria (I)*, 257.
114. Antezana-Pernet, "Peace in the World," 179; Huerta and Veneros, "Mujeres, democracia y participación social," 394; Arrate and Rojas, *Memoria (I)*, 184; Rosemblatt, *Gendered Compromises*, 249.
115. Drake, "International Crises," 134.
116. Amorós, *Allende*, 99–119.
117. Arrate and Rojas, *Memoria (I)*, 234.
118. Amorós, *Allende*, 109.
119. Amorós, 123, 127; Puccio, *Cuarto de siglo*, 31.
120. Teitelboim quoted in Figueroa Clark, *Allende*, 54.
121. See, for example, Marín, *La Vida es hoy*; Amorós, *Miguel Enríquez*, 38; and Lagos, *Memorias (I)*, 95–95.
122. Núñez, Abra, Escobedo, and Claval, *Ricardo Núñez*, 21–22.
123. *LNUH*, 6 April 1957; Arrate and Rojas, *Memoria (I)*, 317; "Communism and the Disturbances," extract, Report by the Political Committee to the 24th Plenary Session of the Central Committee of the PCCh, enclosure, Letter, Chancery, British Embassy, Santiago to Department, 29 May 1957, FO 371/126262/TNA.
124. Arrate and Rojas, *Memoria (I)*, 319; Gazmuri, *Frei*, 443.
125. Arrate and Rojas, *Memoria (I)*, 307–8.
126. Huneeus, *Guerra fría*, 364.
127. Letter, Ivor Pink to Selwyn Lloyd, 9 July 1958, FO 371/132022/TNA.
128. Amorós, *Allende*, 151; Arrate and Rojas, *Memoria (I)*, 322.
129. Amorós, *Allende*, 156.
130. Letter, Ivor Pink to Selwyn Lloyd, 8 September 1958, FO 371/132022/TNA.
131. Puccio, *Cuarto de siglo*, 44.
132. *El Siglo*, 1 September 1958, 3 September 1958.
133. Gazmuri, *Frei*, 463; Amorós, *Allende*, 148.
134. Memorandum, Assistant Secretary of State for Inter-American Affairs to Deputy Under Secretary of State for Economic Affairs, "Strategic Controls on Copper and U.S. Relations with Chile," 18 June 1958, *Foreign Relations of the United States/1958–1960/V.*
135. *El Siglo*, 9 July 1958, 7 July 1958.
136. Soto, interview.

137. Letter, Ivor Pink to Selwyn Lloyd, 25 August 1959, FO 371/132022/TNA.
138. Puccio, *Cuarto de siglo*, 68–75.
139. Figueroa Clark, *Allende*, 61; *El Siglo*, 11 August 1958, 15 August 1958.
140. Pereda, correspondence.
141. Isabel as quoted in Álvarez, *Tati*, 49.
142. Labarca, *Allende*, 144.
143. Beatriz, February 1977, quoted in Álvarez, *Tati*, 27.
144. *El Siglo*, 31 August 1958.
145. *LNUH*, 1 March 1957.
146. *El Siglo*, 24 July 1958, 7 August 1958.
147. *El Siglo*, 7 August 1958, 11 August 1958.
148. Figueroa Clark, *Allende*, 64.
149. Puccio, *Cuarto de siglo*, 46, 61–63; Amorós, *Allende*, 155.
150. Huerta and Veneros, "Mujeres, democracia y participación social," 393.
151. Puccio, *Cuarto de siglo*, 59.
152. Puccio, *Cuarto de siglo*, 83–84.
153. Amorós, *Allende*, 167–70.
154. Pascal Allende, interview. See also del Pozo, *Rebeldes, Reformistas y Revolucionarios*, 133.
155. Victor Irrizarri quoted in *Punto Final*, 30 September 1969.
156. Del Pozo, *Rebeldes, Reformistas y Revolucionarios*, 64–65; Hite, *When the Romance Ended*, 30.
157. Baez, *Preguntas*, 245.
158. Valle and Díaz, *Federación de la Juventud Socialista*, 68n70.
159. Puccio, *Cuarto de siglo*, 95.
160. Jaramillo, correspondence.
161. See *LNUH*, 29 January 1959, 30 January 1959, 2 February 1959.
162. *LNUH*, 29 January 1959.
163. *LNUH*, 15 January 1959.
164. *LNUH*, 2 February 1959.
165. Beatriz quoted in Baez, *Preguntas*, 245.
166. "Entrevista Allende-Debray," 33.
167. Puccio, *Cuarto de siglo*, 95–96.
168. *LNUH*, 29 January 1959.
169. *Gente Joven*, 14 August 1959.
170. *LNUH*, 8 March 1959.
171. *LNUH*, 20 March 1959.
172. *LNUH*, 10 August 1959.
173. Arrate and Rojas, *Memoria (I)*, 334–35.
174. *LNUH*, 5 May 1959, 6 May 1959.
175. *LNUH*, 1 April 1959.
176. *LNUH*, 24 March 1959.
177. *LNUH*, 17 June 1959.
178. *LNUH*, 21 July 1959, 9 August 1959.
179. *LNUH*, 15 July 1959, 17 July 1959; *El Siglo*, 11 August 1959.
180. *LNUH*, 21 July 1959.
181. *LNUH*, 4 August 1959, 8 August 1959.
182. *El Siglo*, 11 August 1959.
183. *El Siglo*, 13 August 1959.

184. *LNUH*, 11 August 1959; *El Siglo*, 12 August 1959; Letter, Pink to Lloyd, 25 August 1959.
185. *LNUH*, 28 July 1959; *El Siglo*, 8 August 1959, 10 August 1959.
186. Letter, Pink to Lloyd, 25 August 1959.
187. *El Siglo*, 19 August 1959; Telegram, British Embassy, Santiago to Foreign Office, 18 August 1959, FO 371/138921/TNA.
188. *El Siglo*, 20 August 1959.
189. Letter, Pink to Lloyd, 25 August 1959.
190. Beatriz quoted in Baez, *Preguntas*, 245.
191. *Gente Joven*, 28 August 1959.
192. *Gente Joven*, 19 November 1959, 3 December 1959.
193. *LNUH*, 8 March 1959.
194. Carmen Paz, Viel, and Gnecco, interview; "Características del 60A. BEATRIZ ALLENDE," 1959, in Álvarez, *Tati*, 52.
195. Collier and Sater, *Chile*, 291.

Chapter 2
1. Lorca Robles, interview.
2. Peña and Funke, interview; Trucco, interview; Amorós, *Miguel Enríquez*, 46.
3. Schlotterbeck, *Beyond the Vanguard*, 7, 11–12; Monsálvez, *El golpe de Estado*, 21; Mattelart, *Atlas social*, 123–26.
4. Palieraki, *¡La revolución ya viene!*, 177, 179, 184.
5. See, for example, *Gente Joven*, 7 January 1960, 29 December 1960; *Renovación* (FEC), March–April 1961; and *El Sur*, 7 February 1960, 15 March 1960, 27 March 1961, 6 April 1961, 4 November 1962.
6. *El Sur*, 21 July 1960.
7. *Gente Joven*, 3 March 1960, 21 April 1960.
8. Valle and Díaz, *Federación de la Juventud Socialista*, 43.
9. Silva and Riquelme, *Una identidad terremoteada*, 153.
10. Boza, correspondence.
11. Trucco, interview, and Ulloa, interview; Amorós, *Miguel Enríquez*, 46.
12. Bernasconi, "Being Decent," 867.
13. *Eva*, 22 January 1960.
14. See, for example, *El Sur*, 21 March 1960.
15. *Eva*, 19 February 1960.
16. Lorca Robles, interview.
17. Benado, interview.
18. Puccio, *Cuarto de siglo*, 101.
19. Lorca Robles, interview.
20. Lorca Robles, interview.
21. Palieraki, *¡La revolución ya viene!*, 182–83; Trucco, interview; Agnic, *Allende*, 74.
22. Peña and Funke, interview; Vivaldi, interview.
23. Labarca, *Allende*, 161.
24. Carmen Paz, Viel, and Gnecco, interview.
25. López and Menke, *Informativo Estadístico ... 1957 a 1960*, 75; *Memoria ... la Universidad de Concepción Correspondiente al Año 1961*.
26. Solari, "Introducción," 34–36; Garretón and Martínez, *Biblioteca del movimiento estudiantil (I)*, 41.
27. *LNUH*, 21 September 1961.

28. Garretón and Martínez, *Biblioteca del movimiento estudiantil (I)*, 41.
29. Palieraki, *¡La revolución ya viene!*, 177–79.
30. *El Sur*, 30 May 1960.
31. Palieraki, *¡La revolución ya viene!*, 158–59; Garretón and Martínez, *Biblioteca del movimiento estudiantil (I)*, 45–56; Muñoz, *69 años*, 97–99.
32. Alessandri, "Introducción," 14–15.
33. Palieraki, *¡La revolución ya viene!*, 175, 178.
34. Trucco, interview.
35. "Salúd Publica" and "El Servicio Nacional de Salud," *Revista Médica de Chile* 87, no. 1 (1959): 57–61; Rosemblatt, *Gendered Compromises*, 129–30.
36. Amrith, *Decolonizing International Health*.
37. "Act of Bogotá," 13 September 1960; *El Mercurio*, 12 January 1961.
38. Cueto and Palmer, *Medicine and Public Health*, 135; Behm, "Educación médica," 203.
39. "Informe Final," *Seminario de Formación Profesional Médica*, 69–72; Alessandri, "Introducción," 15.
40. Urzúa and Mardones, "Aspectos sociales de Chile," 83–89; *LNUH*, 10 August 1961.
41. *El Mercurio*, 10 January 1961.
42. Ulloa, interview.
43. Ulloa, "Recuerdos de juventud."
44. Peña and Funke, interview.
45. Bonilla, "The Student Federation of Chile," 319.
46. Beatriz, *Mujeres*, February 1977, in Álvarez, *Tati*, 73–74.
47. *El Sur*, 1 January 1961; *El Mercurio*, 1 January 1961, 21 May 1961. Earlier reports put the number of dead and missing at five thousand. See *El Sur*, 5 June 1960.
48. *El Sur*, 1 January 1961; *El Mercurio*, 1 January 1961; Collier and Sater, *Chile*, 259.
49. British Embassy, Santiago, "Chile: Annual Review for 1960," 4 January 1960, FO 371/155947/TNA.
50. Lorca Robles, interview; Agnic, *Allende*, 74; *El Siglo*, 28 May 1960.
51. "The University of Concepción: Report on Losses Sustained by the Earthquake of May 21–22, 1960," 31 May 1960, BW 22/13/TNA, and *Memoria . . . Universidad de Concepción Correspondiente al Año 1960*.
52. *El Sur*, 25 May 1960.
53. *El Sur*, 8 June 1960.
54. *El Sur*, 23 May 1960; *El Mercurio*, 1 June 1960.
55. *El Mercurio*, 1 June 1960.
56. "A próposito del cataclismo," *Revista Médica de Chile* 88, no. 6 (1960): 421–22.
57. Puccio, *Cuarto de siglo*, 101–3; Silva and Riquelme, *Una identidad terremoteada*, 38–39.
58. *El Sur*, 23 May 1960; *El Sur*, 27 May 1960.
59. "Seminario sobre Construcción de la Zona Sur" as cited in Behm, "Educación médica," 211–12. See also Silva and Riquelme, *Una identidad terremoteada*, 37.
60. *El Sur*, 23 May 1960, 22 May 1960.
61. *El Sur*, 27 May 1960.
62. *LNUH*, 12 June 1960, 11 June 1960; Puccio, *Cuarto de siglo*, 102–3; Silva and Riquelme, *Una identidad terremoteada*, 147–48.
63. *El Mercurio*, 7 January 1961.
64. *El Mercurio*, 4 June 1960.

65. Agnic, *Allende*, 75.
66. *El Mercurio*, 1 January 1961.
67. See, for example, *El Sur*, 25 May 1960, 27 May 1960, 28 May 1960, 30 May 1960; *El Mercurio*, 1 June 1960, 2 June 1960, 12 June 1960; and *LNUH*, 7 June 1960, 17 June 1960.
68. *El Mercurio*, 1 January 1961.
69. See, for example, *El Siglo*, 31 May 1960, 10 June 1960.
70. See, for example, *LNUH*, 31 May 1960, 20 June 1960, 23 June 1960.
71. *El Sur*, 28 May 1960; *LNUH*, 1 June 1960.
72. *El Sur*, 11 June 1960; *LNUH*, 14 June 1960.
73. Lorca Robles, interview.
74. *LNUH*, 21 March 1961.
75. Sandoval, interview, 15 July 2013.
76. The number of students who went on this trip may be lower. Hernán Sandoval remembered four, although Beatriz recalled six. See Sandoval, interview, 15 July 2013, and Baez, *Preguntas*, 245.
77. Beatriz quoted in Baez, *Preguntas*, 246.
78. Moleiro, *El MIR*, 11, 147–50.
79. Sandoval, interview, 15 July 2013.
80. Beatriz quoted in Baez, *Preguntas*, 237.
81. Moleiro, *El MIR*, 154–58.
82. Sandoval, interview, 15 July 2013.
83. See *Gente Joven*, 7 April 1960, 21 April 1960, 16 June 1960.
84. *Gente Joven*, 7 July 1960.
85. "El Primer Congreso Latinoamericano"; Baez, *Preguntas*, 246; *Gente Joven*, 11 August 1960.
86. On different numbers, see "El Primer Congreso Latinoamericano," and Brown, "Cuba and the Rise of Armed Revolution," 5.
87. *Tricontinental Conference*.
88. "El Primer Congreso Latinoamericano."
89. Sandoval, interview, 15 July 2013.
90. *El Sur*, 16 April 1960.
91. "Discurso al Primer Congreso Latinoamericano de Juventudes."
92. Beatriz quoted in Baez, *Preguntas*, 246–47.
93. Lorca Robles, interview.
94. Beatriz quoted in López, "Ubicar urgente a Señora Hortensia."
95. Jorge Insunza as quoted in *Gente Joven*, 5 May 1960.
96. Baltra Moreno, *Mireya Baltra*, 44–45.
97. Espejo, interview, 31 March 2010; Daza Sepúlveda, interview.
98. Matilde Ladrón de Guevara as quoted in *Revolución*, 22 July 1960.
99. Sources differ on the time Beatriz stayed in Cuba. Sandoval recalls it was two weeks, Beatriz told Luis Baez it was two months, and Labarca suggests it was longer. However, Beatriz passed her exams at the end of the year and so must have arrived back in time to study for them. Sandoval, interview, 15 July 2013; Baez, *Preguntas*, 247; Labarca, *Allende*, 161–62.
100. Sandoval, interview, 15 July 2013; San Martín González, correspondence; Baltra, *Mireya Baltra*, 45.
101. Labarca, *Allende*, 161.
102. *Gente Joven*, 21 July 1960.

103. Beatriz quoted in Baez, *Preguntas*, 247.
104. "El Primer Congreso Latinoamericano."
105. "Discurso al Primer Congreso Latinoamericano de Juventudes."
106. "Discurso pronunciado por el Comandante Fidel Castro ... en el Acto de Clausura del Primer Congreso Latinoamericano de Juventudes"; Baltra, *Mireya Baltra*, 44-46.
107. Sandoval, interview, 15 July 2013.
108. "Resolución del Primer Congreso Latinoamericano de Juventudes," *Revolución*, 8 August 1960. See also *Gente Joven*, 11 August 1960; Sandoval, interview, 15 July 2013; and San Martín González, correspondence.
109. *Gente Joven*, 29 December 1960.
110. *Gente Joven*, 9 February 1961, 27 July 1961.
111. Oscar Waiss, ¿Hacia dónde va Chile?," *Arauco* 2, no. 13 (1960): 10.
112. Taffet, *Foreign Aid*, 70.
113. David Scott Fox, British Embassy, Santiago, "Chile: Annual Review for 1961," 1 January 1962, FO 371/162166/TNA.
114. Loveman, *Chile*, 225.
115. Loveman, 225.
116. David Scott Fox, British Ambassador, Santiago, "The Chilean Communist Party," 13 August 1962, FO 371/162168/TNA.
117. *Gente Joven*, 9 March 1961.
118. Loveman, *Chile*, 225.
119. Rabe, *Most Dangerous Area*, 109; "Las elecciones y los campesinos," *Arauco* 3, no. 16 (1961): 3-4.
120. Puccio, *Cuarto de siglo*, 106-13; Labarca, *Allende*, 162.
121. Agnic, *Allende*, 88, 91-92, 95.
122. *LNUH*, 13 February 1961.
123. *LNUH*, 11 February 1961.
124. *El Sur*, 1 August 1960.
125. Isabel, October 1977, as quoted in Alvaréz, *Tati*, 79; Isabel as quoted in Hite, *When the Romance Ended*, 72.
126. Fox, "Chile: Annual Review for 1961."
127. *El Mercurio*, 9 June 1960.
128. *El Sur*, 12 July 1960.
129. *El Sur*, 14 March 1961.
130. *El Sur*, 18 July 1960, 25 July 1960.
131. Palieraki, *¡La revolución ya viene!*, 115.
132. Salvador Allende, Senate Speech, 27 July 1960, *Cuba, un camino* (Prensa Latina, 1960), CeDInCI.
133. Sandoval, interview, 15 July 2013.
134. Carretero, interview.
135. *LNUH*, 16 January 1961.
136. *Gente Joven*, 27 April 1961.
137. *LNUH*, 11 May 1961, 22 January 1961.
138. *LNUH*, 5 January 1961, 19 January 1961.
139. *LNUH*, 17 April 1961; *¡Cuba no está sola! Diario de Sesiones del Senado: Cuatro voces del socialismo chileno en defense de Cuba de Fidel Castro* (1961), CeDInCI.
140. *LNUH*, 18 April 1961.

141. Suárez and Kruijt, *La Revolución Cubana en Nuestra América*, 21.
142. *Gente Joven*, 11 May 1961.
143. *LNUH*, 17 April 1961, 18 April 1961.
144. *LNUH*, 25 April 1961.
145. *LNUH*, 19 April 1961.
146. *Gente Joven*, 27 April 1961.
147. *LNUH*, 18 April 1961.
148. Alejandro Rojas in Brodsky, *Conversaciones con la FECH*, 107–8; Rojas would switch from the PS to the PCCh in 1964 and serve as president of the Federación de Estudiantes de la Universidad de Chile (FECH) from 1969 to 1972.
149. Carlos Lorca as quoted in Azócar, *Lorca*, 90.
150. *El Sur*, 18 April 1961.
151. *LNUH*, 19 April 1961.
152. See Hove, "The Arbenz Factor," and *El Siglo*, 19 August 1958.
153. *LNUH*, 19 April 1961. On protests in Mexico, see also Zolov, "¡Cuba Sí, Yanquis No!"
154. *El Sur*, 22 April 1961, 26 April 1961.
155. Beatriz quoted Baez, *Preguntas*, 237.
156. *El Sur*, 20 April 1961.
157. *Gente Joven*, 20 April 1960.
158. *Gente Joven*, 27 July 1961.
159. *LNUH*, 2 May 1961.
160. *LNUH*, 3 May 1961, 4 May 1961.
161. *LNUH*, 21 July 1961, 20 November 1961.
162. Rojas quoted in Brodsky, *Conversaciones con la FECH*, 109.
163. Letter, Richard Sykes to Henry Hankey, American Department, Foreign Office, 20 July 1961, FO 371/155948/TNA.
164. Arrate and Rojas, *Memoria (I)*, 341. See also Fox, "Chile: Annual Review for 1961."
165. Arrate and Rojas, *Memoria (I)*, 342–43.
166. Paul Tremblay, Canadian Ambassador, Santiago, to the Secretary of State for External Affairs, Ottawa, "Current Political Climate in Chile," 21 August 1961, FO 371/155949/TNA.
167. See, for example, *LNUH*, 1 March 1961, 21 July 1961.
168. *LNUH*, 24 June 1961.
169. "Current Political Climate in Chile," 21 August 1961.
170. "Current Political Climate in Chile," 21 August 1961.
171. *LNUH*, 21 May 1961.
172. *LNUH*, 23 May 1961.
173. *LNUH*, 6 October 1961, 10 October 1961.
174. Tremblay to the Secretary of State for External Affairs, Ottawa, "Student Strikes in Chile," 20 June 1961, FO 371/155943/TNA.
175. *LNUH*, 21 September 1961.
176. Valle and Díaz, *Federación de la Juventud Socialista*, 44.
177. Ulloa, interview.
178. Palieraki, *¡La revolución ya viene!*, 179–80, 185.
179. Bonilla, "The Student Federation of Chile," 315.
180. Peña and Funke, interview.

181. Ulloa, interview; Sandoval, interview, 15 July 2013.
182. Ulloa, "Recuerdos de juventud." Unfortunately, no copies of *Horizonte* or *Revolución* are held at the University of Concepción or Chile's Biblioteca Nacional.
183. Ulloa, interview; Ulloa, "Recuerdos de juventud." Some recall the name of the nucleus as Espartaco rather than Sierra Maestra. However, Espartaco referred to the nucleus within the regional JS that Miguel Enríquez was part of rather than the nucleus within the Brigada Universitaria Socialista. See Naranjo, *Biografía de Miguel Enríquez*, 8, 29, and Ferrada, "Prólogo," 5–6.
184. Palieraki, *¡La revolución ya viene!*, 115n92.
185. Ulloa, "Recuerdos de juventud." Others in the Sierra Maestra group were Bautista van Schouwen, Jorge Gutierrez, and Claudio Sepúlveda.
186. Palieraki, *¡La revolución ya viene!*, 181.
187. Allende Bussi, "Entre el MIR y Allende"; Amorós, *Miguel Enríquez*, 45, 47, 51.
188. Peña and Funke, interview.
189. Allende Bussi, "Entre el MIR y Allende."
190. Beatriz, *Mujeres*, February 1977, in Álvarez, *Tati*, 73.
191. Bonilla, "The Student Federation of Chile," 314.
192. Palieraki, *¡La revolución ya viene!*, 166.
193. *Gente Joven*, 26 January 1961.
194. Amorós, *Miguel Enríquez*, 39–40.
195. Allend Bussie, "Entre el MIR y Allende."
196. Juan Saavedra Gorriategui, as quoted in Amorós, *Miguel Enríquez*, 55.
197. Pascal Allende quoted in Amorós, *Miguel Enríquez*, 25, 29, 36, 38–39, 40–41; Trucco, interview.
198. Allende Bussi, "Entre el MIR y Allende"; Amorós, *Miguel Enríquez*, 51.
199. Ferrada, "Prólogo," 5–6. According to Ferrada, the MSR also functioned within the regional JS group Espartaco that Miguel was part of.
200. Specifically, Miguel Enríquez's group was close to—if not secretly also part of—the Vanguardia Revolucionaria Marxista (VRM), a Trotskyist group that advocated mass insurrection. According to Palieraki, Miguel's group not only secretly joined the VRM while still in the PS but also formed a small military wing of it known as the Ejército Revolucionario de Trabajadores y de Estudiantes (ERTES). Ferrada refutes this, arguing the MSR did not join the VRM or begin military training until 1964. Paliearki, *¡La revolución ya viene!*, 79–80, 84–85; Ferrada, "Prólogo," 6, 8–9.
201. Ulloa, interview; Ulloa, "Recuerdos de juventud."
202. According to Ferrada, the MSR had twelve members in Concepción by 1963 and eight in Santiago, including Andrés Pascal and Edgardo Enríquez. See Ferrada, "Prológo," 5.
203. Amorós, *Miguel Enríquez*, 56–57; Palieraki, *¡La revolución ya viene!*, 181.
204. Valle and Díaz, *Federación de la Juventud Socialista*, 45.
205. Fox, "The Chilean Communist Party."
206. Fox, "Chile: Annual Review for 1961."
207. David Fox, Dispatch, 26 December 1962, FO 371/167948/TNA.
208. Beatriz's university transcript records list her marks as follows: 1960: 15/14/15/19/15; 1961: 18/15/20/19/18, and 1962: 17/19/15/15/19.
209. Trucco, interview.
210. Taffet, *Foreign Aid*, 72–75.
211. Rabe, *Most Dangerous Area*, 112–14.

Chapter 3

1. Valle and Díaz, *Federación de la Juventud Socialista*, 46–47; Arrate and Rojas, *Memoria (I)*, 367; Álvarez, *Tati*, 88–90.
2. Casals, *La creación de la amenaza roja*, 456.
3. Vexler, "Pulso familiar," *Ercilla*, 20 May 1964.
4. *El Siglo*, 26 August 1963.
5. *El Siglo*, 7 December 1963.
6. Benado, interview.
7. Jeannette Gallo, "Cuatro mujeres retratan a Allende," *El Siglo*, 12 October 1963; Vexler, "Pulso familiar."
8. On the plotting of isolated right-wing coups that the CIA refused to back, see *Covert Action in Chile*, 17.
9. Tad Szulc quoted in Taffet, *Foreign Aid*, 77–78.
10. Gazmuri, *Frei*, 563–65.
11. Eugenio González, "Palabras en la inauguración del año académico," *Boletín de la Universidad de Chile*, no. 47, May 1964, CeDInCI.
12. *El Siglo*, 23 September 1963; *Clarín*, 26 April 1964.
13. *Ercilla*, 3 July 1963.
14. *LNUH*, 6 September 1963.
15. *El Siglo*, 17 May 1964.
16. Casals, *La creación de la amenaza roja*, 374–89.
17. *Covert Action in Chile*, 9, 15–16.
18. Taffet, *Foreign Aid*, 76–78.
19. Taffet, 78.
20. *Ercilla*, 20 May 1964.
21. Palieraki, *¡La revolución ya viene!*, 143–45, 152.
22. Taffet, *Foreign Aid*, 76–77.
23. Pieper Mooney, *Politics of Motherhood*, 48–49; Institute for the Comparative Study of Political Systems, "Chile—An Election Fact Book," enclosure, Letter, Sutherland, British Embassy, Washington to Foreign Office, 11 October 1964, FO 371/167950/TNA.
24. *LNUH*, 20 July 1964; Gazmuri, *Frei*, 545–46, 570.
25. *El Siglo*, 7 December 1963, 20 November 1963, 9 May 1964.
26. *El Siglo*, 29 March 1964, 17 May 1964.
27. Estimates vary between 80,000 and 500,000, but consensus points to 300,000. Gazmuri, *Frei*, 570; Arrate and Rojas, *Memoria (I)*, 372; Blanco, *Frei*, 53–54.
28. *El Siglo*, 17 May 1964.
29. *El Siglo*, 29 March 1964.
30. Palieraki, *¡La revolución ya viene!*, 141, 151; Casals, *La creación de la amenaza roja*, 374–89.
31. Gazmuri, *Frei*, 505, 570; Arrate and Rojas, *Memoria (I)*, 372; Blanco, *Frei*, 56.
32. *Covert Action in Chile*, 9.
33. *Vistazo*, 22 October 1963.
34. *El Siglo*, 29 March 1964.
35. Núñez, interview.
36. Benado, interview.
37. Soto, interview.
38. Huerta and Chávez, *El trabajo*, 128–29.
39. Huerta and Chávez, 128–29; Benado, interview.

40. Benado, interview.
41. Burnett, *Political Groups*, 84.
42. "Discurso del Presidente de la Federación de Estudiantes de Chile, Luis Maira," *Boletín de la Universidad de Chile*, no. 47, May 1964, CeDInCI.
43. *El Siglo*, 20 November 1963.
44. *El Siglo*, 28 April 1964, 17 May 1964.
45. Glazer, "Actitudes y actividades políticas," 287.
46. Beatriz, *Mujeres*, February 1977, in Álvarez, *Tati*, 74.
47. Coloma, interview.
48. Glazer, "Actitudes y actividades políticas," 286-87.
49. "Chile—An Election Fact Book."
50. *Vistazo*, 17 September 1963.
51. Glazer, "Actitudes y actividades políticas," 303-4.
52. Burnett, *Political Groups*, 88.
53. Oyarzún, interview.
54. Glazer, "Actitudes y actividades políticas," 303.
55. Burnett, *Political Groups*, 84; Coloma, interview.
56. Glazer, "Actitudes y actividades políticas," 285, 332.
57. *El Siglo*, 17 May 1964.
58. *Clarín*, 8 May 1964.
59. Jirón, correspondence.
60. *El Siglo*, 21 November 1963.
61. Burnett, *Political Groups*, 83-84.
62. Casals, *La creación de la amenaza roja*, 335-36.
63. Power, "Engendering of Anticommunism," 932-33; "Chile—An Election Factbook."
64. Casals, *La creación de la amenaza roja*, 456.
65. Pieper Mooney, *Politics of Motherhood*, 75.
66. Power, "Engendering of Anticommunism," 937.
67. *Covert Action in Chile*, 9, 15-16.
68. Power, "Engendering of Anticommunism," 931.
69. Casals, *La creación de la amenaza roja*, 374-89.
70. *El Mercurio* quoted in Power, "Engendering of Anticommunism," 940-41.
71. *Eva*, 31 July 1964, 7 August 1964, 14 August 1964, 21 August 1964, 28 August 1964, and 4 September 1964.
72. Casals, *La creación de la amenaza roja*, 458-63.
73. Power, "Engendering of Anticommunism," 940-42, 945-46.
74. *El Siglo*, 27 April 1964.
75. *El Siglo*, 17 May 1964.
76. Casals, *La creación de la amenaza roja*, 465.
77. *El Siglo*, 23 November 1963, 13 December 1963.
78. *El Siglo*, 20 July 1964, 21 July 1964, 31 July 1964.
79. *LNUH*, 20 July 1964.
80. *El Siglo*, 20 November 1963.
81. Power, "Engendering of Anticommunism," 950.
82. *El Siglo*, 4 November 1963.
83. *El Siglo*, 27 October 1963; Arrate and Rojas, *Memoria (I)*, 368.
84. See *El Siglo*, 7 December 1963, 20 November 1963.

85. Gallo, "Cuatro mujeres"; *El Siglo*, 27 October 1963.
86. *El Siglo*, 13 December 1963.
87. Gallo, "Cuatro mujeres."
88. Vexler, "Pulso familiar."
89. Power, "Engendering of Anticommunism," 948; Casals, *La creación de la amenaza roja*, 466; *El Siglo*, 18 July 1964, 9 July 1964.
90. *El Siglo*, 23 November 1963.
91. Benado, interview.
92. Leibner, "Women in Uruguayan Communism," 22.
93. *LNUH*, 20 July 1964.
94. *El Siglo*, 12 December 1963; *LNUH*, 28 December 1963; Power, "Engendering of Anticommunism," 937.
95. See Comando Nacional de la Candidatura Presidencial Dr. Salvador Allende, "Programa del Gobierno Popular," and Tinsman, *Partners in Conflict*, 124.
96. Power, *Right-Wing Women*, 123–24.
97. Casals, *La creación de la amenaza roja*, 465.
98. Power, "Engendering of Anticommunism," 942, 946–47; *El Siglo*, 23 November 1963.
99. *El Siglo*, 13 December 1963; Power, "Engendering of Anticommunism," 946–47.
100. Allende quoted in *El Siglo*, 27 October 1963.
101. *LNUH*, 28 December 1963.
102. *El Siglo*, 27 October 1963.
103. Gallo, "Cuatro mujeres"; Vexler, "Pulso familiar."
104. Tinsman, *Partners in Conflict*, 64.
105. Vexler, "Pulso familiar."
106. Vexler, "Pulso familiar."
107. Gallo, "Cuatro mujeres."
108. *LNUH*, 1 March 1964.
109. Gallo, "Cuatro mujeres."
110. Labarca, *Allende*, 170–72; Tambutti Allende, *Allende, mi abuelo*.
111. Puccio, *Cuarto de siglo*, 121–22.
112. Vexler, "Pulso familiar."
113. *Covert Action in Chile*, 9, 15–16.
114. Special Report, CIA, "Implications of the Recent Elections in Chile," 4 October 1964, CIA, Freedom of Information Act Electronic Reading Room.
115. Petras and Zemelman, *Peasants in Revolt*, 139.
116. Power, "Engendering of Anticommunism," 951.
117. Petras and Zemelman, *Peasants in Revolt*, 10.
118. "Implications of the Recent Elections in Chile."
119. Arrate, interview.
120. Amorós, *Allende*, 204.
121. Isabel as quoted in Hite, *When the Romance Ended*, 72.
122. Tambutti Allende, *Allende, mi abuelo*.
123. "Implications of the Recent Elections in Chile."
124. Letter, Scott Fox to Slater, 22 April 1965, FO 371/179283/TNA.
125. Gazmuri, *Frei*, 537–38.
126. Arrate and Rojas, *Memoria (I)*, 392.
127. Quotation in Valle and Díaz, *Federación de la Juventud Socialista*, 49.

Chapter 4

1. Echeverría and Castillo, *Santiago-París*, 115.
2. Jirón, correspondence, and Jirón, "Homenaje" (2006), AFSA.
3. Pieper Mooney, *Politics of Motherhood*, 75; Arrate and Rojas, *Memoria (I)*, 384.
4. Sorensen, *Turbulent Decade*, 5.
5. Oyarzún, Guiloff, Cabello, and Contreras, interviews; Huerta and Chávez, *El trabajo*, 74.
6. Gálvez, with Parrau, and Ipinza, interviews; Jirón, correspondence.
7. Oyarzún, interview.
8. Oyarzún, interview.
9. Vera, correspondence; Contreras, interview; Carmen Noemi as quoted in Álvarez, *Tati*, 86.
10. Prospectus, *Universidad de Chile: Escuela de Medicina 1960*, 33–35, Museo de Medicina, Facultad de Medicina, Universidad de Chile, Santiago.
11. Gálvez, with Parrau, interview.
12. Oyarzún, interview.
13. Contreras, interview.
14. Guiloff, interview.
15. Tinsman, *Partners in Conflict*, 59.
16. Pieper Mooney, *Politics of Motherhood*, 45, 54–55, 97; Tinsman, *Partners in Conflict*, 58–59.
17. Guiloff and Cabello, interviews.
18. Echeverría and Castillo, *Santiago-París*, 115–16.
19. Connelly, *Fatal Misconception*, 10–11, 210–17.
20. Pieper Mooney, *Politics of Motherhood*, 63, 65, 69.
21. Cabello, interview; Loveman, *Chile*, 245.
22. Cabello, interview.
23. "Agrupación de Médicos Generales de Zona de Chile."
24. Jarpa, "Los 60 años de travesía de los médicos de zona."
25. Sepúlveda, interview.
26. Oyarzún, interview.
27. Oyarzún, interview.
28. Petras and Zemelman, *Peasants in Revolt*, xii, 4–5.
29. Cabello and Oyarzún, interviews.
30. Oyarzún, interview.
31. Cabello, interview.
32. Tinsman, *Partners in Conflict*, 84.
33. Ipinza, interview.
34. Gálvez, with Parrau, interview.
35. Oyarzún and Cabello, interviews.
36. Cabello, interview.
37. Contreras, interview.
38. Trucco, interview.
39. Arrate and Rojas, *Memoria (I)*, 388–90.
40. Núñez, Abra, Escobedo, and Claval, *Ricardo Núñez*, 28. On ideology determining social relations more broadly in Chile at the time, see Salgado, "Making Friends," 301.
41. Benado and Núñez, interviews; Echeverría and Castillo, *Santiago-París*, 116.
42. Núñez, Abra, Escobedo, and Claval, *Ricardo Núñez*, 102; Benado, interview.

43. Benado, interview.
44. Núñez, interview; Núñez, Abra, Escobedo, and Claval, *Ricardo Núñez*, 67.
45. Petras and Zemelman, *Peasants in Revolt*, xiii.
46. Petras and Zemelman, *Peasants in Revolt*, 142.
47. Núñez, interview; Núñez, Abra, Escobedo, and Claval, *Ricardo Núñez*, 66–67.
48. Calderón, interview.
49. Benado, interview.
50. Calderón, interview. On similar feelings of discomfort among members of the MIR from southern Chile who moved to the capital, see Schlotterbeck, *Beyond the Vanguard*, 137–39.
51. Benado, interview.
52. Benado, interview.
53. Núñez and Soto, interviews.
54. Núñez, interview; Pollack, interview.
55. Pollack, interview.
56. Pollack, Benado, and Núñez, interviews.
57. Carmen Paz, Viel, and Gnecco, interview.
58. Jeannette Gallo, "Cuatro mujeres retratan a Allende," *El Siglo*, 12 October 1963.
59. Lorca Robles, interview.
60. Contreras, interview; Álvarez, *Tati*, 86–87.
61. Trucco, interview.
62. Álvarez, *Tati*, 71–72; Contardo, *Raro*, 264–65.
63. Lorca Robles, interview.
64. Cabello, interview.
65. Oyarzún, interview.
66. Gálvez, with Parrau, and Pollack, interviews.
67. Núñez, interview.
68. Garretón and Martínez, *Biblioteca del movimiento estudiantil (III)*, 18–19.
69. Núñez, Abra, Escobedo, and Claval, *Ricardo Núñez*, 54; del Pozo, *Rebeldes, Reformistas y Revolucionarios*, 133.
70. Arrate and Rojas, *Memoria (I)*, 392.
71. Arrate and Rojas, 392; Núñez, Abra, Escobedo, and Claval, *Ricardo Núñez*, 56–59; Pérez, "Guerrilla rural," 182.
72. Benado, interview.
73. Petras and Zemelman, *Peasants in Revolt*, xi, 31, 144.
74. Arrate and Rojas, *Memoria (I)*, 379, 380, 385.
75. Tinsman, *Partners in Conflict*, 86.
76. Tinsman, 88.
77. Taffet, *Foreign Aid*, 80–91; Núñez, Abra, Escobedo, and Claval, *Ricardo Núñez*, 54.
78. Núñez, interview. On strikes of public health workers, university staff, and copper miners in 1966, see Report CH/3/66, Harold Atkin, First Secretary (Labour), 22 December 1966, LAB 13/2129/TNA.
79. *LNUH*, 11 March 1966, 12 March 1966, 13 March 1966.
80. *LNUH*, 17 March 1966.
81. *El Siglo*, 13 March 1966; *LNUH*, 15 March 1966.
82. Núñez, interview.
83. *LNUH*, 13 March 1966; Arrate and Rojas, *Memoria (I)*, 403.
84. *LNUH*, 16 March 1966.

85. Gómez, correspondence; Quiroga, *Compañeros*, 17.
86. Coloma, interview.
87. Núñez, Abra, Escobedo, and Claval, *Ricardo Núñez*, 54, 56.
88. Benado, interview.
89. *LNUH*, 10 March 1966, 13 March 1966.
90. *LNUH*, 21 March 1966.
91. *LNUH*, 22 March 1966.
92. *LNUH*, 16 March 1966.
93. Teitelboim quoted in *LNUH*, 13 March 1966.
94. Huerta, with Oña, interview, 23 March 2010; Huerta and Chávez, *El trabajo*, 65.
95. Palieraki, *¡La revolución ya viene!*, 117-18; Marchesi, *Latin America's Radical Left*, 29-30.
96. See, for example, *Punto Final*, no. 13, October 1966; no. 23, February 1967; no. 25, March 1967; and no. 26, April 1967.
97. *Tricontinental Conference*; Gronbeck-Tedesco, "Left in Transition," 659.
98. Allende, 1966, as quoted in Marchesi, *Latin America's Radical Left*, 71.
99. *Tricontinental Conference*.
100. *Tricontinental Conference*.
101. Marchesi, *Latin America's Radical Left*, 72-73; Report CH/3/67, Atkin, 10 August 1967, LAB 13/2129/TNA; Labarca, *Allende*, 216.
102. *Granma Weekly*, 17 September 1967.
103. Labarca, *Allende*, 213.
104. Marchesi, *Latin America's Radical Left*, 76-78.
105. *Punto Final*, no. 35, August 1967.
106. Núñez, Abra, Escobedo, and Claval, *Ricardo Núñez*, 36.
107. Benado, interview.
108. Huerta and Chávez, *El trabajo*, 129.
109. Núñez, Abra, Escobedo, and Claval, *Ricardo Núñez*, 86.
110. *LNUH*, 22 March 1966.
111. "Chile: Annual Review for 1966," 4 January 1967, FCO 7/337/TNA.
112. "Chile: Annual Review for 1967," 15 January 1968, FCO 7/337/TNA.
113. Palieraki, *¡La revolución ya viene!*, 24.
114. Arrate and Rojas, *Memoria (I)*, 407, 448.
115. Palieraki, *¡La revolución ya viene!*, 258.
116. Arrate and Rojas, *Memoria (I)*, 405.
117. Núñez, Abra, Escobedo, and Claval, *Ricardo Núñez*, 53-54.
118. Garretón and Martínez, *Biblioteca del movimiento estudiantil (III)*, 29. Other groups competing in the election were the Juventud Radical (Radical Youth), which won 869 votes; the Juventud Nacional (National Youth), which won 502 votes; and the MIR, which received 465.
119. Palieraki, *¡La revolución ya viene!*, 90-92.
120. Arrate and Rojas, *Memoria (I)*, 394-95, 396, 400.
121. Palieraki, *¡La revolución ya viene!*, 87-89.
122. Garretón and Martínez, *Biblioteca del movimiento estudiantil (III)*, 29.
123. Palieraki, *¡La revolución ya viene!*, 208, 210-11.
124. Palieraki, 131-33, 135, 136-37.
125. Palieraki, 187-89.
126. Palieraki, 207; Núñez, interview.

127. Palieraki, 134.
128. Núñez, interview.
129. Álvarez, *Tati*, 90.
130. Palieraki, *¡La revolución ya viene!*, 185–86.
131. "Chile Annual Review for 1967," 15 January 1968, FCO 7/337/TNA.
132. Bermeo, *Ordinary People*, 147–48; Garretón and Moulian, *La Unidad Popular*, 24.
133. Lester Spielman, American Labor Attaché, Santiago, "Report on the Economic Situation in Chile," September 1967, LAB 13/2129/TNA.
134. Palieraki, *¡La revolución ya viene!*, 129–32.
135. Oyarzún, interview.
136. Oyarzún, Contreras, and Guiloff, interviews.
137. Oyarzún, interview.
138. Álvarez, *Tati*, 88.
139. Pollack and Lorca Robles, interview; Labarca, *Allende*, 228–29.
140. Jaramillo, correspondence.
141. Carmen Paz, Viel, and Gnecco, interview; Pollack, interview.
142. Funding came from the U.S philanthropic Josiah Macy Foundation, the Quinta Normal municipality, and Chile's Patronato Nacional de la Infancia. Gnecco, correspondence.
143. Gnecco, correspondence; Ipinza, interview.
144. Carmen Paz, Viel, and Gnecco, interview.
145. Ipinza, interview; Montoya-Aguilar, "El Professor Benjamín Viel," 126.
146. Letter, Tati to Querido, February 1969, ABA.
147. Gnecco, correspondence.
148. Carmen Paz, Viel, and Gnecco, interview.
149. Garretón and Martínez, *Biblioteca del movimiento estudiantil (III)*, 30; Arrate and Rojas, *Memoria (I)*, 428.

Chapter 5

1. Carretero, interview.
2. Peredo, interview.
3. Tati to Papote Querido, 10 January 1970, ABA.
4. CIA, Directorate of Intelligence, "Special Report. Cuban Subversive Activities in Latin America: 1959–1968," 16 February 1968, Freedom of Information Act Electronic Reading Room.
5. Information from Bulgarian Ambassador in Havana Stefan Petrov to Bulgarian Leader Todo Zhikov on the Domestic and Foreign Policy of Cuba, 15 August 1968, WCDA.
6. Castro, "Second Declaration of Havana."
7. Guevara, "Crear dos, tres … muchos Vietnam."
8. Barcia, "'Locking Horns,'" 211–12.
9. *Granma Weekly*, 17 September 1967.
10. *Punto Final*, no. 8, January 1966.
11. "Carta de despedida de Elmo Catalán," 19 April 1970, in Bodes, *En la senda del Che*, 115–16.
12. *Punto Final*, no. 35, August 1967.
13. Marchesi, "Revolution beyond the Sierra Maestra," 523–24.

14. Suárez, *Manuel Piñeiro*, 16–17.

15. Rodríguez, *Sin tiempo para las palabras*, 29, 34. See also Villegas, *Pombo*, 261–92. Coco Peredo died on 26 September 1967.

16. "Discurso Pronunciado por el Comandante Fidel Castro ... 18 de octubre de 1967."

17. Haydée Santamaria to Che in Randall, *Haydée Santamaria*, 173.

18. "Special Report. Cuban Subversive Activities in Latin America: 1959-1968."

19. On OLAS's failure to live up to expectations, see Marchesi, *Latin America's Radical Left*, 95, and Huerta, with Oña, interview, 23 March 2010.

20. Huerta and Chávez, *El trabajo*, 221; Quiroga, *Compañeros*, 24.

21. *LNUH*, 12 October 1967, 17 October 1967.

22. *LNUH*, 13 October 1967.

23. *El Siglo*, as quoted in *LNUH*, 16 October 1967.

24. *El Mercurio* and Deputy Patricio Philips as quoted in *LNUH*, 16 October 1967.

25. Huerta, with Oña, interview, 23 March 2010.

26. Edgardo Enríquez, as quoted in Amorós, *Miguel Enríquez*, 87.

27. Coloma, interview.

28. Labarca, *Allende*, 231.

29. See *LNUH*, 11 October 1967, 12 October 1967.

30. "Discurso Pronunciado por el Comandante Fidel Castro ... 18 de octubre de 1967."

31. *Punto Final*, editorial, no. 40, 24 October 1967.

32. *LNUH*, 14 October 1967.

33. Oña, interview, 6 April 2010.

34. Allende as quoted in *Punto Final*, no. 41, 6 November 1967.

35. Allende, "Salvador Allende vino a Cuba a ofrecer condolencias."

36. Oña, interview, 6 April 2010.

37. Beatriz explained to Elena that they chose Luis Fernández Oña as a pseudonym together when walking through Havana's cemetery and picking out names they liked. He used it from 1970 until his death in December 2016. Gálvez, with Parrau, interview.

38. Oña, interview, 29 April 2011. See also Suárez and Kruijt, *La Revolución Cubana en Nuestra América*, 121.

39. Labarca, *Allende*, 210, 246.

40. Oña, interview, 6 April 2010.

41. *Granma Weekly*, 12 November 1967.

42. Beatriz quoted in Baez, *Preguntas*, 247–48.

43. Oña, interview, 6 April 2010.

44. Rodríguez, *Sin tiempo para las palabras*, 23–25, 29–33.

45. *Punto Final*, no. 41, 6 November 1967.

46. Rodríguez, *Sin tiempo para las palabras*, 35–37.

47. *LNUH*, 24 October 1967.

48. *LNUH*, 14 October 1967.

49. *LNUH*, 7 November 1967.

50. Blight and Brenner, *Sad and Luminous Days*, 121–23.

51. Information from Bulgarian Ambassador in Havana Stefan Petrov to Bulgarian Leader Todo Zhikov on the Domestic and Foreign Policy of Cuba, 15 August 1968, WCDA.

52. Blight and Brenner, *Sad and Luminous Days*, xxii, 123, 125.

53. Memorandum of Conversation between Czechoslovak Communist Party Offi-

cial Vladimir Koucky and Communist Party Official Carlos Rafael Rodriguez, Prague, 24 November 1967, WCDA.

54. Parrau, interview.
55. Oña, interview, 6 April 2010.
56. Trapote, interview.
57. Report, Slater, British Embassy, Havana, to Stewart, FCO, "Women in Cuba," 20 May 1968, FCO 7/598/TNA; Guerra, *Visions of Power*, 239-45; Deutsch, "Gender and Sociopolitical Change," 282.
58. Castro, "The Revolution within the Revolution," 9 December 1966, in Stone, *Women*, 48.
59. The target was never reached. By 1974, only 24 percent of women were in the workforce. Stone, *Women*, 13-15. On the Federación de Mujeres Cubanas membership figure, see "Women in Cuba."
60. Deutsch, "Gender and Sociopolitical Change," 283.
61. "Women in Cuba."
62. Deutsch, "Gender and Sociopolitical Change," 283.
63. "Women in Cuba"; *Granma*, 8 March 1968.
64. "Women in Cuba."
65. Estrada, *Tania*.
66. "Women in Cuba."
67. Deutsch, "Gender and Sociopolitical Change," 284-86.
68. *Granma Weekly*, 3 September 1967.
69. *Granma*, 8 March 1968; *Granma Weekly*, 17 March 1968; "Women in Cuba."
70. Huerta, with Oña, interview, 23 March 2010; Oña, interview, 6 April 2010; Trapote, interview.
71. Huerta, with Oña, interview, 23 March 2010; Oña, interview, 6 April 2010.
72. Gómez, correspondence, September-October 2016.
73. Espejo, interview, 18 April 2010.
74. Huerta, with Oña, interview, 23 March 2010; Oña, interview, 6 April 2010; Castillo Estay, "Mucha gente me culpó."
75. Trapote, interview; Gálvez, with Parrau, interview; Espejo, interview, 31 March 2010.
76. Núñez, interview.
77. Jaramillo, correspondence.
78. Núñez, interview; Pollack, interview.
79. Other significant romantic relationships between Chileans and Cubans in the late 1960s and early 1970s were between the Chilean Marxist Marta Harnecker and Manuel Piñeiro and between MIR leader Luciano Cruz and his Cuban wife. On the "romance" of Cuba and Soviet visitors' attachment to the island, see Gorsuch, "'Cuba, My Love.'"
80. Huerta and Chávez, *El trabajo*, 178. See also Marambio, *Las armas*, 41, 48.
81. Cabieses, with Oña, interview.
82. Oña, interview, 6 April 2010.
83. Tati to Amor, adorable, sr Queridísimo, no date, 1969, ABA.
84. Pollack, interview; Núñez, interview.
85. Núñez, interview.
86. Pollack, interview.
87. Pollack and Núñez, interviews.

88. Palieraki, *¡La revolución ya viene!*, 153.
89. Valdés, *El compromiso internacionalista*, 66.
90. Arrate and Rojas, *Memoria (I)*, 425, 427–28.
91. Palieraki, *¡La revolución ya viene!*, 199.
92. Palieraki, 134.
93. Arrate and Rojas, *Memoria (I)*, 428.
94. Huerta, with Oña, interview, 23 March 2010.
95. Oña, interview, 29 April 2011; Castillo Estay, "Mucha gente me culpó."
96. Oña, interviews, 6 April 2010 and 29 April 2011.
97. Cabieses, with Oña, interview; Oña, interview, 6 April; Núñez, Abra, Escobedo, and Claval, *Ricardo Núñez*, 86.
98. Rodríguez, *Sin tiempo para las palabras*, 45–46. Rodríguez cites Benigno as well to argue that Elmo also was able to send a suitcase of money from Salvador Allende to the guerrillas. See Oña, interview, 6 April 2010.
99. Oña, interview, 29 April 2011.
100. Rodríguez, *Sin tiempo para las palabras*, 75. Pedro Valdés has suggested that Jaime Barrios, an economist who worked with Cuba's National Bank from 1960 to 1966, when he returned to Chile, was the direct link to Che and recruited Elmo rather than the latter being the Cubans' primary contact in Chile, but this does not tally with other evidence consulted. It is probably the case that both were in direct communication with Havana. Valdés, *El compromiso internacionalista*, 76–79.
101. Gómez, correspondence. How Catalán helped is unclear. Unverifiable rumors indicate that Che passed through Chile in late 1966 en route to Bolivia. Catalán may well have helped in different ways, either by assisting others, providing documentation, or planting cover stories in the press. See Cortés, *Yo Patán*, 36, 41, and Castañeda, *Compañero*, 348–49.
102. "Carta de despedida," 114.
103. Rodríguez, *Sin tiempo para las palabras*, 74–79; Bodes, *En la senda del Che*, 128; Huerta and Chávez, *El trabajo*, 70; Huerta, with Oña, interview, 23 March 2010.
104. Gómez, correspondence, September–October 2016.
105. Vera and Catalán, *La encrucijada del cobre*, 9–11.
106. Gómez, correspondence.
107. Huerta, with Oña, interview, 23 March 2010.
108. Huerta and Chávez, *El trabajo*, 136.
109. Huerta, with Oña, interview, 23 March 2010.
110. Gómez, correspondence, September–October 2016.
111. Oña, interview, 6 April 2010.
112. Huerta, with Oña, interview, 23 March 2010; Huerta and Chávez, *El trabajo*, 201–2.
113. *El Mercurio*, 18 February 1968.
114. Peredo, interview; *El Mercurio*, 23 February 1968.
115. Carmen Paz, Viel, and Gnecco, interview; Huerta, interview, 20 April 2010; Ipinza, interview; Gnecco, correspondence; Bodes, *En la senda del Che*, 60.
116. Gómez, correspondence, September–October 2016.
117. Rodríguez, *Sin tiempo para las palabras*, 49.
118. On reinforcements on the border, see *El Mercurio*, 17 February 1968.
119. *El Mercurio*, 23 February 1968; Bodes, *En la senda del Che*, 56; Rodríguez, *Sin tiempo para las palabras*, 51.
120. *El Mercurio*, 24 February 1968, 25 February 1968.

121. *El Mercurio*, 23 February 1968; Rodríguez, *Sin tiempo para las palabras*, 52.
122. British Embassy, Santiago, to American Department, FCO, 5 March 1968, FCO 7/345/TNA.
123. *El Mercurio*, 19 February 1968.
124. *El Mercurio*, 17 February 1968.
125. *El Mercurio*, 24 February 1968.
126. *El Mercurio*, 24 February 1968.
127. Gómez, correspondence, September–October 2016.
128. Oña, interview, 9 December 2004; *El Mercurio*, 28 February 1968; British Embassy, Santiago, to American Department, FCO, 5 March 1968, FCO 7/345/TNA; Gómez, correspondence.
129. British Embassy to American Department, 5 March 1968.
130. Gómez, correspondence, September–October 2016.
131. Cabieses, with Oña, interview, 23 March 2010; Oña, interview, 6 April 2010; Uribe, *Operación Tía Victora*, 51–54, 69–71; Rodríguez, *Sin tiempo para las palabras*, 68.
132. Daza Sepúlveda, interview.
133. Huerta, with Oña, interview, 23 March 2010.
134. Oña, interview, 29 April 2011.
135. Codes were deciphered through talking with Luis and in the context in which they were used in 25 surviving letters. On the common use of *becados* to denote Cuban trainees, see *Tricontinental Conference*.
136. Tati to Amor, adorable, sr Queridísimo, no date, 1969, ABA.
137. Oña, interview, 6 April 2010.
138. Rodríguez, *Sin tiempo para las palabras*, 79.
139. Huerta, interview, 20 April 2010.
140. Oña, interview, 6 April 2010.
141. Huerta, with Oña, interview, 23 March 2010.
142. Jirón, correspondence.
143. Parrau, interview; Ipinza, interview; Espejo, interview, 31 March 2010; Jirón, correspondence.
144. Parrau, interview; Huerta, with Oña, interview, 23 March 2010; Gómez, correspondence, September–October 2016.
145. Rodríguez, *Sin tiempo para las palabras*, 108; Bodes, *En la senda del Che*, 60.
146. Rodríguez, *Sin tiempo para las palabras*, 58–71; Bodes, *En la senda del Che*, 60–61; Parrau, interview; Huerta, with Oña, interview, 23 March 2010; Jirón, correspondence; Gómez, correspondence.
147. Rodríguez, *Sin tiempo para las palabras*, 80–83.
148. Gómez, correspondence, September–October 2016.
149. Bodes, *En la senda del Che*, 68–69. Inti's father-in-law, Jesús Lara, insists Inti wrote the manifesto and did not want Cuban help. Lara, *Guerrillero*, 143–44. On Inti's stay in Chile, see Rodríguez, *Sin tiempo para las palabras*, 82.
150. Gómez, correspondence. September–October 2016.
151. On this point, see also Valdés, *El compromiso internacionalista*, 13, 74.
152. Inti Peredo as quoted in *Punto Final*, no. 88, 30 September 1969.
153. Peredo, "Volveremos a las montañas," July 1968.
154. Rodríguez, *Sin tiempo para las palabras*, 115.
155. Peredo, "Volveremos a las montañas."
156. Rodríguez, *Sin tiempo para las palabras*, 166–69.

157. Huerta and Chávez, *El trabajo*, 95–96; Rodríguez, *Sin tiempo para las palabras*, 62.

158. "Comunicado No. 1 al Pueblo Boliviano," 27 March 1967, in Guevara, *América Latina*, 395.

159. Peredo, "Volveremos a las montañas."

160. Inti Peredo as quoted in *Punto Final*, no. 88, 30 September 1969.

161. Peredo, "Volveremos a las montañas."

162. Huerta and Chávez, *El trabajo*, 225–26.

163. "Discurso Pronunciado por el Comandante Fidel Castro ... 18 de octubre de 1967." For echoes of this message in Chile, see *Punto Final*, no. 41, 6 November 1967.

164. Nicolás Guillén, "Che Comandante," in *Punto Final*, no. 41, 6 November 1967. For the original poem, see *Bohemia*, 3 November 1967.

165. On sacrifice, see Pérez, *To Die in Cuba*, 331–39. On the idea of being *consecuente*, albeit related to the MIR, see Palieraki, *¡La revolución ya viene!*, 153.

166. Peredo, "Volveremos a las montañas."

167. Rodríguez, *Sin tiempo para las palabras*, 118.

168. Rodríguez, 85–87. Two weeks is calculated based on their leaving on 20 July and arriving on 2 August 1968.

169. Bodes, *En la senda del Che*, 68.

170. Huerta and Chávez, *El trabajo*, 73, 172–76.

171. Carmen Paz, Viel, and Gnecco, interview.

172. Gálvez, with Parrau, interview.

173. Rodríguez, *Sin tiempo para las palabras*, 80. Beatriz was already there when Félix arrived at the end of August. Huerta, with Oña, interview, 23 March 2010. Oña could not recall exact dates, simply remembering that Beatriz "came and went" in 1968–69. It is possible she returned to Chile between August and December. Oña, interview, 6 April 2010.

174. Carretero, interview.

175. Estrada, interview, 19 April 2011.

176. Peredo, interview; Rodríguez, *Sin tiempo para las palabras*, 135–36; Huerta and Chávez, *El trabajo*, 190.

177. Oña, interview, 6 April 2010.

178. De la Guardia, interview. On training, see also Huerta, interview, 20 April 2010.

179. Rodríguez, *Sin tiempo para las palabras*, 158.

180. *Punto Final*, no. 88, 30 September 1969.

181. Estrada, *Tania*, 117–19.

182. López, "Ubicar urgente a Señora Hortensia."

183. Huerta, with Oña, interview, 23 March 2010.

184. Gómez, correspondence, September–October 2016.

185. *El Mercurio*, 18 February 1968.

186. Oña, interview, 29 April 2011.

187. Gómez, correspondence, September–October 2016; Oña, interview, 6 April 2010.

188. De la Guardia, interview. On training for urban recruits, see Rodríguez, *Sin tiempo para las palabras*, 135.

189. Rodríguez, *Sin tiempo para las palabras*, 127.

190. Huerta, with Oña, interview, 23 March 2010.

191. Huerta with Oña, interview, 23 March 2010; Huerta and Chávez, *El trabajo*, 180.

192. Rodríguez, *Sin tiempo para las palabras*, 118. Recollections of numbers range from under one hundred to almost two hundred. Félix told Mónica González that there were close to one hundred. González, *Chile. La conjura*, 150.

193. Rodríguez, *Sin tiempo para las palabras*, 117; de la Guardia, interview; Huerta, interview, 20 April 2010.

194. Huerta, with Oña, interview, 23 March 2010.

195. Rodríguez, *Sin tiempo para las palabras*, 124; Guevara, *Bolivian Diary*, 46, 54–55.

196. Rodríguez, *Sin tiempo para las palabras*, 125; Huerta and Chávez, *El trabajo*, 185.

197. Bodes, *En la senda del Che*, 70–71.

198. Huerta and Chávez, *El trabajo*, 184.

199. Huerta and Chávez, 181.

200. Rodríguez, *Sin tiempo para las palabras*, 136–41.

201. Rodríguez, 137–43.

202. Huerta, with Oña, interview, 23 March 2010.

203. Rodríguez, *Sin tiempo para las palabras*, 137–38; Tati to Querido, February 1969, ABA.

204. Peredo, interview.

205. Gómez, correspondence, 14 May 2018; Tati to Papote Querido, 10 January 1970, ABA; Tati to Papote, 5 February 1970, ABA.

206. Bussi, interview.

207. Tati to Papote Querido, queridible amor mío, Tesoro, January 1969, ABA.

208. Tati to Lindo Mío, 19 February 1969, ABA.

209. Tati to Amor Mío, 17 February 1969, ABA.

210. Tati to Amor, March 1969, ABA.

211. Tati to Amor; Tati to Papote queridúsimo amor mío, 17 March 1969, ABA.

212. Tati to Querido, February 1969, ABA.

213. Tati to Papote Querido, 22 February 1969, ABA.

214. Tati to Amor, March 1969.

215. Tati to Amor.

216. Tati to Amor, adorable, sr Queridísimo, no date, ca. February 1969, ABA.

217. Gómez, correspondence, 14 May 2018.

218. Espejo, interview, 31 March 2010.

Chapter 6

1. Tati to Amor Mío, 17 February 1969, ABA.
2. Garretón and Moulian, *La Unidad Popular*, 24, 164.
3. Arrate and Rojas, *Memoria (I)*, 406.
4. Report CH/3/67, Atkin, 10 August 1967, LAB 13/2129/TNA.
5. Arrate and Rojas, *Memoria (I)*, 439–40.
6. "Chile: Annual Review for 1968," 13 January 1969, FCO 7/1126/TNA.
7. Beatriz quoted in Baez *Preguntas*, 243.
8. Arrate and Rojas, *Memoria (I)*, 416–17.
9. Alejandro Rojas in Brodsky, *Conversaciones con la FECH*, 114.
10. Inés Pepper as quoted in Azócar, *Lorca*, 33–34.
11. Rojas quoted in Brodsky, *Conversaciones con la FECH*, 125; Ennio Vivaldi as quoted in Azócar, *Lorca*, 41.
12. Vivaldi, "Pero está la presencia de Carlos."

13. Coloma, interview; Azócar, *Lorca*, 31.
14. Schlotterbeck, *Beyond the Vanguard*, 68.
15. Rojas quoted in Brodsky, *Conversaciones con la FECH*, 113.
16. Marchesi, "Southern Cone Cities," 66–67; Marchesi, "Imaginación política."
17. Núñez, Abra, Escobedo, and Claval, *Ricardo Núñez*, 77–78.
18. Carlos Lorca, *Bohemia*, 1972, quoted in Azócar, *Lorca*, 90.
19. Huerta and Chávez, *El trabajo*, 130–31.
20. "Entrevista Allende-Debray," 35.
21. Valle and Díaz, *Federación de la Juventude Socialista*, 52.
22. Coloma, interview.
23. Rigo Quezada quoted in Azócar, *Lorca*, 25; Coloma, interview.
24. Huerta and Chavez, *El trabajo*, 67.
25. Pascal Allende, interview.
26. Coloma, interview; Ipinza, interview.
27. Tati to Amor, Tesoro, April 1969, ABA.
28. Discussed by Rojas in Brodsky, *Conversaciones con la FECH*, 127.
29. Espejo, interview, 31 March 2010.
30. Tati to Papote Querido, Viejo recordado, no date, ABA.
31. Ipinza, interview.
32. Tati to Papote Querido e Ingrato, 15 June 1970, ABA.
33. Espejo, interview, 31 March 2010.
34. Huerta, with Oña, interview, 23 March 2010.
35. Tati to Amor, adorable, sr Queridísimo, no date, ca. February 1969, ABA.
36. Huerta, interview, 20 April 2010; Huerta and Chávez, *El trabajo*, 121; Soto, *Allende en el recuerdo*, 26–27.
37. Espejo, interview, 31 March 2010.
38. Tati to Amor, adorable, sr Queridísimo.
39. Espejo, interview, 31 March 2010.
40. Ipinza, interview.
41. Sepúlveda Carvajal, interview.
42. Vivaldi, interview.
43. Ipinza, interview.
44. Discussed by Fernando Martínez in Brodsky, *Conversaciones con la FECH*, 167.
45. Espejo, interview, 31 March 2010.
46. Echeverría and Castillo, *Santiago-París*, 97.
47. Vivaldi, interview.
48. Ipinza, interview.
49. Espejo, interview, 31 March 2010.
50. Ipinza, interview.
51. Tati to Papote Querido y Ingrato. Emphasis in original.
52. Ipinza, interview.
53. Pascal Allende, "El MIR, 35 años (Parte 2)"; Núñez, Abra, Escobedo, and Claval, *Ricardo Núñez*, 83.
54. Azócar, *Lorca*, 28.
55. Azócar, 28; Coloma, interview; Pérez, "Guerrilla rural," 183, 185–93, 196–99; Quiroga, *Compañeros*, 29–33.
56. Coloma, interview; Quiroga, *Compañeros*, 33–34; Arrate and Rojas, *Memoria (I)*, 434.
57. Coloma, interview.

58. Quiroga, *Compañeros*, 42–43; Coloma, interview.
59. Calderón, interview; Coloma, interview.
60. Tati to Amor Mío, 17 February 1969, ABA.
61. Coloma, interview. Quiroga suggests Joel Marambio, Socialist deputy for San Fernando and Santa Cruz and father to Max Marambio, rather than the ELN supplied it. Quiroga, *Compañeros*, 31.
62. Quiroga, *Compañeros*, 44–45, 52–53; Azócar, *Lorca*, 30–31; Valdés, *El compromiso internacionalista*, 120.
63. Marambio, *Las armas*, 62; Pascal Allende, "El MIR, 35 años (Parte 2)."
64. Marambio, *Las armas*, 61.
65. Pascal Allende, "El MIR, 35 años (Parte 2)."
66. Tati to Amor Mío.
67. Palieraki, *¡La revolución ya viene!*, 227–28n22; Pascal Allende, "El MIR, 35 años (Parte 2)."
68. Pascal Allende, interview; Pascal Allende, "El MIR, 35 años (Parte 2)"; Oña, interview, 6 April 2010.
69. Tati to Amor Mío.
70. Tati to Amor, adorable, sr Queridísimo; on mistakes made during bank raids, see also Pascal Allende, "El MIR, 35 años (Parte 2)."
71. Pascal Allende, interview.
72. Oña, interview, 29 April 2011.
73. Haslam, *Assisted Suicide*, 29.
74. See Tati to Amor Mío, 17 February 1969; Tati to Papote, 5 February 1970; and Letter, Tati to Papote Querido e Ingrato, 15 June 1970.
75. See, for example, Tati to Amor Mío.
76. Rodríguez, *Sin tiempo para las palabras*, 155–56.
77. Rodríguez, 210, 212–13.
78. Wright, *Latin America in the Era of the Cuban Revolution*, 77–78, 103–4.
79. Suárez and Kruijt, *La Revolución Cubana en Nuestra América*, 56–58, 124, 125; Erisman, *Cuba's Foreign Relations*, 73–77; Blight and Brenner, *Sad and Luminous Days*.
80. Daza Sepúlveda, interview.
81. Huerta, interview, 20 April 2010.
82. Tati to Querido Papote, 6 October 1969; Tati to Papote Querido, 10 December 1969, ABA.
83. Oña, interview, 29 April 2011.
84. Rodríguez, *Sin tiempo para las palabras*, 218, 219. On the lack of an explanation, see also Huerta, interview, 20 April 2010, and off-the-record interview with ELN member.
85. Rodríguez Ostria argues that this preoccupation with infiltration was misguided. Bolivian security forces' source of information—and a further motive for Havana's withdrawal—probably came from a Cuban based in Paris who defected in April 1969 and shared intelligence with the CIA. Rodríguez, *Sin tiempo para las palabras*, 205, 212–13, 218–22.
86. Rodríguez, 183–235.
87. "The Black Riders" (1918), in Bly, *Neruda and Vallejo*, 178–79. On Beatriz reading this poem, see López, "Ubicar urgente a Señora Hortensia."
88. Rodríguez, *Sin tiempo para las palabras*, 238–48.
89. Peredo, interview.

90. Rodríguez, *Sin tiempo para las palabras*, 248-65.
91. Tati to Querido Papote, 6 October 1969, and Tati to Papote Querido, 10 December 1969, ABA.
92. Tati to Papote Querido, 10 January 1970, ABA.
93. "Amor mío," undated, ABA; Neruda, *The Captain's Verses*, 47.
94. Tati to Papote Querido, 10 January 1970.
95. Tati to Papote Querido.
96. Letter, Tati to Papote, December 1969, ABA.
97. Parrau, interview; Rodríguez, *Sin tiempo para las palabras*, 266-67.
98. *Punto Final*, no. 88, 30 September 1969. On new middle-class recruits and Inti as revered martyr, see Rodríguez, *Sin tiempo para las palabras*, 278, 281, 296, 308.
99. Full lyrics (in Spanish) can be found online at http://www.cancioneros.com/nc/4572/0/volveremos-a-la-montana-victor-jara. Although the song does not appear on any of Victor Jara's LPs, see a recording at the University of Valparaíso in May 1970 at https://www.youtube.com/watch?v=eUjKCmYhhg4.
100. Valdés, *El compromiso internacionalista*, 122; Álvarez, *Tati*, 114-15.
101. Echeverría and Castillo, *Santiago-París*, 116-17.
102. Rodríguez, *Sin tiempo para las palabras*, 274, 281-306, 308, 620; Valdés, *El compromiso internacionalista*, 125.
103. *Punto Final*, no. 89, 14 October 1969. Although a false attribution, Guevara had written the verse out, changing certain words and missing four lines of the original in a notebook he took to Bolivia. See Pérez Guillén, "Ernesto Che Guevara y León Felipe."
104. Rodríguez, *Sin tiempo para las palabras*, 274, 278.
105. Rodríguez, 353.
106. For names of those in the ELN guerrilla column at Teoponte, see Rodríguez, 617-31.
107. Rodríguez, 312-13, 326-36.
108. Rodríguez, 333-37.
109. Peredo, interview.
110. Huerta and Chávez, *El trabajo*, 215-16, 220.
111. Daza Sepúlveda, interview.
112. Tati to Papote Querido, 25 June 1970, ABA.
113. Peredo, interview.
114. Huerta, with Oña, interview, 23 March 2010.
115. Azócar, *Lorca*, 54-56.
116. Arrate and Rojas, *Memoria (I)*, 445-46; Núñez, Abra, Escobedo, and Claval, *Ricardo Núñez*, 105.
117. Quotation from Amorós, *Allende*, 248-49.
118. Pereda, correspondence.
119. Oña, interview, 29 April 2011; Huerta, with Oña, interview, 23 March 2010; Estrada, interview, 19 April 2011.
120. Calderón, interview.
121. Coloma, interview.
122. Huerta and Chávez, *El trabajo*, 117-19; González, *Chile. La conjura*, 151.
123. "Carta a Taty," January 1974, CDC-0002/AFSA; Echeverría and Castillo, *Santiago-París*, 118-19.
124. Pascal Allende, interview; Pascal Allende, "El MIR, 35 años (Parte 2)"; Haslam, *Assisted Suicide*, 51-52.

125. Tati to Papotísimo Recordado, 26 January 1970, ABA.
126. Tati to Papote Querido, 11 March 1970, ABA.
127. Tati to Papote, 5 February 1970.
128. Tati to Papote Papote Querido, 27 May 1970, ABA.
129. Tati to Papote Querido, 25 June 1970.
130. Carretero, interview.

Chapter 7
1. Tati to Papotísimo Recordado, 26 January 1970, ABA. Emphasis in original.
2. Tati to Papotísimo Recordado.
3. Soto, interview; Soto, *Allende en el recuerdo*, 30–33; Labarca, *Allende*, 265–66; *LNUH*, 7 May 1970.
4. Tati to Papote Papote Querido, 27 May 1970, ABA.
5. Tati to Papote Papote Querido.
6. *LNUH*, 3 May 1970.
7. Arrate, interview; Labarca, *Allende*, 267.
8. *LNUH*, 11 May 1970.
9. Tati to Papote Papote Querido.
10. Tati to Papote Querido, 11 March 1970, ABA.
11. Tati to Papote Papote Querido.
12. Vivaldi, interview; Azócar, *Lorca*, 60–61.
13. Contreras, interview.
14. Tati to Papote Querido, 15 June 1970, ABA.
15. Del Pozo, *Rebeldes, Reformistas y Revolucionarios*, 140–41; Soto, interview.
16. "Programa básico de gobierno de la Unidad Popular"; Garretón and Moulian, *La Unidad Popular*, 161–62.
17. "Las primeras 40 medidas," González and Fontaine, *Míl días*, 961–63; Figueroa Clark, *Allende*, 25.
18. *LNUH*, 3 June 1970.
19. *LNUH*, 12 June 1970; *El Siglo*, 8 June 1970, 11 June 1970.
20. Tati to Papote Querido, 25 June 1970, ABA.
21. Tati to Papote Querido, 15 June 1970.
22. Tati to Papote Querido, 15 June 1970.
23. Reports CH/2/65, Carlin, First Secretary (Labour), British Embassy, Santiago, 5 November 1965, and CH/3/67, Harold Atkin, First Secretary (Labour), British Embassy, Santiago, 10 August 1967, LAB 13/2129/TNA.
24. Núñez, Abra, Escobedo, and Claval, *Ricardo Núñez*, 90–91.
25. *LNUH*, 12 May 1970.
26. *LNUH*, 12 May 1970.
27. *LNUH*, 3 May 1970, 11 May 1970.
28. *LNUH*, 14 May 1970.
29. Parrau, interview; Gómez, correspondence, September–October 2016; "Entrevista Allende-Debray," 42.
30. Labarca, *Allende*, 174.
31. Quiroga, *Compañeros*, 44, 47–48.
32. Tati to Papote Querido, 11 March 1970, and Tati to Papote Querido, 15 June 1970; Ipinza, interview.
33. Huerta, with Oña, interview, 23 March 2010.
34. Gómez, correspondence, September–October 2016; Quiroga, *Compañeros*, 48.

35. Gómez, correspondence, September–October 2016. On Allende's initial reticence, see also Cortés, *Yo Patán*, 40.
36. Quiroga, *Compañeros*, 48.
37. Quiroga, 42–44.
38. Huerta and Chávez, *El trabajo*, 115–16.
39. Espejo, interview, 31 March 2010.
40. Coloma, interview.
41. Baez, *Preguntas*, 238.
42. Discussed by Rojas in Brodsky, *Conversaciones con la FECH*, 133.
43. Coloma, interview.
44. Espejo, interview, 31 March 2010; Torres, interview.
45. Carmen Paz, Viel, and Gnecco, interview.
46. Beatriz quoted in Baez, *Preguntas*, 238.
47. Beatriz quoted in Baez, 238–39.
48. Coloma, interview.
49. Parrau, interview.
50. Álvarez, *Tati*, 128.
51. Daza Sepúlveda, interview.
52. Carretero, interview; Oña, interview, 6 April 2010.
53. Castro's advice was disseminated through various channels. See, for example, Memorandum of Conversation, Galo Plaza and Allende, 2 November 1970, Tomás Moro, enclosure, Rogers to Nixon, 29 December 1970, box 2196/RG59/NARA; "Conversación del embajador N. B. Alekseev con Volodia Teitelboim," 14 October 1970, in Ulianova and Fediakova, "Chile en los archivos de la URSS," 412; and Memorandum, Gerrity to Merriam, "The Chilean Candidate," 28 October 1970, in *Subversion in Chile*, 85.
54. Carretero, interview.
55. Oña, interview, 6 April 2010; Harmer, *Allende's Chile*, 52–53.
56. Oña, interview, 6 April 2010.
57. Off-the-record interview with ELN member.
58. Huerta, with Oña, interview, 23 March 2010.
59. Oña, interviews, 9 and 16 December 2004; conversations with Oña, March–April 2010.
60. Oña, interviews, 3 September 2005, 2 May 2006, 6 April 2010, and 29 April 2011.
61. Ruben, interview.
62. On Allende's efforts to bring the MIR into government, see Pascal Allende, "El MIR, 35 años (Parte 3)."
63. Quiroga, *Compañeros*, 49, 51, 52–53; Labarca, *Allende*, 269–70; Gómez, correspondence, September–October 2016.
64. Ruben, interview; Oña, interviews, 2004–6; Estrada, interview, 19 April 2011; Quiroga, *Compañeros*, 58, 77–78.
65. Oña, interview, 6 April 2010; Ruben, interview; Gómez, correspondence, September–October 2016.
66. See, for example, Power, *Right-Wing Women*, 142–43, and Cortés, *Yo Patán*, 86–88.
67. For a fuller discussion of U.S. policy toward Chile, see Harmer, *Allende's Chile*, 58–62.
68. Quiroga, *Compañeros*, 53, 55, 56.

69. Labarca, *Allende*, 275.
70. Carretero, interview.
71. Marchesi, *Latin America's Radical Left*, 121.
72. Núñez, Abra, Escobedo, and Claval, *Ricardo Núñez*, 116–18; Arrate and Rojas, *Memoria (II)*, 45.
73. Salazar, *Conversations con Carlos Altamirano*, 248–52. For a discussion of Allende's foreign policy team, see Harmer, *Allende's Chile*, 78–80.
74. Gálvez, with Parrau, interview.
75. Jaramillo, correspondence.
76. Soto, interview.
77. Huerta, with Oña, interview, 23 March 2010; Labarca, *Allende*, 261, 26–63, 292; Marambio, *Armas de ayer*, 142.
78. Labarca, *Allende*, 282, 292, 331.
79. Marambio, *Armas de ayer*, 139.
80. Jaramillo, correspondence; Espejo, interviews, 31 March and 18 April 2010; Oña, interview, 6 April 2010; Ruben, interview; Estrada, interview, 19 April 2011; Pey, interview.
81. Espejo, correspondence.
82. Espejo, interviews, 31 March and 18 April 2010; Jaramillo, correspondence.
83. Modak, interview.
84. Arrate, interview; Ruben, interview; Modak, interview; Espejo, interviews, 31 March and 18 April 2010; Daza Sepúlveda, interview.
85. Espejo, interview, 18 April 2010.
86. Allende Bussi, "Mi padre."
87. Espejo, interview, 18 April 2010.
88. Beatriz quoted in Baez, *Preguntas*, 239.
89. Arturo Jirón, "Homenaje" (2006), AFSA; Huerta, with Oña, interview, 23 March 2010; Trapote, interview.
90. Espejo, interview, 31 March 2010; Pollack, interview.
91. Espejo, interview, 31 March 2010.
92. Ruben, interview; Espejo, interview, 31 March 2010.
93. Permanent analysts included Jorge Klein (PCCh), Manuel Contreras (PCCh), Guillermo Cumsille Garib (PCCh), Claudio Jimeno (PS), and René Bendit (PS). González, *Chile. La conjura*, 147–53; Huerta and Chávez, *El trabajo*, 113–25; Labarca, *Allende*, 328; Huerta, interview, 20 April 2010.
94. Huerta and Chávez, *El trabajo*, 114.
95. Allende Bussi, "Mi padre."
96. Huerta and Chávez, *El trabajo*, 113; Labarca, *Allende*, 329–30.
97. Huerta and Chávez, *El trabajo*, 115; Huerta, with Oña, interview, 23 March 2010; Huerta, interview, 20 April 2010.
98. Jirón, correspondence.
99. Ipinza, interview.
100. Jirón, "Homenaje" (2006), AFSA.
101. Cabello, interview; Cabello, "Mi recuerdo de Beatriz."
102. Almeyda, "Foreign Policy of the Unidad Popular," 84; Almeyda, "Exposición del Ministro de Relaciones Exteriores, Señor Clodomiro Almeyda, ante la Comisión de Relaciones Exteriores del Senado," 22 December 1970, enclosure, Circular, MRE, 25 January 1971, Discursos: S. Allende Gossens/1971/AMRE. See also Harmer, *Allende's Chile*, 78–80.

103. Pey, interview; Vázquez and Cubillas, interview, 11 September 2005.
104. Coloma, interview.
105. Letter, Tati to Papote Querido, 15 June 1970, ABA.
106. Memcon, Galo Plaza, and Allende, 2 November 1970, enclosure, Memorandum, Rogers to Nixon, 29 December 1970, box 2196/RG59/NARA.
107. Carretero, interview; Harmer, *Allende's Chile*, 66.
108. Oña, interview, 6 April 2010; Labarca, *Allende*, 298.
109. Harmer, *Allende's Chile*, 66–67; Trapote, interview.
110. Marchesi, *Latin America's Radical Left*, 120; Quiroga, *Compañeros*, 108.
111. National Security Decision Memorandum 93, "Policy towards Chile," 9 November 1970, doc. 175, in *Foreign Relations of the United States*, vol. 21. See also Harmer, *Allende's Chile*, 69–70, 78–96, 124–30.
112. Marchesi, *Latin America's Radical Left*, 101, 102–3; Quiroga, *Compañeros*, 108; Harmer, *Allende's Chile*, 95.
113. Marchesi, *Latin America's Radical Left*, 105.
114. Rodríguez, *Sin tiempo para las palabras*, 570; Azócar, *Lorca*, 70.
115. Peredo, interview.
116. Huerta, interview, 20 April 2010; Schreiber, *La mujer que vengó al Ché*, 9–10, 89, 143, 175, 206, 211; Rodríguez, *Sin tiempo para las palabras*, 572–73.
117. Barreiro, interview and correspondence.
118. Parrau, interview; Espejo, interview, 31 March 2010; Labarca, *Allende*, 317.
119. Espejo, interview, 31 March 2010.
120. Parrau, interview; Jaramillo, correspondence; Echeverría and Castillo, *Santiago-París*, 148.
121. Parrau, interview.
122. Barreiro, interview and correspondence. Three of the nine were reintegrated into the MLN-T's hierarchy at the end of 1971. See also Marchesi, *Latin America's Radical Left*, 108, and Alonso, "Uruguayos en Chile," 12–13.
123. Barreiro, interview and correspondence; Marchesi, *Latin America's Radical Left*, 108–9.
124. Jaramillo, correspondence.
125. Allende told the British he had offered this sum of money though there is no other evidence to corroborate this offer on the Uruguayan side. Hildyard to FCO, 1 July 1971; Hildyard to FCO, 16 July 1971; Hildyard to FCO, 23 August 1971, FCO 7/2091/TNA; Aldrighi, *El caso Mitrione*, 325–26; Jaramillo and Espejo, correspondence.
126. Hildyard to Hunter, 30 June 1971, FCO 7/2091/TNA.
127. Douglas-Home to British Embassy, Santiago, 19 September 1971, FCO 7/2092/TNA.
128. Allende Bussi, "Mi padre."
129. Echeverría and Castillo, *Santiago-Paris*, 148.
130. "Entrevista Allende-Debray," 31–62.
131. Oña, interviews, 6 April 2010 and 29 April 2011.
132. Quiroga, *Compañeros*, 154.
133. Carter, interview.
134. Oña, interviews, 6 April 2010 and 29 April 2011; Huerta, with Oña, interview, 23 March 2010.
135. Echeverría and Catsillo, *Santiago-París*, 147.
136. Arrate and Rojas, *Memoria (II)*, 46.
137. Azócar, *Lorca*, 87–88.

138. Deutsch, "Gender and Sociopolitical Change," 297; del Pozo, *Rebeldes, Reformistas y Revolucionarios*, 212.
139. Parrau, interview; San Martín, correspondence.
140. Hite, *When the Romance Ended*, 74; Labarca, *Allende*, 281–87.
141. Gálvez, with Parrau, interview; Oña, interview, 29 April 2011.
142. Oña, interview, 29 April 2011.
143. Espejo, interview, 18 April 2010; Labarca, *Allende*, 286.
144. Labarca, *Allende*, 264–65, 325.
145. Espejo, interview, 18 April 2010. On arguments and criticism, see also Pey, interview, and Labarca, *Allende*, 260.
146. Labarca, *Allende*, 287.
147. Espejo, interview, 18 April 2010; Oña interview, 29 April 2011; Ruben, interview.
148. Labarca, *Allende*, 291.
149. Labarca, 293–94.
150. Beatriz quoted in Baez, *Preguntas*, 244.
151. Vázquez and Cubillas, interview, 11 September 2005.
152. Del Pozo, *Rebeldes, Reformistas y Revolucionarios*, 181–87.
153. Beatriz quoted in Baez, *Preguntas*, 243–44.
154. Del Pozo, *Rebeldes, Reformistas y Revolucionarios*, 246.
155. Arrate and Rojas, *Memoria (II)*, 46, 58.
156. Pieper Mooney, *Politics of Motherhood*, 102.
157. "Entrevista Allende-Debray," 50.
158. *Eva*, 8–14 October 1971.
159. Petras and Zemelman, *Peasants in Revolt*, xii.
160. Arrate and Rojas, *Memoria (II)*, 35, 46, 58.
161. Pey, interview; Salazar, *Conversaciones con Carlos Altamirano*, 226; Marambio, *Las armas*, 72.
162. Tati to Papote Papote Querido.
163. Quiroga, *Compañeros*, 71–74; Calderón, interview; Ulloa, interview.
164. Quiroga, *Compañeros*, 72–73.
165. Debray as quoted in Arrate and Rojas, *Memoria (II)*, 40.
166. Salazar, *Conversaciones con Carlos Altamirano*, 347; *La VOP*, 15; Pomar, "La Vanguardia Organizada del Pueblo," 1497, 1502–4.
167. Barreiro, interview; Coloma as quoted in Quiroga, *Compañeros*, 119; Oña, interview, 9 December 2004.
168. Arrate and Rojas, *Memoria (II)*, 47–48.
169. Arrate and Rojas, 47–53; Garretón and Martínez, *Biblioteca del movimiento estudiantil (III)*, 96; Quiroga, *Compañeros*, 118.
170. Quiroga, *Compañeros*, 120.
171. Beatriz quoted in Baez, *Preguntas*, 242.
172. Espejo, interview, 31 March 2010.
173. Castro to Allende, 21 May 1971, in Castro, "Salvador Allende, un ejemplo que perdura."
174. Huerta, with Oña, interview, 23 March 2010; Oña, interview, 6 April 2010.

Chapter 8

1. Espinosa, "'La batalla de la merluza'"; Angell, "Social Class and Political Mobilisation," 34; Loveman, *Chile*, 251; Soto, *Último día*, 35; Garretón and Martínez, *Biblioteca del movimiento estudiantil (III)*, 95–99.

2. Garretón Merino and Martínez Bengoa, *Biblioteca del movimiento estudiantil (III)*, 106–8.

3. Carassai, "Dark Side of Social Desire," 41.

4. Garretón and Moulian, *La Unidad Popular*, 152–53.

5. Espinosa, "'La batalla de la merluza,'" 35.

6. Quotation from Figueroa Clark, *Allende*, 117.

7. Garretón and Moulian, *La Unidad Popular*, 150–55.

8. Casals, "Estado, contrarrevolución y autoritarismo," 99; Angell, "Social Class and Political Mobilisation," 4.

9. Power, *Right-Wing Women*, 147.

10. Arrate and Rojas, *Memoria (II)*, 66–67. On the women's march, related violence, and its broader significance, see also Trumper, *Ephemeral Histories*, 43–64.

11. *Tribuna*, 4 December 1971, in González and Fontaine, *Míl días (I)*, 251–52. See also Power, *Right-Wing Women*, 153.

12. Power, *Right-Wing Women*, 148.

13. Deutsch, "Gender and Sociopolitical Change," 304; Power, *Right-Wing Women*, 150.

14. *Paula*, no. 96, September 1971.

15. Manzano, "Sex, Gender and the Making of the 'Enemy Within,'" 5, 23; Zalaquett, *Chilenas en armas*, 11.

16. Schlotterbeck, *Beyond the Vanguard*, 77.

17. Zalaquett, *Chilenas en armas*, 15.

18. *Paula*, no. 98, September 1971.

19. See, for example, Cowan, *Securing Sex*, and Manzano, "Sex, Gender and the Making of the 'Enemy Within.'"

20. Power, *Right-Wing Women*, 228–29; Deutsch, "Gender and Sociopolitical Change," 302; "Marcha de las mujeres," *Tribuna*, 4 December 1971, in González and Fontaine, *Mil días (I)*, 251–52.

21. Oña, interview, 6 April 2010; Labarca, *Allende*, 298.

22. See, for example, "Numero extraordinario de niños," *Paula*, October 1971; and Espejo interview, 31 March 2010.

23. Trapote, interview.

24. Oña, interview, 9 April 2010.

25. Espejo, interview, 31 March 2010.

26. Benado, interview; Gálvez, with Parrau, interview.

27. Pieper Mooney, *Politics of Motherhood*, 111; Deutsch, "Gender and Sociopolitical Change," 293.

28. Carmen Gloria Aguayo quoted in *Eva*, 16–22 July 1971. On negative attitudes toward the women's liberation movement in the United States, see also Power, *Right-Wing Women*, 176.

29. "Programa básico de la Unidad Popular"; Deutsch, "Gender and Sociopolitical Change," 294.

30. Maravall, *Las mujeres*, 52–53, 57.

31. Maravall, 53, 77.

32. *Eva*, 16–22 July 1971; Deutsch, "Gender and Sociopolitical Change," 301.

33. Power, *Right-Wing Women*, 217–18.

34. Deutsch, "Gender and Sociopolitical Change," 293.

35. Tupper, *Historias de clandestinidad*, 41.

36. Deutsch, "Gender and Sociopolitical Change," 296–97; Pieper Mooney, *Politics*

of Motherhood, 114; Angell, "Social Class and Political Mobilization," 28; Maravall, *Las mujeres*, 54.

37. Deutsch, "Gender and Sociopolitical Change," 298; Maravall, *Las mujeres*, 71–72; Power, *Right-Wing Women*, 135; Pieper Mooney, *Politics of Motherhood*, 110.

38. Deutsch, "Gender and Sociopolitical Change," 297–98; Maravall, *Las mujeres*, 53.

39. Maravall, *Las mujeres*, 60, 73–74.

40. Maravall, 51, 57–58, 306.

41. Pieper Mooney, *Politics of Motherhood*, 103, 115.

42. "Las primeras 40 medidas del gobierno popular," in González and Fontaine, *Mil días (II)*, 961–63; Deutsch, "Gender and Sociopolitical Change," 295.

43. Pieper Mooney, *Politics of Motherhood*, 115, 127.

44. Daza Sepúlveda, interview.

45. Espejo, interview, 18 April 2010.

46. Labarca, *Allende*, 321; Daza Sepúlveda, interview.

47. Baltra, *Mireya Baltra*, 91–93.

48. Quiroga, *Compañeros*, 173.

49. Castro, 2 December 1971, "Acto de despedida," in *Cuba-Chile*, 473–88.

50. Power, *Right-Wing Women*, 160.

51. "Acto de despedida."

52. Pascal Allende, interview.

53. Barreiro, interview.

54. Carretero, interview; Oña, interview, 9 April 2010.

55. Carassai, "Dark Side of Social Desire," 40.

56. Carretero, interview.

57. Garcés, *Allende y la experiencia chilena*, 276.

58. *El Siglo*, 26 July 1973, in González and Fontaine, *Mil días*, 763.

59. Pey, interview.

60. Marchesi, *Latin America's Radical Left*, 121; Schlotterbeck, *Beyond the Vanguard*, 134–40.

61. Daza Sepúlveda, interview; Arrate and Rojas, *Memoria (II)*, 72.

62. Arrate and Rojas, *Memoria (II)*, 72.

63. Marchesi, *Latin America's Radical Left*, 122; Schlotterbeck, *Beyond the Vanguard*, 104–5.

64. Pascal Allende, interview; Estrada, interview, 13 December 2004.

65. Gómez, correspondence, September–October 2016.

66. Daza Sepúlveda, interview.

67. Allende Bussi, "Entre el MIR y Allende." On the relationship, see Pascal Allende, "El MIR, 35 años (Parte 3)."

68. Memorandum of Conversation, "Meeting with [redacted]," 17 August 1971, Chile Declassification Project, Virtual Reading Room, Freedom of Information Act, U.S. Department of State.

69. Tarud, *Historia de una vida*, 204.

70. Labarca, *Allende*, 331–32; Arrate and Rojas, *Memoria (II)*, 88; Marchesi, *Latin America's Radical Left*, 123.

71. Huerta, interview, 20 April 2010.

72. Marchesi, *Latin America's Radical Left*, 107–8.

73. Barreiro, interview and correspondence.

74. Parrau, interview.

75. Marchesi, *Latin America's Radical Left*, 122; Labarca, *Allende*, 333; Harmer, *Allende's Chile*, 185.

76. Labarca, *Allende*, 333–34.

77. Espejo, interview, 31 March 2010.

78. Vázquez and Cubillas, interview, 11 September 2005; Debray as quoted by Haslam, *Assisted Suicide*, 32.

79. Marchesi, *Latin America's Radical Left*, 125–26.

80. Allende Bussi, "Mi padre." For a similar evaluation of Allende's decision, see Cortés, *Yo Patán*, 73.

81. Parrau, interview; Oña, interview, 3 September 2005; Harmer, *Allende's Chile*, 134. On collaboration before late 1972, see Marchesi, *Latin America's Radical Left*, 126.

82. Marchesi, *Latin America's Radical Left*, 108.

83. Barreiro, interview and correspondence.

84. Marchesi, *Latin America's Radical Left*, 130–32; Dinges, *Condor Years*, 51. On the JCR's aims, see "A los pueblos de América Latina: Declaración conjunta (MLN, ERP, ELN, MIR)," no date, CeDInCI.

85. Peredo, interview.

86. Barreiro, interview.

87. Echeverría and Castillo, *Santiago-París*, 150.

88. Carretero, interview.

89. Allende Bussi, "Mi padre."

90. Harmer, *Allende's Chile*, 221. For the reach this idea had, see Kissinger, *Years of Upheaval*, 378.

91. Espejo, interview, 18 April 2010.

92. See, for example, del Pozo, *Rebeldes, Reformistas y Revolucionarios*, 251–52.

93. Espejo, interview, 18 April 2010.

94. Angell, "Social Class and Political Mobilisation," 9.

95. Del Pozo, *Rebeldes, Reformistas y Revolucionarios*, 251–52; Arrate and Rojas, *Memoria (II)*, 83; Angell, "Social Class and Political Mobilisation," 38.

96. "Conversación del embajador A. V. Basov con Luis Corvalán y Volodia Teitelboim," 13 September 1972, in Ulianova and Fediakova, "Chile en los archivos de la URSS," 441–43; CIA Information Cable, 14 September 1972, doc. 307, in *Foreign Relations of the United States*, vol. 21; Quiroga, *Compañeros*, 84.

97. Angell, "Social Class and Political Mobilisation," 10–11, 24; Loveman, *Chile*, 254.

98. Medina, *Cybernetic Revolutionaries*, 141–51.

99. "Marcelino" as quoted in del Pozo, *Rebeldes, Reformistas y Revolucionarios*, 256.

100. Del Pozo, *Rebeldes, Reformistas y Revolucionarios*, 256; Angell, "Social Class and Political Mobilisation," 45–47.

101. Angell, "Social Class and Political Mobilisation," 4, 32.

102. Barreiro, interview and correspondence; Marchesi, *Latin America's Radical Left*, 108–9.

103. Quiroga, *Compañeros*, 82–83; Salazar, *Conversaciones con Carlos Altamirano*, 246.

104. Fermandois, *La revolución inconclusa*, 595–96, 652–58, 721–24.

105. Ruben, interview; Salazar, *Conversaciones con Carlos Altamirano*, 287. On the MIR's opposition, see Pascal Allende, "El MIR, 35 años (Parte 3)."

106. For a full discussion of Allende's trip, see Harmer, *Allende's Chile*, 192–202.

107. See, for example, "Informe sobre la situación chilena elaborado por el Instituto de América Latina de la Academia de Cincias de la URSS," ca. July 1972, in Ulianova and Fediakova, "Chile en los archivos de la URSS," 424–44.

108. Tati to Querida Tenchita, 2 May 1977, Fondo Tencha 2/2/AFSA.

109. Fidel Castro, 13 December 1972, published as "Castro, Allende Exchange Speeches," CSD.

110. See Harmer, *Allende's Chile*, 141–42, 200.

111. Castro to Allende, 2 February 1972, in Castro, "Salvador Allende, un ejemplo que perdura."

112. Castro to Allende, 6 September 1972, in Castro, "Salvador Allende, un ejemplo que perdura."

113. Memorandum of conversation, Luis Fernández Oña and Salvador Allende, as summarized in Oña, interview, 29 April 2011.

114. Oña, interview, 29 April 2011.

115. Espejo, interview, 18 April 2010. No record of these documents has surfaced.

116. Loveman, *Chile*, 250; Navia and Osorio, "'Make the Economy Scream'?"

117. Azócar, *Lorca*, 97.

118. Arrate and Rojas, *Memoria (II)*, 115; Quiroga, *Compañeros*, 138.

119. Arrate and Rojas, *Memoria (II)*, 114.

120. Angell, "Social Class and Political Mobilisation," 17–18.

121. Arrate and Rojas, *Memoria (II)*, 118–19.

122. Fermandois, *La revolución inconclusa*, 665–68.

123. Quiroga, *Compañeros*, 99; Pascal Allende, "El MIR, 35 años (Parte 4)"; Schlotterbeck, *Beyond the Vanguard*, 156–57.

124. Quiroga, *Compañeros*, 94–96.

125. Fermandois, *La revolución inconclusa*, 708; Quiroga, *Compañeros*, 97–98, 102, 122, 134; *La Prensa*, 5 August 1973, *Las Noticias de Última Hora*, 9 July 1973 and 5 September 1973, *El Siglo*, 31 August 1973, all in González and Fontaine, *Mil días (I)*, 747–48, 768–69, 810.

126. Loveman, *Chile*, 256.

127. *El Siglo*, 2 September 1973, in González and Fontaine, *Míl días (I)*, 823.

128. Quiroga, *Compañeros*, 91, 138; Arrate and Rojas, *Memoria (II)*, 139.

129. Quiroga, *Compañeros*, 98.

130. Labarca, *Allende*, 350–51.

131. Transcript, Cuban embassy staff, Raúl Castro, Buro Político et al., 13 September 1973, anonymous private collection, Havana (hereafter Transcript, 13 September 1973).

132. Arrate and Rojas, *Memoria (II)*, 125; Soto, *Último día*, 31.

133. Quiroga, *Compañeros*, 103.

134. Núñez, Abra, Escobedo, and Claval, *Ricardo Núñez*, 119.

135. See, for example, *El Mercurio*, 11 July 1973, in González and Fontaine, *Míl días (I)*, 749–50.

136. "Discurso del Secretario General del Partido Socialista, Carlos Altamirano," 9 September 1973, in González and Fontaine, *Míl días (II)*, 1276–81.

137. Quiroga, *Compañeros*, 105.

138. Gómez, correspondence, September–October 2016 and 18 January 2017.

139. Quiroga, *Compañeros*, 88–89, 90–91.

140. Quiroga, *Compañeros*, 76, 136; Transcript, 13 September 1973.

141. Fermandois, *La revolución inconclusa*, 727; Labarca, *Allende*, 388n22.

142. Colonel Manuel Díaz Escobar Figueroa, Oficina del Agregado Militar y Aereo, Mexican Embassy, Santiago, 31 October 1973, III-6009-1(4a)/AHGE/SRE.

143. Quiroga, *Compañeros*, 251.

144. Barreiro, interview and correspondence.

145. Quiroga, *Compañeros*, 103, 131.

146. Oña, interview, 16 December 2004.

147. Marchesi, *Latin America's Radical Left*, 110; Barreiro, interview and correspondence.

148. Del Pozo, *Rebeldes, Reformistas y Revolucionarios*, 263.

149. Fermandois, *La revolución inconclusa*, 727.

150. Oña, interview, 6 April 2010.

151. Espejo, interview, 31 March 2010.

152. Soto, *Último día*, 74.

153. Gálvez, with Parrau, interview.

154. Oña, interview, 9 April 2010.

155. Transcript, 13 September 1973.

156. Oña, interview, 9 April 2010.

157. Ruben, interview; Figueroa Clark, *Allende*, 121.

158. Figueroa Clark, *Allende*, 120, 125.

159. Ruben, interview.

160. Labarca, *Allende*, 371–72.

161. Oña, interview, 29 April 2011.

162. Gálvez, with Parrau, interview.

163. Labarca, *Allende*, 389, 423.

164. Oña, interview, 9 April 2010; Conversations with Oña, March–April 2010.

165. Gálvez, with Parrau, interview; Oña, interview, 9 April 2010.

166. Espejo, interview, 31 March 2010.

167. Roció Montes, "El yerno de Allende que se convirtió en ermitaño," *La Tercera*, 22 September 2012.

168. Huerta and Chávez, *El trabajo*, 120–21; Labarca, *Allende*, 330; Huerta, with Oña, interview, 23 March 2010; Huerta, interview, 20 April 2010.

169. Labarca, *Allende*, 311, 337–47; Gaitán, *Compañero Presidente*.

170. Letter, Gloria to her mother, 7 July 1973, as cited in Labarca, *Allende*, 362–63, and Labarca, *Allende*, 364.

171. Espejo, interview, 18 April 2010.

172. *La Segunda*, 5 September 1973 and 8 September 1973, in González and Fontaine, *Míl días*, 865–66, 901–4.

173. Labarca, *Allende*, 377–79; Soto, *Último día*, 64–65; Garcés, *Allende y la experiencia chilena*, 374.

174. Oña, interview, 9 April 2010; Espejo, interviews, 31 March and 18 April 2010; Gálvez, with Parrau, interview; "Carta de la Payita."

175. Beatriz quoted in López, "Ubicar urgente a Señora Hortensia."

176. Oña, interview, 9 April 2010; Modak, interview; Labarca, *Allende*, 390.

177. López, "Ubicar urgente a Señora Hortensia."

178. Quiroga, *Compañeros*, 190–91; Soto, *Último día*, 68; Labarca, *Allende*, 383, 386.

179. Transcript, 13 September 1973.

180. Allende, "Últimas palabras," 11 September 1973, Archivo Salvador Allende Gossens.

181. Labarca, *Allende*, 395–96; Quiroga, *Compañeros*, 188; Soto, *Último día*, 67–85; Huerta and Chávez, *Trabajo*, 125–26.
182. Soto, *Último día*, 73.
183. Soto, 73; Labarca, *Allende*, 398.
184. Echeverría and Catillo, *Santiago-París*, 152–53.
185. Transcript, 13 September 1973; Oña, interview, 9 April 2010.
186. Transcript, 13 September 1973.
187. Beatriz quoted in López, "Ubicar urgente a Señora Hortensia."
188. Modak, interview; Transcript, 13 September 1973; Soto, *Último día*, 84; Labarca, *Allende*, 398–99.
189. Modak, interview; Labarca, *Allende*, 400.
190. Beatriz quoted in López, "Ubicar urgente a Señora Hortensia."
191. Modak, interview; Labarca, *Allende*, 400. It is unclear why Verónica and Cecilia did not leave with them.
192. Quiroga, *Compañeros*, 150–53.
193. Transcript, 13 September 1973.
194. Modak, interview.
195. Jerez, *Ilusiones y quebrantos*, 346.
196. Modak interview; Oña, interview, 29 April 2011.
197. Modak, interview; Oña, interview, 29 April 2011, and 9 April 2010; Transcript, 13 September 1973.
198. Transcript, 13 September 1973.
199. Transcript, 13 September 1973; Oña, interview, 9 April 2010.
200. Transcript, 13 September 1973.
201. Transcript, 13 September 1973.
202. Transcript, 13 September 1973; Oña, interview, 9 April 2010.
203. Transcript, 13 September 1973.
204. Tencha to Tati, 12 September 1973, Cartas/AFSA.
205. "Carta de la Payita"; Modak, interview.
206. Transcript, 13 September 1973.
207. Espejo, interview, 31 March 2010.
208. López, "Ubicar urgente a Señora Hortensia."
209. Transcript, 13 September 1973.
210. Huerta, with Oña, interview, 23 March 2010.
211. Allende Bussi, "Mi padre."
212. Gómez, correspondence, September–October 2016.

Chapter 9

1. Transcript, Cuban embassy staff, Raúl Castro, Buro Político et al., 13 September 1973, anonymous private collection, Havana (hereafter Transcript, 13 September 1973); de la Guardia, interview; Oña, interview, 9 April 2010.
2. Espejo, interview, 31 March 2010.
3. Wright and Oñate, "Chilean Political Exile," 145.
4. Allende Bussi, "Entrevista en exclusiva con Beatriz Allende."
5. Dorfman, *Feeding on Dreams*, 65–66.
6. Jirón, "Homenaje" (2006), AFSA.
7. Hernán [Sandoval] to Tati, 7 November 1973, ABA.
8. *Bohemia*, 21 September 1973.
9. Transcript, 13 September 1973.

10. Oña, interview, 9 April 2010.
11. Oña, interview, 9 April 2010; de la Guardia, interview.
12. Oña, interview, 9 April 2010; Transcript, 13 September 1973.
13. Espejo, interview, 18 April 2010.
14. *Granma*, 19 September 1973.
15. Castro, 28 September 1973, in Timossi, *Grandes Alamedas*, 166–69.
16. Fingland, British Embassy, Havana, to Hunter, Latin America Department, FCO, 11 October 1973, FCO 7/2465/TNA.
17. Pérez, *To Die in Cuba*, 339, 350–51.
18. Carlos [Rafael Rodríguez] to Tati, 17 September 1973, CDC-0001/AFSA.
19. This image was extensively used for the coup's first anniversary. See, for example, *Granma*, 4 September 1974.
20. Espejo, interview, 18 April 2010.
21. Castro, 28 September 1973, in Timossi, *Grandes alamedas*, 182–84; Marín, "'Eladio,' el escolta de Allende"; Quiroga, *Compañeros*, 207.
22. Embamex to Relaciones, 16 September 1973, III/6015-2(1a)/AHGE/SRE. See also Quiroga, *Compañeros*, 216–17.
23. Espejo, interview, 18 April 2010.
24. Memorandum, la Barreda Morenao, Director Federal de Seguridad, 16 September 1973, "Hortensia Bussi de Allende (1)," VP/IPS/DFS/AGN.
25. See "Estado de Puebla," DFS-11-IX-73; "Estado de Yucatan," DFS-12-IX-73; "Estado de Michoacan," DFS-15-IX-73, all in "Salvador Allende," VP/IPS/DFS/AGN; "Amembassy Mexico to Secstate," 18 September 1973, CFP/DOS; and *Granma*, 13 September 1973.
26. "Lista de personas que salieron en el avión numero dos con destino a México, el día 19 de septiembre 73"; "Relación de personas que salen en el avión no. 3 con destino a México, el día 20 de septiembre de 1973"; "Relación de las personas que viajan en el avión no. 4 con destino a México D.F. el día 25 de septiembre de 1973"; DelegaMex New York to SRE, 28 September 1973, all in III-6015-2(1a)/AHGE/SRE.
27. Rojas, "El exilio político chileno," 102.
28. Oña, interview, 9 April 2010; Labarca, *Allende*, 415–16.
29. "Cubana de Aviación," 24 September 1973, "Hortensia Bussi de Allende," VP/IPS/DFS/AGN. The same file shows she returned to Mexico on 1 October 1973; *Bohemia*, 28 September 1973.
30. Maldonado, EmbaMex, Havana, to Relaciones Exteriores, 29 September 1973, III-3213-2/AHGE/SRE.
31. Heitman, EmbaChile, Washington, D.C., to Señor Ministro, 16 November 1973, Vol: 169, EEUU/Oficios Conf./R/AMRE.
32. On Hortensia's prominence and significance worldwide, see Kelly, *Sovereign Emergencies*, 95, 102–3, 151–53.
33. Fernández Fredes, interview.
34. Tencha to Tati, 12 September 1973, CDC-0011/AFSA.
35. *El Comercio*, 21 September 1973, III-6008-1(2a)/AHGE/SRE; Memorandum, la Barreda Morenao, 16 September 1973; Labarca, *Allende*, 454–55.
36. Beatriz, 28 September 1973, in Timossi, *Grandes alamedas*, 48.
37. Oña, interview, 9 April 2010.
38. Beatriz, 28 September 1973, in Timossi, *Grandes alamedas*, 49, 54, 60.
39. Tati to Tío Ramón [Huidobro], 18 September 1973, AFSA.
40. "Homenaje a Salvador Allende y al pueblo chileno (1973)."

41. Lorca Robles, interview.
42. Fernández Fredes, interview.
43. Fernández Fredes, interview.
44. Hernán to Tati, 7 November 1973.
45. Fernández Fredes, interview.
46. Oña, interview, 6 April 2010; Espejo, interview, 18 April 2010.
47. Letter, Tati to Pillayo [Gerardo Vidaurre], 30 August 1974, ABA; "Materia: Pauta de Acción del Comité para los Meses Futuros," enclosure, Fernández to Compañero Arturo Espinoza, Instituto Cubano de Amistad con los Pueblos, 11 March 1975, CMSA; Intelligence Memorandum, CIA, "Anti-Junta Activity Outside Chile," 14 August 1974, Central Intelligence Agency Records Search Tool, National Archives and Records Administration, United States.
48. Estrada, interview, 19 April 2011.
49. Tati to Pillayo, 30 August 1974.
50. Fernández Fredes, interview.
51. "Notes: Chile Solidarity Committee with the Anti-fascist Resistance," 18 December 1973, TAM.132/box 35/folder 47/TL; Tati to Pillayo, 30 August 1974.
52. Arrate and Rojas, *Memoria (II)*, 176, 191, 212, 258–59, 261; Berguño, Emba-Chile, Paris, to Señor Ministro, "Anuncio de la llegada de Carlos Altamirano a La Habana," 7 January 1974, Vol. 80, Francia/Oficios Sec.-Conf.-Res./E-R/1974 (hereafter Vol. 80), AMRE.
53. Carretero, interview.
54. "Anti-Junta Activity."
55. "Estatutos del Comité Chileno de Solidaridad con la Resistencia Antifascista," no date, CMSA.
56. "Declaración de la Izquierda Chilena," 12 February 1974, *Casa*, March 1974.
57. "Decisiones du Bureau du Comité reuni le 4 decembre a 14 H 30," as cited in Durán, EmbaChile, Paris, to Señor Ministro, 22 March 1974, Vol. 80/AMRE; Arrate, interview; Brown, "Meeting in Cuba with Beatriz Allende and other rep's [*sic*] of UP [Unidad Popular] resistance outside Chile," 14 May 1974, TAM.132/box 35/folder 47/TL; Margarita [Tati] to Laura Allende, 11 March 1975, ABA.
58. Brown, "Meeting in Cuba."
59. "Anti-Junta Activity."
60. Margarita to Laura Allende, 11 March 1975; Tati to Pedro, 23 October 1974; Tati to Lino, 11 March 1975; Tati to Carlos Altamirano, 21 July 1975 and 6 November 1975, ABA.
61. Margarita to Laura Allende, 11 March 1975; Tati to Carlos Altamirano, 21 July 1975; Tati to compañeros, Oficina de Roma, 24 February 1976; Tati to Carlos Altamirano, 4 October 1977, ABA.
62. Tati to Pedro [Vuskovic], 1 September 1974, ABA.
63. "Anti-Junta Activity"; Ulianova, "La nueva inserción internacional." On Czechoslovakian intelligence services providing documentation, see also Zourek, *Checoslovaquia y el Cono Sur*, 272.
64. "Anti-Junta Activity." On money being sent via Peru, see Maria Elena to Tati, 13 February 1974, ABA.
65. Echeverría and Castillo, *Santiago-París*, 164.
66. Tati to Pedro, 17 November 1974, ABA.
67. "Anti-Junta Activity."
68. "AmEmbassy, Rome, to SecState," 30 October 1973, CFP/DOS.

69. Zourek, *Checoslovaquia y el Cono Sur*, 265–75.
70. Tati to Altamirano, 15 January 1974, ABA.
71. Espejo, interview, 31 March 2010.
72. Espejo, interview, 18 April 2010.
73. Transcript, 13 September 1973; Espejo, interview, 18 April 2010.
74. "Carta a Taty," January 1974, CDC-0002/AFSA.
75. Espejo, interview, 31 March 2010.
76. Tati to Pillayo, 30 August 1974.
77. Peña and Funke, interview; Ipinza, interview.
78. Guiloff, interview.
79. Cueto and Palmer, *Medicine and Public*, 203; Peña and Funke, interview.
80. "Represión contra los médicos," April 1975; "Notes: Chile Solidarity Committee."
81. Hite, *When the Romance Ended*, 40–41; Roberts, *Deepening Democracy?*, 94; del Pozo, *Allende*, 18–19.
82. Daza Sepúlveda, interview.
83. Hernán to Tati, 7 November 1973.
84. Tambutti Allende, *Allende, mi abuelo*.
85. Carter, interview.
86. María Elena Carrera as quoted in Wright and Oñate, *Flight from Chile*, 159.
87. "Notes: Chile Solidarity Committee." On the Izquierda Chilena's efforts to give direction to campaigns, see also "Carta circular a los comités y organizaciones de solidaridad con Chile," May 1974, Chile Solidarity Campaign/1/1/LHA/PHM.
88. Rioseco, EmbaChile, Stockholm, to Señor Ministro, "Remite recortes de prensa," 28 December 1973, Suecia/Oficios Ord.-Conf./1973/AMRE; "Anti-Junta Activity"; "Enérgica Protesta de Chile," *El Mercurio*, 20 December 1973.
89. Arrate, interview.
90. Arrate, interview; "Declaración de la Izquierda Chilena," 12 February 1974.
91. Hernán to Tati, 7 November 1973.
92. Allende Bussi, "Entrevista en exclusiva con Beatriz Allende."
93. Oña, interview, 29 April 2011.
94. Berguño, EmbaChile, Paris, to Señor Ministro, "Anuncio de la llegada de Carlos Altamirano a La Habana."
95. Informe 223/74, CIEX, "Propaganda comunista contra o Chile. 'Libro Negro.' Beatriz Allende," 18 April 1974; Informe 519/74, CIEX, "Actividades de Hortensia Bussi de Allende," 6 November 1974, Fundo CEMVDHC, Comissão Estadual da Memória e Verdade Dom Helder Câmara, Brazil.
96. "Conferencia de prensa de la Sra. Hortensia Bussi Vda. De Allende," 11 November 1973; Drapa, Deputy Director General (Ops.) Security Service [Canada] to de Barrera Moreno, 25 February 1974, "Hortensia Bussi de Allende," VP/IPS/DFS/AGN.
97. "Memorandum," enclosure, Besa, Director General, Ministerio de Relaciones Exteriores to Encargado de Negocios de Chile, 7 March 1974, Suecia/Oficios., Tel., Aerog./E-R/1974/AMRE.
98. Durán, EmbaChile, Paris, to Señor Ministro, 12 July 1974, Vol. 80/AMRE.
99. See, for example, Durán, EmbaChile, Paris, to Señor Ministro, 11 July 1974, Vol. 80/AMRE.
100. Rioseco to Señor Ministro, 28 December 1973, Suecia/Oficios Ord.-Conf.-Aerogramas.-Telex/1973/AMRE.
101. Memorandum Confidencial de la Cancilleria Chilena (Distributed by Centro

de Informaciones—Comité Chileno de Solidaridad con la Resistencia Antifascista), 9 December 1974, FOL/5/3/2/AN.

102. Durán to Señor Ministro, 17 October 1974, Vol. 80/AMRE.

103. See, for example, Pedro Vuskovic to Tati, 11 May 1974, ABA.

104. "Memo from Carolyn Dietchman to Beatriz et al.," 5 August 1974, FOL/9/17/2/AN.

105. Brown, "Meeting in Cuba."

106. *Granma*, 6 September 1973, 10 September 1973.

107. Echeverría and Castillo, *Santiago-París*, 186–87; Tati to Jorge Arrate, 11 and 26 October 1974, ABA.

108. "3219 (XXIX). Protection of Human Rights in Chile," 6 November 1974, United Nations: Documents.

109. Beatriz, "Información" and "Informe de Alarcón respecto a la resolución aprobada en la ONU con relación a Chile," 26 October 1974, ABA.

110. Beatriz to Jorge [Arrate], 26 October 1974, ABA.

111. Tati to Ricardo [Alarcón], 3 December 1974, ABA.

112. Tati to Pillayo, 30 August 1974.

113. Michael Dover, National Coordinating Centre for Solidarity with Chile, U.S., to Jose Velasquez, Izquierda Chilena, Committee for Mexico, 25 July 1974, TAM.132/box 40/folder 3/TL.

114. María Elena to Tati, 25 October 1973, ABA.

115. Guaraní to Tati, 30 August 1974, ABA. On the significance placed on solidarity by the PS's leadership in Chile, see also PS Central Committee, "Documento de Marzo."

116. "Carta a Taty," January 1974.

117. Tupper, *Historias de clandestinidad*, 30–31.

118. "Memorandum, Gespräch Erich Honecker mit Orlando Millas, am 10.10.1974," DY30/IV/B2/20/102/Bundesarchiv.

119. Power, "The US Movement in Solidarity with Chile," 47.

120. See, for example, "Declaración de la Izquierda Chilena," 12 February 1974.

121. Allende Bussi, "Entrevista en exclusiva con Beatriz Allende."

122. Numbers of Chilean exiles range from 1,300 to 1,400 for mid-1974. See Brown, "Meeting in Cuba," and Tati to Pillayo, 30 August 1974. In 1975, the Cubans referred to "more than 1,500" Chilean exiles on the island. See "Amembassy, Caracas, to SecState," 23 October 1975, CFP/DOS. Casa de Chile documents refer to 2,000 exiles in Cuba; see Rojas, "El exilio político chileno," 58.

123. Pancho to Guillermo Perez, San Jose, 6 February 1975, CMSA; "Notes: Chile Solidarity Committee."

124. "Fidel Castro Addresses Cuban Workers Congress," 16 November 1973, CSD; French, British Embassy, Havana, to Douglas-Home, 28 November 1973, FCO 7/2465/TNA.

125. Maldonado, EmbaMex, Havana to Relaciones Exteriores, 23 November 1973, III-3213-2/AHGE/SRE.

126. Daza Sepúlveda, interview.

127. Fernández Fredes, interview.

128. Torres, interview.

129. San Martín González, correspondence. See also Guzmán, *Telón de azucar*.

130. "Anti-Junta Activity."

131. Espejo, interview, 18 April 2010; San Martín González, correspondence; Arrate, interview; Tati to Pillayo, 30 August 1974.

132. Fernández Fredes, interview.
133. Cabieses, interview.
134. Fernández Fredes, interview.
135. "Anti-Junta Activity."
136. Estrada, interview, 19 April 2011; Carretero, interview.
137. Fernández Fredes, interview.
138. Soto, interview.
139. Torres, interview.
140. Fernández Fredes, interview.
141. San Martín González, correspondence. On Alamar, see Randall, *No se puede*, 120–21.
142. Fernández Fredes, interview.
143. San Martín González, correspondence.
144. Espejo, interview, 18 April 2010.
145. Oña, interview, 29 April 2011.
146. Espejo, interview, 18 April 2010.
147. Oña, interview, 29 April 2011; Guerra, with Oña, interview.
148. Roció Montes, "El yerno de Allende que se convirtió en ermitaño," *La Tercera*, 22 September 2012.
149. San Martín González, correspondence; Ruben, interview.
150. Oña, interview, 6 April 2010.
151. Carmen Castillo, "Prólogo," in Álvarez, *Tati*, 14.
152. María Elena to Tati, 13 February 1974, ABA.
153. Tati to Jaime, 2 July 1975, ABA.
154. Pillayo to Tati, 11 June 1974, ABA.
155. Tati to Ricardo [Alarcón], 22 October 1974, ABA.
156. Castillo, "Prólogo," 14.
157. Echeverría and Castillo, *Santiago-París*, 186–87.
158. Tati to Ricardo, 22 October 1974; Hart Daválos, *Homenaje a Miguel Enríquez*, 1, 16, 18.
159. "A los pueblos de América Latina. Declaración conjunta (MLN, ERP, ELN, MIR)," CeDInCI.
160. Jorge to Tati, "Informe sobre situación producida en la oficina de Roma," 4 December 1974, ABA.

Chapter 10

1. Tati to Carlos and Tati to Carlos Altamirano, 5 August 1975; Flyer, "Fondos para un Chile Libre," no date, ABA.
2. Tati to Carlos Altamirano, 6 November 1975, ABA.
3. Tati to Compañeros, Oficina Roma, 24 February 1976, ABA.
4. Tati to Carlos, 1 March, 1976, ABA.
5. Hernán del Canto to Tati, no date [ca. November 1975], ABA.
6. Tati to Danilo, 31 March 1976, ABA. Emphasis in original.
7. Tati to Lucho, 1 July 1977, ABA.
8. Orlando to Tati, 23 October 1975, CDC-0004/AFSA.
9. "Declaración de los partidos que integran la Unidad Popular y el Movimiento de Izquierda Revolucionaria," 23 December 1973, in *Casa*, March 1974.
10. "Sintesis de la situación de los Derechos Humanos en Chile," May 1975, FOL/4/9/1/AN.

11. Ingersoll to SecState, 10 July 1975, CFP/DOS.
12. Exequiel Ponce, as quoted by Máximo Pacheco Matte, in Arrate and Rojas, *Memoria (II)*, 227.
13. Margarita [Beatriz] to Laura, and Tati to Lino, 11 March 1975, ABA. Emphasis in original.
14. Tati to Ricardo Alarcón, 1 October 1975, ABA.
15. *Juventud Rebelde*, 15 April 1975; *Bohemia*, 25 April 1975.
16. Arrate and Rojas, *Memoria (II)*, 226–27, 248.
17. Tati to Jaime, 2 July 1975, ABA.
18. Arrate and Rojas, *Memoria (II)*, 274–75.
19. Arrate and Rojas, 274–75.
20. Furci, *Crisis of the Chilean Socialist Party*, 11.
21. Tati to Carlos Altamirano, 21 July 1975, ABA.
22. Comité Central del Partido Socialista de Chile, "Documento de Marzo."
23. "Anti-Junta Activity Outside Chile" 14 August 1974, Central Intelligence Agency Records Search Tool, National Archives and Records Administration, United States.
24. "Memorandum, Gespräch Erich Honecker mit Orlando Millas, am 10.10.1974," DY30/IV/B2/20/102/Bundesarchiv.
25. Beatriz to Gustavo Ruz, 7 April 1977, ABA.
26. Tati to Orlando, 30 December 1975, FOL/3/17/8/AN; Arrate and Rojas, *Memoria (II)*, 246.
27. "El ultraizquierdismo, caballo de Troya del imperialismo" (1975) as quoted in Arrate and Rojas, *Memoria (II)*, 234–35.
28. Edgardo Condeza to Tati, 9 December 1975; Beatriz Allende to Adonis Sepúlveda, 3 January 1976, ABA.
29. Orlando to Tati, 7 October 1975, CDC-0010/AFSA.
30. Tati to Edgardo, February 1976, ABA.
31. For discussion of previous pleas, see Tati to Cloro, 26 October 1976, ABA.
32. "Mensaje de Benjamin [Andrés Pascal Allende] a Prima," 23 December 1974, CDC-0038/AFSA.
33. "A los pueblos de América Latina: Declaración conjunta (MLN, ERP, ELN, MIR)," no date, CeDInCI.
34. Orlando to Tati, 7 October 1975.
35. Félix Luna Mederos (Partido Comunista de Cuba) to Beatriz Allende, 17 February 1976, ABA.
36. Cloro to Tati, 12 October 1975, ABA.
37. Tati to Jaime, 12 May 1975, and Jaime to Taty, 31 May 1975, ABA.
38. "Comisión organizadora del movimiento mexicano por la paz y la coordinación de agrupaciones e instituciones progresistas," 29 June 1975, "Laura Allende Gossens," VP/IPS/DFS/AGN.
39. "Informe para las delegadas al evento propiciado por las Naciones Unidas en el año internacional de la mujer," June 1975, FOL/3/11/11/AN.
40. "Informe de la delegación de la Unidad Popular que concurrió a la reunión del buro de coordinación, a nivel de ministros de estados del Movimiento de Los Países No Alineados: Argelia, 30 de mayo–2 de junio de 1976," FOL/3/13/16/AN.
41. "La resistencia popular vencerá," Havana, 15 June 1975, TAM.132/box 34/folder 47/TL.
42. Tati to Cloro, 10 June 1976, ABA.
43. Tati to Marta Mele (Caracas), 5 July 1976, ABA.

44. Tati to Lucho, 13 March 1977, ABA.
45. Convenio, Casa de Chile de Mexico and Comite, 11 February 1975, CMSA; Beatriz to Compañeros, Chile Solidarity Campaign, 16 December 1976, Chile Solidarity Campaign/30/2/LHA/PHM.
46. Tati to Danilo and Isabel, 7 April 1976, CCA; Tati to Jaime, 15 April 1976, ABA.
47. Tati to Danilo, 31 March 1976, ABA. Emphasis in original.
48. Tati to Orlando, 11 June 1975, FOL/9/16/27/AN. On plans to publish an English version of the bulletin in Canada, see Tati to Lucho, 13 March 1977, ABA.
49. Tati to Danilo and Isabel, 15 April 1976, CCA.
50. Tati to Danilo and Isabel, 7 April 1976.
51. Sergio Barría Pérez to Tati, 16 February 1976, ABA.
52. Arrate and Rojas, *Memoria (II)*, 237–38.
53. Dinges, *Condor Years*, 145–47.
54. Dinges, 143.
55. Dinges, 10–17.
56. Contreras quoted in Dinges, 12.
57. Dinges, 15.
58. Tati to Lucho, 23 February 1977, ABA.
59. Orlando to Tati, 7 October 1975.
60. Tati to Cloro, 26 October 1977, ABA.
61. Espejo, interview, 18 April 2010.
62. Collier and Sater, *Chile*, 360.
63. Benado, interview; Arrate and Rojas, *Memoria (II)*, 226–7; Núñez, Abra, Escobedo, and Claval, *Ricardo Núñez*, 172.
64. Durán, EmbaChile, Paris, to Señor Ministro, 22 March 1974, Vol. 80, Francia/Oficios Sec.-Conf.-Res./E-R/1974, AMRE.
65. "Anti-Junta Activity."
66. For example, see "Información acerca de chilenos asilados en México," 2 July 1975, "Laura Allende Gossens," and "Actividades de la Sra. Hortensia Bussi Vda. de Allende," 25 and 30 December 1974, "Hortensia Bussi de Allende," VP/IPS/DFS/AGN.
67. Tati to Lucho, 23 February 1977, ABA.
68. Tati to Carlos Antonio, 3 and 24 March 1977, ABA.
69. Tati to Carlos Antonio, 8 March 1977, ABA.
70. Tati to Lucho, 17 February 1977, ABA; Yankelevich, *México, país refugio*, 275n42.
71. Juan Gabriel to Tati, 25 November 1976, ABA.
72. Juan Gabriel to Tati, 14 December 1976, and Tati to Lucho, 23 February 1977, ABA; *Washington Post*, 20 December 1976.
73. *Democrat and Chronicle* (Rochester, NY) 16 February 1977; *Washington Post*, 17 February 1977.
74. Ingersoll to SecState, 10 July 1975.
75. *El Mercurio*, 10 March 1977.
76. See, for example, Tati to Jorge, 26 October 1974; Tati to Carlos Antonio, 8 March 1977, ABA; and Orlando to Tati, 29 March 1977, FOL/12/2/24/AN.
77. Tati to Carlos Antonio, 8 March 1977.
78. Tati to Moi, 25 November 1976, ABA.
79. Almeyda to Tati, 16 November 1976, ABA.
80. Tati to Lucho, 17 February 1977.
81. Beatriz to Alejandro [Witker], 11 March 1977; Beatriz to Osvaldo Puccio, 11 May 1977; Tati to Pedro Vuskovic, 23 October 1974, all in ABA.

82. Tati to Carlos Antonio, 10 June 1977, ABA.
83. Moyn, *Last Utopia*.
84. Oña, interview, 9 April 2010.
85. Kirk, "Normalization of Sexual Diversity," 34–36; Lumsden, *Machos, Maricones, and Gays*, 57–59, 65–69.
86. Kirk, "Normalization of Sexual Diversity," 34–36; Smith and Padula, *Sex and Revolution*, 170.
87. Huerta and Chávez, *El trabajo*, 134.
88. Kirk, "Normalization of Sexual Diversity," 32–34, 41–44; Lumsden, *Machos, Maricones, and Gays*, 73–74.
89. Kirk, "Normalization of Sexual Diversity," 32.
90. Smith and Padula, *Sex and Revolution*, 173.
91. Espejo, interview, 18 April 2010.
92. On Chilean homophobia in the 1960s and 1970s, particularly on the left, see Contardo, *Raro*, 253–394; Barr-Melej, *Psychedelic Chile*, 83–84; and Hugo Robles, "History in the Making," 36–44.
93. Sandoval, interview, 23 July 2010.
94. Tati to Carlos Antonio, 24 March 1977. Emphasis in original.
95. Beatriz to Osvaldo Puccio, 11 May 1977.
96. Conversations with Oña, March–April 2010.
97. Fernández Allende, correspondence.
98. On exiles, see Lecourt-Kendall, "Relaciones de genero," 120.
99. Conversations with Oña; Oña, interview, 9 April 2010.
100. Fernández Fredes, interview; Tati to Lucho, 13 March 1977.
101. Randall, *No se puede*, 131–36.
102. Randall, 154.
103. Smith and Padula, *Sex and Revolution*, 147, 158.
104. Fernández Allende, correspondence; Álvarez, *Tati*, 207.
105. Randall, *No se puede*, 153.
106. *Bohemia*, 14 March 1975.
107. Tati to Carlos Antonio, 8 March 1977.
108. Guerra, with Oña, interview.
109. Benado, interview.
110. Tati to Jorge Arrate, 11 October 1974; Tati to Antonio, 27 May 1977; Tencha to Tati, 10 June 1977; Tati to Danilo, 31 March 1976, ABA.
111. Tati to Carlos Antonio, 8 March 1977.
112. Antonio Carvallo to Tati, 20 April 1977; Tati to Carlos Antonio, 11 May 1977; Beatriz to Osvaldo Puccio, 11 May 1977, ABA.
113. Tati to Carlos Antonio, 10 June 1977.
114. Fernández Fredes, interview.
115. Gálvez, with Parrau, interview.
116. Beatriz to Osvaldo and Miriam, 27 September 1977, ABA.
117. Conversations with Oña.
118. Tati to Carlos Antonio, 1977, ABA.
119. Tati to Carlos Antonio, 24 March 1977.
120. Tati to Lucho, 1 July 1977.
121. Jaramillo, correspondence; Gálvez, with Parrau, interview.
122. Fernández, interview.
123. Espejo, interview, 18 April 2010.

124. Vásquez-Bronfman and Araújo, *La maldición de Ulises*, 23–24.

125. Espejo, interview, 18 April 2010.

126. *Granma*, 9 September 1977; "Manifestaciones de apoyo a Chile," *Granma*, 12 September 1977.

127. *Granma*, 9 September 1977.

128. Daza Sepúlveda, interview.

129. Tati to Lucho, 22 February 1977, ABA; López, "Ubicar urgente a Señora Hortensia."

130. Tati to Lucho, 13 March 1977.

131. Tati to Lucho, 1 July 1977.

132. Beatriz to Jaimito, 1 July 1977, ABA.

133. Arrate and Rojas, *Memoria (II)*, 238–39.

134. Ricardo Alvarado to Beatriz, 30 August 1976; Tati to Estimado compañero, 1 October 1976, ABA.

135. Clodomiro Almeyda to Orlando, 10 August 1976, FOL/12/2/22/AN.

136. Rolando Calderón to Tati, 10 August 1976, ABA.

137. Partido Socialista de Chile, "Planteamientos del Secretario General Sobre Cuestiones Primordiales de Definición Política y orgánica," September 1976, ABA; Arrate and Rojas, *Memoria (II)*, 245, 250–52, 284–88.

138. Tati to Moi, 25 November 1976.

139. Tati to Lucho, 17 February and 13 March 1977; Tati to Carlos Antonio, 8 March 1977, ABA.

140. Tati to Lucho, 18 August 1977, ABA; Fernández Fredes, interview.

141. Tati to Carlos Altamirano, 4 October 1977, ABA.

142. Alejandro Rojas in Brodsky, *Conversaciones con la FECH*, 155.

143. Benado, interview.

144. "Memorandum, Gespräch Hermann Axen mit Anselmo Sule am 6. September 1977," DY30/IV/B2/20/102/Bundesarchiv.

145. Arrate and Rojas, *Memoria (II)*, 252–53; Collier and Sater, *Chile*, 364.

146. Coloma, interview; Benado, interview; Modak, interview.

147. Daza Sepúlveda, interview; Pascal Allende, interview; Ulloa, interview.

148. Ulloa, interview.

149. Espejo, interview, 18 April 2010.

150. Carretero, interview.

151. Sandoval, interview, 23 July 2015.

152. Estrada, interview, 19 April 2011; de la Guardia, interview; Ruben, interview.

153. Estrada, interview, 19 April 2011.

154. Ruben, interview.

155. Arrate and Rojas, *Memoria (II)*, 279.

156. Huerta, with Oña, interview, 23 March 2010.

157. Tencha to Tati, 10 June 1977, ABA.

158. Espejo, interview, 18 April 2010.

159. Modak, interview.

160. Jirón, correspondence.

161. Espejo, interview, 18 April 2010.

162. Estrada, interview, 19 April 2011.

163. Daza Sepúlveda, interview.

164. Oña, interview, 9 April 2010.

165. Tati to Carlos Altamirano, 4 October 1977.

166. Beatriz to Dr. Pérez Carballas, 4 October 1977, ABA.
167. Daza Sepúlveda, interview.
168. Beatriz to Osvaldo and Miriam, 27 September 1977.
169. Carretero, interview.
170. Oña, interview, 9 April 2010; Fernández Allende, correspondence.
171. Fernández Fredes, interview.
172. Ruben, interview.
173. Guerra, with Oña, interview.
174. Daza Sepúlveda, interview.
175. Oña, interview, 9 April 2010. On the letter's content, see also Fernández Allende, correspondence.

Onward March

1. Estrada, interview, 19 April 2011; Francisco Fernández, interview; Oña, interview, 9 April 2010; *Granma*, 11 October 1977.
2. Pérez, *To Die in Cuba*, 350–51.
3. *New York Times*, 13 October 1977.
4. *Granma*, 13 October 1977; Estrada, interview, 19 April 2011.
5. Tupper, *Historias de clandestinidad*, 14.
6. Castillo quoted in Lazzara, "Militancy Then and Now," 5.
7. *La Segunda*, 13 October 1977.
8. Maravall, *Las mujeres*, 25, 211–301; Centro Cultural por la memoria "La Monche," *Voces transgresoras*, 62–67.
9. See Zalaquett, *Chilenas en armas*; Robles, "Memorias de la clandestinidad"; Maravall, *Las mujeres*; and Tupper, *Historias de clandestinidad*.
10. Garcés, *Allende y la experiencia chilena*, 277.
11. Schlotterbeck, *Beyond the Vanguard*, 105.
12. Carmen Castillo quoted in Echeverría, *Vuelo de la memoria*, 232.
13. Collier and Sater, *Chile*, 377.
14. Garretón as quoted in Hite, *When the Romance Ended*, 41.
15. Tencha to Luis, 7 December 1983, Luis Fernández Oña private archive, Havana.
16. Espejo, interview, 18 April 2010.
17. Sandoval, interview, 23 July 2013.
18. Peña and Funke, interview.
19. Parrau, interview.
20. Vivaldi, interview.
21. Coloma, interview; Arrate, interview.
22. Moyn, *Last Utopia*, 4, 8.
23. Borstelmann, *The 1970s*; Ferguson, "Crisis, What Crisis?," 12.
24. Ferguson, "Crisis, What Crisis?," 3–8, 19–20.
25. Westad, *The Cold War*, 391; Prashad, *Darker Nations*, xviii.
26. Núñez, interview; Figueroa Clark, "Chilean Internationalism"; Cortés, *Yo Patán*.
27. Moyano, "El Golpe de Estado," 157–68; Loveman, "The Political Left in Chile," 24, 30.
28. Coloma, interview; Perry, "'With a Little Help,'" 88–89.
29. Pinto Vallejos, "¿Y la historia les dio la razón?," 186–205.
30. Loveman, "The Political Left in Chile," 27–29.
31. Roberts, *Deepening Democracy?*, 122, 125.
32. Figueroa Clark, "The Forgotten History."

33. Collier and Sater, *Chile*, 377–78.
34. Roberts, *Deepening Democracy?*, 119, 141–42.
35. Zalaquett, *Chilenas en armas*, 326. On Chile's "memory wars," see Stern, *Battling for Hearts and Minds* and *Reckoning with Pinochet*, and Weld, "Writing Political Violence."
36. Allende Bussi, "Mi padre."
37. Allende Bussi; Guevara, "Crear dos, tres … muchos Vietnam"; Labarca, *Allende*, 426.
38. Loveman, "The Political Left in Chile," 36.
39. Collier and Sater, *Chile*, 373–74.
40. Roberts, *Deepening Democracy?*, 153.
41. Roberts, 195–96; Moyano, "El Golpe de Estado," 150–74.
42. Tupper, *Historias de clandestinidad*, 15.
43. Zalaquett, *Chilenas en armas*, 326.
44. Roberts, *Deepening Democracy?*, 142.
45. Roberts, 181.
46. Beatriz Allende, interview by Regis Debray, 1974, as cited in *El Mercurio*, 14 October 1977.
47. "A un año de las tomas feministas."
48. "El ayer y hoy de la ola feminista."
49. León, "Súper lunes feminista."

Bibliography

Primary Sources
ARCHIVES
Argentina
  Centro de Documentación e Investigación de la Cultura de Izquierdas,
    Buenos Aires
Chile
  Archivo Fundación Salvador Allende, Santiago
  Archivo General Histórico, Ministerio de Relaciones Exteriores, Santiago
  Archivo Nacional, Santiago
  Biblioteca Central Luis David Cruz Ocampo, Universidad de Concepción,
    Concepción
  Biblioteca Nacional de Chile, Santiago
  Museo Nacional de Medicina, Facultad de Medicina, Universidad de Chile,
    Santiago
Cuba
  Archivo Beatriz Allende, Havana
  Casa Memorial Salvador Allende, Havana
  Luis Fernández Oña, Private Archive, Havana
  Prensa Latina
Germany
  Stifung Archiv der Parteien und Massenorganisationen der DDR im
    Bundersarchiv, Berlin
Mexico
  Archivo General de la Nación, Mexico City
  Archivo Histórico Genaro Estrada, Secretaria de Relaciones Exteriores,
    Mexico City
  Casa de Chile Archive, Private Collection
United Kingdom
  Hennessy Collection, University of Nottingham
  Labour History Archive, People's History Museum, Manchester
  National Archives, Kew
United States
  National Archives and Records Administration, College Park, Maryland
  Tamiment Library and Robert F. Wagner Labor Archives, New York University,
    New York

INTERVIEWS AND CORRESPONDENCE
All interview recordings and correspondence are in the author's possession. In cases where the person who introduced the author to an interviewee sat in on the interview, at times joining in the conversation, this is indicated as "with [individual's name]."
Carmen Paz Allende, Cecilia Viel, and Gilda Gnecco, interview, 14 April 2010 (Chile)
Jorge Arrate, interview, 15 July 2013 (Chile), and email correspondence, 15 August
  2017
Fernando Barreiro, interview, 15 January 2018 (via Skype), and email
  correspondence, January–September 2018

Edith Benado, interview, 22 October 2017 (Chile)
María Lina Boza, email correspondence, 1 September 2013
Ana María Bussi, interview, 9 April 2010 (Chile)
Felipe Cabello, interview, 20 July 2017 (via Skype)
Manuel Cabieses, interview, with Luis Fernández Oña, 25 March 2010 (Chile)
Rolando Calderón, interview, 17 October 2017 (Chile)
Juan and Nancy Carretero, interview, 18 April 2011 (Cuba)
Patricia Carter, interview, 9 July 2013 (Chile)
Hernán Coloma, interview by Javiera Soto, 28 January 2015 (Chile)
Marcela Contreras, interview, 21 August 2013 (London)
Sonia Daza Sepúlveda, interview, 18 March 2013 (Mexico City)
ELN member, off-the-record interview, 7 April 2010 (Chile)
Patricia Espejo, interview, 31 March and 18 April 2010 (Chile), and email correspondence, 3 September 2018
Ulises Estrada, interview, 13 December 2004 and 19 April 2011 (Cuba)
Alejandro Fernández Allende, email correspondence, May 2017
Francisco Fernández Fredes, interview, 8 July 2013 (Chile)
Elena Gálvez, interview, with Celsa Parrau, 8 April 2010 (Chile)
Gilda Gnecco, email correspondence, 26 October 2016
Fernando Gómez, email correspondence, September–October 2016, 18 January 2017, and 14 May 2018
Patricio de la Guardia, interview, 21 April 2011 (Cuba)
Neida Guerra, interview, with Luis Fernández Oña, 19 April 2011 (Cuba)
Roberto Guiloff, interview, 18 July 2017 (London)
Félix Huerta, interview, 23 March 2010, with Luis Fernández Oña; and 20 April 2010 (Chile)
Manuel Ipinza, interview, 22 July 2013 (Chile)
Isabel Jaramillo, interview, 24 November 2004 and 21 September 2005 (Cuba), and email correspondence, March–September 2018
Arturo Jirón, email correspondence, 30 July 2013
María Eugenia Lorca Robles, interview, 16 July 2013 (Chile)
Frida Modak, interview, 22 March 2013 (Mexico City)
Ricardo Núñez Muñoz, interview, 9 November 2017 (via Skype)
Luis Fernández Oña, interview, 9 and 16 December 2004, 3 September 2005, 15 April and 2 May 2006 (Havana), 6 and 9 April 2010 (Chile), 29 April 2011 (Havana)
Manuel Oyarzún, interview, 11 July 2013 (Chile)
Celsa Parrau, interview, 1 April 2010 (Chile)
Andrés Pascal Allende, interview, 7 April 2010 (Chile)
Jorge Peña Delgado and Silvia Funke, interview, 18 July 2013 (Chile)
Guaraní Pereda, email correspondence, 2 July 2018
Osvaldo "Chato" Peredo, interview, 7 August 2018 (via Skype)
Victor Pey, interview, 11 July 2013 (Chile)
Benny Pollack, interview, 20 September 2017 (via telephone)
Ruben, interview, 21 July 2013 (Chile)
Hernán Sandoval, interview, 15 and 23 July 2013 (Chile)
Enrique San Martín González, email correspondence, 30 August 2013
Cecilia Sepúlveda Carvajal, interview, 24 July 2013 (Chile)
Oscar Soto Guzmán, interview, 24 September 2013 (Spain)
Beatriz Torres, interview, 23 June 2016 (via Skype)

Irina Trapote, interview, 27 April 2011 (Cuba)
Marcelo Trucco, interview, 15 July 2013 (Chile)
Ariel Ulloa, interview, 19 July 2013 (Chile)
Michel Vázquez y Nelly Cubillas, interview, 11 September 2005 and 24 April 2011 (Cuba)
Luís Vera Sobrino, email correspondence, 19 July 2017
Ennio Vivaldi, interview, 24 July 2013 (Chile)

JOURNALS, MAGAZINES, AND NEWSPAPERS

Chile
- *Arauco, PS*
- *Boletín de la Universidad de Chile*
- *Boletín del Servicio Nacional de Salud*
- *Clarín*
- *Cuadernos Médico Sociales*
- *Ercilla*
- *Eva*
- *Gente Joven*
- *La Nación*
- *Las Noticias de Última Hora*
- *Paula*
- *Punto Final*
- *Renovación*
- *Revista Médica de Chile*
- *La Segunda*
- *El Siglo*
- *El Sur*
- *La Tercera*
- *Las Últimas Noticias*
- *Vea*
- *Vistazo*

Cuba
- *Bohemia*
- *Casa*
- *Granma*
- *Granma Weekly*
- *Juventud Rebelde*
- *Pensamiento Crítico*
- *Revolución*

DOCUMENTARY FILMS

Guzmán Urzúa, Camila, dir. *El telón de azúcar*. France/Cuba, 2005.
Tambutti Allende, Marcia, dir. *Allende, mi abuelo Allende*. Chile, 2015.

ONLINE SOURCES

All online sources were accessed in 2010–2019.

"Act of Bogotá," 13 September 1960. The Avalon Project. http://avalon.law.yale.edu/20th_century/intam08.asp.
"Agrupación de Médicos Generales de Zona de Chile." http://mgz.cl/quienes-somos/.
Allende Bussi, Beatriz. "Entre el MIR y Allende siempre hubo diálogo político." *Juventud Rebelde*, 1974. http://www.archivochile.com/Miguel_Enriquez/Doc_sobre_miguel/MEsobre0018.pdf.
———. "Entrevista en exclusiva con Beatriz Allende." *Exprés Español* (Frankfurt), March 1974. https://studylib.es/doc/8465754/entrevista-en-exclusiva-con-beatriz-allende-¿qué-ha-pasado.
———. "Mi Padre." *Boletín Informativo de la Juventud Socialista*, DDR, 1977. http://www.allendevive.cl/phocadownload/beatriz_padre.pdf.
Allende Gossens, Salvador. "Salvador Allende vino a Cuba a ofrecer condolencias por la muerte del Che: Entrevista de 1967." *La Fogata*. http://www.lafogata.org/chile/a13.htm.
Archivo-Chile. Centro de Estudios Miguel Enríquez (CEME). www.archivo-chile.com.

Archivo Salvador Allende Gossens. Marxists Internet Archive. https://www.marxists.org/espanol/allende/.

"A un año de las tomas feministas: ¿Cómo han avanzado las demandas de las mujeres en las universidades?" *El Desconcierto*, 17 April 2019. https://www.eldesconcierto.cl/2019/04/17/a-un-ano-de-las-tomas-feministas-como-han-avanzado-las-demandas-de-las-mujeres-en-las-universidades/.

"El ayer y hoy de la ola feminista: Alondra Carrillo y Teresa Valdés analizan el movimiento en Chile." CNN Chile, 19 March 2019. https://www.cnnchile.com/lodijeronencnn/el-ayer-y-hoy-de-la-ola-feminista-alondra-carrillo-y-teresa-valdes-analizan-el-movimiento-en-chile_20190319/.

Biblioteca Virtual Salvador Allende Gossens, https://www.facebook.com/BibliotecaSAG/.

Cabello, Felipe. "Mi recuerdo de Beatriz Allende." *Generación 1967*, 12 December 2017. https://medicina1967.blogspot.com/2017/12/felipe-cabello-mis-recuerdos-de-beatriz.html.

Carrera, María Elena. Interview by Alfonso Pérez Guíñez, Biblioteca del Congreso Nacional de Chile, 20 November 2008. https://vimeo.com/27018454.

"Carta de la Payita, Miria Contreras Bell, a Beatriz Tati Allende." *The Clinic*, 4 September 2003. https://www.facebook.com/notes/biblioteca-virtual-salvador-allende-gossens/carta-de-la-payita-miria-contreras-bell-a-beatriz-tati-allende/339944596117381/.

Castro, Fidel. "Salvador Allende, un ejemplo que perdura." *Granma*, 26 June 2008. http://www.granma.cu/granmad/secciones/ref-fidel/art25.html.

———. "The Second Declaration of Havana." 4 February 1962. http://www.walterlippmann.com/fc-02-04-1962.pdf.

Castro Speech Data Base, Latin American Network Information Center. http://lanic.utexas.edu/la/cb/cuba/castro.html.

Chile Declassification Project. Virtual Reading Room, Freedom of Information Act, U.S. Department of State. https://foia.state.gov/Search/Results.aspx?collection=CHILE&searchText=*

Comando Nacional de la Candidatura Presidencial Dr. Salvador Allende. "Programa del Gobierno Popular." No date. http://www.bcn.cl/obtienearchivo?id=documentos/10221.1/23629/1/ll_00002_Programa_Gobierno.pdf.

Comité Central del Partido Socialista de Chile. "Documento de Marzo," March 1974. http://www.blest.eu/pp/ps_mar74.html (link no longer available).

Covert Action in Chile: 1963-1973. Washington, DC: U.S. Government Printing Office, 1975. https://www.intelligence.senate.gov/sites/default/files/94chile.pdf.

"La dictadura, gran maquina del olvido, convirtió a Chile en país de la amnesia general." Carmen Castillo, diálogo con Ximena Bedregal. https://www.jornada.com.mx/1999/04/05/carmen-castillo.htm.

"Discurso pronunciado por el Comandante Fidel Castro Ruz, Primer Ministro del Gobierno Revolucionario, en el Acto de Clausura del Primer Congreso Latinoamericano de Juventudes, el 6 de Agosto de 1960." http://www.cuba.cu/gobierno/discursos/1960/esp/f060860e.html.

"Discurso pronunciado por el Comandante Fidel Castro Ruz, Primer Secretario del Comité Central del Partido Comunista de Cuba y Primer Ministro del Gobierno Revolucionario, en la Velada Solemne en Memoria del Comandante Ernesto Che Guevara, en la Plaza de la Revolución, el 18 de octubre de 1967." http://www.cuba.cu/gobierno/discursos/1967/esp/f181067e.html.

Fernández Allende, Alejandro. "Emotivo homenaje de Alejandro Fernández Allende su madre Tati Allende al presentar su libro." https://www.youtube.com/watch?v=xD1lVOLRyoU&app=desktop.

Ferrada de Noli, Marcello. "Prólogo a Orígenes del Movimiento de Izquierda Revolucionaria (MIR). La Universidad de Concepción" (2016). http://media3.libertarianbooks.se/2018/11/Origenes-del-Movimiento-de-Izquierda-Revolucionaria-MIR-Marcello-Ferrada-de-Noli.pdf.

Foreign Relations of the United States, 1969–1976. Vol. E-10, *Documents on American Republics, 1969–1972.* https://history.state.gov/historicaldocuments/frus1969-76ve10.

Foreign Relations of the United States, 1969–1976. Vol. 21, *Chile, 1969–1973.* https://history.state.gov/historicaldocuments/frus1969-76v21.

Freedom of Information Act Electronic Reading Room, Central Intelligence Agency. https://www.cia.gov/library/readingroom/.

Fundo CEMVDHC—Comissão Estadual da Memória e Verdade Dom Helder Câmara. http://200.238.112.225/index.php/comissao-da-verdade.

"Generación 1967." https://medicina1967.blogspot.com.

Guevara, Ernesto Che. "Crear dos, tres ... muchos Vietnam: Mensaje a los pueblos del mundo a través de la *Tricontinental*," 16 April 1967. https://www.marxists.org/espanol/guevara/04_67.htm.

———. "Discurso al Primer Congreso Latinoamericano de Juventudes," 28 July 1960. Archivo Chile. http://www.archivochile.com/America_latina/Doc_paises_al/Cuba/Escritos_del_Che/escritosdelche0022.PDF.

"Homenaje a Salvador Allende y al pueblo chileno (1973)." Noticero ICAIC Latinoamericano, 3 October 1973. Vimeo. https://vimeo.com/193161293 (link no longer available).

Jarpa, María José. "Los 60 años de travesía de los médicos de zona." *La Tercera*, 17 July 2015. http://www.latercera.com/noticia/los-60-anos-de-travesia-de-los-medicos-de-zona/.

León, Pilar. "Súper lunes feminista: comienza la víspera del 8M." diarioUchile, 4 March 2019. https://radio.uchile.cl/2019/03/04/super-lunes-feminista-comienza-la-vispera-del-8m/.

López, Luis Ignacio. "Ubicar urgente a Señora Hortensia de Allende. Ha Fallecido Su Hija Beatriz." *Primera Plana*, 20 October 1977. *Allende Vive*. http://allendevive.cl/phocadownload/beatriz_imagen.pdf.

Marín, Francisco. "'Eladio,' el escolta de Allende." *Proceso*, 27 June 2014. http://www.proceso.com.mx/375853/eladio-el-escolta-de-allende.

Naranjo Sandoval, Pedro. *Biografía de Miguel Enríquez E.* (1999). Centro de Estudios "Miguel Enríquez" (CEME), Archivo Chile. http://www.archivochile.com/entrada.html.

Pascal Allende, Andrés. "El MIR, 35 años." *Punto Final*, 11 August 2000. http://puntofinal.cl/000811/nactxt.html.

———. "El MIR, 35 años (Parte 2)." *La Haine*, no date. https://www.lahaine.org/internacional/historia/mir35parte2.htm.

———. "El MIR, 35 años (Parte 3)." *La Haine*, no date. https://www.lahaine.org/internacional/historia/mir35parte3.htm.

———. "El MIR, 35 años (Parte 4)." *La Haine*, 13 October 2000. https://www.lahaine.org/internacional/historia/mir35parte4.htm.

Peredo, Inti. "Volveremos a las montañas," July 1968. http://www.ruinasdigitales.com/cristianismoyrevolucion/cyrintiperedovolveremosalasmontaas99/.
Pérez Guillén, Daily. "Ernesto Che Guevara y León Felipe: Una amistad entrañable." *Juventud Rebelde*, 28 November 2015. http://www.juventudrebelde.cu/cuba/2015-11-28/ernesto-che-guevara-y-leon-felipe-una-amistad-entranable/.
"El Primer Congreso Latinoamericano de Juventudes: Entrevista a Otto Vargas, secretario general del PCR." PCR: Partido Comunista Revolucionario de la Argentina, 2 October 2010. http://www.pcr.org.ar/nota/temas-ideológicos/el-primer-congreso-latinoamericano-de-juventudes.
"Programa básico de la Unidad Popular," 17 December 1969. https://www.marxists.org/espanol/allende/1969/diciembre17.htm.
"Represión contra los médicos," April 1975. Sala Virtual, Arzobispado de Santiago, Fundación y Archivo de la Vicaria de la Solidaridad. http://www.vicariadelasolidaridad.cl/node/27801.
State Department Central Foreign Policy Files (1973–1977). National Archives and Records Administration, Access to Archival Databases. https://aad.archives.gov/aad/series-description.jsp?s=4073.
The Tricontinental Conference of African, Asian, and Latin American Peoples: A Staff Survey Prepared for the Subcommittee to Investigate the Administration of the Internal Security Act and Other Internal Security Laws of the Committee on the Judiciary United States Senate. Washington, DC: U.S. Government Printing Office, 1966. http://www.latinamericanstudies.org/tricontinental.htm.
Ulloa, Ariel. "Recuerdos de juventud." *1000 Historias*, 1 April 2013. http://1000-historias-borrador.blogspot.co.uk/2013/04/recuerdos-de-juventud.html.
United Nations: Documents. http://www.un.org/en/documents/index.shtml.
Vivaldi, Dr. Ennio. "Pero está la presencia de Carlos y está también la ausencia de Carlos." *1000 Historias*, June 2013. http://1000-historias-borrador.blogspot.co.uk/2013/07/pero-esta-la-presencia-de-carlos-y-esta.html.
Wilson Center Digital Archive. https://digitalarchive.wilsoncenter.org.

MEMOIRS, TESTIMONIES, AND OTHER PUBLISHED PRIMARY SOURCES

Agnic Krstulovic, Ozren. *Allende, el hombre y el político: Memorias de un secretario privado*. Santiago: RIL Editores, 2008.
Alessandri R., Hernán. "Introducción al Estudio de la Educacción Médica." In *Seminario de Formación Profesional Médica: Antecedentes, Documentos e Informe Final, 13–19*. Santiago: Editorial Universitaria, S.A., 1960.
Allende Gossens, Salvador. *La realidad médico-social de Chile*. Santiago: Ministerio de Salubridad, Prevensión y Asistencia Social, 1939.
———. *Salvador Allende: Obras escogidas*. Edited by Victor Pey, Joan E. Garés, and Gonzalo Martner. Santiago: Siglo XX, 1992.
Almeyda Medina, Clodomiro. "The Foreign Policy of the Unidad Popular Government." In *Chile at the Turning Point: Lessons of the Socialist Years, 1970–1973*, edited by Federico G. Gil, Ricardo Lagos E., and Henry A. Landsberger, 76–103. Philadelphia, PA: ISHI, 1979.
Altamirano, Carlos. *Dialéctica de una derrota*. México: Siglo Veintiuno Editores, 1977.
Baez, Luis. *Preguntas indiscretas*. Havana: Ediciones Prensa Latina, 1999.
Baltra Moreno, Mireya. *Mireya Baltra: Del quiosco al Ministerio del Trabajo*. Santiago: LOM, 2014.
Behm Rosas, Hugo. "Educación Médica: Sintesis bibliografica nacional e

internacional." In *Seminario de Formación Profesional Médica: Antecedentes, Documentos e Informe Final, 201-31*. Santiago: Editorial Universitaria, S.A., 1960.
Blanco, Guillermo. *Eduardo Frei: El hombre de la patria joven*. Santiago: Instituto Chileno de Estudios Humanísticos, 1984.
Bly, Robert. *Neruda and Vallejo: Selected Poems*. Translated by Robert Bly, John Knoepfle, and James Wright. Boston, MA: Beacon Press, 1971.
Bonilla, Frank. "The Student Federation of Chile: 50 Years of Political Action." *Journal of Inter-American Studies* 2, no. 3 (1960): 311–34.
Brodsky B., Ricardo. *Conversaciones con la FECH*. Santiago: CESOC, 1988.
Cabieses Donoso, Manuel. *Autobiografía de un rebelde*. Santiago: Punto Final, 2015.
Castillo, Carmen E. *Un día de octubre en Santiago*. Santiago: LOM, 2013.
Castillo Estay, Nancy. "Mucha gente me culpó cuando se suicidó la Tati." *La Tercera: Reportajes*, 14 October 2007.
Cavalla Rojas, Antonio, ed. *Fuimos testigos (60 años de la FECH)*. Santiago: El Buen Aire S.A., 2016.
Cortés I., Manuel. *Yo Patán: Memorias de un Combatiente*. Santiago: Ceibo Ediciones, 2015.
Corvalán, Luis. *El gobierno de Salvador Allende*. Santiago: LOM, 2003.
Cuba-Chile. Havana, 1972.
Dorfman, Ariel. *Feeding on Dreams: Confessions of an Unrepentant Exile*. Boston: Mariner Books/Houghton Mifflin Harcourt, 2011.
Echeverría, Mónica, and Carmen Castillo. *Santiago-París: El vuelo de la memoria*. Santiago: LOM, 2002.
Echeverría Yáñez, Mónica. *El vuelo de la memoria*. Txalaparta, Mexico: Editores independientes, 2002.
"Entrevista Allende-Debray." Special issue: "Allende habla con Debray," *Punto Final* 126, no. 16 (1971): 25–63.
Foreign Relations of the United States, 1958–1960. Vol. 5, *American Republics*, microfiche supplement. Washington, DC: U.S. Government Printing Office, 1991.
Frank, Waldo. *South American Journey*. London: Victor Gollancz, 1944.
Gaitán, Gloria. *El Compañero Presidente*. Bogotá: Ediciones Alfonso Renteria Mantilla, 1973.
Garretón Merino, Manuel A., and Javier Martínez Bengoa. *Biblioteca del movimiento estudiantil*. Tomo I, *Universidades chilenas: Historia, reforma e intervención*. Santiago: Ediciones Sur, 1985.
———. *Biblioteca del movimiento estudiantil*. Tomo III, *La Reforma en la Universidad de Chile*. Santiago: Ediciones Sur, 1985.
González Pino, Miguel, and Arturo Fontaine Talavera, eds. *Los mil días de Allende (Tomos I y II)*. Santiago: Centro de Estudios Públicos, 1997.
Guevara, Ernesto Che. *América Latina: Despertar de un continente*. Melbourne: Ocean Press, 2002.
———. *Bolivian Diary*. London: Pimlico, 2000.
Hart Dávalos, Armando. *Homenaje a Miguel Enríquez, Discurso leído por Armando Hart Dávalos, miembro del Buró Político, el 21 de octubre de 1974, en el teatro Lázaro Peña*. Havana: De la Cultura Ediciones, 1990.
Huerta, Félix, and Jaime Chávez. *El trabajo es vivir: Conversaciones de Félix Huerta con Jaime Chávez*. Santiago: Ediciones Ruben Darío, 2011.
Informativo Estadístico: Alumnado de la Universidad de Chile en 1967. Santiago: Instituto de Investigaciones Estadísticas, Universidad de Chile, 1967.

"Informe Final." In *Seminario de Formación Profesional Médica: Antecedentes, Documentos e Informe Final*, 69–82. Santiago: Editorial Universitaria, S.A., 1960.

Jerez Ramírez, Luis. *Ilusiones y quebrantos: Desde la memoria de un militante socialista*. Santiago: Editorial Forja, 2007.

Kissinger, Henry A. *Years of Upheaval*. London: Weidenfeld and Nicolson, 1982.

Lagos Escobar, Ricardo. *Memorias I. Mi vida: De la infancia a la lucha contra la dictadura*. Santiago: Debate/Penguin Random House Grupo Editorial, 2014.

Lara, Jesús. *Guerrillero Inti Peredo*. Cochabamba, Bolivia: Editorial Canelas, S.A., 1980.

Lazo, Carmen, and Eliana Cea. *La Negra Lazo: Memorias de una pasión política*. Santiago: Planeta, 2005.

Lazzara, Michael James. "Militancy Then and Now: A Conversation with Carmen Castillo." *Journal of Latin American Cultural Studies* 21, no. 1 (2012): 1–14.

López T., Carmen and Menke T., Luis *Informativo Estadístico: Alumnado de la Educación Superior en Chile desde 1957 a 1960*. Santiago: Instituto de Investigaciones Estadísticas, Universidad de Chile, 1967.

Marambio, Max. *Las armas de ayer*. Santiago: Random House Mondadori, 2007.

Marín, Gladys. *La vida es hoy*. Havana: Casa Editora Abril, 2004.

Mattelart, Armand. *Atlas social de las comunas de Chile*. Santiago: Editorial del Pacifico, S.A., 1965.

Memoria: Presentada por el Directorio de la Universidad de Concepción Correspondiente al Año 1960.

Memoria: Presentada por el Directorio de la Universidad de Concepción Correspondiente al Año 1961.

Montoya-Aguilar, Carlos, "El professor Benjamín Viel, su cátedra B de higiene y medicina preventiva, y el centro de demostración de medicina integral." *Cuadernos M de higiene y* 47, no. 2 (2007): 126 y m.

Muñoz Labraña, Carlos. *69 años: Historia de la Facultad de Medicina*. Concepción: Universidad de Concepción, 1993.

Naranjo, Pedro, Mauricio Ahumada, Mario Garcés and Julio Pinto, eds. *Miguel Enríquez y el proyecto revolucionario en Chile: Discursos y documentos del Movimiento de Izquierda Revolucionaria*. Santiago: LOM, 2004.

Neruda, Pablo. *The Captain's Verses/Los versos del Capitán: The Love Poems*. Translated by Donald Walsh. New York: New Directions Publishing, 2009.

Núñez, Ricardo. *El gran desencuentro. Una mirada al socialismo chileno, la Unidad Popular y Salvador Allende*. Santiago: Fondo de cultura económica, 2014.

Núñez, Ricardo, Joaquín Fernández Abra, Alvaro Góngora Escobedo, and Patricia Arancibia Claval. *Ricardo Núñez: Trayectoria de un socialista de nuestros tiempos*. Santiago: Ediciones Universidad Finis Terrae, 2013.

Puccio, Osvaldo. *Un cuarto de siglo con Allende: Recuerdos de su secretario privado*. Providencia: Editorial Emisión, 1985.

Randall, Margaret. *No se puede hacer la revolución sin nosotras*. Havana: Casa de las Américas, 1978.

Salazar, Gabriel. *Conversaciones con Carlos Altamirano: Memorias críticas*. Santiago: Debate, 2010.

Soto Guzmán, Oscar. *Allende en el recuerdo*. Madrid, Spain: Sílex ediciones, 2013.

———. *El último día de Salvador Allende*. Santiago: Aguila Chilena de Ediciones, 1999.

Stone, Elizabeth, ed. *Women and the Cuban Revolution: Speeches and Documents by Fidel Castro, Vilma Espín and Others*. New York: Pathfinder Press, 1981.
Suárez Salazar, Luis, ed. *Manuel Piñeiro: Che Guevara and the Latin American Revolutionary Movements*. Melbourne: Ocean Press, 2001.
Suárez Salazar, Luis, and Dirk Kruijt, eds. *La Revolución Cubana en Nuestra América: El internacionalismo anónimo*. Havana: Ruth Casa Editorial, 2015.
Subversion in Chile: A Case Study in U.S. Corporate Intrigue in the Third World. Nottingham, England: Spokesman Books, 1972.
Tarud Siwady, Raúl. *Historia de una vida*. Santiago: Planeta Chilena, 2002.
Timossi, Jorge. *Grandes alamedas. El combate del Presidente Allende*. Havana: Editorial de Ciencias Sociales, 1974.
Ulianova, Olga, and Eugenia Fediakova, eds. "Chile en los archivos de la URSS: Comité Central del PCUS y del Ministerio de Relaciones Exteriores de la URSS." *Estudios Publicos* 72 (1998): 391–476.
Urzúa M., Hernán, and Francisco Mardones R. "Aspectos sociales de Chile y su relación con los problemas de Salud." In *Seminario de Formación Profesional Médica: Antecedentes, Documentos e Informe Final*, 83–93. Santiago: Editorial Universitaria, S.A., 1960.
Vera, Mario, and Elmo Catalán. *La encrucijada del cobre*. Santiago: Confederación Nacional de Trabajadores del Cobre, 1965.
Villegas, Harry. *Pombo. A Man of Che's Guerrilla: With Che Guevara in Bolivia*. New York: Pathfinder, 1997.

Secondary Sources
Aldrighi, Clara. *El caso Mitrione*. Montevideo: Ediciones Trilce, 2007.
Alonso, Jimena. "Uruguayos en Chile: De la solidaridad al exilio (1970–1973)." IX Jornadas de Sociología de la UNLP, 5 al 7 de diciembre de 2016, Ensenada, Argentina, *Memoria Académica*. http://www.memoria.fahce.unlp.edu.ar/trab_eventos/ev.8862/ev.8862.pdf.
Álvarez, Vergara Marco. *Tati Allende. Una revolucionaria olvidada*. Santiago: Pehuén, 2017.
Ameringer, Charles D. *The Socialist Impulse: Latin America in the Twentieth Century*. Gainesville: University Press of Florida, 2009.
Amorós, Mario. *Allende. La Biografía*. Santiago: Ediciones B., 2013.
———. *Miguel Enríquez: Un nombre en las estrallas. Biografía de un revolucionario*. Santiago: Ediciones B., 2014.
Amrith, Sunil S. *Decolonizing International Health: India and Southeast Asia, 1930–65*. Basingstoke: Palgrave Macmillan, 2006.
Angell, Alan. "The Left in Latin America since c. 1920." In *Latin America since 1930: Economy, Society and Politics*, edited by Leslie Bethell. Vol. 6, Part 2. Cambridge History of Latin America. Cambridge: Cambridge University Press, 1994.
———. "Social Class and Popular Mobilisation in Chile: 1970–1973." *A Contracorriente* 7 (2010): 1–51.
Antezana-Pernet, Corinne. "Peace in the World and Democracy at Home: The Chilean Women's Movement in the 1940s." In *Latin America in the 1940s: War and Postwar Transitions*, edited by David Rock, 166–86. Berkeley: University of California Press, 1994.
Arrate, Jorge, and Eduardo Rojas. *Memoria de la izquierda chilena: Tomo I (1850–1970)*. Santiago: Ediciones B., 2003.

———. *Memoria de la izquierda chilena: Tomo II (1970–2000)*. Santiago: Ediciones B, 2003.

Azócar Valdés, Juan. *Lorca: Vida de un socialista ejemplar*. Santiago: Ediciones Radio Universidad de Chile, 2015.

Barcia, Manuel. "'Locking Horns with the Northern Empire': Anti-American Imperialism at the Tricontinental Conference of 1966 in Havana." *Journal of Transatlantic Studies* 7, no. 3 (2009): 208–17.

Barr-Melej, Patrick. *Psychedelic Chile: Youth, Counterculture, and Politics on the Road to Socialism and Dictatorship*. Chapel Hill: University of North Carolina Press, 2014.

———. *Reforming Chile: Cultural Politics, Nationalism, and the Rise of the Middle Class*. Chapel Hill: University of North Carolina Press, 2002.

Bermeo, Nancy. *Ordinary People in Extraordinary Times: The Citizenry and the Breakdown of Democracy*. Princeton, NJ: Princeton University Press, 2003.

Bernasconi, Oriana. "Being Decent, Being Authentic: The Moral Self in Shifting Discourses of Sexuality across Three Generations of Chilean Women." *Sociology* 44, no. 5 (2010): 860–75.

Blight, James G., and Philip Brenner. *Sad and Luminous Days: Cuba's Struggle with the Superpowers after the Missile Crisis*. Lanham, MD: Rowman & Littlefield, 2002.

Bodes, José. *En la senda del Che: Biografía de Elmo Catalán*. Havana: Ediciones Prensa Latina, 2009.

Borstelmann, Thomas. *The 1970s: A New Global History from Civil Rights to Economic Inequality*. Princeton, NJ: Princeton University Press, 2012.

Brown, Jonathan C. *Cuba's Revolutionary World*. Cambridge, MA: Harvard University Press, 2017.

Burnett, Ben G. *Political Groups in Chile: The Dialogue between Order and Change*. Austin: University of Texas Press, 1970.

Cabrera Infante, Guillermo. *Mea Cuba*. London: Faber and Faber, 1994.

Carassai, Sebastián. "The Dark Side of Social Desire: Violence as Metaphor, Fantasy and Satire in Argentina, 1969–1975." *Journal of Latin American Studies* 47, no. 1 (2015): 31–63.

Carr, Barry. *Marxism and Communism in Twentieth-Century Mexico*. Lincoln: University of Nebraska Press, 1992.

Carr, Barry, and Steve Ellner. *The Latin American Left: From the Fall of Allende to Perestroika*. Boulder: Westview Press/Latin American Bureau, 1993.

Casals Araya, Marcelo. *El alba de una revolución. La izquierda y el proceso de construcción estratégica de la "vía chilena al socialismo, 1956-1970*. Santiago: LOM, 2010.

———. *La creación de la amenaza roja. Del surgimiento del anticomunismo en Chile a la "campaña del terror" de 1964*. Santiago: LOM, 2016.

———. "Estado, contrarrevolución y autoritarismo en la trayectoria política de la clase media professional chilena. De la oposición a la Unidad Popular al fin de los Colegios Profesionales (1970–1981)." *Izquierdas*, no. 44 (2018): 91–113.

Castañeda, Jorge G. *Compañero. The Life and Death of Che Guevara*. London: Bloomsbury, 1997.

———. *Utopia Unarmed: The Latin American Left after the Cold War*. New York: Vintage Books, 1994.

Caulfield, Sueann. "The History of Gender in the Historiography of Latin America." *Hispanic American Historical Review* 81, nos. 3-4 (2001): 449-90.
Centro Cultural por la memoria "La Monche." *Voces transgresoras: Memorias de mujeres a cuarenta años del golpe en Chile*. Concepción, Chile: Ediciones Escaparate, 2015.
Chase, Michelle. *Revolution within the Revolution: Women and Gender Politics in Cuba, 1952-1962*. Chapel Hill: University of North Carolina Press, 2015.
Colburn, Forrest D. *The Vogue of Revolution in Poor Countries*. Princeton, NJ: Princeton University Press, 1994.
Colley, Linda. *The Ordeal of Elizabeth Marsh: A Woman in World History*. New York: Anchor Books, 2008.
Collier, Simon, and William Sater. *A History of Chile, 1808-2002*. Cambridge: Cambridge University Press, 2004.
Connelly, Matthew James. *Fatal Misconception: The Struggle to Control World Population*. Cambridge, MA: Belknap, 2008.
Contardo, Óscar. *Raro: Una historia gay de Chile*. Santiago: Editorial Planeta, 2011.
Cowan, Benjamin A. *Securing Sex: Morality and Repression in the Making of Cold War Brazil*. Chapel Hill: University of North Carolina Press, 2016.
Cueto, Marcos, and Steven Palmer. *Medicine and Public Health in Latin America: A History*. New York: Cambridge University Press, 2015.
Del Pozo, José. *Allende: Cómo su historia ha sido relatada. Un ensayo de historiografía ampliada*. Santiago: LOM, 2017.
———. *Rebeldes, Reformistas y Revolucionarios: Una historia oral de la izquierda chilena en la época de la Unidad Popular*. Santiago: Ediciones Documentas, 1992.
Deutsch, Sandra McGee. "Gender and Sociopolitical Change in Twentieth-Century Latin America." *Hispanic American Historical Review* 71, no. 2 (1991): 259-306.
Dinges, John. *The Condor Years: How Pinochet and His Allies Brought Terrorism to Three Continents*. New York: New Press, 2004.
Drake, Paul W. "International Crises and Popular Movements in Latin America: Chile and Peru from the Great Depression to the Cold War." In *Latin America in the 1940s: War and Postwar Transitions*, edited by David Rock, 109-40. Berkeley: University of California Press, 1994.
Erisman, H. Michael. *Cuba's Foreign Relations in a Post-Soviet World*. Gainesville: University Press of Florida, 2000.
Espinosa Muñoz, Francisca. "'La batalla de la merluza': Política y consumo alimenticio en el Chile de la Unidad Popular (1970-1973)." *Historia* 51, no. 1 (2018): 31-54.
Espuña, Margarita. *Tati Allende: La hija revolucionaria del presidente chileno*. Barcelona: RBA, 2010.
Estrada, Ulises. *Tania: Undercover in Bolivia with Che Guevara*. Melbourne: Ocean Press, 2005.
Falabella Luco, Soledad. "Gabriela Mistral y Winétt de Rokha: Género, discurso, sexualidad y cultura letrada pública a principios del siglo XX en Chile." In *Historia de las mujeres en Chile (Tomo 2)*, edited by Ana María Stuven and Joaquín Fermandois, 281-318. Santiago: Taurus, 2013.
Ferguson, Niall. "Crisis, What Crisis? The 1970s and the Shock of the Global." In *The Shock of the Global: The 1970s in Perspective*, edited by Niall Ferguson, Charles S. Maier, Erez Manela, and Daniel J. Sargent, 1-21. Cambridge, MA: Belknap Press of Harvard University Press, 2011.

Fermandois H., Joaquín. *La Guerra Fría*. Valparaiso, Chile: Universidad Católica de Valparaiso-Chile, 1975.

———. *Mundo y fin de mundo: Chile en la política mundial, 1990–2004*. Santiago: Universidad Católica de Chile, 2005.

———. *La revolución inconclusa. La izquierda chilena y el gobierno de la Unidad Popular*. Santiago: Centro de Estudios Públicos, 2013.

Figueroa Clark, Victor. "The Forgotten History of the Chilean Transition: Armed Resistance against Pinochet and US Policy toward Chile in the 1980s." *Journal of Latin American Studies* 47, no. 3 (2015): 491–520.

———. *Salvador Allende: Revolutionary Democrat*. London: Pluto Press, 2013.

Frens-String, Joshua. "Communists, Commissars, and Consumers: The Politics of Food on the Chilean Road to Socialism." *Hispanic American Historical Review* 98, no. 3 (2018): 471–501.

Furci, Carmelo. *The Chilean Communist Party and the Road to Socialism*. London: Zed Books, 1984.

———. *The Crisis of the Chilean Socialist Party (PSCh) in 1979*. Working Papers: 11. London: University of London Institute of Latin American Studies, 1984.

Garcés, Joan E. *Allende y la experiencia chilena. Las armas de la política*. Santiago: Ediciones BAT, 1991.

Garretón, Manuel A., and Tomás Moulian. *La Unidad Popular y el conflict político en Chile*. Santiago: Ediciones Minga, 1983.

Gazmuri Riveros, Cristián. *Eduardo Frei Montalva y su época*. Santiago: Aguilar, 2000.

Gil, Federico G., Ricardo Lagos E., and Henry A. Landsberger, eds. *Chile at the Turning Point: Lessons of the Socialist Years, 1970–1973*. Philadelphia, PA: ISHI, 1979.

Glazer, Myron. "Las actitudes y actividades políticas de los estudiantes de la Universidad de Chile." In *Estudiantes y política en América Latina*, edited by Aldo E. Solari, 273–335. Caracas, Venezuela: Monte Ávila Editores, 1968.

González, Mónica. *Chile. La conjura: Los mil y un días del golpe*. Santiago: Ediciones B, 2000.

Gordon, Mari, Jo Buhle, and Nancy Schrom Dye. "The Problem of Women's History." In *Liberating Women's History: Theoretical and Critical Essays*, edited by Berenice A. Carroll. Chicago: University of Illinois Press, 1976.

Gorsuch, Anne E. "'Cuba, My Love': The Romance of Revolutionary Cuba in the Soviet Sixties." *American Historical Review* 120, no. 2 (2015): 497–526.

Gosse, Van. *Where the Boys Are: Cuba, Cold War America and the Making of a New Left*. London: Verso, 1993.

Gould, Jeffrey L. "Solidarity under Siege: The Latin American Left, 1968." *American Historical Review* 114, no. 2 (2009): 348–75.

Grandin, Greg. *The Last Colonial Massacre: Latin America in the Cold War*. Chicago: University of Chicago Press, 2011.

Grandin, Greg, and Gilbert M. Joseph, eds. *A Century of Revolution: Insurgent and Counterinsurgent Violence during Latin America's Long Cold War*. Durham, NC: Duke University Press, 2010.

Green, James N. "'Who Is the Macho Who Wants to Kill Me?' Male Homosexuality, Revolutionary Masculinity, and the Brazilian Armed Struggle of the 1960s and 1970s." *Hispanic American Historical Review* 92, no. 3 (2012): 437–69.

Gronbeck-Tedesco, John A. "The Left in Transition: The Cuban Revolution in US

Third World Politics." *Journal of Latin American Studies* 40, no. 4 (2008): 651–73.

Guerra, Lillian. *Visions of Power in Cuba: Revolution, Redemption, and Resistance, 1959–1971*. Chapel Hill: University of North Carolina Press, 2012.

Guterl, Matthew Pratt. "Comment: The Futures of Transnational History." *American Historical Review* 118, no. 1 (2013): 130–39.

Harmer, Tanya. *Allende's Chile and the Inter-American Cold War*. Chapel Hill: University of North Carolina Press, 2011.

———. "Two, Three, Many Revolutions? Cuba and the Prospects for Revolutionary Change in Latin America, 1967–1975." *Journal of Latin American Studies* 45, no. 1 (2013): 61–89.

Harmer, Tanya, and Alfredo Riquelme Segovia, eds. *Chile y la Guerra Fría global*. Santiago: Ril Editores, 2014.

Haslam, Jonathan. *The Nixon Administration and the Death of Allende's Chile: A Case of Assisted Suicide*. London: Verso, 2005.

Hite, Katherine. *When the Romance Ended: Leaders of the Chilean Left, 1968–1998*. New York: Columbia University Press, 2000.

Hove, Mark T. "The Arbenz Factor: Salvador Allende, U.S.-Chilean Relations, and the 1954 U.S. Intervention in Guatemala." *Diplomatic History* 31, no. 4 (2007): 623–63.

Huerta Malbrán, María Antonieta, and Diana Veneros Ruiz-Tagle. "Mujeres, democracia y participación social: Las múltiples representaciones del contrato social." In *Historia de las mujeres en Chile (Tomo 2)*, edited by Ana María Stuven and Joaquín Fermandois, 385–430. Santiago: Taurus, 2013.

Huneeus, Carlos. *La guerra fría chilena: Gabriel González Videla y la ley maldita*. Santiago: Random House Mondadori SA, 2009.

Hutchison, Elizabeth Quay, Thomas Miller Klubock, Nara B. Milanich, and Peter Winn, eds. *The Chile Reader: History, Culture, Politics*. Durham, NC: Duke University Press, 2014.

Iber, Patrick. *Neither Peace nor Freedom: The Cultural Cold War in Latin America*. Cambridge, MA: Harvard University Press, 2015.

Jobet, Julio César. *El Partido Socialista de Chile*. Santiago: Ediciones Prensa Latina, 1971.

Joseph, Gilbert M. "What We Now Know and Should Know: Bringing Latin America More Meaningfully into Cold War Studies." In *In From the Cold: Latin America's New Encounter with the Cold War*, edited by Gilbert M. Joseph and Daniela Spenser, 3–46. Durham, NC: Duke University Press, 2008.

Joseph, Gilbert M., and Daniela Spenser, eds. *In from the Cold: Latin America's New Encounter with the Cold War*. Durham, NC: Duke University Press, 2008.

Keller, Renata. "The Latin American Missile Crisis." *Diplomatic History* 39, no. 2 (2015): 195–222.

Kelly, Patrick William. *Sovereign Emergencies: Latin America and the Making of Global Human Rights Politics*. Cambridge: Cambridge University Press, 2018.

Kessler-Harris, Alice. "Why Biography?" *American Historical Review* 114, no. 3 (2009): 625–30.

Kirkwood, Julieta. *Ser política en Chile. Las feministas y los partidos*. Santiago: FLACSO, 1986.

Kohl, James, and John Litt. *Urban Guerrilla Warfare in Latin America*. Cambridge, MA: MIT Press, 1974.

Kornbluh, Peter. *The Pinochet File: A Declassified Dossier on Atrocity and Accountability*. New York: New Press, 2003.

Kruijt, Dirk. *Cuba and Revolutionary Latin America: An Oral History*. London: Zed Books, 2017.

Labarca, Eduardo. *Salvador Allende: Biografía sentimental*. Edición ampliada y definitive. Santiago: Editorial Catalonia, 2014.

Labbens, Jean. "Las universidades latinoamericanas y la movilidad social." In *Estudiantes y política en América Latina*, edited by Aldo E. Solari, 111–32. Caracas, Venezuela: Monte Ávila Editores, 1968.

Lambe, Jennifer. "Drug Wars: Revolution, Embargo, and the Politics of Scarcity in Cuba, 1959–1964." *Journal of Latin American Studies* 49, no. 3 (2017): 489–516.

Leavy, Patricia. *Oral History*. New York: Oxford University Press, 2011.

Leibner, Gerardo. *Camaradas y compañeros: Una historia política y social de los comunistas del Uruguay*. 1st ed. Montevideo, Uruguay: Ediciones Trilce, 2011.

———. "The Italian Communist Party between 'Old Comrades in Arms' and the Challenges of the New Armed Left." In *Toward a Global History of Latin America's Revolutionary Left*, edited by Tanya Harmer and Alberto Martín Álvarez. Gainesville: University Press of Florida, forthcoming.

———. "Women in Uruguayan Communism: Contradictions and Ambiguities." *Journal of Latin American Studies* 50, no. 3 (2018): 643–72.

Lepore, Jill. "Historians Who Love Too Much: Reflections on Microhistory and Biography." *Journal of American History* 88, no. 1 (2001): 129–44.

Lindo-Fuentes, Héctor. "Educational Television in El Salvador and Modernisation Theory." *Journal of Latin American Studies* 41, no. 4 (2009): 757–92.

Liss, Sheldon B. *Marxist Thought in Latin America*. Berkeley: University of California Press, 1984.

Loveman, Brian. *Chile: The Legacy of Hispanic Capitalism*. New York: Oxford University Press, 2001.

———. "The Political Left in Chile, 1973–1990." In *The Latin American Left: From the Fall of Allende to Perestroika*, edited by Barry Carr and Steve Ellner, 23–39. Boulder, CO: Westview Press, 1993.

Löwy, Michael, ed. *Marxism in Latin America from 1909 to the Present: An Anthology*. Atlantic Highlands, NJ: Humanities Press, 1992.

Lumsden, Ian. *Machos, Maricones, and Gays: Cuba and Homosexuality*. Philadelphia, PA: Temple University Press, 1996.

Maravall Yáguez, Javier. *Las mujeres en la izquierda chilena durante la Unidad Popular y la dictadura militar (1970–1990)*. Madrid: Ediciones UAM, 2014.

Marchesi, Aldo. "Escribiendo La Guerra Fría Latinoamericana: Entre El Sur 'Local' y El Norte 'Global.'" *Estudos Históricos* (Rio de Janeiro) 30, no. 60 (2017): 187–202.

———. "Imaginación política del antiimperialismo: Intelectuales y política en el Cono Sur a fines de los sesenta." *EIAL* 17, no. 1 (2006): 135–60.

———. *Latin America's Radical Left: Rebellion and Cold War in the Global 1960s*. New York: Cambridge University Press, 2018.

———. "Revolution beyond the Sierra Maestra: The Tupamaros and the Development of a Repertoire of Dissent in the Southern Cone." *The Americas* 70, no. 3 (2014): 523–24.

———. "Southern Cone Cities as Political Laboratories of the Global Sixties: Montevideo (1962–1968); Santiago de Chile (1969–1973); Buenos Aires (1973–1976)." *EIAL* 28, no. 2 (2018): 54–79.

Markarian, Vania. *Uruguay, 1968: Student Activism from Global Counterculture to Molotov Cocktails*. Oakland: University of California Press, 2017.

Medina, Eden. *Cybernetic Revolutionaries: Technology and Politics in Allende's Chile*. Cambridge, MA: MIT Press, 2011.

Moleiro, Moisés. *El MIR de Venezuela*. Havana: Guairas, Instituto del Libro, 1967.

Monsálvez Araneda, Danny Gonzalo. *El golpe de Estado de 1973 en Concepción: Violencia política y control social*. Concepción, Chile: Editorial Universidad de Concepción, 2017.

Montero, Claudia. "Cincuenta años de prensa de mujeres en Chile, 1900–1950." In *Historia de las mujeres en Chile (Tomo 2)*, edited by Ana María Stuven and Joaquín Fermandois, 319–54. Santiago: Taurus, 2013.

Monzano, Valeria. *The Age of Youth in Argentina: Culture, Politics, and Sexuality from Perón to Videla*. Chapel Hill: University of North Carolina Press, 2014.

———. "Sex, Gender and the Making of the 'Enemy Within' in Cold War Argentina." *Journal of Latin American Studies* 47, no. 1 (2015): 1–29.

Moyano B., Cristina. "El Golpe de Estado y la erosión de los mapas cognitivos: Renovación socialista y efectos en la postdictadura." In *A 40 años del Golpe de Estado en Chile*, edited by Cristina Moyano B, 149–76. Santiago: Editorial USACH, 2013.

Moyn, Samuel. *The Last Utopia: Human Rights in History*. Cambridge, MA: Belknap Press of Harvard University Press, 2012.

Navia, Patricio, and Rodrigo Osorio. "Las encuestas de opinión pública en Chile antes de 1973." *Latin American Research Review* 50, no. 1 (2015): 117–39.

———. "'Make the Economy Scream'? Economic, Ideological and Social Determinants of Support for Salvador Allende in Chile." *Journal of Latin American Studies* 49, no. 4 (2017): 771–87.

Olcott, Jocelyn. *International Woman's Year: The Greatest Consciousness-Raising Event in History*. New York: Oxford University Press, 2017.

Palieraki, Eugenia. *¡La revolución ya viene! El MIR chileno en los años sesenta*. Santiago: LOM, 2014.

Pensado, Jaime M. *Rebel Mexico: Student Unrest and Authoritarian Political Culture during the Long Sixties*. Stanford, CA: Stanford University Press, 2013.

Pérez, Cristián. "Guerrilla rural en Chile: La Batalla del Fundo San Miguel (1968)." *Estudios Públicos* 78 (2000).

Pérez, Louis A. *To Die in Cuba: Suicide and Society*. Chapel Hill: University of North Carolina Press, 2005.

Perry, Mariana. "'With a Little Help from My Friends': The Dutch Solidarity Movement and the Chilean Struggle for Democracy." *European Review of Latin American and Caribbean Studies* 101 (2016): 75–96.

Petras, James F., and Hugo Zemelman Merino. *Peasants in Revolt: A Chilean Case Study, 1965–1971*. Austin: University of Texas Press, 1972.

Pieper Mooney, Jadwiga E. *The Politics of Motherhood: Maternity and Women's Rights in Twentieth-Century Chile*. Pittsburgh, PA: University of Pittsburgh Press, 2009.

Pinto Vallejos, Julio. "¿Y la historia les dio la razón? El MIR en dictadura, 1973–1981." In *Su revolución contra nuestra revolución izquierdas y derechas en el Chile de Pinochet (1973–1981)*, edited by Verónica Valdivia Ortiz de Zárate, Rolando Álvarez, and Julio Pinto Vallejos, 153–206. Santiago: LOM, 2006.

Pomar Rodríguez, Jorge Andrés. "La Vanguardia Organizada del Pueblo (VOP):

Origen, subversion y aniquilamiento. ¡El pan que con sangre fue quitado, con sangre sera recuperado!" In *200 años de Iberoamérica (1810-2010): Congreso Internacional: Actas del XIV Encuentro de Latinoamericanistas Españoles, Santiago de Compostela, 15-18 de septiembre de 2010*, edited by Eduardo Rey Tristán and Patricia Calvo González, 1496–506. Santiago de Compostela, Spain: Universidad de Santiago de Compostela Publicaciones D.L., 2010.

Power, Margaret. "The Engendering of Anticommunism and Fear in Chile's 1964 Presidential Election." *Diplomatic History* 32, no. 5 (November 2008): 931–53.

———. *Right-Wing Women in Chile: Feminine Power and the Struggle against Allende: 1964-1973*. University Park: Pennsylvania State University Press, 2002.

———. "The US Movement in Solidarity with Chile in the 1970s." *Latin America Perspectives* 36, no. 6 (2009): 46–66.

———. "Who but a Woman? The Transnational Diffusion of Anti-Communism among Conservative Women in Brazil, Chile and the United States during the Cold War." *Journal of Latin American Studies* 47, no. 1 (2015): 93–119.

Prashad, Vijay. *The Darker Nations: A People's History of the Third World*. A New Press People's History. New York: New Press, 2007.

Purcell, Fernando. "Guerra Fría, motivaciones y espacios de interacción: El caso del Cuerpo de Paz de Estados Unidos en Chile, 1961-1970." In *Chile y la Guerra Fría global*, edited by Tanya Harmer and Alfredo Riquelme Segovia, 71-111. Santiago: RIL Editores, 2014.

Purcell, Fernando, and Marcelo Casals. "Espacios en disputa: El Cuerpo de Paz y las unviersidades sudamericanas durante la Guerra Fría en la década de 1960." *História Unisinos* 19, no. 1 (2015): 1–11.

Purcell, Fernando, and Alfredo Riquelme. *Ampliando miradas: Chile y su historia en un tiempo global*. Santiago: RIL Editores, 2009.

Quiroga Zamora, Patricio, *Compañeros. El GAP: la escolta de Allende*. Santiago: Aguilar, 2001.

Rabe, Stephen G. *The Killing Zone: The United States Wages Cold War in Latin America*. New York: Oxford University Press, 2012.

———. *The Most Dangerous Area in the World: John F. Kennedy Confronts Communist Revolution in Latin America*. Chapel Hill: University of North Carolina Press, 1999.

Randall, Margaret. *Haydée Santamaría, Cuban Revolutionary: She Led by Transgression*. Durham, NC: Duke University Press, 2015.

Riquelme Segovia, Alfredo. "La Guerra Fría en Chile: Los intrincados nexos entre lo nacional y lo global." In *Chile y la Guerra Fría global*, edited by Tanya Harmer and Alfredo Riquelme Segovia, 11–43. Santiago: RIL Editores, 2014.

———. "*La vía chilena al socialismo* y las paradojas de la imaginación revolucionaria." *Araucaria: Revista Iberoamericana de Filosofía, Política y Humanidades* 17, no. 34 (2015): 203–30.

Roberts, Kenneth M. *Deepening Democracy? The Modern Left and Social Movements in Chile and Peru*. Stanford, CA: Stanford University Press, 1998.

Robles, Victor Hugo. "History in the Making: The Homosexual Liberation Movement in Chile." *NACLA Report on the Americas* 31, no. 4 (1998): 36–44.

Robles Recabarren, Javiera. "Memorias de la clandestinidad: Relatos de la militancia femenina del Frente Patriótico Manuel Rodríguez." *Revista Nomadías* 19 (2015): 85-103.

Rodríguez Ostria, Gustavo. *Sin tiempo para las palabras: Teoponte, la otra guerrilla guevarista en Bolivia*. Cochabamba, Bolivia: Grupo Editorial Kipus, 2006.
Rojas Flores, Jorge. *Historia de la infancia en Chile republican: 1810-2010*. Santiago: Ocho Libros, 2010.
Rojas Mira, Claudia, and Alessandro Santoni. "Geografía política del exilio chileno: Los diferentes rostros de la solidaridad." *Perfiles Latinoamericanos* 41 (2013): 123–42.
Rolle, Claudio, ed. *1973: La vida cotidiana de un año crucial*. Santiago: Editorial Planeta, 2003.
Rosemblatt, Karin Alejandra. *Gendered Compromises: Political Cultures and the State in Chile, 1920-1950*. Chapel Hill: University of North Carolina Press, 2000.
Salgado, Alfonso. "Making Friends and Making Out: The Social and Romantic Lives of Young Communists in Chile (1958-1973)." *The Americas* 76, no. 2 (2019): 299–326.
Schell, Patience A. "Beauty and Bounty in Che's Chile." In *Che's Travels: The Making of a Revolutionary in 1950s Latin America*, edited by Paulo Drinot, 53–87. Durham, NC: Duke University Press, 2010.
Schlotterbeck, Marian E. *Beyond the Vanguard: Everyday Revolutionaries in Allende's Chile*. Oakland: University of California Press, 2018.
Schreiber, Jürgen. *La mujer que vengó al Ché Guevara. La historia de Monika Ertl*. Buenos Aires, Argentina: Capital Intelectual, 2010.
Scott, Joan, W. *Gender and the Politics of History*. Rev. ed. New York: Columbia University Press, 1999.
———. "Gender: A Useful Category of Historical Analysis." *American Historical Review* 91, no. 5 (1986): 1053–75.
Silva Avaria, Bárbara, and Alfredo Riquelme. *Una identidad terremoteada. Comunidad y territorio en el Chile de 1960*. Santiago: Ediciones Universidad Alberto Hurtado, 2018.
Smith, Lois M., and Alfred Padula. *Sex and Revolution: Women in Socialist Cuba*. New York: Oxford University Press, 1996.
Solari, Aldo. "Introducción: La universided en América Latina." In *Estudiantes y política en América Latina*, edited by Aldo E. Solari, 9–110. Caracas, Venezuela: Monte Ávila Editores, 1968.
Sorensen, Diana. *A Turbulent Decade Remembered: Scenes from the Latin American Sixties*. Stanford, CA: Stanford University Press, 2007.
Stern, Steve. *Battling for Hearts and Minds: Memory Struggles in Pinochet's Chile, 1973-1988*. Durham, NC: Duke University Press, 2006.
———. *Reckoning with Pinochet: The Memory Question in Democratic Chile, 1989-2006*. Durham, NC: Duke University Press, 2010.
Stuven, Ana María, and Joaquín Fermandois, eds. *Historia de las mujeres en Chile (Tomo 2)*. Santiago: Taurus, 2013.
Suri, Jeremi. *Power and Protest: Global Revolution and the Rise of Détente*. Cambridge, MA: Harvard University Press, 2003.
Sznajder, Mario, and Luis Roniger. *The Politics of Exile in Latin America*. New York: Cambridge University Press, 2009.
Taffet, Jeffrey L. *Foreign Aid as Foreign Policy: The Alliance for Progress in Latin America*. New York: Routledge, 2007.
Thomson, Alistair. "Making the Most of Memories: The Empirical and Subjective

Value of Oral History." *Transactions of the Royal Historical Society* 9 (1999): 291–301.

Tinsman, Heidi. *Partners in Conflict: The Politics of Gender, Sexuality, and Labor in the Chilean Agrarian Reform, 1950–1973*. Durham, NC: Duke University Press, 2002.

Trumper, Camilo D. *Ephemeral Histories: Public Art, Politics, and the Struggle for the Streets in Chile*. Oakland, CA.: University of California Press, 2016.

Tupper, Sofía. *Historias de clandestinidad. Cuatro testimonios (1973–1992)*. Santiago: Ediciones B., 2016.

Ulianova, Olga. "Algunas reflexiones sobre la Guerra Fría desde el fin del mundo." In *Ampliando Miradas: Chile y su historia en un tiempo global*, edited by Fernando Purcell and Alfredo Riquelme, 235–59. Santiago: RIL Editores, 2009.

Uribe, Hernán. *Operación Tía Victora: Cómo Entregamos el "Diario del Che Guevara" a Cuba*. Mexico City: Editorial Villicaña S.A., 1987.

Valdés Navarro, Pedro. *El compromiso internacionalista: El Ejército de Liberación Nacional. Los elenos chilenos, 1966–1971. Formación y identidad*. Santiago: LOM, 2018.

Valle H., Jorge, and José Díaz G. *Federación de la Juventud Socialista: Apuntes históricos, 1935–1973*. Santiago: Ediciones Documentas, 1987.

Vásquez, Ana, and Ana María Araújo. *La maldición de Ulises: repercusiones psicológicas del exilio*. Santiago: Editorial Sudamericana, 1990.

La VOP: Vanguardia Organizada del Pueblo (1969–1971): Historia de una guerrilla olvidada en tiempos de la Unidad Popular. Santiago: Colecciones Memoria Negra, 2012.

Weld, Kirsten. "The Spanish Civil War and the Construction of a Reactionary Historical Consciousness in Augusto Pinochet's Chile." *Hispanic American Historical Review* 98, no. 1 (2018): 77–115.

———. "Writing Political Violence into History." *Latin American Research Review* 48, no. 2 (2013): 175–83.

Westad, Odd Arne. *The Cold War: A World History*. London: Allen Lane, 2017.

Winn, Peter. *Weavers of Revolution: The Yarur Workers and Chile's Road to Socialism*. New York: Oxford University Press, 1986.

Wright, Thomas C. *Latin America in the Era of the Cuban Revolution*. Westport: Praeger, 2001.

Wright, Thomas C., and Rody Oñate. "Chilean Political Exile." In *Exile and the Politics of Exclusion in the Americas*, edited by Luis Roniger, James N. Green, and Pablo Yankelevich, 145–62. Portland, OR: Sussex Academic Press, 2011.

———. *Flight from Chile: Voices of Exile*. Albuquerque: University of New Mexico Press, 1998.

Yankelevich, Pablo. *México, país refugio: La experiencia de los exilios en el siglo 20*. Mexico City: Instituto Nacional de Atropología e Historia, 2002.

Zalaquett, Cherie. *Chilenas en armas: Testimonios e historia de mujeres militares y guerrilleras subversivas*. Santiago: Catalonia, 2009.

Zolov, Eric. "¡Cuba Sí, Yanquis No! The Sacking of the Instituto Cultural México-Norteamericano in Morelia, Michoacán, 1961." In *In From the Cold: Latin America's New Encounter with the Cold War*, edited by Daniela Spenser and Gilbert M. Joseph, 214–52. Durham, NC: Duke University Press, 2008.

———. "Expanding Our Conceptual Horizons: The Shift from an Old to a New Left in Latin America." *A Contracorriente* 5, no. 2 (2008): 47–73.

———. "Introduction: Latin America in the Global Sixties." *The Americas* 70, no. 3 (2014): 349–62.
Zourek, Michal. *Checoslovaquia y el Cono sur 1945–1989: Relaciones políticas, económicas y culturales durante la Guerra Fría*. Prague: Editorial Karolinum, 2014.

PAPERS, THESES, AND DISSERTATIONS

Brown, Jonathan C. "Cuba and the Rise of Armed Revolution in Argentina." Conference paper presented at Global Histories of Latin America's Revolutionary Left, London School of Economics, 26–27 February 2016.
Figueroa Clark, Victor. "Chilean Internationalism and the Sandinista Revolution, 1978–1990." PhD diss., London School of Economics, 2011.
Kirk, Emily J. "The Normalization of Sexual Diversity in Revolutionary Cuba." PhD diss., University of Nottingham, 2015.
Lecourt-Kendall, Yazmín. "Relaciones de género y liderazgo de mujeres dentro del Partido Comunista de Chile." Master's thesis, Universidad de Chile, 2005.
Miqueles, Gloria. "Women in Arms: An Approach to the Women Members of the Manuel Rodriguez Patriotic Front—FPMR." Conference paper presented at Birkbeck, University of London, 20 September 2013.
Rojas Mira, Claudia Fedora. "El exilio político chileno: La Casa de Chile en México (1973–1993). Una experiencia singular." PhD diss., Universidad de Santiago de Chile, 2013.
Salgado, Alfonso. "Exemplary Comrades: The Public and Private Life of Communists in Twentieth-Century Chile." PhD diss., Columbia University, 2016.

Index

Page numbers in italics refer to illustrations.

abortions, 87–88, 224
Adriazola Veizaga, David "Dario," 147
age of youth, 10–11
Aguirre Cerda, Pedro, 22, 28
agrarian reform: Chileans and Cuba's, 35, 40; Frei and, 69, 82, 84, 89, 91; 1950s and, 28–29; opposition to, 196, 215; revolutionary differences on, 101; and rural land seizures, 135–36, 141, 148, 178–79, 191; Salvador Allende and, 30, 31, 99
Aguayo, Carmen Gloria, 187
Ahumada, Jaime, 59
Ahumada, Verónica, 208
aid to Chile: after 1960 earthquake, 48–49; from U.S., 64, 69, 96. *See also* United States
Alamar, 231
Alarcón, Ricardo, 227
Alarcón Ramírez, Daniel, 118–19. *See also* escape of Guevara column survivors
Alessandri, Arturo, 31
Alessandri, Jorge: elections and, 31, 32, 74, 156, 160–61, 279; presidency of, 11, 46, 53, 64, 160–61
Algarrobo, Allende home at, 20, *21*, 90, 118
Algeria, 40, 198, 243–44
Allende, Hortensia Bussi de: about, 2, 19, 23; Allende presidency and, 175–76, 177; as exile, 216–17, 218, 246, 322n29; Beatriz's children and, 267–68; Beatriz's relationship with, 22, 176, 217, 257; Chilean coup and, 209; death of Salvador Allende and, 211; election of 1964 and, *67*, 79–80, 81, 82; health of, 22; as mother, 19–20; post-coup resistance and, 222, 225, 229, 246
Allende Bussi, Beatriz Ximena: aftermath of death of, 267–74; background and overview of, 1–5, 8–10; birth and childhood of, 2, 19–23, *21*, 26; births of children of, 185–86, *186*, 218–19, *219*; Chilean citizenship stripping of, 225; conclusions on, 263–67, 271–72, 273, 274; death of, 3, 6, 258–61, 262–64, 266–67, 268; as doctor, 104–5; education of, 22, 23–24, 37 (*see also* University of Chile; University of Concepción); gender norms and, 15–16, 22, 25–26, 185–87; Guevara and, 109–10; health of, 154, 252–53; on her father, 270–71; marriage to Fernández Oña of, 162, *176*, 250–51, 260; marriage to Julio of, 104, 106, 116–17; 1960 trip to Latin America, 49–52, 291n76; political awakening of, 18, 19, 24, 30, 31–32, 33, 37–38, 65; political comparison to father of, 12–13; radicalization of, 84–85, 94–95, 103–4, 105, 107–8, 117; relationship with father of, 15, 22, 42, *111*, *166*; relationship with Fernández Oña of, 6–7, 115–16, 118, 123–24, 129, *130*, 131–32, *133*; relationship with mother of, 22, 176, 217, 257; as a revolutionary, 127–28, 135–36, 138, 141, 144, 174–75, *190*; scholarship on, 5–6; social life of, 90–91, *93*; as victim, 262–63, 264, 267; young romances of, 92–94. *See also specific events, groups, people, and places*
—in exile, 213–14, 229, 231, *232*, 232–33, *259*; Chilean dictatorship resistance and, 233–35, 236–44, 254–57, 266–67; international solidarity and, 217–22, 225–28, *226*, 263; personal difficulties of, 249–54, 256–58; security and, 245–48
Allende Bussi, Carmen Paz: Allende presidency and, 175; on Beatriz, 19, 20, 22, 23; birth and childhood of, 19, *21*, 23, 31; Chilean coup and, 205; election of 1964 and, *67*, 79–80; exile of, 209, 233; on her father, 23, 77,

::: 353

79–80; visits to University of Concepción of, 42
Allende Bussi, Maria "Isabel": about, 66, 175, 220; Allende presidency and, 175; as exile, 257; childhood of, 21, 22, 23, 31–32; Chilean coup and, 207, 208–9, 210; election of 1964 and, 54, 67, 80, 82; on her father, 23; politics and, 25, 26, 54, 273
Allende Gossens, Laura, 20, 76, 122, 143, 179, 239, 242, 254
Allende Gossens, Salvador: background and overview of, 1, 2, 3, 8, 18, 19, 21, 23; on Chile, 16; Chilean coup and, 207–8; Cuba and, 34–35, 36, 55, 112–13, 152; death and legacy of, 205, 209, 211, 215–18, 271, 322n19; election of 1952 and, 31–33, 64; election of 1958 and, 74; election of 1961 and, 54; election of 1964 and, 66, 67, 68, 69, 71–72, 74, 76, 78–82; election of 1970 and, 151–53, 154–55, 156–61, 164–65; as father, 22–23; fear of Beatriz's actions implicating, 132–34; Fernández Oña and, 112, 124, 199–200; gender and, 15–16, 25–26, 205, 212; Guevara and, 109, 110; Guevara column survivors rescue operation and, 121, 304n98; infidelities of, 23, 42, 80, 177, 205; Latin American revolution and, 98, 99, 143; medical profession and, 23; Paredes and, 139; politics of, 12–13, 18, 27, 95, 137; presidency of (*see* presidency of Salvador Allende); public health and, 28, 43; relationship with Beatriz of, 15, 22, 42, 111, 166, 199, 204–5, 212; scholarship on, 6; as senator, 27, 28, 29, 30, 42; Socialist Party and, 29–30
Alliance for Progress, 64, 68, 69, 96
Almeyda, Clodomiro, 92, 95, 169–70, 239, 241–42, 255
Almeyda Socialists, 270
Altamirano, Carlos: about, 117, 119, 120, 179, *199*; Beatriz and, 152; Chilean coup and, 202, 209; post-coup resistance and, 222, 237, 239, 240, 241, 255, 257, 258; PS and, 177, 192; Salvador Allende and, 177
Álvarez Vergara, Marco, 5–6

Ambrosio, Rodrigo, 135
Amnesty International, 268
Ampuero, Raul, 30
Anaconda, 97
Anderson, Jack, 247
Angola, 243, 267
anticommunism: Allende and, 32–33; Chilean form of, 224; election of 1964 and, 68, 70, 75; El Salvador massacre and, 97–98; prevalence of, 27, 29–30, 57
anti-imperialism, 43, 95, 99, 136–37, 155, 171
Antonio, Carlos, 253
Arauco, 92
Araya, Arturo, 201
Arbenz, Jacobo, 36, 50
Argentina: Allende presidency and, 170, 171, 193–94, 203; Beatriz in, 49; coup in, 237–38, 244–45; earthquake aid from, 48; ELN and, 145, 148, 158; MIR and, 143; post-Chilean coup solidarity and, 222
Armas Cruz, Rodolfo, 85
armed forces, Chilean. *See* military, Chilean
arms, Cuban: attempt to return, 210, 211; transfers from Cuba of, 162–63, 189–90, 203
arms searches by Chilean armed forces, 201
Arrate, Jorge, 155, 268, 269
asylum, 121–22, 171–72, 209–10, 222. *See also* exiles
"Ausencia" (Neruda), 147

Bachelet, Michelle, 273
Baltra, Mireya, 51, 78–79, 188
Barrientos, René, 109, 144
Barrios, Jaime, 207, 304n100
Barr-Melej, Patrick, 11
Batista, Fulgencio, 33–34
"battle for production," 178
Bay of Pigs invasion, 54, 55–57
beards, 35
beauty, celebration of, 22, 41
Benado Calderón, Edith, 71–72, 92, 95, 100, 186, 252
"Benigno." *See* Tamayo Núñez, Leonardo

Benítez, Julio, 257
Bermeo, Nancy, 9
Betancourt, Rómulo, 49–50
Blest, Clotario, 57
Bolivia: Beatriz and, 106, 131, 132–35; Catalán and, 119–20; escape of ELN survivors from, 112, 118–23, 124–25, 304n98, 304n100; guerrilla insurgencies in, 106, 108–9, 112–13, 119–21, 125–26, 129–34; nationalist military regime of, 171; post-Guevara ELN in, 144–50, 159, 195; women in, 128
Bolivia Libre training camp, 129–30, 307n192
Bolivian Communist Party (PCB), 108, 113
Bolshevik Revolution anniversary, 113
Bonilla, Óscar, 204
Bordes, Inés, 68
Bossay, Luis, 31
Boza, Maria Lina, 41
Brazil: Beatriz in, 49; earthquake aid from, 48; left-wing groups from, 40, 145; right-wing dictatorship in, 171, 225, 245
Brazilian exiles, 171
Brigada Universitaria Socialista (BUS): about, 2, 59, 60–61, 106–7; Beatriz and, 63, 65, 71, 90–92, 93, 103, 117; El Salvador massacre and, 96, 97; guerrilla training camp of, 159; members of, 100, 109, 120, 155, 180, 220, 252, 256
Britain, 48, 173, 314n125
Bunke, Tamara "Tania," 115, 128
BUS. *See* Brigada Universitaria Socialista
Bussi, Anna María, 131
Bussi de Allende, Hortensia. *See* Allende, Hortensia Bussi de

Cabello, Felipe, *86*, 89
Cabieses, Manuel, 118–19, 120, 230, 242
Caffarena, Elena, 24
Calderón, Rolando: about, 91–92, 141, 152; Allende presidency and, 168, *199*, 205, 208; in exile, 255; GAP and, 179, 202; as member of Central Committee, 117
Campusano, Julieta, 24, 256

Campus Oriente, 138–40
Camú, Arnoldo: Allende presidency and, 168, 180, *199*; Beatriz and, 113–14; Chilean coup and, 204, 205, 208; death of, 222; ELN and, 124, 125, 130, 147–48
Canales, Alfredo, 197
Cañaveral, El, 177–78, 188, 204
Capitalismo y subdesarrollo en América Latina (Frank), 137
Carballas, Pérez, 258–59
Cardoso, Fernando Henrique, 137
Carrera, María Elena, 224–25, 233
Carretero, Juan: Allende's presidency and, 164, 170, 174, 195; Beatriz and, 106, 127, 161, 190, *190*, 257, 262; post-coup resistance and, 220
Carretero, Nancy, 260
Carter, Jimmy, 237, 268
Casals, Marcelo, 11, 75, 78
Castillo, Carmen: Beatriz and, 140, 163, 234, 263, 266; ELN and, 148–49, 172; on female militancy, 16; Salvador Allende and, 195
Castillo Velasco, Fernando, 140
Castro, Fidel: Beatriz and, 112, 161–62, *162*, 182, 186, 188–89, 219; Beatriz's death and, 261, 262; Chilean coup and, 214–15; Confederación de Trabajadores de Cuba speech of, 229; Cuban Revolution and, 34, 35; El Salvador and, 97; guerrilla insurgencies and, 145; Guevara and, 107, 109, 110, 126; homophobia and, 249; influence of, in Chile, 57, 157; Latin American Youth Congress and, 52; on revolution in Chile, 108; Salvador Allende and, 34, 36, 161–63, 164; Salvador Allende presidency and, 170, 183–84, 188, 189–90, 198–99, *199*; Soviet Union and, 113; women and, 14, 114
Castro, Juana, 75
Castro, Raúl, 36–37, 50, 213–14
Catalán, Elmo: Beatriz and, 129, 148, 151; death of, 149–50; ELN and, 130, 131, 146, 151; Guevara column survivors escape and, 119–21, 122, 124–25, 127, 304n98, 304nn100–101; legacy of, 155

Catholic Church, 32–33, 61, 69, 88
Catholics, 10–11, 149
Catholic University, 136, 148, 223
CENOP (Centro de Estudios Nacionales de Opinión Pública), 168, 169, 207
Central Única de Trabajadores (CUT): Chilean coup and, 201; election of 1972 and, 196, 197; El Salvador massacre and, 96; solidarity for Cuba and, 36, 55, 57
Centro de Estudios Nacionales de Opinión Pública (CENOP), 168, 169, 207
Cerro Castillo, 177
children's rights, 187, 188
Chile: aid to, 48–49, 64, 69, 96; Communist Party in (*see* Communist Party, Chilean); coup of (*see* coup, military, of Chile); ; democracy and, 3, 9, 12, 29, 66, 135, 265, 266, 270; economy of, 103, 200; elections (*see* elections); exiles in, 171–72, 193–94, 195; feminist movement of, 273–74; guerrilla insurgency unsuitability of, 106–8, 119; history of, 9; Left of (*see* Left, Chilean); neoliberal reform and, 269; political awakening in (*see* political awakening in Chile); political change in, 53–54, 57–59, 63–64, 135–37; postdictatorial, 271–72, 273–74; protests of 1980s in, 267; reform in, 87, 95–96, 135–36; revolutionary upheaval in (*see* revolutionary upheaval in Chile); rioting in, 26, 286n77; and solidarity with Cuba, 35–37, 55–57; student movement of twenty-first century in, 272–73. *See also specific aspects, events, groups, and movements*
Chilean Committee of Solidarity with the Antifascist Resistance. *See* Comité Chileno de Solidaridad con la Resistencia Antifascista
Chilean-Cuban Cultural Institute, 57
"Chileanization" of mines, 84
Chilean Left Abroad (Izquierda Chilena en el Exterior), 220–21, 222, 235
"Chilean road to socialism," 2, 12, 156–57, 189, 191
Chile Democrático, 220–21

Chile Informativo, 219–20, 227, 243, 244
China, 50, 62, 269
Christian Democratic Party (PDC): about, 9, 20; Allende presidency and, 183, 184; Chilean coup and, 201, 206; congress and, 82; and solidarity with Cuba, 36; election of 1958 and, 31, 32; election of 1961 and, 53; election of 1964 and, 66, 68–69, 70–71, 74, 75, 82–83; election of 1965 and, 82; election of 1970 and, 151, 156, 157–58; election of 1971 and, 181; election of 1972 and, 196; El Salvador and, 97; fall of Chilean dictatorship and, 270; FECH and, 36, 40, 42, 58–59, 63, 94, 101; Frei reformist government and, 84–85, 94–95, 135; Left differences and, 101, 102, 103; "Revolution in Liberty" and, 69, 96, 97, 100–101, 156; Socialist Party and, 95; Tricontinental Conference and, 98; UP and, 180–81; U.S. support of, 64
Christian Democratic Youth (JDC), 70–71
CIA: Allende presidency and, 167, 181; Chilean elections and, 71, 81, 82, 164; Chilean exiles and, 230, 240; Latin America and, 55, 106, 109; post-Chilean coup resistance and, 221, 246
class hatred, 271
coal miners, 42, 45, 47, 56
CODE (Confederación Democrática), 187, 279
Código de la Familia, 251–52
Cold War: background and overview of, 4, 12; Chilean struggles of, 33, 40, 63, 180, 193, 224, 268; Chile earthquake aid and, 48; communism and, 29; Cuba and, 33, 55, 171; election of 1964 and, 66, 71, 72, 78, 79, 82–83; repression, 97; women/gender and, 16, 185
Colley, Linda, 4
Coloma, Hernán, 97, 109, 160, 256, 268
Colombia, 48, 99, 227, 240
Comisión National Agraria Socialista (CONAS), 91
Comité Chileno de Solidaridad con la Resistencia Antifascista: about, 218, 219–21; Beatriz and, 218, 236, 255–56,

258; exiles and, 229, 231; funds stolen from, 242; human rights and, 238, 242–43; international support for, 227, 248; priorities of, 225, 229; remembrance of Chilean coup and, 254
Communist Party, Bolivian, 108
Communist Party, Cuban, 114, 247
Communist Party, Chilean (PCCh): 1950s unrest and, 30; Allende presidency and, 177, 178, 179, 191–92, 198, 201–2, 203; anticommunism and Ley Maldita, 29; background and overview of, 12, 13; Bolshevik Revolution anniversary and, 113; Chilean coup and, 209, 211; conclusions on, 266; and solidarity with Cuba, 36, 55–56; elections and, 53, 165; escape of Guevara column survivors and, 121, 122; Frei and, 97–98; growth of, 100–101; Guevara and, 109; Left differences and, 101, 102; MIR and, 191–92, 234, 240; Moreno and, 80; MUI and, 62; popular rebellion and, 270; post-coup resistance and, 221, 222, 228, 240, 241, 255, 270; UP and, 154; Vietnam War and, 137; women in, 92. *See also* Left, Chilean; *and specific members*
Communist Party, U.S., 242
Communist Youth (JJCC), 83, 181
CONAS (Comisión National Agraria Socialista), 91
Concepción, 39, 46–47
Conceptión Students' Federation (FEC), 57, 58–59, 62, 118
Condeza, Edgardo, 240
Condor System, 245
Confederación Democrática (CODE), 187, 279
Confederación de Trabajadores de Cuba (Cuban Workers Confederation, 229
Confederación Nacional de Campesinos e Indígenas Ránquil, 117, 141–42
Congreso Latinoamericano de Estudiantes, 101
Conservative Parties, 31, 53
Consultorio Ismael Valdés, 104–5, 138, 301n142
continental revolution, 99–100, 107, 108, 126–27, 147, 148–49, 150

contraception, 87–88
Contreras, Isabel "Mitzi," 261, 267
Contreras, Manuel, 245
Contreras, Marcela, 223
Contreras de Ropert, Miria "Paya": Allende presidency and, 162–63, 165–66, 177, 188; Beatriz and, 161, 176–77, 205; Chilean coup and, 199–200, 206–7, 208; coup remembrance services and, 216, 254; exile of, in Cuba, 258
Convention on University Reform, 94–95
Coordinadora Nacional de Regionales, 239
Coordinating Revolutionary Junta (JCR), 194–95, 196, 241, 244–45
copper: foreign dependency and, 28, 96, 119–20; labor unrest and, 27, 200, 227; nationalization of, 69, 84, 170, 178
Corbalán, Salomón, 36, 81, 91
cordones industriales, 197
Corvalán, Luis, 177, 202
coup, military, of Argentina (1976), 244–45
coup, military, of Chile: Allende presidency contingency planning for, 180, 196–200, 204–6; asylum seeking due to, 209–11; Castro and, 189–90; division among Left groups and, 190–93; event of, 206–9, 211–12; fate of Allende associates and, 222–23; overview of, 2–3, 183–84; remembrance services of, 217–18, 254; rumors and plotting of, before 1973, 158, 160, 164, 197; solidarity with revolutionaries and, 193–96; Tanquetazo and aftermath and, 200–205; women and, 208, 212
coup attempt of Chile (Tanquetazo), 200–202, 203, 205
Crespo, Demid. *See* Fernández Oña, Luis
Cristiana, Izquierda, 191
Cruz, Luciano, 61, 102–3, 118, 303n79
Cuba: Allende presidency and, 170–71, 182, 192 (*see also* Castro, Fidel); Bay of Pigs invasion and, 54, 55–57; Beatriz's 1959 trip to, 50–52, 291n99; Beatriz's 1967 trip to, 105, 106, 110–13, *111*,

114–16; Beatriz's 1968 trip to, 127–29, *130*, 306n173; Beatriz's 1970 trip to, 161–62, 170; Beatriz's 1971 trip to, 181–82; Beatriz's relationship with, 33, 34, 37, 153; Chilean coup and, 192, 197, 198–200, 202, 207–8, 211 (*see also* Castro, Fidel); Chilean coup impact on, 214–16; Comité Chileno and, 219–20; Communist Party in, 114, 247; economy of, 229; El Salvador massacre and, 97–98; escape of ELN from Bolivia and, 118–19, 122–23; foreign policy of, 161; guerrilla insurgencies and, 98, 131, 145; homophobia in, 249–50; household labor in, 251; Latin America Youth Congress and, 50–52; microphone scanning of, 167; post–Chilean coup connections to, 247–49; post–Chilean coup exile life in, 229–34, *232*, 263–64; post–Chilean coup resistance solidarity of, 216–18, 219–22, 227, 236–37, 241–44, 254, 257; Soviet Union and, 54–55, 113, 145, 269; sugar harvest of, 153; transition to Communism struggles of, 229–30; women in, 114–15, 251–52, 303n59. *See also* Cuban Revolution

CUBALSE-12, 221

Cuban Institute of Friendship with Peoples (ICAP), 56, 60, 219, 231

Cuban Revolution: about, 68; gender and, 14–15, 114–15, 128; homophobia and, 249; influence on Chile of, 6–7, 11–12, 33–37, 40, 54, 100; solidarity for, 35–37, 55–57

Cuban Revolution Defense and Solidarity Movement, 55–57

Cuban Women's Federation (FMC), 114, 116, 219, 251–52, 303n59

Cuban Workers Confederation, 229

CUT. *See* Central Única de Trabajadores

Darricarrere, Rafael, 42, 43, 44–45, 46
Davis, Angela, 227
Daza Sepúlveda, Sonia, 145, 223, 230, 254, 256, 258
Debray, Régis, 34, 98, 137, 151, 174, 180
del Canto, Hernán, 237

democracy, constitutional, 3, 9, 12, 29, 66, 135, 265, 266, 270
Democrat and Chronicle, 247
Democratic Confederation (CODE), 187, 279
demonstrations against Bay of Pigs invasion, 56–57
Dependencia y desarrollo en América Latina (Cardoso and Faletto), 137
dependency theory, 92, 137
dictatorship in Chile: background and overview of, 2–3; Beatriz suicide and, 262–63, 264; Chilean exiles and, 216–17; fall of, 270; health care and, 223; infiltration and surveillance by, 244, 246; Letelier and, 245, 247; Pinochet's 1977 speech and, 256; reform and, 269; repression of, 223–24, 227–28, 238–39, 243, 245; resistance to (*see* resistance to Chilean dictatorship); targeting of Beatriz by, 225–27
Dinges, John, 245
Dirección de Inteligencia Nacional, 246
Dirección Interna, 239–40, 255
direct observed treatment (DOT), 88
dogs of Beatriz Allende, 175, 224
Dominican Republic, 98, 99
Dorfman, Ariel, 213
Dorticós, Osvaldo, 112, 214, 215
Dunalistair College, 22

earthquakes of 1960: about, 9, 40–41, 45–47, 290n47; reconstruction after, 47–49, 53, 58, 69
Echeverría, Luis, 216
Echeverría, Mónica, 222
Edwards, Augustín, 164
Eisenhower, Dwight, 40, 55
Ejército de Liberación Nacional (ELN): about, 108–9, 271; Beatriz and, 128–29, 145–47, 151, 171–72; Bolivian insurgencies of, 112, 131, 132–35; conclusions on, 150–51; in Cuba, 127; difficulties within, 144–49, 309n85; election of 1970 and, 158, 159; escape from Bolivia of members of, 112, 118–23, 124–25, 304n98, 304n100; Guevara "heirs" and, 125–27; JCR

358 ::: INDEX

and, 195; Paredes and, 139; Quintanilla and, 172; Salvador Allende presidency and, 163, 171–72, 179; San Miguel occupation and, 142; Teoponte insurgency and, 149–50; Teoponete survivors of, 171; training of, 129–30, 307n192; Vietnam War and, 126, 137

Ejército Revolucionario de Trabajadores y de Estudiantes (ERTES), 294n200

Elections: of 1958, 30–33, 279; of 1961, 53–54; of 1964; of 1965, 82; of 1966, 101, 300n118; of 1970, 151–53, 154–61, 164–65, 187, 279; of 1972, 196; of 1973, 187, 188, 200, 279; participation in, 9; reform of, 31, 33, 53–54

—1964 presidential: Allende family and, 65–66, *67*, 79–82; background and overview of, 64, 65–70, 82–83; Beatriz and, 65–66, *67*, 70–72, 74, 77, 79–80; women and, 65, 74–79, 81, 279; youth and, 70–74

ELN. *See* Ejército de Liberación Nacional

El Salvador, strike and massacre in, 96–98, 103, 119

embassies of Cuba: Chilean coup and, 199–200, 207–8, 209–12; post-coup resistance and, 225, 244, 247, 248; revolutionary support for Chile and, 194

Encrucijada del Cobre, La (Catalán), 120

Enríquez, Edgardo, 103, 244

Enríquez, Marco Antonio, 61

Enríquez, Miguel: about, 61–62, 102–3, 152; Allende presidential security and, 163, 169, 192–93, 194; BUS and, 60–61, 63; Chilean coup and, 207; death and legacy of, 233–34, 241, 267; election of 1964 and, 65; gender and, 15; Guevara and, 109; MIR and, 118, 141, 143, 152, 163; post-coup, 222–23, 227–28

Ercilla, 27, 48, 65, 77

Ertl, Monika "Imilla," 172

escape of Guevara column survivors, 118, 120–23, 124–25, 304n98, 304n100

Espejo, Patricia: about, 139, 258; Allende presidency and, 166–67, 172, 186, 194, 195, 196, 200, 203, 205; Beatriz and, 139, 140, 253–54, 257, 268; Chilean coup and, 205, 209–11, 216; election of 1970 and, 160; as exile, 209–11, 213, 214, 232, *232*, *258*; military training of, 182; MIR and, 160; post-coup resistance and, 222–23

Espín, Vilma, 36, 50, 114, 214, 252

Espinosa Muñoz, Francisca, 183

Espuña, Margarita, 6

Estrada, Ulises, 192, *199*, 212, 220, 230–31, 257, 262

Estrella, the, 90

Ethiopia, 267

Europe, Western, Beatriz trips to, 225–26, 243

Eva, 41, 75, 179, 187

exiles: about, 253; in Chile, 171–72, 193–94, 195; Chilean, 213–14, 216, 224–25, 229–33, 240, 244, 325n122. *See also specific exiles*

exports, 28, 54, 64

Exprés Español, 228

Faivovich, Jaime, 242

Faletto, Enzo, 92, 137

Family Code, 251–52

Family Ministry, 187

family planning, 87–88, 105

FAR (Fuerzas Armadas Revolucionarias), 193–94

Farga, Victorino, 85, 88

FBI, 246, 247

FECH. *See* Federación de Estudiantes de la Universidad de Chile

Federación de Estudiantes Concepción (FEC), 57, 58–59, 62, 118

Federación de Estudiantes de la Universidad de Chile (FECH): about, 61, 63, 136, 293n148; Convention of University Reform and, 94–95; elections and, 72, 151, 160; El Salvador massacre and, 96; Left differences and, 101, 102, 103; social inequality and, 42, 58–59; support for Cuba of, 36; U.S. and, 40

Federación de Mujeres Cubanas (FMC), 114, 116, 219, 251–52, 303n59

Federation of Students at the University of Chile (FECH). *See* Federación de Estudiantes de la Universidad de Chile

Felipe, León, 149

Fernandez, Maya Alejandra: as an adult, 273; as a child, 185–86, *186*, 205, 206, 210, 211, 250, 260–61

Fernández Allende, Alejandro Salvador, 218–19, *219*

Fernández Fredes, Francisco, 220, 229, 230, 231, 256

Fernández Oña, Luis: about, 1, 110–12, 302n37; Allende presidency and, 171, 174, 182, 190, *199*, 199–200, 201, 203, 204, 205; Beatriz's death and, 258, 264, 267; Beatriz's marriage to, 162, 175, *176*, 177, 198, 249, 250–51, 256, 260; Beatriz's 1967 trips to Cuba and, 110–12, 114; Beatriz's relationship with, 6–7, 115–16, 118, 123–24, 129, *130*, 131–32, *133*, *134*, *138*, *144*, *153*, *161*, *263*; Chilean coup and, 206, 209–10, 211; as diplomat to Chile, 170, 171; escape of Guevara column survivors and, 119, 120, 121, 122; as father, 115, 185, *219*, 251, 261, 267; Guevara diary and, 123; health of, 252, 260; Hortensia Allende and, 176; intelligence work of, in Chile, 118, 123, 143–44, 146, 162–63, 167; life of after Beatriz's death, 267–68; post-coup, 214, 216, 225, 232–33, 257, 264

Ferrada, Marcello, 62, 294nn199–200, 294n202

Festival of Youth (FRAP), 32

Figueroa Clark, Victor, 270

First National Congress on Education and Culture, Cuba, 249

FMC (Federación de Mujeres Cubanas), 114, 116, 219, 251–52, 303n59

Foro Abierto, 59

FPMR (Frente Patriotico Manuel Rodríguez), 270, 272

France, 127, 225, 226

Frank, Andre Gunder, 137

Frank, Waldo, 27

Franulic, Lenka, 48

FRAP. *See* Frente de Acción Popular

Frei, Eduardo, and administration: agrarian reform and, 89, 91; Allende family and, 20; criticism of, 135–36, 156, 158, 265; early presidency of, 82–83; economy and, 103; elections and, 31, 66, 68–71, 75–76, 78, 81, 164, 279; escape of Guevara column survivors and, 121, 122; health care reform and, 84–85, 87–89, 105, 140; radicalization during presidency of, 84–85, 95–96, 97–98, 100–101, 135; U.S. and, 96

Frente de Acción Popular (FRAP): about, 30; solidarity of, with Cuba, 36, 55; election of 1958 and, 30–31, 32–33; election of 1961 and, 53; election of 1964 and, 63–66, 68, 71–72, 74, 76–78, 81, 83; election of 1970 and, 156; guerrilla asylum and, 121; Left disagreements and, 58, 59, 101; U.S. and, 96

Frente del Pueblo, 30

Frente Interno (Internal Front), 179–80, 257

Frente Patriotico Manuel Rodríguez (FPMR), 270, 272

Fuerzas Armadas Revolucionarias (FAR), 193–94

Fundo San Miguel occupation, 141–42

Funke, Silvia, 60

Gaitán, Gloria, 205

Gaitán, Jorge Eliécer, 205

Gallo, Jeanette, 77, 79, 80

Gálvez, Elena, 90, 127, 203, 205, 206, 210, 253

GAP. *See* Grupo de Amigos Personales

Garcés, Joan, 168, 190, 265

García Incháusteguí, Mario, 170, 207, 210

Garretón, Manuel Antonio, 267

gender norms: Allende presidency and, 184–85, 205; Beatriz's challenges to, 3, 22, 25–26, 129, 185–86, 212, 273; changing of, 15, 269; Chilean coup and, 210, 212; Cuba and, 114–15, 116, 128, 250, 251–52; education and, 23–24; guerrilla warfare and, 115, 128, 129, 212; politics in Chile and, 24, 75, 77–78, 187–88; power structures

and, 14–16; professions and, 24–25; of society, 41, 75
Gente Joven, 35, 37, 53
Gil, Federico, 9
Gnecco, Gilda, 105, 127, 160
Gómez, Carlos, 119–20, 150, 257
Gómez, Fernando: about, 119–20; Beatriz and, 129, 134, 212; election of 1970 and, 158–59; ELN and, 119–20, 121, 125, 146, 202; GAP and, 159, 192, 202; Marambio dispute with, 192
González Córdoba, Luis Renato, 215–16
González Videla, Gabriel, 29, 98
Gould, Jeffrey, 15
Grandin, Greg, 4
Granma, 115, 254, 262
Grau, Rodulfo Gallart. *See* Fernández Oña, Luis
Grupo de Amigos Personales (GAP): Allende presidency and, 166, 167, 168, 177; anti-coup preparations and, 175, 196, 202–3; Chilean coup and, 206, 207, 233; Cuba and, 162–64, 201; establishment of, 158–59, 166, 167; Frente Interno and, 179–80; González Córdoba and, 215–16; MIR and, 192; MLN-T and, 172; Santiago garage of, 173, 189, 194; strength of, 202–3
Guardia, Patricio de la, 210
Guardia Vieja, 67, 80, 90, 117, 152, 154, 175
Guatemala, 36, 145
Guerra, Neida and Sergio, 260–61
Guerra de Guerrillas (Guevara), 98
guerra fría, la, 4
guerrilla cinema, 76
Guerrilla Decade, 106, 123, 144, 150
guerrilla insurgencies: in Bolivia, 106, 108–9, 131, 132–35, 149–50, 171; in Cuba, 35; growth of, 98–100, 105; in Uruguay, 141; women and, 114–15, 128–29, 184–85
Guevara, Che: Beatriz's identification with, 117, 127–28, 129, 148; Catalán and, 119, 304nn100–101; as "Christ in the mountains," 149, 310n103; class hatred and, 271; death of, 9, 106, 109–10, 112, 113, 117, 145, 214, 267; diary of, 123, 130; ELN and, 108–10, 113, 115,

118, 120, 123, 126, 146, 148, 172; gender and, 14; *Guerra de Guerrillas*, 98; influence in Chile of, 57, 109–10, 157; Latin American Youth Congress and, 51, 52; message to Tricontinental, 107, 126, 137, 271; romanticization of, 125–27; Salvador Allende and, 34
Guillén, Nicolás, 56, 120, 126–27
Guzmán, Hector, *86*

Harnecker, Marta, 220, 303n79
Harrington, Michael, 247
Hart, Armando, 36, 234
health care. *See* public health
"Heraldos Negros, Los" (Vallejo), 146
Herrera, Felipe, 168
hierarchies, revolutionary, 14–15
"Himno de la Mujer Allendista," 76
Hite, Katherine, 8
homophobia, 94, 249–50
Honecker, Erich, 240
Horizonte, 26, 60
Hospital San José, 89
Hospital San Juan de Dios, 73, 85–88, *86*, 87, 88, 90, 138
Hotel Presidente, 230, 231
housing of Chilean exiles in Cuba, 230, 231
housing problem in Chile, 178–79
Huerta, Enrique, 158, 172–73
Huerta, Félix: about, 100, 142; Allende presidency and, 168, 169, 177, 196, 205; Beatriz and, 124, 129, 212, 306n173; election of 1970 and, 152, 158, 160; ELN and, 120, 121, 126, 127, 130, 142, 150, 307n192
Huerta Díaz, Ismael, 198
Huidobro, Ramon, 168, 218
human rights, 227, 237, 238, 243, 247–48, 268–69
Hungary, 30

Ibáñez del Campo, Carlos, 11, 26, 29, 30, 32
Iber, Patrick, 12
ICAP (Instituto Cubano de Amistad con los Pueblos), 56, 60, 219, 231
imperialism, 43, 56, 97–98, 99, 107, 126, 136, 228

imports, 28, 53, 54, 64
inclusive nationalism, 28
infant mortality, 19, 27, 28, 58
inflation, 53, 58, 200
Institute for a New Chile, 268, 269
Instituto Chileno-Cubano de Cultura, 57
Instituto Cine Popular, 76
Instituto Cubano de Amistad con los Pueblos (ICAP), 56, 60, 219, 231
Instituto de Biología, Concepción, 60
"Instituto Lenin," 40
integrated medicine, 23, 44, 105
Internal Front (Frente Interno), 179–80, 257
International Commission of Enquiry into Crimes of the Military Junta in Chile, 242, 247, 248
internationalism, 3, 107, 117, 118, 121, 151
International Telephone and Telegraph (ITT) documents, 6, 196
International Women's Day, 118, 252, 273–74
internship, medical, of Beatriz, 87–89
internships, rural medical, 88–89
Ipinza, Manuel, 90, 105, 138–40, 141, 169, 223
Italy, 225
Izquierda Chilena en el Exterior (Chilean Left Abroad), 220–21, 222, 235

Jackson, Geoffrey, 173, 314n125
Jara, Víctor, 148, 273
Jaramillo, Isabel, 34, 104, 166–67, 172, 173, 214, 232, *232*, 244, 253, 261
JCR (Junta Coordinadora Revolucionaria), 194–95, 196, 241, 244–45
Jeep. *See* Land Rover jeep
JDC (Juventud Democrata Cristiana), 70–71
Jimeno, Claudio, 168, 205, 313n93
Jirón, Arturo, *86*, 90, 124, 125, 169, 213, 258
JJCC (Juventudes Communistas de Chile), 83, 181
Jorquera, Carlos, 199–200
José Marti medal, 198
Joseph, Gilbert, 4

Josiah Macy Foundation, 301n142
JS. *See* Juventud Socialista
Julien, Nancy, 208, 209
Julio, Renato: about, 92, 103; on Central Committee, 117; marriage to Beatriz of, 104, 106, 116–17; Nicaragua and, 269; pre-marriage relationship with Beatriz, 92–94, *93*; PS congress and, 95
Junta, Chilean. *See* dictatorship in Chile
Junta Coordinadora Revolucionaria (JCR), 194–95, 196, 241, 244–45
Juventud Democrata Cristiana (JDC), 70–71
Juventudes Communistas de Chile (JJCC), 83, 181
Juventud Nacional, 300n118
Juventud Radical, 300n118
Juventud Socialista (JS): about, 10, 59, 168; Beatriz and, 19, 138, 200; Cuba and, 33; elections and, 31, 95; Frei administration and, 83, 179; MSR and, 294n199; national conferences of, 40, 137

Kennedy, Robert, 103
Kennedy, John F., administration, 64, 69
KGB (Soviet Committee for State Security), 205, 247
Kirkwood, Julieta, 5, 25
Kissinger, Henry, 171
Klein, Jorge, 205, 313n93
Klein-Saks Plan, 27

Labarca, Amanda, 24
Labarca, Eduardo, 6, 207
labor unrest. *See* strikes, labor
Lagos Salinas, Ricardo, 9, 239
land occupations. *See* land seizures
land reform, 54, 64, 179, 196
Land Rover jeep (Beatriz's), 121, 124, 125, 140
Landsberger, Henry, 9
land seizures, 27, 58, 91, 99, 135–36, 141–42, 152, 178–79, 191
Lara, Jesús, 305n149
Latin American Congress of Students, 101

Latin American Solidarity Organization (OLAS), 99–100, 107, 108, 109, 110, 122, 150–51
Latin American Youth Congress, 37, 50–52
La Victoria settlement, 27, 36
Law for the Permanent Defense of Democracy, 29, 30, 31
Lazo, Carmen, 24
Leavy, Patricia, 7
Left, Chilean: background and overview of, 11–14; Cuban Revolution and, 33–37; division in, 154, 165, 178–80, 190–93, 195–96, 197; faction reunification of 1950s of, 30; gender and, 14–15; military training and preparation of, 141–44; post-coup resistance and, 224–25, 227–28, 234–37, 239–42, 255; renovation of, 269–70, 271; Salvador Allende's posthumous message to, 217–18. *See also specific groups and members*
Left-Wing University Movement (MUI), 62–63
Leibner, Gerardo, 78
Leigh, Gustavo, 204
Leighton, Bernardo, 246
Lenin, Vladimir, 60, 61
Leoni, Raúl, 100
Lepore, Jill, 4–5
lesbians, 249
Letelier, Orlando, 204, 239, 241, 245–46, 247–48, 268
Ley Maldita, 29, 30, 31
Leyton, Eugenio, 139, 167
Liberal Party, 31, 53, 66
liberation theology, 149
life expectancy, in Chile, 28, 69
Llanquique, 88–89
Lorca, Carlos, 137, 142, 152, 168, 200, 205, 239
Lorca Robles, María Eugenia, 42, 46, 48–49
Loti, 185, 211, 214, 219, 233, 249–50
Loveman, Brian, 271

Maira, Luis, 247, 248, 256
Maisonette school, la, 22, 23
malnutrition, 28, 44, 58, 105

Mandel, Ernst, 61
Manuel Rodriguez Patriotic Front (FPMR), 270, 272
Manzano, Valeria, 10
Mao Zedong, 22
MAPU (Movimiento de Acción Popular Unitario), 135, 151, 154, 191–92, 200, 201, 255, 269
Marambio, Joel, 309n61
Marambio, Max, 163, 174, 192, 210, 309n61
Maravall Yáguez, Javier, 188
March of the Empty Pots, 77, 184
Martí, José, 128
Marxism: Beatriz and, 147, 258, 263; Cold War and, 4; Concepción study group and, 60–61; Linares congress and, 95; PDC and, 95; PS questioning of, 240, 249, 269; Right and, 184, 185; Salvador Allende and, 18; university students and, 45; Venezuelan MIR and, 50
masculinity, 14–15, 185, 190, 249, 251–52
Matthews, Herbert, 34
Mazola Collazo, Giraldo, 56
medicina integral, 23, 44, 105
médico general de zona (MGZ), 88–89
Melipilla province, 88, 89, 91
Mercurio, El, 47, 48, 55, 75, 122, 247
Merino, José, 204
Mexico: Allende presidency and, 163, 171, 198; Beatriz and, 123, 233, 243, 257–58; Chilean coup and, 210, 211; Chilean exiles and, 209, 216, 225, 231, 248, 253–54; Cuba and, 57, 119, 170; earthquake aid from, 48; Hortensia in, 216, 257, 268; post–Chilean coup, 267–68; solidarity and resistance and, 221, 239, 242, 243–44, 246, 247
MGZ (médico general de zona), 88–89
micro-brigades, 229, 231
microphone scanning, 167–68
military, Chilean: Allende presidency and, 13, 164, 180, 196, 198, 200, 202, 204, 206; arms raids and, 201, 203; Castro's advice on, 161; Chilean coup and, 1–2, 208, 209, 210, 211 (*see also*

INDEX ::: 363

coup, military, of Chile); coup-plotting within, 158, 197; Tacnazo and, 158; university students and, 59; violence and, 212, 222–23, 228, 262–63, 266

military preparations to defend Allende presidency, 13, 165, 179–80, 189–91, 192, 202–3

military training: Beatriz and, 114–15, 129, *130*, 185, 212; of Chilean exiles, 230–31, 257, 278; ELN and, 108, 130, 141, 149; GAP and, 163; JCR and, 194; Latin American revolutionaries and, 106, 112, 116, 119–20, 129–30, 307n192; Latin American Youth Conference and, 50, 52; MIR and, 143, 180, 190, 192; Organa and, 141–42, 159; young socialists and, 100, 106–7

mines, 28, 39, 45, 84, 200

Ministerio del Interio, Cuba, 111, 163

MIR. *See* Movimiento de Izquireda Revolucionaria

Miranda, Hugo, 96–97

Mistral, Gabriela, 24

MLN-T. *See* Movimiento de Liberación Nacional-Tupamaro

Modak, Frida, 167, 208, 209, 257–58

modernization and modernity: Allende government and, 168; of Chile, 22, 40, 45–46, 47, 89, 265; Frei government and, 136; modernization theory and, 68; PDC and, 68–69; Soviet Union and, 113; universities and, 43; women and, 78, 79, 274; youth and, 10

Moneda, La: Allende presidency at, 164, 165–69, 191, 197, 200; coup at, 206–9, 211; Frei presidency at, 100

Monsálvez, Danny, 39

Montero, Raúl, 204

Montoneros, 193–94, 195

Moreno, Inés, 42, 76, 80, 188

motherhood, 16, 25, 75, 79, 185–86, 263

Movimiento de Acción Popular Unitario (MAPU), 135, 151, 154, 191–92, 200, 201, 255, 269

Movimiento de Defensa y Solidaridad con la Revolución Cubana, 55–57

Movimiento de Izquireda Revolucionaria (MIR), Chilean: about, 102–3, 139; Allende presidency and, 163, 167, 168, 171, 172, 173, 178–79, 191–92, 195, 200, 206; Argentinian coup and, 244–45; armed operations and, 103, 107, 143–44, 180; background and overview of, 2, 12; Beatriz and, 124, 132, 134, 141, 143–44, 166, 169, 177, 192–93, 260, 272; Chilean coup and, 207, 209, 212; Cuba and, 104; elections and, 118, 152–53, 156, 160, 165, 300n118; ELN and, 125; JCR and, 194–95; Left differences and, 102–4, 138; military's targeting of, 222–23; Operation Retorno and, 270; PCCh and, 191–92, 197, 234, 240; preparations for coup, 191–92, 201, 204; origins of, 60–62; post-coup resistance and, 220, 221, 223, 234–35, 240, 241–42; University of Chile and, 183; UP and, 191–92, 239; VOP and, 181

Movimiento de Izquireda Revolucionaria (MIR), Venezuelan, 50

Movimiento de Liberación Nacional-Tupamaro (MLN-T): about, 141, 143, 167; Allende presidency and, 172–74, 181, 193, 194, 195, 314n122; in Argentina, 244; Castro and, 189; ELN and, 148; preparations for coup, 197, 203

Movimiento Socialista Revolucionario (MSR), 62–63, 294nn199–200, 294n202

Movimiento Universitario de Izquierda (MUI), 62–63

Moyn, Samuel, 248, 268–69

MSR (Movimiento Socialista Revolucionario), 62–63, 294nn199–200, 294n202

National Agrarian Commission, 141

National Board of Kindergartens, 169

National Compesino and Indigenous Confederation Ránquil, 117, 141–42

National Coordinating Center in Solidarity with Chile (NCCSC), 227, 236, 242

National Feminine Command, 76

National Health Service (SNS), 28, 58, 223

National Intelligence Directorate, 246

nationalism, 18, 28, 224

National Liberation Army (ELN). *See* Ejército de Liberación Nacional
National Party (PN), 156, 181
National Socialist Agrarian Commission (CONSA), 91
National Women's Secretariat, 187–88
NCCSC (National Coordinating Center in Solidarity with Chile), 227, 236, 242
neoliberalism, 3, 269
Neruda, Pablo, 20, 147
New Song (Nueva Canción) movement, 14, 90
New York Times, 66
Nicaragua, 269, 270
nicknames, 7–8
Ñico López, 258
Nixon, Richard: and administration, 164, 171, 196, 269
Noemi, Carmen, 93
Non-Aligned Movement, 40, 242, 243
"Non-Capitalist Road to Development," 135
Noticias de Última Hora, Las (*LNUH*), 34, 36, 48, 100, 104
Nueva Canción (New Song) movement, 14, 90
Nuevo La Habana, 178
Núñez, Ricardo: about, 92; on Beatriz, 103; PS and, 101, 117, 165; radicalization of, 94, 95, 96, 97, 100

O'Higgins, Bernardo, 203
OLAS (Organización Latinoamericana de Solidaridad), 99–100, 107, 108, 109, 110, 122, 150–51
Olivares, Augusto, 168, 177, 199–200
Oña. *See* Fernández Oña, Luis
Operation Condor, 245
Operation Retorno, 270
Organa: Beatriz and, 142, 144; election of 1970 and, 158, 160; establishment of, 141–42; Salvador Allende security and, 163, 179; training camp of, 159
Organización de Solidaridad con los Pueblos de Asia, África y América Latina (OSPAAAL), 98; and Tricontinental Conference, 98–99, 107, 150–51, 152, 245
Organización Latinoamericana de Solidaridad (OLAS), 99–100, 107, 108, 109, 110, 122, 126, 150–51, 152
Organization of American States (OAS), 36–37, 43, 48, 111, 170
Organized Vanguard of the People (VOP), 181
OSPAAAL. *See* Organización de Solidaridad con los Pueblos de Asia, África y América Latina
Ostria, Rodríguez, 309n85
Otero, Lisandro, 171
Oyarzún, Manuel, 86, *86*, 87, 89

Padula, Alfredo, 251
Palieraki, Eugenia, 59, 61, 69, 102, 143, 294n200
Palme, Olaf, 225
Paraguay, 49, 171, 245
parallel power, 197
Paredes, Eduardo "Coco": about, 139, 140, 154; Allende presidency and, 168, 181, 193, 203, 205; coup and, 207, 212; election of 1970 and, 158, 160, 164; post-coup, 222
Parque Cousiño, 70
Parra, Ángel, 90, 204
Parra, Violeta, 24, 90, 123, 272–73
Parrau, Celsa: Allende presidency and, 161, 172, 193, 194, 204; Beatriz and, 114, 193; coup and, 208; ELN and, 124–25; post-coup and, 268
Partido Comunista de Chile (PCCh). *See* Communist Party, Chilean
Partido Demócrata Cristiano (PDC). *See* Christian Democratic Party
Partido Nacional (PN), 156, 181
Partido Radical (PR). *See* Radical Party
Partido Revolucionario de los Trabajadores–Ejército Revolucionario del Pueblo (PRT-ERP), 193–94
Pascal Allende, Andrés: Beatriz and, 33, 65; Carmen Castillo and, 168–69; on Enríquez, 61; MIR and, 103, 143, 152–53; MSR and, 62; post-coup and, 241, 254, 294n202
Patria y Libertad, 184, 196, 200, 201, 202
Patronato Nacional de la Infancia, 301n142
Paula, 184, 185

PCB (Bolivian Communist Party), 108, 113
PCCh. *See* Communist Party, Chilean
PDC. *See* Christian Democratic Party
Pedraza, Elena, 254
Peña Delgado, Jorge, 42, 45, 59–60, 223, 268
Peña de los Parra, 90
People's Assembly in Concepción, 192
People's Front, 30
Pepper, Inés, 136
Pereda, Guaraní, 227
Peredo, Guido Alvaro "Inti": Beatriz and, 151; death and legacy of, 146, 148; ELN and, 108–9, 128, 131; rescue of, 125–27, 305n149
Peredo, Osvaldo "Chato," 146–47, 149–50, 151, 171–72, 195
Peredo, Roberto "Coco," 108, 139, 302n15
Pérez Molina, Sergio, 103
Peru, 40, 48, 52, 99, 108, 146, 171, 210–11, 222, 233
Pey, Victor, 24, 168, 191, 199–200
Pickering, Guillermo, 201
Pincheira, Ricardo, 168, 180, 205, 206, 207
Piñeiro, Manuel: about, 36, 111, 116, 118, 127, 145, 163, 220, 303n79; Allende presidency and, 170, *199*, 204–5; Beatriz and, 37, 112, 161, 124, 219; Fernández Oña and, 124, 146, 264; post-coup and, 214, 220
Pinochet, Augusto, 3, 29, 204, 237, 256, 270. *See also* dictatorship in Chile
Pinto, Aníbal, 28
Pizarro, Daniel, *86*
Plan Santiago, 197–98, 201
plebiscites, 206, 270
PL 480 aid program, 69
Población Andalién, 49
poblaciónes, 11, 49, 57, 58, 61, 71–72, 91, 95, 103, 136, 138, 157, 169, 178, 208
poder popular, 192, 196, 197, 200
political awakening in Chile: context of, 26–30; Cuba and, 33–37; mobilization, 30–33
Pollack, Benny and Gloria, *93*
polyclinics, 140

"Pombo." *See* Tamayo Núñez, Leonardo
Ponce, Exequiel, 180, 208, 239, 240
Popular Action Front. *See* Frente de Acción Popular
"Populare" cigarettes, 153
Popular Front, 28, 29, 33
popular rebellion, 270
population control, 88
Portocarrero, René, 178
poverty, 3, 18, 27–28, 39, 45, 47, 54, 72–73, 74, 78, 84, 88, 105, 136
Power, Margaret, 75
Prats, Carlos, 168, 198, 201, 203–4, 246
Premio Lenin de la Paz, 198
Prensa, La, 208
Prensa Latina, 35, 98, 123, 210, 262
presidency of Salvador Allende: anti-Allende collaborators and, 164; coup preparations of, 197–200, 204–6; coup of, 206–9, 211–12; establishment of, 165–69; family life during, 175–78; first year overview of, 178–79; military defense of, 179–80, 189–91; and post-coup asylum seeking, 209–11; revolutionary solidarity of, 169–75; Right opposition to, 180–81, 196–97, 200; Tanquetazo and aftermath and, 200–204; women and, 184–89
—and Beatriz Allende: family life and, 175–77; foreign relations and, 170–73; revolutionary solidarity and, 194–95, 196; secretariat and, 165, 166, 167–69, 181–82, 188–89; security and, 161–64
Prieto Figueroa, Luis Beltrán, 49
PRT-ERP (Partido Revolucionario de los Trabajadores–Ejército Revolucionario del Pueblo), 193–94
public health: Allende presidency and, 169, 175; Beatriz's vocation for, 86, 104–5, 258; campaigning and, 72; Chilean dictatorship and, 223, 271; earthquakes reconstruction and, 69; Frei reforms and, 84–85, 87–89, 105, 140; medical students and, 43–45, 73, 84–85, 87–89, 140; unrest about, 58
Puccio, Osvaldo, 34–35, 80–81, 109–10, 143, 165, 253, 260
Puente, Eliana, 76

Puerto Montt massacre, 135, 158, 181
Punto Cero, 129–30, *130*
Punto Final: Cuban Revolution and, 98; guerrilla insurgencies and, 112, 118–19, 148; Guevara and, 110, 123, 126, 149, 310n103; Vietnam War and, 107
Purcell, Fernando, 11

Qué Pasa?, 119
Quintanilla Pereira, Roberto, 172
Quiroga, Patricio, 203, 309n61

radicalization in Chile: growth of, 94–98; Latin America and, 98–101; revolutionary differences and, 101–3; of students, 136–37
Radical Party, 9, 27, 31, 154, 221
Radio Portales, 193
Ramírez, Alicia, 26
Randall, Margaret, 251
reconstruction, earthquake, 47–49, 53, 58, 69
religious shifts, 149
resistance to Chilean dictatorship: challenges and disillusionments of, 236–42, 254; within Chile, 254–57, 267, 269–70; communication and, 222, 243–44; financing of, 221–22, 233, 236–37, 244, 246, 247, 255; garnering solidarity for, 224–28, 242–44; goals of, 221; groups of, 218–21; security and, 246–48; setbacks of, 244–49; women and, 16
Resoluciones 47 and 48, 115, 251
Revista Médica de Chile, 44
Revolución, 51, 60
revolutionary internationalism, 18, 107, 117, 118, 151
Revolutionary Left Movement (MIR). *See* Movimiento de Izquireda Revolucionaria
Revolutionary Marxist Vanguard (VRM), 62, 294n200
Revolutionary Socialist Movement (MSR), 62–63, 294nn199–200, 294n202
revolutionary upheaval in Chile: Campus Oriente and, 138–40; ELN and, 144–51, 309n85; military preparations of, 141–44; overview of, 135–38
"Revolution in Liberty," 69, 96, 97, 100–101, 156
Revolution in the Revolution (Debray), 98
Right: about, 9, 14; during Allende presidency, 196, 201, 202, 228; elections and, 32, 156; OLAS and, 99; resurgence of, 158, 180–81, 196. *See also specific groups and members*
right-wing paramilitary violence, 158, 184, 196, 201, 266
Ríos, Juan Antonio, 28
rioting of 1957 in Chile, 26, 30, 286n77
Riquelme, Alfredo, 12
Riquelme, Samuel, 211, 222
Roberts, Kenneth, 271
Rocca, Marco Antonio, 58–59
Rodríguez, Aniceto, 95, 117, 151, 304n98
Rodríguez, Carlos Rafael, 204–5, 215, 258
Rodríguez, Luis, 34
Rojas, Alejandro, 56, 136, 151, 160
Rojas, Gonzalo, 220
Rojas, Manuel, 20
Ruiz, César, 204

Saldaña, Rodolfo "Saúl," 125, 127
Salinas, Luis Adolfo, 144
Sánchez, Celia, 232
Sandinistas, 269, 270
Sandoval, Hernán, 49, 52, 103, 223–24, 250, 253, 268
San Martín González, Enrique, 230
San Miguel occupation, 141–42, 158
Santa Adriana, 58
Santa Cruz, Hernán, 168
Santamaria, Haydée, 36, 99, 109
Santiago: about, 69, 72–73; election of 1964 and, 69–70
Santucho, Mario Roberto, 194
scare campaign of 1964 elections, 75–76, 80, 81, 82
Schlotterbeck, Marian, 39
Schneider, René, 164–65, 174
Schouwen, Bautista van, 61, 62, 102–3, 152, 222

scope of this biography, 8
Scott, Joan, 15, 16
Second Vatican Council, 69
Secretaría Nacional de la Mujer, 187–88
secretariat of Allende presidency, 165–67, 172, 173
security detail for Salvador Allende: during campaign, 158–59; during presidency (*see* Grupo de Amigos Personales)
Sepúlveda, Cecilia, 139
Sepúlveda, Mario, 201
Servicio Nacional de Salud (SNS), 28, 58, 223
Sierra Maestra, 35, 36, 112
Sierra Maestra nucleus of Brigada Universitaria Socialista, 60, 62–63, 294n183, 294n185
Siglo, El: earthquake aid and, 48; elections and, 32, 68, 76, 77, 80; guerrilla rescue operation and, 121; on Guevara, 109; shutting down of, 29
16 de Julio de Liberación Nacional, 193
Smith, Lois, 251
SNS (Servicio Nacional de Salud), 28, 58, 223
"social debt," 42–43
Socialist Party (PS), Chilean: Allende presidency and, 177, 179, 191, 192, 197, 198, 200, 201, 202, 203, 204; background and overview of, 2, 3, 12, 13; Beatriz and, 138, 220, 227, 236, 242, 256; Chilean coup and, 206, 207, 208, 211; Cuba and, 33, 36, 55–56, 57; elections and, 83, 100, 151, 158, 165; Enríquez and, 60, 65; Frente Interno and, 179–80, 191; growth of, 95–97, 100, 117–18; Havana plenum of, 239, 240; "Instituto Lenin" and, 40; JCR and, 194, 195; Julio and, 92; Left differences and, 30, 101, 102, 269; MIR and, 143, 191–92, 200, 234; MUI and, 62; of 1940s, 29–30; of 1980s, 270, 271; Organa and, 141–42, 144; post-coup resistance and, 221, 222, 223, 237, 239, 240–41, 255, 257; riots of 1957 and, 26; Salvador Allende and, 18, 30; Schneider and, 165; UP and,
154; Vietnam War and, 137; women and, 77, 266
Socialist University Brigade (BUS). *See* Brigada Universitaria Socialista
Socialist Youth (JS), Chilean. *See* Juventud Socialista (JS), Chilean
social question, the, 27, 44–45
societal unrest of 1950s, 26–27, 28–29
solidarity: of Allende presidency, 172–74; for Cuba, 35–37, 55–57; post-Chilean coup resistance and, 216–18, 219–22, 227, 236–37, 241–44, 254, 257; rally in Cuba against Chilean coup, 214, 215–16, *217*, 217–18
Sorensen, Diana, 85
Soto, Oscar "Cacho," 154, 208
sources for this biography, 7
Soviet Committee for State Security (KGB), 205, 247
Soviet Union: Beatriz in, 113; Chile and, 48, 68, 198, 210; Cuba and, 54–55, 113, 145, 269; KGB and, 205, 247; Salvador Allende and, 18, 113, 198; women in, 75
Steeger, Adalberto, 85
Stitchkin, David, 46
strikes, labor: during Allende presidency, 178, 197, 200; earthquakes of 1960 and, 47; of 1940s and 1950s, 27, 29; of 1960s, 58, 96, 103, 141, 158; youth and, 11
strikes, student, 58
sugar harvest of Cuba, 153
suicide of Beatriz Allende, 3, 6, 258–61, 262–64, 266–67, 268
Sule, Anselmo, 256
Sur, El, 40, 43, 47, 55, 57
survivors of Guevara column, escape of, 118, 120–23, 124–25, 304n98, 304n100
Sweden, 225–26, *226*, 237

Tacnazo, 158
Tamayo Núñez, Leonardo, 118–19, 121, 122, 130, 145, 304n98. *See also* escape of Guevara column survivors
Tanquetazo and aftermath, 200–202, 203, 205
Teitelboim, Volodia, 30, 98

Teoponte insurgency, 149–50, 171
theological shifts, 149
Third World project, 13, 113, 269
Tinsman, Heidi, 89, 96
Tohá, Jaime, 254
Tohá, José, 184
tomas. See land seizures
Tomás Moro, 175, 176, 202, 209, 224
Tomic, Radomiro, 156, 181, 279
Tormo, Cecilia, 208
Torres, Juan José, 171
Track II, 164
transition to democracy in Chile, 270–72
Trapote, Irina, 114, 115, 116, 170–71
Tricontinental Conference. *See* Organización de Solidaridad con los Pueblos de Asia, África y América Latina
Tropas Especiales of Cuba, 163, 210, 232
Trotsky, Leon, 61
Trotskyist Party, 62, 102
Trucco, Marcelo, 90
tuberculosis (TB), 22, 88
Tupamaros. *See* Movimiento de Liberación Nacional–Tupamaro
Tupper, Sophia, 263, 272
26th of July Movement, 37, 50, 102

Ugalde, Ana Eugenia, 76–77
Ulloa, Ariel, 60, 62, 180, 222, 257
UN (United Nations), 198, 227, 242, 256
UNICEF (United Nation's Educational, Scientific, and Cultural Organization), 58
Unidad de la Izquierda, 151
Unidad Popular (UP): about, 154, 175; Allende presidency and, 177, 178–79, 180, 183, 196–97; Basic Program of, 156–57, 187; Chilean coup and, 206; conclusions on, 265–66; election of 1970 and, 154, 155–58, 159–60, 161, 165; MIR and, 183, 191–92, 239; PDC and, 180–81; post-coup resistance and, 220, 239, 241, 256; Tupamaros and, 172; University of Chile and, 183; VOP and, 181; women and, 184–85, 187–88
Union of Chilean University Federations, 101

United Nations (UN), 198, 227, 242, 256
United Nation's Educational, Scientific, and Cultural Organization (UNESCO), 43
United States: aid to Chile of, 48, 64, 69, 96; Allende presidency and, 164, 170, 171, 174, 180, 196; Beatriz in, 227; Chilean coup and, 228; Chilean dependency on, 28; Chilean election of 1964 and, 68–69, 71, 75–76; Chilean investments of, 31; Chilean protests against, 55–57, 96; Chilean solidarity and, 242, 243, 244, 248; Condor System and, 245; invasion of Dominican Republic by, 98, 99; Latin America and, 40, 68, 109; Tricontinental Conference and, 99
University of Chile: Beatriz in medical school at, 65, 84–89, *86*, 90, 104; Campus Oriente and, 138–40; election of 1964 and, 66–68, 71; radicalization and, 102; student occupation of, 136; women and, 24, 37
University of Concepción: about, 37, 39–40, 41–42; Beatriz at, 39, 41–42, 43, 45, 55, 59–60, 62, 63; and solidarity with Cuba at, 60; earthquakes of 1960 and, 46, 48–49; School of Medicine at, 43, 44–45; settlement communities and, 136
university reform, 11, 94, 138, 148
Urbano, 118–19. *See also* escape of Guevara column survivors
Uruguay, 48, 49, 50, 77, 141, 171, 172, 173, 193, 245, 314n125

Valdés, Gabriel, 20
Valdés, Juan Gabriel, 247
Valdés, Pedro, 304n100
Valdivia, Rita, 145, 186
Vallejo, César, 146
Valparaiso, 26, 54, 76, 137, 174, 181, 200
Vanguardia Organizada del Pueblo (VOP), 181
Vanguardia Revolucionaria Marxista (VRM), 62, 294n200
Vargas, Félix, 150
Vegara, Marta, 24

Vekemens, Roger, 69
Venezuela, 48, 49–50, 53, 57, 99, 100, 145, 227
Vexler, Erica, 65, 77
vía chilena al socialismo, la, 2, 12, 156–57, 189, 191
Victory Train, 31
Viel, Benjamin, 86, 104, 105
Viel, Cecilia, 19, 20
Vietnam, 96, 98, 105, 107, 113, 121, 126, 137, 145, 152, 170, 198, 207, 213, 214, 225, 234, 242
Villalón, Luis, 93–94
Villa project, La, 140
Villegas Tamayo, Harry, 118–19. *See also* escape of Guevara column survivors
volunteering, youth. *See* youth, volunteering of
Volveremos a las montañas, 125, 127, 148, 305n149
voter participation, 29

wages, 29, 53, 58, 96
Washington Post, 6, 196
Weld, Kirsten, 8
West Germany, 48, 225
Whitelaw, William, 167, 173, 244–45
Whitten, Les, 247
women: Allende presidency and, 165, 172, 175, 184–89; background and overview of, 14–16; in Bolivia, 128; Chilean coup and, 208, 210, 212; in Cuba, 114–15, 203, 249, 251–52, 303n59; as depicted in history, 1, 5, 6, 264; dictatorship and, 224, 264; education and, 24, 37; elections and, 65, 66, 69, 74–80, 81, 82, 83, 279; equality and, 29, 186–87, 251, 273–74; guerrilla insurgencies and, 128–29; health of, 28, 87–88, 105; as medical students, 86; as militants in democracy, 272; political Right and, 32; in politics, 14–16, 24, 25–26, 77–78; position in Chile, 20, 22, 23, 24–25, 92, 96; in postdictatorial Chile, 273–74; regulation of, 41; solidarity and resistance of, 242–43; twenty-first century feminist movement and, 273–74; UP opposition of, 183–84
Workers' Congress, 229
Workers' Revolutionary Party–Revolutionary Army of the People (PRT-ERP), 193–94
World Federation of Democratic Youth, 11, 50, 56
World Health Organization, 44

youth, political participation of: background and overview of, 9–11; Cuban Revolution and, 35, 37; elections and, 32, 70–74; growth of, 58–59; international movement of, 49–53; Latin American Youth Congress and, 37, 50–52. *See also specific political youth groups*
youth, volunteering of, 48–49, 57, 61, 70, 71, 72–73, 74, 85, 91, 136, 169

Zahler, Adrés, *86*
Zalaquett, Cherie, 270
Zamorano, Antonio, 31, 32, 279
Zenith Radio, 162, 163
Zepeda, Horacio, *86*
Zolov, Eric, 14
Zujovic, Edmundo Pérez, 181
Zuna de Echeverría, Maria Esther, 216

www.ingramcontent.com/pod-product-compliance
Lightning Source LLC
Chambersburg PA
CBHW051744030925
32039CB00002B/39